D0968753

On Emerson

On Emerson

The Best from *American Literature*

Edited by Edwin H. Cady and Louis J. Budd

Duke University Press Durham and London 1988

Printed in the United States of America
on acid-free paper ∞
Library of Congress Cataloging in Publication Data
appears on the last printed page of this book.

Contents

Series Introduction

From Vol. 1, no. 1, in March 1929 to the latest issue, the front cover of *American Literature* has proclaimed that it is published "with the Cooperation of the American Literature Section [earlier Group] of the Modern Language Association." Though not easy to explain simply, the facts behind that statement have deeply influenced the conduct and contents of the journal for five decades and more. The journal has never been the "official" or "authorized" organ of any professional organization. Neither, however, has it been an independent expression of the tastes or ideas of Jay B. Hubbell, Clarence Gohdes, or Arlin Turner, for example. Historically, it was first in its field, designedly so. But its character has been unique, too.

Part of the tradition of the journal says that Hubbell in founding it intended a journal that should "hold the mirror up to the profession"—reflecting steadily its current interests and (ideally) at least sampling the best work being done by historians, critics, and bibliographers of American literature during any given year. Such remains the intent of the editors based at Duke University; such also through the decades has been the intent of the Board of Editors elected by the vote of members of the professional association—"Group" or "Section."

The operative point lies in the provisions of the constitutional "Agreements" between the now "Section" and the journal. One of these provides that the journal shall publish no article not approved by two readers from the elected Board. Another provides that the Chairman of the Board or, if one has been appointed and is acting in the editorial capacity at Duke, the Managing Editor need publish no article not judged worthy of the journal. Historically, again, the members of the successive Boards and the Duke editor have seen eye-to-eye. The Board has tended to approve fewer than one out of every ten submissions. The tradition of the journal dictates that it keep a slim back-log. With however much revision, therefore, the journal publishes practically everything the Board approves.

Founder Hubbell set an example from the start by achieving the almost total participation of the profession in the first five numbers of *American Literature*. Cairns, Murdock, Pattee, and Rusk were involved in Vol. 1, no. 1, along with Boynton, Killis Campbell, Foerster, George Philip Krapp, Leisy, Mabbott, Parrington, Bliss Perry, Louise Pound, Quinn, Spiller, Frederick Jackson Turner, and Stanley Williams on the editorial side. Spiller, Tremaine McDowell, Gohdes, and George B. Stewart contributed essays. Canby, George McLean Harper, Gregory Paine, and Howard Mumford Jones appeared as reviewers. Harry Hayden Clark and Allan Gilbert entered in Vol. 1, no. 2. Frederic I. Carpenter, Napier Wilt, Merle Curti, and Grant C. Knight in Vol. 1, no. 3; Clarence Faust, Granville Hicks, and Robert Morss Lovett in Vol. 1, no. 4; Walter Fuller Taylor, Orians, and Paul Shorey in Vol. 2, no. 1.

Who, among the founders of the profession, was missing? On the other hand, if the reader belongs to the profession and does not know those present, she or he probably does not know enough. With very few notable exceptions, the movers and shakers of the profession have since the beginning joined in cooperating to create and sustain the journal.

The foregoing facts lend a special distinction to the best articles in *American Literature*. They represent the many, often tumultuous winds of doctrine which have blown from the beginnings through the years of the decade next to last in this century. Those articles often became the firm footings upon which present structures of understanding rest. Looking backward, one finds that the argonauts were doughty. Though we know a great deal more than they, they are a great deal of what we know. Typically, the old best authors wrote well—better than most of us. Conceptually, even ideologically, we still wrestle with ideas they created. And every now and again one finds of course that certain of the latest work has reinvented the wheel one time more. Every now and again one finds a sunburst idea which present scholarship has forgotten. Then it appears that we have receded into mist or darkness by comparison.

Historical change, not always for the better, also shows itself in methods (and their implied theories) of how to present evidence, structure an argument, craft a scholarly article. The old masters were far from agreed—much to the contrary—about these matters.

But they are worth knowing in their own variety as well as in their instructive differences from us.

On the other hand, the majority of *American Literature*'s authors of the best remain among us, working, teaching, writing. One testimony to the quality of their masterliness is the frequency with which the journal gets requests from the makers of textbooks or collections of commentary to reprint from its pages. Now the opportunity presents itself to select without concern for permissions fees what seems the best about a number of authors and topics from the whole sweep of *American Literature.*

The fundamental reason for this series, in other words, lies in the intrinsic, enduring value of articles that have appeared in *American Literature* since 1929. The compilers, with humility, have accepted the challenge of choosing the best from well over a thousand articles and notes. By "best" is meant original yet sound, interesting, and useful for the study and teaching of an author, intellectual movement, motif, or genre.

The articles chosen for each volume of this series are given simply in the order of their first publication, thus speaking for themselves and entirely making their own points rather than serving the compilers' view of literary or philosophical or historical patterns. Happily, a chronological order has the virtues of displaying both the development of insight into a particular author, text, or motif and the shifts of scholarly and critical emphasis since 1929. But comparisons or trend-watching or a genetic approach should not blur the individual excellence of the articles reprinted. Each has opened a fresh line of inquiry, established a major perspective on a familiar problem, or settled a question that had bedeviled the experts. The compilers aim neither to demonstrate nor undermine any orthodoxy, still less to justify a preference for research over explication, for instance. In the original and still current subtitle, *American Literature* honors literary history and criticism equally—along with bibliography. To the compilers this series does demonstrate that any worthwhile author or text or problem can generate a variety of challenging perspectives. Collectively, the articles in its volumes have helped to raise contemporary standards of scholarship and criticism.

This series is planned to serve as a live resource, not as a homage to once vibrant but petrifying achievements in the past. For several sound reasons, its volumes prove to be weighted toward the more recent articles, but none of those reasons includes a presumed superiority of insight or of guiding doctrine among the most recent generations. Some of the older articles could benefit now from a minor revision, but the compilers have decided to reprint all of them exactly as they first appeared. In their time they met fully the standards of first-class research and judgment. Today's scholar and critic, their fortunate heir, should hope that rising generations will esteem his or her work so highly.

Many of the articles published in *American Literature* have actually come (and continue to come) from younger, even new members of the profession. Because many of those authors climb on to prominence in the field, the fact is worth emphasizing. Brief notes on the contributors in the volumes of their series may help readers to discover other biographical or cultural patterns.

Edwin H. Cady
Louis J. Budd

Melville as a Critic of Emerson

William Braswell

I

BECAUSE the critical remarks of one eminent author concerning another are rarely without interest, students of American literature regret that there is apparently no record of Ralph Waldo Emerson's opinion of Herman Melville.[1] That Emerson owned at least one of Melville's works is shown by the presence of *Typee* among the preserved books of his library. Yet there is no evidence that he read the volume.[2] We are more fortunate, however, in regard to our knowledge of what Melville thought of Emerson.

Until now a letter that Melville wrote to E. A. Duyckinck on March 3, 1849, has been the only generally known source from which one could learn Melville's opinion of Emerson. In the incomplete reproduction of that letter in Meade Minnigerode's *Some Personal Letters of Herman Melville and a Bibliography,*[3] one reads that Melville had recently heard Emerson lecture[4] and that he considered Emerson "more than a brilliant fellow." He had been told that Emerson was difficult to understand because of his abstruseness, but on this occasion he had found him quite clear. He jested concerning Emerson's reputed sobriety. And he made a statement that astonishes anyone familiar with the thought of the two men: he charged Emerson with insinuating "that had he lived in those days when the world was made, he might have offered

[1] After discussing Emerson's criticism of various other novelists, John T. Flanagan says, in "Emerson as a Critic of Fiction," *Philological Quarterly,* XV, 39 (Jan., 1936): "Of Melville . . . there is no record." So far as I have been able to discover, this statement is correct.

[2] I have not seen Emerson's copy of *Typee;* but Mrs. Marian E. Kent, of the Concord Antiquarian Society, has informed me by letter that it is a reprint, published in 1848, of Wiley and Putnam's Revised Edition of the novel. She says, "There are no annotations in this book, and I am unable to learn when it came into Ralph Waldo Emerson's possession."

[3] (New York, 1922), pp. 32-34.

[4] He heard one of the five lectures (unpublished) on "Mind and Manners in the Nineteenth Century" which Emerson delivered in Boston during Jan. and Feb., 1849. See Luther Stearns Mansfield, *Herman Melville: Author and New Yorker, 1844-1851* (an unpublished doctoral dissertation at the University of Chicago, 1936), pp. 178-179, and James Elliot Cabot, *A Memoir of Ralph Waldo Emerson* (Boston, 1899), II, 753.

some valuable suggestions." He censured Emerson on that point, whereas he himself, in his recently published *Mardi,* had shown more discontent over the universe than Emerson expressed in all his published works.[5]

On the whole, Melville wrote so capriciously of "this Plato who talks thro' his nose" that one is not surprised to discover in the manuscript of the letter his confession that he knew practically nothing about Emerson. Minnigerode's version of the letter curiously omits[6] the following important passage: ". . . I had only glanced at a book of his once in Putnam's store—that was all I knew of him, till I heard him lecture."[7] This statement of his unfamiliarity with Emerson's works, together with the fact that he had heard only one of Emerson's lectures, convinces one that at the time of writing the letter Melville was hardly qualified to pass judgment upon the merits of his famous contemporary. The comments on Emerson in the letter, therefore, should not be taken very seriously.

In *Pierre,* published three years after the letter was written, there is a passage which might be considered a severe condemnation of Emerson as well as the other New England Transcendentalists. In writing of "the talismanic secret" by which one reconciles "this world with his own soul," Melville says:

> Certain philosophers have time and again pretended to have found it; but if they do not in the end discover their own delusion, other people soon discover it for themselves, and so those philosophers and their vain philosophy are let glide away into practical oblivion. Plato, and Spinoza, and Goethe and many more belong to this guild of self-impostors, with a preposterous rabble of Muggletonian Scots and Yankees, whose vile brogue still the more bestreaks the stripedness of their Greek and German Neoplatonical originals.[8]

Harsh as this stricture is, one cannot but be impressed by the illustrious company in which the Transcendentalists are damned. After

[5] On this point, and on other points in this article pertaining to Melville's religious thought, see William Braswell, *Herman Melville and Christianity* (an unpublished doctoral dissertation at the University of Chicago, 1934).

[6] Minnigerode indicates that an omission has been made.

[7] The manuscript of this letter is in the Duyckinck Collection, in the New York Public Library.

[8] *Pierre,* p. 290. All references to Melville's works are to the Constable Edition (London, 1922-1924).

publishing *Pierre,* Melville apparently did not express himself in print on either Emerson or the Transcendentalists as a school.[9]

He did, however, write some comments upon Emerson which he did not mean to publish, and which have not been published until now. These appear in three volumes of Emerson's essays that Melville bought secondhand: *Essays: First Series* and *Essays: Second Series,* which he obtained in the early sixties,[10] and *The Conduct of Life,* which he obtained in 1870.[11] Judging from the markings in these books, one concludes that Melville probably did not read some of the essays; there is no evidence, for instance, that he read "Compensation," "Self-Reliance," or "The Over-Soul," which are among the sixteen unmarked essays of the thirty essays[12] contained in the three volumes. The fourteen other essays, however, are marked here and there with pencil;[13] and of these the following eight are annotated in Melville's handwriting: "Spiritual Laws," "Prudence," "Heroism," "The Poet," "Culture," "Worship," "Considerations by the Way," and "Illusions."[14] By considering the markings and annotations, one discovers some interesting facts about Melville's attitude toward Emerson. One should remember, of course, that the annotations are not to be thought of as notes for

[9] Carl Van Vechten's theory that *The Confidence-Man* is a satire on the Transcendentalists seems to me unfounded. See his article "The Later Work of Herman Melville," *Double Dealer,* III, 19 (Jan., 1922).

[10] On the verso side of the front cover of the *Essays: First Series* there is inscribed in pencil in Melville's hand, "H Melville/March 22d 1862/N. Y." The other volume contains the same inscription except that the year is given as "1861" instead of "1862." It seems probable that Melville bought both books at the same time and merely made a careless error when writing the date of the year in one of them.

The copy of *Essays: First Series* labeled "New Edition" and also "Fourth Edition," was published in Boston, by James Munroe and Company, in 1847. The copy of *Essays: Second Series,* "Third Edition," was published by the same house in 1844. Both are cheaply bound. When I examined these two volumes, they, together with Melville's copy of *The Conduct of Life,* were in the possession of Mrs. Eleanor Melville Metcalf, of Cambridge, Mass., by whose kind permission I had access to them. They are now in the Harvard College Library.

[11] This volume is inscribed in Melville's hand, "H. Melville/Nov 1870/N. Y." (There is the barest possibility that the third figure in the date of the year may be "9" instead of "7.") The title-page states that this copy is of both the "Author's Edition" and the "Second Edition"; the book was published in London, by Smith, Elder, and Co., in 1860.

[12] This figure includes the lecture on "New England Reformers."

[13] Melville marked passages in various ways: he underscored, he drew marginal lines, he used brackets and other symbols. Occasionally he marked a passage in two or three ways.

[14] The six essays that are marked but not annotated are "Art," "Character," "Manners," "Power," "Wealth," and "Beauty."

a systematic treatise on Emerson's philosophy: they are merely opinions that Melville recorded immediately after reading particular passages in Emerson's essays.

Although any grouping of these incidental observations would be arbitrary, they can be treated in a fairly coherent way under three general topics: first, comments on Emerson's ideas concerning the poet; second, praise of Emerson's views on life; and third, unfavorable criticism of Emerson's ideas concerning the problem of evil.[15]

II

The annotations on passages concerning men of letters show that Melville, like Emerson, was more concerned with thought in literature than with craftsmanship. The two men were in agreement on the timeless, universal qualities in the works of great men. In "Spiritual Laws" Emerson wrote:

> We are always reasoning from the seen to the unseen. Hence the perfect intelligence that subsists between wise men of remote ages. A man cannot bury his meaning so deep in his book, but time and like-minded men will find them. Plato had a secret doctrine, had he? What secret can he conceal from the eyes of Bacon? of Montaigne? of Kant? Therefore, Aristotle said of his works, "They are published and not published."[16]

Melville drew a line beside this passage and annotated, "Bully for Emerson!—Good." A similar idea in Emerson's "The Poet" brought forth another favorable comment. In writing of a conversation "on a recent writer of lyrics," Emerson said: "But when the question arose, whether he was not only a lyrist, but a poet, we were obliged to confess that he is plainly a contemporary, not an eternal man."[17] Melville marked heavily the words "contemporary, not an eternal man" and observed concerning them, "A noble expression, with a clear strong meaning."

He was likewise impressed by Emerson's eulogy of the poets as "liberating gods" who, with their figurative writing, open new worlds for other men. Beginning with "We are like persons who come out of a cave or cellar into the open air," Melville marked in "The Poet" the rest of the long paragraph in which that sentence

[15] Since no chronological development is discernible in the annotations, I have set aside the element of time in an effort to achieve more unity in considering them.

[16] *Essays: First Series*, p. 131.

[17] *Essays: Second Series*, pp. 9-10.

appears[18] and wrote the following praise: "All this is nobly written, and proceeds from noble thinking, and a natural sympathy with greatness."

He did not agree, however, with all Emerson's statements concerning creative artists. Although he concurred in the wisdom of a man's following his peculiar bent, he opposed the view that a man's ambition and powers are commensurate. In "Spiritual Laws" he marked the following sentences as "True":

He [each man] inclines to do something which is easy to him, and good when it is done, but which no other man can do. He has no rival. For the more truly he consults his own powers, the more difference will his work exhibit from the work of any other.

But the sentences immediately succeeding these he marked as "False":

His ambition is exactly proportioned to his powers. The height of the pinnacle is determined by the breadth of the base. Every man has this call of the power to do somewhat unique, and no man has any other call.[19]

In connection with Melville's opinion of this passage, one recalls his writing to Duyckinck in 1850:

Can you send me about fifty fast-writing youths. . . . If you can I wish you would, because since I have been here I have planned about that number of future works and can't find enough time to think about them separately.[20]

Another point upon which the two men's views conflicted is the effect upon the artist of the stimulants that are sometimes used to produce what Emerson called "animal exhilaration." After enumerating in "The Poet" several of the "*quasi*-mechanical substitutes for the true nectar" which help a man "to escape the custody of that body in which he is pent up, and of that jail-yard of individual relations in which he is enclosed," Emerson went on to affirm:

Hence a great number of such as were professionally expressors of Beauty, as painters, poets, musicians, and actors, have been more than others wont to lead a life of pleasure and indulgence; all but the few who received the true nectar; and, as it was a spurious mode of attain-

[18] *Essays: Second Series,* pp. 33-34.
[19] *Essays: First Series,* p. 126.
[20] Minnigerode, *op. cit.,* p. 71.

ing freedom, as it was an emancipation not into the heavens, but into the freedom of baser places, they were punished for that advantage they won, by a dissipation and deterioration.[21]

Melville marked this passage and wrote at the bottom of the page:

> No no no.—Titian—did he deteriorate?—Byron?—did he.—Mr E. is horribly narrow here. He has his Dardanelles for his every Marmora.[22] But he keeps nobly on, for all that!

If Emerson had had an opportunity to answer the questions in this annotation, he probably would have answered in the affirmative. He seems to have left no comment upon Titian; but he made numerous references to Byron, several of which show that although he admired that poet very much as a rhetorician, he held the not uncommon view that Byron's intellect was "depraved" and his will "perverted."[23]

In the paragraph on the harm of intoxicants to poets, Emerson went on to say:

> So the poet's habit of living should be set on a key so low and plain, that the common influences should delight him. His cheerfulness should be the gift of the sunlight; the air should suffice for his inspiration, and he should be tipsy with water.[24]

Melville annotated, "This makes the Wordsworthian poet—not the Shakespearean."[25] Although Emerson ranked Wordsworth very high,[26] he, like Melville, considered Shakespeare supreme among poets. For all his love of Shakespeare, however, he felt that the

[21] *Essays: Second Series,* pp. 30-31.

[22] *Lippincott's Gazetteer* defines the Dardenelles as "a narrow strait between Europe and Asia, connecting the Sea of Marmora and the arm of the Mediterranean known as the Aegean Sea. . . ."

[23] See the *Journals of Ralph Waldo Emerson,* ed. Edward Waldo Emerson and Waldo Emerson Forbes (Boston, 1909-1914), II, 4; VII, 163, 285; VIII, 89; and *The Complete Works of Ralph Waldo Emerson* (Centenary ed.; Boston, 1903-1904), II, 355, and XII, 319.

[24] *Essays: Second Series,* p. 32.

[25] The paragraph preceding the one just quoted from "The Poet" also caused Melville to refer to Wordsworth. This paragraph begins: "It is a secret which every intellectual man quickly learns, that beyond the energy of his possessed and conscious intellect, he is capable of a new energy (as of an intellect doubled on itself), by an abandonment to the nature of things. . . ." Melville noted in regard to this thought, "Wordsworth, 'One impulse from a vernal wood' &c" (the quoted words are from Wordsworth's well-known poem "The Tables Turned").

[26] See *Journals,* X, 68-69, where Emerson expresses his delight at Wordsworth's being acknowledged the greatest of English poets since Milton. For a good brief criticism by Emerson of Wordsworth's merits and faults, see *Works,* V, 297-298.

great dramatist's "profane life" and his "using his genius for the public amusement" had prevented him from filling the highest office of the poet.[27]

Melville's reaction to Emerson's argument that the poet should not indulge the senses but should become "tipsy with water" reminds one of the letter that Melville had written to Duyckinck in regard to Emerson. Here Melville replied to Duyckinck's complaint concerning Emerson's sobriety:

Ah, my dear Sir, that's his misfortune, not his fault. His belly, Sir, is in his chest, and his brains descend down into his neck, and offer an obstacle to a draughtful of ale or a mouthful of cake. . . .[28]

Melville's delight in conviviality is well known to all who are familiar with his life and works. The fact that he once entertained visions of paradise as a place where he might drink champagne with Hawthorne[29] sets him apart from Emerson; for although Emerson "placed wine before guests of discreet age and habit and took it with them, seldom more than one glass,"[30] he on one occasion recorded his regret that during the preceding year he had spent "say $20 in wine and liquors," only to the detriment of the drinkers, whereas that sum "would have bought a beautiful print that would have pleased for a century; or have paid a debt. . . ."[31] The conflicting views of the two authors concerning indulgence of the senses

[27] *Works*, IV, 218-219. In connection with Melville's comment on the Wordsworthian and the Shakespearean poets, it is interesting to note an opinion that Emerson expressed at the age of twenty-three. "It would seem," he wrote, that "the boisterous childhood, careless of criticism and poetry, the association of vulgar and unclean companions, were necessary to balance the towering spirit of Shakespeare, and that Mr. Wordsworth has failed of pleasing by being too much a *poet*" (in a letter to "Miss Emerson" (?), June 30, 1826; *Journals*, II, 106).

[28] Minnigerode, *op. cit.*, p. 34. Viola Chittenden White, *Symbolism in Herman Melville's Writings* (an unpublished doctoral dissertation at the University of North Carolina, 1934), p. 75, points out the similarity of this conceit of Melville's and one in Burton's *Anatomy of Melancholy*.

[29] During the composition of *Moby Dick* Melville wrote to Hawthorne: "If ever, my dear Hawthorne, in the eternal times that are to come, you and I shall sit down in Paradise, in some little shady corner by ourselves; and if we shall by any means be able to smuggle a basket of champagne there (I won't believe in a Temperance Heaven), and if we shall then cross our celestial legs in the celestial grass that is forever tropical, and strike our glasses and our heads together, till both musically ring in concert,—then, O my dear fellow-mortal, how shall we pleasantly discourse of all the things manifold which now so distress us,—when all the earth shall be but a reminiscence, yea, its final dissolution an antiquity" (Julian Hawthorne, *Nathaniel Hawthorne and his Wife: A Biography*, Boston, 1884, I, 402-403).

[30] Edward Waldo Emerson, *Emerson in Concord: A Memoir* (Boston, 1888), pp. 154-155.

[31] *Journals*, II, 468.

are quite in keeping with their differences in temperament as evidenced in the austerity of Emerson's essays and poems and in the spirit of revelry in parts of Melville's novels, notably *Mardi.*

As Melville took exception to the puritanical standards of living prescribed in "The Poet," so he objected to statements made there in regard to the poet's understanding and interpretation of life. Emerson said:

> For as it is dislocation and detachment from the life of God, that makes things ugly, the poet, who reattaches things to nature and the Whole,—re-attaching even artificial things, and violations of nature, to nature, by a deeper insight,—disposes very easily of the most disagreeable facts.[32]

Melville underlined "disposes very easily of the most disagreeable facts" and commented, "So it would seem. In this sense, Mr E. is a great poet." Further on in the essay Emerson asserted concerning the poet:

> He uses forms according to the life, and not according to the form. This is true science. The poet alone knows astronomy, chemistry, vegetation, and animation, for he does not stop at these facts, but employs them as signs. He knows why the plain, or meadow of space, was strown with these flowers we call suns, and moons, and stars; why the great deep is adorned with animals, with men, and gods. . . .[33]

Melville marked the last sentence, underscoring "He knows," and wrote, "Would some poet be pleased to tell us 'why.' Will Mr E.?" The unhappy result of Melville's search for some purpose in the universe explains his attitude toward Emerson's faith in the poet's vision. Melville agreed with Emerson that poets are "liberating gods" in that they present wise views on certain aspects of life, but he did not share Emerson's enthusiasm over the poet's ability to reconcile man to the deepest mysteries.

His criticism of Emerson on this point is related to his remarks about various opinions of Emerson concerning life in general.

III

In several instances Melville recorded a favorable opinion of Emerson's ideas about particular aspects of the individual and of society.

[32] *Essays: Second Series,* p. 20.

[33] *Ibid.,* p. 23.

He was delighted by Emerson's giving veracity and honesty the first place among the virtues. In "Illusions" Emerson declared:

I look upon the simple and childish virtues of veracity and honesty as the root of all that is sublime in character. Speak as you think, be what you are, pay your debts of all kinds. I prefer to be owned as sound and solvent, and my word as good as my bond, and to be what cannot be skipped, or dissipated, or undermined, to all the *eclat* in the universe. This reality is the foundation of friendship, religion, poetry, and art.[34]

Melville enclosed the last sentence in brackets and annotated, "True & admirable! Bravo!" for he too embodied in his writings the idea that Emerson here expressed. The necessity of being true to oneself is emphasized in the works of both men.

This fact explains the concurrence of their ideas in regard to the fundamental nature of heroism. Melville was impressed by the following passage in the *Essays:*

Self-trust is the essence of heroism. It is the state of the soul at war, and its ultimate objects are the last defiance of falsehood and wrong, and the power to bear all that can be inflicted by evil agents. . . . Its jest is the littleness of common life. That false prudence which dotes on health and wealth is the butt and merriment of heroism.[35]

Melville drew a marginal line beside these sentences and observed, "This is noble again."[36] Besides seeing in the lives of others the truth of these remarks by Emerson, he was aware that his own struggle in the late forties and the early fifties, his most productive period, was characterized by such a heroic spirit as Emerson defined.

Personal experience served also to make him agree with Emerson that great truth is learned only through suffering. In "Considerations by the Way" Emerson wrote that we daily pray "to be conventional," saying:

Supply, most kind gods! this defect in my address, in my form, in my fortunes, which puts me a little out of the ring: supply it, and let me be like the rest whom I admire, and on good terms with them. But the

[34] *The Conduct of Life,* p. 201.

[35] "Heroism," *Essays: First Series,* p. 229. The omission indicated, together with a few sentences preceding those quoted, is also marked.

[36] On the preceding page he underlined: "Heroism feels and never reasons, and therefore is always right . . . ," and wrote in the margin, "Alas for the truth again!" But he erased this remark, which happens still to be discernible. Perhaps he made the erasure because he felt that the remainder of the passage sufficiently qualified the underscored words.

wise gods say, No, we have better things for thee. By humiliations, by defeats, by loss of sympathy, by gulfs of disparity, learn a wider truth and humanity than that of a fine gentleman.[37]

Concerning the last sentence Melville commented, "Nothing can be truer or better said." By not writing books that would make him popular and financially prosperous, and by writing instead books containing the truth learned by just such means as "the wise gods" stipulated,[38] he himself had sacrificed the possibility of becoming "a fine gentleman."

Various other passages that Melville marked without annotating are obviously in accord with what he believed. For instance, he underlined "adversity is the prosperity of the great,"[39] and "Every man's task is his life-preserver";[40] and he heavily marked an old Persian proverb which Emerson praised:

> Fooled thou must be, though wisest of the wise:
> Then be the fool of virtue, not of vice.[41]

The annotations and markings referred to show quite clearly that Melville appreciated many of Emerson's opinions relative to personal integrity and fortitude. He was gratified by Emerson's argument that strong character is based upon self-reliance.

He felt, however, that Emerson went too far in his praise of self-reliance when he spoke disparagingly of the benefits to be derived from the study of foreign cultures. His attitude toward Emerson's views on traveling throws some light on that point. In writing of Americans' going to Europe for culture, Emerson queried, "You do not think you will find anything there which you have not seen at home?"[42] This statement caused Melville to observe, "Yet, possibly, Rome or Athens has something to show or suggest that Chicago has not." Since traveling had contributed much to Melville's own education, such a comment on his part seems only natural. The sights that he had seen were partly responsible for

[37] *The Conduct of Life*, p. 162. The phrase "by gulfs of disparity" is underlined. Lower on the page this sentence is also underlined: "A rich man was never insulted in his life: but this man [who becomes wise] must be stung."

[38] See William Braswell, "The Satirical Temper of Melville's *Pierre*," *American Literature*, VII, 424-426 (Jan., 1936).

[39] "Worship," *The Conduct of Life*, p. 145.

[40] *Ibid.*, p. 144.

[41] "Illusions," *The Conduct of Life*, p. 202. At the end of his tragic life Pierre, a symbol of Melville's own spiritual life, calls himself "the fool of Truth, the fool of Virtue, the fool of Fate" (*Pierre*, p. 499).

[42] "Culture," *The Conduct of Life*, p. 90.

the difference between his cosmic view and that of Emerson; and it was this difference which caused Melville to write his most severe criticism of Emerson.

IV

He found a great deal to criticize in Emerson's views upon the problem of evil. Since from the time of writing *Mardi* (1849) he himself had shown great concern over the suffering and wretchedness in the universe, it is not surprising that he found fault with Emerson's relatively unperturbed attitude in regard to the matter.

In the first place, he objected to what he considered an insinuation by Emerson that man himself is responsible for the origin of his ills. In "Heroism" Emerson said:

> The disease and deformity around us certify the infraction of natural, intellectual, and moral laws, and often violation on violation to breed such compound misery. A lockjaw that bends a man's head back to his heels, hydrophobia, that makes him bark at his wife and babes, insanity, that makes him eat grass; war, plague, cholera, famine, indicate a certain ferocity in nature, which, as it had its inlet by human crime, must have its outlet by human suffering.[43]

Melville marked the last part of this passage and commented:

> Look squarely at this, & what is it but mere theology—Calvinism?—The brook shows the stain of the banks it has passed thro. Still, these essays are noble.

Melville's use of the word "Calvinism" indicates that he perceived in the passage evidence of Emerson's belief in the fall of man through his own agency.[44] This dissenting comment came naturally

[43] *Essays: First Series*, pp. 226-227.

[44] As a youth Emerson had accepted the story of Adam's entailing sin upon all mankind. On Feb. 22, 1822, Emerson wrote concerning evil: "What is its origin? The sin which Adam brought into the world and entailed upon his children" (*Journals*, I, 115). On Nov. 23 of the same year a new note appears: "it should be remembered that we wisely assume the righteousness of the Creator in placing man in a probationary state. We do not seek with vain ambition to question the abstruse and unsearchable ground of this ordination, because it is plain matter of fact that we are incompetent to the discussion" (*ibid.*, I, 195). About a year later he wrote to ask his Aunt Mary Moody Emerson a number of questions, among them: "what is the origin of evil?" (Cabot, *op. cit.*, I, 103).

But as a mature man he wrote: "We say Paradise was; Adam fell; the Golden Age, and the like. We mean man is not as he ought to be; but our way of painting this is on Time and we say *was*" (under Aug. 21, 1837, *Journals*, IV, 287). The fall of man, he observed, is "the discovery we have made that we exist" (*Works*, III, 75).

enough from one who, brought up to believe in the doctrine of the fall, had in maturity come to the conclusion that God is responsible for the presence of evil as well as for the presence of good.

Similarly Melville was perturbed, for understandable reasons, by Emerson's belief that by obeying the immutable natural laws, which Emerson thought to be at one with a Beneficent Tendency of the universe, man attains goodness, whereas by disobeying them he becomes depraved.[45] So Emerson maintained when he wrote: "it is the undisciplined will that is whipped with bad thoughts and bad fortunes."[46] This statement caused Melville to accuse Emerson again of being theological: "Jumps into the pulpit from off the tripod here," Melville annotated. Another passage concerning the punishment that a man suffers for his sins evoked a humorous comment. In "Spiritual Laws" Emerson wrote:

> Our dreams are the sequel of our waking knowledge. The visions of the night bear some proportion to the visions of the day. Hideous dreams are exaggerations of the sins of the day.[47]

Melville annotated the last sentence thus: "Meaning, of course, the sins of *indigestion.*"

Like Emerson, Melville believed that man can improve his condition if he will but live by the best that is in him. Both *Redburn* and *White Jacket,* especially the latter, contain forcible argument to that effect. But Melville was not nearly so sanguine as Emerson concerning man's ability to overcome evil. He stressed much more than Emerson the fact that there is a difference between man and man. To quote Babbalanja, the philosopher in *Mardi,* some men are governed less by their "moral sense" than by their "instinctive passions," which fact makes it "easier for some men to be saints, than for others not to be sinners."[48] Babbalanja says concerning the man who is not a criminal: "That he is not bad, is not of him. Potter's clay and wax are all moulded by hands invisible. The soil decides the man."[49] Reduced to the ultimate, such a view might be held to show that Melville was a Necessitarian; but he, like Emerson, had no definite philosophical system. Suffice it here to

[45] See Chester Eugene Jorgenson, "Emerson's Paradise under the Shadow of Swords," *Philological Quarterly,* XI, 281-282 (July, 1932).

[46] "Illusions," *The Conduct of Life,* pp. 200-201.

[47] *Essays: First Series,* p. 132.

[48] *Mardi,* II, 156.

[49] *Ibid.,* II, 251.

say that he was more fully aware of the undesirable elements in human nature than Emerson was.

In an annotation already noted Melville said that if the tendency to dispose easily of disagreeable facts is a sign of poetic power, Emerson is a great poet. His dissatisfaction with Emerson's minimizing some of the harsher aspects of nature is evident in other marginal remarks. In the essay on "Prudence" Emerson declared: "The drover, the sailor, buffets it all day, and his health renews itself at as vigorous a pulse under the sleet, as under the sun of June."[50] Melville commented: "To one who has weathered Cape Horne as a common sailor what stuff all this is." The vivid description in *White Jacket* of the hardships and the danger encountered in rounding Cape Horn contains this statement concerning the Cape: "Lucky it is that it comes about midway in the homeward-bound passage, so that the sailors have time to prepare for it, and time to recover from it after it is astern."[51]

That Melville considered Emerson prejudiced in his treatment of unpleasant facts is likewise shown by an annotation upon a passage which proclaims the trustworthiness of man. "Trust men," wrote Emerson, "and they will be true to you; treat them greatly, and they will show themselves great, though they make an exception in your favor to all their rules in trade."[52] Melville observed, "God help the poor fellow who squares his life according to this." In *The Confidence-Man* (1857) Melville had written one of the severest satires ever directed at the idea that man is innately good and deserving of trust. Later works indicate that he came to hold a more favorable view of human nature, but he never found enough goodness in mankind to justify such an assumption as Emerson's.

His criticism of Emerson on these matters is merely a part of his criticism of Emerson's optimism in regard to the problem of evil. Emerson believed that evil is temporary. "Good is positive," he asserted. "Evil is merely privative, not absolute: it is like cold, which is the privation of heat."[53] Believing in a universal scheme that tends toward absolute good, Emerson made some statements

[50] *Essays: First Series,* p. 216. Emerson, however, did not deny the ferocities of nature. In "Fate" he recorded: "But Nature is no sentimentalist,—does not cosset or pamper us. We must see that the world is rough and surly. . . . The cold, inconsiderate of persons, tingles your blood, benumbs your feet, freezes a man like an apple" (*Works,* VI, 6-7).

[51] *White Jacket,* p. 137.

[52] "Prudence," *Essays: First Series,* p. 215.

[53] *Works,* I, 124.

that Melville thought ridiculous. In Emerson's assertion that "the first lesson of history is the good of evil"[54] Melville underlined "the good of evil" and wrote: "He still bethinks himself of his optimism—he must make that good somehow against the eternal hell itself."[55] Emerson's saying that "we use defects and deformities to a sacred purpose, so expressing our sense that the evils of the world are such only to the evil eye,"[56] caused Melville to inquire:

> What does the man mean? If Mr Emerson travelling in Egypt should find the plague-spot come out on him—would he consider that an evil sight or not? And if evil, would the eye be evil because it seemed evil to his eye, or rather to his sense using the eye for instrument?

A passage in "Spiritual Laws" had a similar effect upon Melville. "The good," Emerson wrote, "compared to the evil which he [a man] sees, is as his own good to his own evil."[57] Melville annotated:

> A perfectly good being, therefore, would see no evil.—But what did Christ see?—He saw what made him weep.—Howard, too, the "Philanthropist" must have been a very bad man—he saw, in jails, so much evil. To annihilate all this nonsense read the Sermon on the Mount, and consider what it implies.[58]

The Sermon on the Mount was for Melville the "greatest real miracle of all religions" because it shows Christ's vivid awareness of the evil in the world and expresses his "inexhaustible . . . tenderness and loving-kindness" for mankind.[59]

The annotations upon the subject of evil help to explain the most important critical remark that Melville made concerning Emerson. In "The Poet" Melville marked the passage beginning, "Language is fossil poetry,"[60] and wrote:

[54] "Considerations by the Way," *The Conduct of Life*, p. 157.

[55] The use of "hell" here is figurative, for Melville did not believe in eternal punishment. See *Mardi*, II, 33.

[56] "The Poet," *Essays: Second Series*, p. 20. To continue Emerson's passage: "In the old mythology, mythologists observe, defects are ascribed to divine natures, as lameness to Vulcan, blindness to Cupid, and the like, to signify exuberances." In this sentence Melville underlined "defects" and "signify exuberances," and in the margin he commented: " 'Defects' signify 'exuberances.'—My Dear Sir!"

[57] *Essays: First Series*, p. 133.

[58] One can see that where Melville wrote the last sentence he had written and erased some other remark.

[59] *Pierre*, pp. 289-290.

[60] *Essays: Second Series*, p. 24.

This is admirable, as many other thoughts of Mr Emerson's are. His gross and astonishing errors & illusions spring from a self-conceit so intensely intellectual and calm that at first one hesitates to call it by its right name. Another species of Mr Emerson's errors, or rather blindness, proceeds from a defect in the region of the heart.

By expressing admiration for much of Emerson, and by censuring at the same time what appeared to Melville to be intellectual smugness and an imperfect appreciation of the suffering of mankind, this comment sums up very well Melville's criticism of Emerson.[61] In spite of what the praise implies, the censure shows that between the two men's interpretations of truth there was a gulf.

V

How to account for that gulf is a problem which can be partially solved by a brief survey of certain factors in the lives of the two authors.

There is a real contrast between Emerson's long academic training and Melville's brief training. And there is a great difference between the types of people the two were associated with as young men: Melville's experiences on the high seas and on foreign soil brought him into contact with a wider variety of evils than was

[61] All except three of Melville's annotations upon Emerson have been considered. For anyone who may be curious, here are those three annotations:

In "Heroism," *Essays: First Series*, p. 232, Emerson wrote: "It is told of Brutus, that when he fell on his sword, after the battle of Philippi, he quoted a line of Euripides,—'O virtue! I have followed thee through life, and I find thee at last but a shade.' I doubt not the hero is slandered by this report. The heroic soul does not sell its justice and its nobleness." Melville commented: "The meaning of the exclamation imputed to Brutus is here wrested from its obvious import. The struggle in which he was foiled was for mankind, & not for himself."

In "Worship," *The Conduct of Life*, pp. 127-128, Emerson quoted from Chaucer to show "Chaucer's extraordinary confusion of heaven and earth in the picture of Dido:—

> She was so fair,
> So young, so lusty, with her eyen glad,
> That if that God that heaven and earthe made
> Would have a love for beauty and goodness,
> And womanhede, truth, and seemliness,
> Whom should he loven but this lady sweet?
> There n' is no woman to him half so meet.

With these grossnesses, we complacently compare our own taste and decorum." Melville underlined "these grossnesses" and observed: "The idea in the quoted lines is perfect poetry—therefore very far from blasphemous or gross—as it seems to me."

In "The Poet," *Essays: Second Series*, p. 29, Emerson wrote: "As the traveller who has lost his way, throws his reins on his horse's neck, and trusts to the instinct of the animal to find his road, so must we do with the divine animal who carries us through this world." Melville annotated: "This is an original application of the thought."

afforded by polite society of Boston and Cambridge. His financial failure as a novelist also taught him some bitter truth.

Yet it would be dangerous to assert that the hardships and the distress which Melville suffered were more difficult to bear than those which came to Emerson in his quiet surroundings. Mental defectiveness in one brother, temporary insanity in another, consumption that preyed upon himself and others in his family, deaths of loved ones, all caused Emerson sorrow; but they did not lessen his basic optimism.

The difference in the religious training of the two men is probably one of the chief reasons why one's outlook on life was much brighter than the other's. It is significant that Emerson was born and reared in a Unitarian world, whereas Melville spent his early years under the influence of the Reformed Theology. Emerson was taught to believe that the Deity is benevolent and that man is good. Melville was instructed in the Calvinistic views that God is a jealous God and that man is corrupt. Moreover, because of the place it gave to Christ, Melville's religious training was more emotional in effect than Emerson's. In both cases the teachings had an abiding influence.

Perhaps even more important than religious training, however, is the constitutional factor. At the age of thirty Emerson wrote in his journal:

> Men seem to be constitutionally believers and unbelievers. There is no bridge that can cross from a mind in one state to a mind in the other. All my opinions, affections, whimsies, are tinged with belief,—incline to that side. . . . But I cannot give reasons to a person of a different persuasion that are at all adequate to the force of my conviction. Yet when I fail to find the reason, my faith is not less.[62]

There is a notable contrast between this autobiographical passage and a shrewd analytical comment that Hawthorne made upon Melville. After a long talk with Melville, with whom he had conversed many times before, Hawthorne wrote in his journal in 1856:

> He can neither believe, nor be comfortable in his unbelief; and he is too honest and courageous not to try to do one or the other. If he were a religious man, he would be one of the most truly religious and reverential; he has a very high and noble nature, and [is] better worth immortality than most of us.[63]

[62] *Journals,* III, 210.

[63] Julian Hawthorne, *op. cit.,* II, 135.

Emerson's optimism had an unshakable basis in his intuition: physical facts and logic were secondary matters with him. Although during the early part of his career as a novelist Melville derived occasional ecstasy from intuitional thinking, he was temperamentally disposed to trust more to his understanding than to his intuition.

For that reason one might expect certain important influences from his reading. He was more affected by the arguments of skeptical philosophers than Emerson was. The attitudes of the two men toward Hume is enlightening. Emerson admitted that Hume's logic had proved invulnerable to all attacks upon it; yet he referred to Hume's arguments as "calumnies upon our nature."[64] Melville, on the other hand, said that although Hume was "the most skeptical of philosophical sceptics, yet" he was "full of that firm, creedless faith that embraces the spheres."[65]

The constitutional tastes of Emerson and Melville as well as the influences of their reading are implied in Emerson's fondness for Plotinus, who minimized the importance of evil in the universal scheme, and Melville's fondness for such works as Ecclesiastes. When praising that book, Melville wrote: "that mortal man who hath more of joy than sorrow in him, that mortal man cannot be true—not true, or undeveloped."[66] This assertion, written before Melville annotated Emerson's essays, is not unlike an opinion that he expressed some years after that experience. When writing to thank an English correspondent for a copy of Thomson's *The City of Dreadful Night, and Other Poems,* he said:

> As to the pessimism [of Thomson's poetry], although neither pessimist nor optimist myself, nevertheless I relish it in the verse, if for nothing else than as a counterpoise to the exorbitant hopefulness, juvenile and shallow, that makes such a bluster in these days, at least in some quarters.[67]

This taste for pessimism in literature helps to explain why at the very end of his life Melville read sympathetically certain passages in the works of Schopenhauer.[68] An admirer of Schopenhauer—

[64] *Journals,* I, 292; see also *ibid.,* I, 290; *ibid., passim;* and Cabot, *op. cit.,* I, 104-105.

[65] *Redburn,* p. 377.

[66] *Moby Dick,* II, 181.

[67] Letter to James Billson, Jan. 22, 1885, *The* [London] *Nation and the Athenaeum,* XXIX, 712 (Aug. 13, 1921).

[68] See Braswell, *Herman Melville and Christianity,* chap. ix, for a discussion of some of the markings in the seven volumes of Schopenhauer that Melville owned.

a philosopher whom Emerson called "odious"[69]—would hardly approve of some of the ideas in Emerson's essays.

On the whole, in the light of all the facts noted concerning the two men, Melville's criticism of Emerson seems very much what one might have expected. That Melville censured Emerson's attitude toward evil is no more surprising than that he praised such qualities as Emerson's mastery of rhetoric and his love of goodness.

[69] *Works,* VIII, 138.

Emerson and Quakerism

Frederick B. Tolles

A VAST deal of learned ink has flowed on the subject of the origins of Emerson's thought. We have had studies of his indebtedness to Asian philosophy, to Plato and the Neo-Platonists, to Swedenborg, to Goethe and the German philosophers, and so on through a large corpus of scholarly writings. And we have had various estimates of his relation to, or his place in, the Puritan tradition. There is one more thread, however, which remains to be picked up before the final statement is made concerning the influences which moulded Emerson's thinking. And once this thread is picked up and laid in its proper place it will be found in a measure to clarify and define Emerson's relation to Puritanism.

Emerson himself furnished the clue, and it is rather surprising that the commentators have so generally neglected it. On one occasion when his kinsman, the Reverend David Greene Haskins, asked him to define his religious position, Emerson answered "with greater deliberateness, and longer pauses between his words than usual, 'I am more of a Quaker than anything else. I believe in the "still, small voice," and that voice is Christ within us.' "[1]

The significant parallelism between the religion of the Friends and the ideas which were abroad in New England in the thirties

[1] David Greene Haskins, *Ralph Waldo Emerson: His Maternal Ancestors, with Some Reminiscences of Him* (Boston, 1886), p. 48.

There is some reason to believe that Emerson may have made this, or a similar statement more than once to his friends. For we find Daniel Ricketson, the New Bedford historian and poet, writing to a friend in 1895, thirteen years after Emerson's death, "I can say in the words of my friend Ralph Waldo Emerson, 'If I am anything, I am a Quaker' " (*Daniel Ricketson and His Friends*, ed. Anna Ricketson and Walton Ricketson, Boston, 1902, p. 261). Of course Ricketson may here be quoting, consciously or unconsciously, from Haskins's book or from E. W. Emerson's *Emerson in Concord* (Boston, 1889, p. 48) in which the statement in question was reprinted.

There is, however, additional evidence that Emerson's contemporaries were in the habit of thinking of him as a Quaker. Miss Geraldine Endsor Jewsbury of Manchester, England, wrote to Jane Carlyle in 1848: "Emerson has taken his departure . . . I don't fancy he took to me. I am too tumultuous for him . . . I had far rather the Quaker liked me" (*Selections from the Letters of Geraldine Endsor Jewsbury to Jane Welsh Carlyle*, ed. Mrs. Alexander Ireland, London, 1892, pp. 235-236). It is possible, to be sure, that Miss Jewsbury may have used the term "Quaker" in a general sense with reference merely to Emerson's quiet demeanor, and that she intended it to carry no religious connotation. I give the evidence for what it is worth.

and forties was apparent to Emerson and his contemporaries if it has not been to subsequent scholars.[2] George Bancroft, writing in 1837, implied a comparison between Quakerism and Transcendentalism when he contrasted them both with the philosophy of Locke.[3] Emerson read the second volume of Bancroft's *History* with its famous panegyric on the Quakers soon after it appeared, and was pleased to note that "the huge world has at last come round to . . . George Fox and William Penn; time-honoured John Locke received kicks."[4] A few years later (1842) Emerson contributed to the *Dial* a paper on Transcendentalism in which he quoted part of a letter written by a Quaker, as follows:

> It is very interesting to me to see, as I do, all around me here, the essential doctrines of the Quakers revived, modified, stript of all that puritanism and sectarianism had heaped upon them, and made the foundation of an intellectual philosophy, that is illuminating the finest minds and reaches the wants of the least cultivated.[5]

Emerson commented thus:

> The identity, which the writer of this letter finds between the speculative opinions of serious persons at the present moment, and those entertained by the first Quakers, is indeed so striking as to have drawn a very general attention of late years to the history of that sect. . . . Of course, in proportion to the depth of the experience, will be its independence on time and circumstances, yet one can hardly read George Fox's Journal, or Sewel's History of the Quakers, without many a rising of joyful surprise at the correspondence of facts and expressions to states of thought and feeling with which we are very familiar.[6]

[2] The only recent writer who, to my knowledge, has given his serious attention to this correspondence is Mr. Henry Seidel Canby (*Classic Americans,* New York, 1931, p. 155). He tends to make light of the similarity, maintaining that "the Quakers were content with inner light, but Emerson, sprung from a harsher discipline, and a stronger will, rationalizes this inner light and lifts it out of mysticism into a doctrine for intelligent men." I shall not here take issue with this statement; some objections to it, however, will appear in the sequel.

Mr. Van Wyck Brooks appears to be aware of the importance of Quakerism in Emerson's background of ideas, but he limits his consideration of it to a few passing allusions patched together from scattered entries in the *Journals* (see *The Life of Emerson,* New York, 1932, p. 45; and *The Flowering of New England,* New York, 1936, p. 199).

[3] *History of the United States* (Boston, 1837), II, chap. xvi. Octavius Brooks Frothingham (*Transcendentalism in New England,* New York, 1876, pp. 117-120) comments briefly on this passage.

[4] *Journals of Ralph Waldo Emerson,* ed. Edward Waldo Emerson and Waldo Emerson Forbes (Boston and New York, 1909-1914), IV, 304. Henceforth these will be cited simply as *Journals.*

[5] *Uncollected Writings,* ed. Charles C. Bigelow (New York, 1912), p. 62.

[6] *Ibid.,* p. 63.

Thoreau, too, had some inkling of it, for in 1843 he wrote to his sister on hearing a Quaker sermon by Lucretia Mott, "It was a good speech,—Transcendentalism in its mildest form."[7]

This affinity, so clearly recognized by Emerson and his contemporaries, and so overlooked by later students, will bear investigation. But before we proceed to examine Emerson's work for traces of Quaker influence, let us indulge in a side-glance at the intellectual tradition to which both Emerson and the Quakers belonged.

The sect of Quakers arose in the middle of the seventeenth century as a by-product of the Puritan movement. When Puritanism, which had been conceived and brought forth in rebellion against an established ecclesiastical order, hardened in its turn into an equally rigid ecclesiastical system, George Fox appeared on the scene, took up the banner of protestantism once more, and carried it to an advanced position whither few were willing to follow. Feeling that the English people had forsaken the fountain of living waters and had hewed them out broken cisterns which could hold no water, he carried the Lutheran principle of the priesthood of all believers to its logical conclusion: whereas the Puritans had "purified" the church of prayer-books, vestments and music, the Quakers wished to go one step further and purify the church of the clergy. "Some seek truth in books, some in learned men, but what they seek for is in themselves,"[8] wrote William Penn. Thus Fox and the other primitive Friends began where the other reformers had left off, and Quakerism must therefore be regarded not only as a revolt against the Puritan church but also, and at the same time, a further extension of the basic reforming spirit which underlay Puritanism.

The position of Emerson with reference to Puritanism was curiously and significantly like that of the first Friends. In England the ascendency of the Puritans came to an abrupt end in 1660; but in America and particularly in New England, where Puritanism had driven its roots into the granite bedrock, it lingered on for two hundred years.[9] As Parrington has it, "there was no vigorous attack, but only a tedious decay."[10] Before any vigorous concerted attack

[7] *Familiar Letters* (Concord ed., Boston, 1929), p. 97.

[8] Quoted by Bancroft, *History of the United States*, II, 338.

[9] A few courageous voices like those of Anne Hutchinson and Roger Williams were lifted up at the outset against the iron-clad sway of "God's unworthy Prophets," but they were voices in the wilderness, and for the most part they went unheard.

[10] *Main Currents in American Thought* (New York, 1927), I, 148.

was possible there had to be a leader; and in the second third of the nineteenth century, after the way had been opened by the Unitarian movement, the leader appeared in the person of Ralph Waldo Emerson.

In Emerson's youth the old religion "still dwelt like a Sabbath peace in the country population of New England, [teaching] privation, self-denial, and sorrow."[11] In 1841, when Dr. Ezra Ripley, the pastor of the Concord church, died at the patriarchal age of ninety years, Emerson was able to say:

> He was identified with the ideas and forms of the New England Church, which expired about the same time with him, so that he and his coevals seemed the rear guard of the great camp and army of the Puritans, which, however in its last days declining into formalism, in the heyday of its strength had planted and liberated America.[12]

Like George Fox, who rejected priestly authority and bade men look for recourse to "that of God in themselves," Emerson turned away from churches and placed his emphasis on the self-reliant individual. But the analogy does not stop there. Quakerism, as we have seen, was at once a protest against the existing Puritan establishment and a continuation of the nonconforming principle from which Puritanism took its rise. It was so also with Emerson. It is not enough merely to see that he turned his back upon his Puritan inheritance; it must also be recognized that he took that inheritance as a point of departure from which to continue on the old road of nonconformity along which his Puritan ancestors had started. Emerson himself understood the true nature of his position when he wrote in his *Journals* on the occasion, already mentioned, of Dr. Ripley's death:

> Great, grim, earnest men, I belong by natural affinity to other thoughts and schools than yours, but my affection hovers respectfully about your retiring footprints, your unpainted churches, strict platforms, and sad offices; the iron-gray deacon and the wearisome prayer rich with the diction of ages.
>
> Well, the new is only the seed of the old. What is this abolition and non-resistance and temperance but the continuation of Puritanism, though

[11] *Journals,* V, 543.

[12] *Lectures and Biographical Sketches,* p. 383. All references are to the Centenary Edition of Emerson's *Works* (Boston and New York, 1903-1904).

it operate inevitably the destruction of the church in which it grew, as the new is always making the old superfluous?[13]

The fundamental agreement which is seen to exist between the attitude of Emerson and that of the Quakers is therefore due in part, at least, to the similarity of the historical circumstances out of which they grew. Both took their rise in a reaction against, and at the same time a logical development from, Puritanism, and the delay which attended the ultimate revolt in New England can only be ascribed to the firmer hold which Puritanism had on the New England mind.

We know that Emerson admired and respected the Quakers as a sect. "I have sometimes thought," he said in 1869:

and indeed I always do think, that the sect of the Quakers in their best representatives appear to me to have come nearer to the sublime history and genius of Christ than any other of the sects. They have kept the traditions perhaps for a longer time, kept the early purity, did keep it for a longer time; and I think I see this cause, I think I find in the language of that sect, in all the history and all the anecdotes of its leaders and teachers, a certain fidelity to the Scriptural character.[14]

We also know that he remembered certain individuals among the Quakers with deepest gratitude. "I refer now," he wrote in 1836:

to last evening's lively remembrance of the scattered company who have ministered to my highest wants: Edward Stabler,[15] Peter Hunt, Sampson Reed, my peasant Tarbox, Mary Rotch, Jonathan Phillips, A. B. Alcott,—even Murat has a claim,—a strange class, plain and wise, whose charm to me is wonderful, how elevating! . . . Theirs is the true light of all our day. They are the argument for the spiritual world, for their spirit is it. Nothing is impossible, since such communion has already been. Whilst we hear them speak, how frivolous are the distinctions of fortune! and the voice of fame is as unaffecting as the tinkle of the passing sleigh-bell.[16]

[13] *Journals,* VI, 53.

[14] From a lecture on "Natural Religion" delivered at Horticultural Hall in Boston on April 4, 1869 (*Uncollected Lectures,* ed. Clarence Gohdes, New York, 1932, p. 57).

[15] This name appears in the published *Journals* as *Stubler.* The editors, in transcribing the MS, apparently misread the name, for the man here referred to was certainly Edward *Stabler* (1769-1831), a Quaker preacher who practiced the trade of druggist in Alexandria (see William Stabler, *A Memoir of the Life of Edward Stabler,* Philadelphia, 1846). I have not seen the MS, but a glance at any facsimile of Emerson's handwriting will show that he habitually neglected to close his *a*'s, a fact which would easily account for the error. Moreover, I am informed by the City Records Office in Alexandria that the name *Stubler* is unknown there.

[16] *Journals,* IV, 51-52.

The names in this list which concern us are those of two Quakers, Edward Stabler and Mary Rotch.[17] I purpose now to indicate something of Emerson's indebtedness to these two persons, adding, as a third branch of the inquiry, a discussion of the influence of Quaker writers upon his intellectual development.

It is worthy of note at the outset that the years during which he was subject to the direct influence of Quakerism (roughly 1827-1836) were the formative years of his intellectual life. They were the years immediately preceding his first publication—a period during which we can watch the growth of his characteristic ideas as they germinated and began to bear fruit in the *Journals*.

Emerson's method of composition is sufficiently well known. He was continually extracting from his reading, his intercourse with friends, his observations of nature, and his own ceaseless reflections the precious metal from which to coin ideas. He stamped each day's coinage with his own likeness, and committed it to the "savings-bank"—his *Journals*—where he had always a reserve fund available upon which to draw for the material of his essays. It is, therefore, chiefly to the *Journals* that we must look for guidance in determining the scope and direction of the Quaker influence on Emerson's writings.

About Edward Stabler and Emerson's relations with him we know very little. He makes his first appearance in the *Journals* in an entry dated May 12, 1828:

> It was said of Jesus that "he taught as one having authority," a distinction most palpable. There are a few men in every age, I suppose, who teach thus. Stabler the Quaker, whom I saw on board the boat in Delaware Bay, was one.[18]

Emerson must have encountered Stabler on his way back to Boston from the South whither he had gone, late in 1826, for his health's sake. He was in Alexandria in May, 1827, and proceeded from there to Philadelphia by boat. Presumably he struck up an acquaintance with the old Quaker, and immediately engaged him, as was his

[17] Six years later, in 1842, he made another list in which the names of actual persons mingle with those of characters in literature. Most of the names are new, but those of his two Quaker friends reappear. "I have a company who travel with me in the world," he writes, "and one or other of whom I must still meet, whose office none can supply to me: Edward Stabler; my Methodist Tarbox; Wordsworth's Pedlar; Mary Rotch; Alcott; Manzoni's Fra Cristoforo; Swedenborg; Mrs. Black; and now Greaves, and his disciple Lane; supreme people who represent, with whatever defects, the Ethical Idea" (*Journals,* VI, 240-241).

[18] *Journals,* II, 296.

custom, in serious talk. Few things are as ephemeral as conversations with chance acquaintances, and, except for a few fragments, this conversation between the young divinity student and the old Quaker itinerant is lost.

Of the two scraps of this conversation which Emerson later preserved only one has significance for us. In the spring of 1831 he was giving a good deal of thought to the notion of compensation, and Stabler's words, as he remembered them, played directly into this train of thought. In his *Journals* for June 29, 1831, he wrote:

> Is not the law of compensation perfect? . . . Old Stabler, the Quaker in the Baltimore steamboat, said to me, that, if a man sacrificed his impurity, purity should be the price with which it would be paid; if a man gave up his hatred, he should be rewarded with love—'tis the same old melody and it sounds through the vast of being.[19]

Seven years later, when he was casting about for material to incorporate into his address before the graduating class of the Divinity School at Cambridge, he came across this entry, and it appears, thus phrased, in that address: "He who does a good deed is instantly ennobled. He who does a mean deed is by the action itself contracted. He who puts off impurity, thereby puts on purity."[20]

As to what further intellectual stimulus Emerson received from Stabler we can only conjecture.[21] It seems not unreasonable, however, to attribute to his influence the strong interest which Emerson later manifested in the Society of Friends.

We pass from the shadowy figure of Edward Stabler to a consideration of Emerson's reading in the literature of Quakerism. He was reading about George Fox in Sewel's *History of the Quakers* early in 1830. The first reference in the *Journals* runs as follows:

> And there is some confused idealism in the conversation of a soldier with Geo. Fox [Sewel's *History of the Quakers,* vol. I, p. 85]. "Christ did not

[19] *Journals,* II, 389. Cf. the following passage from a letter of Stabler, dated 8th mo. 30, 1828: "If we would give up our pride, we should have humility in place of it. Our obduracy might be exchanged for tenderness of heart; and our fierceness, for gentleness, &c" (William Stabler, *Memoir of the Life of Edward Stabler,* p. 151).

[20] *Nature, Addresses and Lectures,* p. 122.

[21] The only other reference to Stabler in the *Journals* is another fragment of their conversation which Emerson suddenly remembered in 1833: "Stabler said the difference between Brother Witherlee's preaching and his was this: Brother W. said, 'If you do not become good you shall be whipt,' and himself said, 'If you will become good you shall not be whipt' " (*Journals,* III, 228). He never converted this anecdote into ready currency for the essays, but left it drawing interest in the "savings-bank."

suffer outwardly," said Fox. [The Soldier asked him] "whether there were not Jews, Chief Priests and Pilate outwardly?"[22]

The saintly career of George Fox made a deep impression upon Emerson. Fox's name figures in many of those lists, so frequent in the *Journals,* of men whom Emerson especially revered, alongside those of Jesus, Plato, Michelangelo, Shakespeare, Swedenborg, and others. The character of George Fox made a strong appeal to him because of the Quaker's basic conviction that "though he read of Christ and God, he knew them only from the like spirit in his own soul."[23]

Two years later Emerson picked Sewel up again, and read further in the history of the Friends, although it does not appear that he read the entire work.[24] His reading at this time is of especial interest in view of the circumstances in which he found himself. It was the hour of decision. He had told his congregation at the Second Church in Boston "that he could no longer administer the Lord's Supper as a divinely appointed, sacred ordinance of religion . . . that he could henceforth conduct the service only as a memorial service, without attributing to it any deeper significance."[25] The parish was not willing to sanction any change in the rite, feeling that "it would be tantamount to admitting that they were no longer Christians."[26] Accordingly, he was faced with the choice between resigning his charge and continuing to administer a sacrament with which he had no sympathy. "The objection to conforming to usages which have become dead to you," he later wrote, "is that it scatters your force."[27] He found his objection to conforming to

[22] *Journals,* II, 335. There may be some confused idealism here, but there is also some confused reporting. As the incident stands in Sewel, *The History of the Rise, Increase, and Progress of the Society of Friends* (London, 1833), pp. 106-107, the soldier denied that there was such a person as Jesus. Fox asked, "Did he not suffer in Jerusalem?" The soldier answered, "Not outwardly." Then Fox asked, "Were there not Jews, Chief Priests, and Pilate outwardly?" The soldier was perplexed, and refused to answer.

Traces of Emerson's reading in Sewel appear in at least two of the sermons which he preached as minister of the Second Church in Boston during the next two years. See *Young Emerson Speaks,* ed. A. C. McGiffert, Jr. (Boston, 1938), pp. 134, 186.

[23] Quoted by Emerson in a speech at the second annual meeting of the Free Religious Association in Boston, May 28, 1869 (*Miscellanies,* p. 488).

[24] His notes (*Journals,* II, 497-500) are all based on the first volume. This is not surprising, considering his habit of reading for "lustres" only.

[25] These are the words he used, years later, in telling the story to Charles Eliot Norton (*Letters of Charles Eliot Norton,* ed. Sara Norton and M. A. DeWolfe Howe, Boston, 1913, I, 509).

[26] *Ibid.*

[27] "Self-Reliance," *Essays, First Series,* p. 54.

this usage insuperable, and he fled to the White Mountains for a few weeks to settle the matter with his conscience.

Among the books which he took with him were Sewel's *History of the Quakers* and Tuke's *Memoirs of the Life of Fox.*[28] He filled several pages in his *Journals* with notes on these two books. And, significantly enough, these notes follow directly after a long passage of self-examination in which we can actually watch the progress of his mind from doubt and perplexity to certainty and decision. "I know very well," he says at the end:

that it is a bad sign in a man to be too conscientious, and stick at gnats. The most desperate scoundrels have been the over-refiners. Without accommodation society is impracticable. But this ordinance is esteemed the most sacred of religious institutions, and I cannot go habitually to an institution which they esteem holiest with indifference and dislike.[29]

In the notes which follow he refers almost at once to Fox's attitude towards the Communion rite. It is hard to escape the conclusion that his purpose in reading these particular books at this time was to find a source of moral strength and reassurance for the decision which he was about to make. When he returned to Boston in September, his mind was made up. It was a memorable and a heroic decision, for he knew that henceforth all but a few liberal pulpits in New England were forever closed to him. By this decision America lost a preacher and gained a man of letters.

Here again, one of Emerson's contemporaries saw clearly what subsequent generations have failed to recognize. A lifelong Quaker friend wrote in 1840:

Yr refusal to administer the Lord's Supper years ago, & your late omission of public prayer are both spoken of with an irrecognition of the existence of Quakers which is too ridiculous.[30]

On September 9, 1832, Emerson delivered from the pulpit of the Second Church a well-ordered exposition of his views on the Lord's Supper, announcing at the close of the sermon his intention of re-

[28] Neither Emerson nor his editors name this book specifically, but "Fox's Life" (*Journals,* II, 499) can only refer to Tuke's *Memoirs* inasmuch as it was the only biography of Fox which had been written by 1832. All of Emerson's notes can be traced to Sewel except this: "He also wrote to them [the magistrates] about the evil of putting to death for stealing." The source of this statement is Henry Tuke, *Memoirs of the Life of Fox* (Philadelphia, 1815), p. 35.

[29] *Journals,* II, 497.

[30] *Records of a Lifelong Friendship: Ralph Waldo Emerson and William Henry Furness,* ed. Horace Howard Furness (Boston, 1910), p. 13.

signing his charge. The sermon opens with a brief historical review of the age-old controversy over the Eucharist, a controversy almost coeval with the rite itself, and Emerson does not forget to mention in this connection that "it is now near two hundred years since the Society of Quakers denied the authority of the rite altogether, and gave good reasons for disusing it."[31] The arguments which he adduces in support of his decision are precisely those which the Quakers had used,[32] and his conclusion expresses an attitude towards Christianity which is entirely consonant with the religion of the Friends:

> I am not engaged to Christianity by decent forms, or saving ordinances; it is not usage, it is not what I do not understand, that binds me to it,—let these be the sandy foundations of falsehoods. What I revere and obey in it is its reality, its boundless charity, its deep interior life, the rest it gives to mind, the echo it returns to my thoughts, the perfect accord it makes with my reason through all its representation of God and His Providence; and the persuasion and courage that come out thence to lead me upward and onward. Freedom is the essence of this faith. It has for its object simply to make men good and wise. Its institutions then should be as flexible as the wants of men. That form out of which the life and suitableness have departed should be as worthless in its eyes as the dead leaves that are falling around us.[33]

Emerson's contact, through his reading, with the Friends' way of life had borne fruit in the most decisive action of his life. It is no wonder that his brother ministers found his behavior rather "Quakerish," and even hinted at mental derangement![34]

He did not forget what he had read in Sewel's *History*. Among the notes which he took in 1832 on the life of George Fox we find this: "He taught that the Scriptures could not be understood but by the same spirit that gave them forth."[35] Looking into Sewel, we find that a certain priest at Nottingham had told his congregation that they were to try all doctrines, religions, and opinions by the Scriptures.

> George Fox hearing this, felt such mighty power and godly zeal working in him, that he was made to cry out, "O no, it is not the Scripture, but

[31] *Miscellanies,* p. 4.

[32] See, for instance, Robert Barclay, *An Apology for the True Christian Divinity* (1st ed., London, 1678), Proposition XIII.

[33] *Miscellanies,* p. 21.

[34] James Elliot Cabot, *A Memoir of Ralph Waldo Emerson* (Boston, 1887), I, 158.

[35] *Journals,* II, 498.

it is the Holy Spirit, by which the holy men of God gave forth the Scriptures, whereby opinions, religions, and judgments are to be tried."[36]

In his very first published work Emerson made use of this idea without acknowledging the source: viz., "Every scripture is to be interpreted by the same spirit which gave it forth,'—is the fundamental law of criticism."[37] And many years later (1854), in an address on the Fugitive Slave Law, he said, apropos of attempts made to justify slavery by quoting the Bible:

These things show that no forms, neither constitutions, nor laws, nor covenants, nor churches, nor bibles, are of any use in themselves. . . . To interpret Christ it needs Christ in the heart. The teachings of the Spirit can be apprehended only by the same spirit that gave them forth.[38]

In January, 1835, he was reading about George Fox again: "Bitter cold days, yet I read of that inward fervor which ran as fire from heart to heart through England in George Fox's time."[39] His immediate object this time was to collect material for a lecture on the life of Fox which he was to deliver in Boston before the Society for the Diffusion of Useful Knowledge on February 26, 1835. This lecture has never been published, but a few sentences abstracted from it are printed in an appendix to J. E. Cabot's *Memoir*.[40] Emerson apparently went back to Sewel and Tuke for his biographical information, and he incorporated into his lecture many of the notes which he had made on these authors in 1832. The lecture does not add materially to Emerson's literary stature or to our knowledge of the contents of his mind, and may well be suffered to remain in manuscript. We may, however, note that in this lecture he described Fox as "a realist, even [ever?] putting a thing for a name."[41]

[36] Sewel, *History*, I, 58. This was one of George Fox's ruling ideas; one finds it constantly reiterated in the pages of his *Journal*. The thought can be traced back to the German mystics of the sixteenth and early seventeenth centuries—Sebastian Franck, Caspar Schwenkfeld and, above all, Jacob Boehme—the spiritual forerunners of George Fox and the Quakers (see Rufus M. Jones, *Spiritual Reformers in the 16th & 17th Centuries*, London, 1914, pp. 60-61, 73-74, 170, 225, and *passim*). We know, from frequent references in the essays and the *Journals*, that Emerson was a reader of Boehme. He may have read, in John Sparrow's preface to the *Aurora* (edition of 1656, which he was reading in August, 1835 [*Journals*, III, 524]), that no one "can . . . understand the Holy Scriptures but by the same Gifts of the Holy Spirit in the Soul" (quoted by Jones, *Spiritual Reformers*, p. 225).

[37] *Nature, Addresses and Lectures*, p. 35.

[38] *Miscellanies*, p. 234.

[39] *Journals*, III, 432.

[40] II, 713-714.

[41] *Ibid.*, II, 713. This phrase goes back to "a reformer, putting ever a thing for a form," in his earlier notes on Fox (*Journals*, II, 500).

He must have recognized his own kinship and that of his like-minded contemporaries with the founder of Quakerism, for he used the phrase again: "Realist seems the true name for the movement party among our Scholars here. I at least endeavor to make the exchange evermore, of a reality for a name."[42]

His interest in George Fox did not cease with the delivery of this lecture. On the contrary, there are a number of references to Fox scattered through the *Journals* for 1835, indicating that his life and teachings were constantly before Emerson's mind during that year. For instance:

> Some persons in Rhode Island saying to George Fox, that, if they had money enough, they would hire him to be their minister, he said, "Then it was time for him to be gone, for if their eye was to him, or to any of them, then would they never come to their own teacher."[43]

No doubt he copied down this anecdote because it perfectly reflected his own feeling about the ministry. "I have sometimes thought," he wrote elsewhere, "that in order to be a good minister it was necessary to leave the ministry."[44]

Again he observed: "George Fox's chosen expression for the God manifest in the mind is the Seed. He means the seed of which the Beauty of the world is the Flower, and Goodness is the Fruit."[45] Emerson made frequent use of this expression in his essays,[46] for, like so many other utterances of Fox, it harmonized perfectly with his own thinking.

At the same time that he was preparing his lecture on Fox, he wrote in his *Journals:*

> The Quaker casts himself down a passive instrument of the Supreme Reason, and will not risque silencing it by venturing the cooperation of his Understanding. He therefore enacts his first thought, however violent or ludicrous, nor stays to consider whether the purport of his vision may not be expressed in more seemly and accustomed forms.[47]

If one did not know that Emerson's thoughts had been running in this vein for some time, one would be tempted to see in this pas-

[42] *Journals,* IV, 459.

[43] *Journals,* III, 493-494. This anecdote is found in Fox's *Journal,* ed. Norman Penney (London, 1924), p. 290; and is excerpted thence into Tuke's *Memoirs* (ed. cited), p. 232.

[44] *Journals,* II, 491.

[45] *Journals,* III, 497.

[46] See, for example, "Intellect," *Essays, First Series,* p. 332, and note; and "Character," *Lectures and Biographical Sketches,* pp. 96-97.

[47] *Journals,* III, 433.

sage—suggested, surely, by his acquaintance with Fox's life—the germ of "Self-Reliance." Here, at any rate, was remarkable corroboration of his own convictions, for he had long held that our first and third thoughts coincide,[48] and that "our first thought is rendered back to us by the trumpets of the Last Judgment."[49]

We lie [he wrote] in the lap of immense intelligence, which makes us receivers of its truth and organs of its activity. When we discern justice, when we discern truth, we do nothing of ourselves, but allow a passage to its beams. If we ask whence this comes, if we seek to pry into the soul that causes, all philosophy is at fault. Its presence or its absence is all we can affirm. Every man discriminates between the voluntary acts of his mind and his involuntary perceptions, and knows that to his involuntary perceptions a perfect faith is due.[50]

To say that Emerson owed his doctrine of self-reliance exclusively to the Quakers would be to disregard most of the evidence; nevertheless, he himself recognized the identity of his teaching with the Quaker doctrine of the Inner Light. In George Fox he found a kindred spirit—a religious teacher who posited his religion on man's "involuntary perceptions"—a preacher whose preaching consisted in calling men to "that of God in themselves."

George Fox was not the only one among the early Quakers whose career interested Emerson. Strangely enough, the bizarre figure of the enthusiast James Nayler appealed to him, and he referred to Nayler's dying words as one of the few utterances in literature "of the highest moral class."[51]

In 1830, the same year in which he first picked up Sewel's *History,* he was reading Thomas Clarkson's *Life of William Penn.*[52] He respected in Penn as in Fox the unquestioning readiness to accept the precepts of the New Testament literally, and he saw in Penn's career a moving affirmation of the practicability of the New Testament way of life.

I wish the Christian principle, the *ultra* principle of non-resistance and returning good for ill, might be tried fairly. William Penn made one

[48] *Journals,* II, 435-436.
[49] "Self-Reliance," *Essays, First Series,* p. 45.
[50] *Ibid.,* pp. 64-65.
[51] *Journals,* V, 112. He marked this speech in his copy of Sewel's *History,* and twice quoted it in full: once, in the 1835 lecture on George Fox, and again, in a paper on "Transcendentalism" written for the *Dial* in 1842 (reprinted in *Uncollected Writings,* p. 64).
[52] *Journals,* II, 328.

trial. The world was not ripe, and yet it did well. An angel stands a poor chance among wild beasts; a better chance among men: but among angels best of all. And so I admit of this system that it is, like the Free Trade, fit for one nation only on condition that all adopt it. Still a man may try it in his own person, and even his sufferings by reason of it shall be its triumphs.[53]

He recognized the unison between Penn's religion and his own when he wrote:

To be at perfect agreement with a man of most opposite conclusions you have only to translate your language into his. The same thought which you call *God* in his nomenclature is called *Christ.* In the language of William Penn, moral sentiment is called *Christ.*[54]

Penn's name, nearly always in a favorable context, appears many times in the essays as well as in the *Journals.* Emerson was not blind to the flaws in Penn's character; he regarded him as an imperfect agent of unalterable laws. In "The Sovereignty of Ethics" he wrote:

Truth gathers itself spotless and unhurt after all our surrenders and concealments and partisanship—never hurt by the treachery or ruin of its best defenders, whether Luther or William Penn or St. Paul. We answer, when they tell us of the bad behavior of Luther or Paul: "Well, what if he did? Who was more pained than Luther or Paul?" Shall we attach ourselves violently to our teachers and historical personalities, and think the foundation shaken if any fault is shown in their record? But how is the truth hurt by their falling from it?[55]

The genesis of this passage is found in a conversation with a Quaker of New Bedford:

Truth. It is not wise to talk, as men do, of reason as the gift of God bestowed, etc., or, of reasoning from nature up to nature's God, etc. The intellectual power is not the gift, but the presence of God. Nor do we reason to the being of God, but God goes with us into nature, when we go or think at all. Truth is always new and wild as the wild air, and is alive. The mind is always true, when there is mind, and it makes no difference that the premises are false, we arrive at true conclusions.

Mr. Arnold, with whom I talked at New Bedford, saw as much as

[53] *Ibid.*, II, 418-419. [54] *Ibid.*, II, 478.
[55] *Lectures and Biographical Sketches*, pp. 195-196.

this, and when Penn's treacheries were enumerated, replied, "Well, what if he did? it was only Penn who did it."[56]

It is worth noting that although the thought first occurred to his mind with reference to Penn, Emerson characteristically generalized it, applying it to Luther and St. Paul.

Emerson's interest in the Abolition movement gave him further contact with Quakers and Quakerism. His early *Journals* testify that he had been incensed against slavery as early as 1822; the Abolition movement in this country was not formally inaugurated until 1831. Emerson, however, chose to keep silence on this subject until 1844, when he delivered an address on the anniversary of the emancipation of the Negroes in the British West Indies. His objection to slavery was exactly the same as that of the Quakers: "Because every man has within him something really divine, therefore is slavery the unpardonable outrage it is."[57] Again he wrote:

Yesterday, had I been born and bred a Quaker, I should have risen and protested against the preacher's words. I would have said that in the light of Christianity is no such thing as slavery. The only bondage it recognizes is that of sin.[58]

In the 1844 address he acknowledged the priority of the Quakers in the movement for the liberation of the slaves, and gave due credit to John Woolman and other Quakers for their part in the development of the anti-slavery sentiment. He was acquainted with Woolman's *Journal,* and had a copy of it in his library, the gift of his friend John Greenleaf Whittier.[59] He had a great admiration for Lucretia Mott,

[56] *Journals,* IX, 14-15. James Arnold (1781-1868) was a wealthy Quaker merchant of New Bedford who had joined the Unitarian Church of that city under circumstances which will be noticed below.

[57] *Journals,* III, 390.

[58] *Ibid.,* III, 447.

[59] Professor H. J. Cadbury has called my attention to a letter from Whittier to Emerson which was discovered by accident in a secret drawer after the contents of Emerson's study had been removed to the Concord Antiquarian Society building. The letter is dated 12th mo. 12, 1852, and refers to a mutual interchange of books between the two writers: "I feel guilty in respect to the Bhagavad Gita, but it is too late to repent: & I will keep it even until I restore it to thee personally in exchange for Geo. Fox." Evidently the Quaker poet had lent Emerson the *Journal* or some other writing of George Fox. This incident is significant, showing as it does, that Emerson's interest in Fox persisted in 1852. See Professor Cadbury's note in the *Bulletin of the Friends' Historical Association,* XXIV, 48-49 (Spring, 1935).

Emerson saw Whittier occasionally, at the meetings of the Saturday Club and elsewhere, and a number of letters passed between them, but they were never intimate friends. There was too great a gulf between them with respect to intellectual background and

the Abolitionist and Feminist[60] leader whom he met several times in later life, and he called her "the flower of Quakerism."[61]

In 1858 Emerson was lecturing in Philadelphia. Mrs. Mott was in the audience, and wrote afterwards to a friend:

We have been greatly pleased with listening to R. W. Emerson. His lecture on "The Law of Success" is full of gems. . . . I spoke to Emerson after the lecture, thanking him for it; he replied, "I got some leaves out of your book," adding, "from your New Bedford friends." I remembered that his mind was enlightened beyond his pulpit ordinances about the time of the enlightened Mary Newall's coming out, and I doubt not she had some influence on him.[62]

This brings us to the last and most important of the Quaker influences which in some measure determined the character and direction of Emerson's thought. During the winter of 1833-1834 Emerson supplied the pulpit of his cousin, the Reverend Orville Dewey, minister of the Unitarian Church in New Bedford. The reason for this congregation's willingness to accept a preacher of Emerson's heterodox views is significant. As the historian of the church puts it:

It is doubtful if there was another congregation in New England so well prepared to receive Emerson's message as this one was at that time, because of the large influx of liberal Friends that came into it during Dr. Dewey's ten years ministry bringing so much of their free spirit with them.[63]

There had been a schism in the New Bedford Friends' Meeting ten years before, and the liberal party had seceded in a body, joining the Unitarian Church. Among them was Miss Mary Rotch, a wealthy Quakeress who had been one of two elders removed from office by the Friends' Meeting in 1824. When asked in England who his chief friends in America were, Emerson made this reply: "I find

habits. For an amusing anecdote illustrating the disparity of their views on the subject of prayer, see Albert Mordell, *Quaker Militant* (Boston, 1933), p. 295.

[60] In his lecture on "Woman," he noted that "the Quakers have the honour of having first established, in their discipline, the equality of the sexes" (*Miscellanies,* p. 415). In the unpublished lecture on George Fox he gives the Quakers credit for having led the way in other humanitarian and reform movements such as Temperance, Pacifism, Prison Reform, the abolition of oaths, and the establishment of freedom of conscience.

[61] *Journals,* VIII, 110.

[62] Anna D. Hallowell, *James and Lucretia Mott* (Boston, 1884), p. 385.

[63] E. Stanton Hodgin, *One Hundred Years of Unitarianism in New Bedford* (New Bedford, 1924), p. 37. This writer adds, with a penetration which we have not met elsewhere: "The transcendentalism that Emerson was proclaiming was intellectualized Quakerism, pure and simple" *(loc. cit.).*

many among the Quakers. I know one simple old lady in particular whom I especially honour. She said to me, 'I cannot think what you find in me which is worth notice.' Ah," continued Emerson, "if she had said yea, and the whole world had thundered in her ear nay, she would still have said yea."[64]

Emerson had many serious conversations with Miss Rotch, and was a frequent visitor at her house.[65] It may have been at her home that he first became acquainted with the custom to which he refers in "Social Aims":

It is an excellent custom of the Quakers, if only for a school of manners,—the silent prayer before meals. It has the effect to stop mirth, and introduce a moment of reflection. After the pause, all resume their usual intercourse from a vantage-ground.[66]

It is also possible, as M. D. Conway suggests, that it was "the vision of Mary Rotch leaving church when the Last Supper was to be commemorated which first cast a blight upon that rite in Emerson's eyes."[67] These, of course, are only conjectures, but we have positive evidence of his indebtedness to her in respect of her religious views, an indebtedness which the student of Emerson cannot overlook.

First, however, it will be necessary to refer to the circumstances which surrounded Miss Rotch's resignation from the Friends' Meeting. The New Bedford Friends in 1823 were undergoing a miniature schism which foreshadowed the general rift between Liberal (or

[64] W. Hale White, "What Mr. Emerson Owed to Bedfordshire," *Athenaeum*, No. 2846, pp. 602-603 (1882).

[65] It has traditionally been supposed that Emerson lodged at her house when he came to New Bedford to preach. This tradition was founded on Charles T. Congdon's statement (*Reminiscences of a Journalist*, Boston, 1880, p. 34) that Emerson stayed "in the home of a Quaker lady, just below ours." W. E. Emery, writing in the New Bedford *Morning Mercury* (Jan. 2, 1933, p. 4) on "Emerson's Home in New Bedford, Mass.," questions the accuracy of this tradition, and points out, on the basis of Congdon's statement, that it is more likely that Emerson stayed at the house of Mrs. Deborah Brayton, a Quaker lady who kept a boarding house not far from Congdon's residence. He adds that he has authoritative corroboration of his conjecture from an independent source. It is, of course, a matter of supreme unimportance; the important thing is that Emerson knew Miss Rotch, and profited from his acquaintance with her.

[66] *Letters and Social Aims*, p. 86.

[67] Moncure Daniel Conway, *Emerson at Home and Abroad* (London, 1883), p. 69. W. E. Emery *(loc. cit.)* denies that Mary Rotch's example had any influence on Emerson's refusal to administer the Lord's Supper, stating that his renunciation of the rite had taken place two years before he knew her. Mr. Emery overlooks the fact that Emerson had preached in New Bedford earlier, in 1827 (Cabot, *Memoir*, p. 131), and very likely had made Miss Rotch's acquaintance at that time.

Hicksite) and Orthodox Friends throughout the country later in the decade. The seeds of dissent were planted by the preaching of Mary Newhall (or Newall), who came to New Bedford in 1822, and immediately began to preach advanced doctrines. Her sermons were popular with the majority of the Friends, but the conservative element among the elders frowned upon her preaching and tried to silence her. Among her adherents were Mary Rotch and Elizabeth Rodman, themselves elders; and when they went so far as to rise and join in her prayers, the inevitable conflict was precipitated. The "old lights" finally succeeded in expelling the two ladies from the Select Meeting, and, as we have seen, they joined the Unitarian Church, together with a number of their supporters.[68]

When Emerson was in New Bedford in 1834, he read the account of the proceedings against Miss Rotch with great interest.

> I have been much interested lately in the MS Record of the debates in the Quaker Monthly Meetings here in 1823, when Elizabeth Rodman and Mary Rotch were proposed to be removed from the place of Elders for uniting in the prayers of Mary Newhall. I must quote a sentence or two from two of these speakers. "February, 1823: M. N. rose in the meeting and began with, 'As the stream does not rise higher than the fountain,' etc.; spoke of the Mosaic dispensation in which the performance of certain rituals constituted the required religion; the more spiritual dispensation of our Saviour; of the advent of Christ; and the yet more inward and spiritual dispensation of the present day. These dispensations she compared to the progressive stages of the human heart in the work of religion, from loving our neighbor as ourselves to loving our enemies, and lastly arriving at that state of humility when self would be totally abandoned and we could only say, Lord be merciful to me a sinner."[69]

Knowing that all was grist that came to his mill, one looks for a reflection of this passage in Emerson's published writings. It is not far to seek. In his first book, *Nature,* which he was writing at this very time, we find the following:

> The exercise of the Will, or the lesson of power, is taught in every event. From the child's successive possession of his several senses up to

[68] It is possible to follow the course of this interesting conflict through the eyes of contemporaries. See *The Diary of Samuel Rodman,* ed. Z. W. Pease (New Bedford, 1927), *passim;* and *Life in New Bedford a Hundred Years Ago: A Chronicle of the Social, Religious and Commercial History of the Period as Recorded in a Diary Kept by Joseph R. Anthony,* ed. Z. W. Pease (New Bedford, 1922), *passim.*

[69] *Journals,* III, 265-266. Note that he quotes only *one* of the speakers. Unfortunately the MS which he saw has disappeared, so that we are unable to conjecture what other speech it was that caught his attention.

the hour when he saith, "Thy will be done!" he is learning the secret that he can reduce under his will not only particular events but great classes, nay, the whole series of events, and so conform all facts to his character.[70]

We find the same germinal idea, developed in a different way, in a lecture on "War," delivered in 1838:

War and peace thus resolve themselves into a mercury of the state of cultivation. At a certain stage of his progress, the man fights, if he be of a sound body and mind. At a certain higher stage, he makes no offensive demonstration, but is alive to repel injury, and of an unconquerable heart. At a still higher stage, he comes into the region of holiness; passion has passed away from him; his warlike nature is all converted into an active medicinal principle; he sacrifices himself, and accepts with alacrity wearisome tasks of denial and charity; but, being attacked, he bears it and turns the other cheek, as one engaged, throughout his being, no longer to the service of an individual but to the common soul of all men.[71]

There can be little doubt that this conception of successive stages of resignation, leading up to complete humility and submission, was suggested by the speech of Mary Newhall which he read in the Quaker records.

Returning to Mary Rotch, I will preface my discussion of her influence on Emerson by a quotation from the Reverend Orville Dewey who knew and admired her:

Her religious opinions were of the most catholic stamp, and in one respect they were peculiar. The Friends' idea of the "inward light" seemed to have become with her coincident with the idea of the Author of all light; and when speaking of the Supreme Being, she would never say "God," but "that Influence." That Influence was constantly with her; and she carried the idea so far as to believe that it prompted her daily action, and decided for her every question of duty.[72]

This sense of the indwelling presence of God, and of its all-sufficiency as a guide to conduct is illustrated by an anecdote which Emerson delighted to tell on occasions when the stream of conversation threatened to lose itself in the sands of theological debate. A little girl had asked Miss Rotch if she might do something. Miss Rotch asked her, "What does the voice in thee say?" The child disappeared, and presently returned to announce that "the little

[70] *Nature, Addresses and Lectures,* pp. 39-40.
[71] *Miscellanies,* pp. 166-167.
[72] *Autobiography and Letters of Orville Dewey, D.D.,* ed. Mary E. Dewey (Boston, 1883), p. 68.

voice says no." "That," said Emerson, "starts the tears to one's eyes."[73] Be that as it may, this theory of the immanence of God and of the individual's private responsibility for his conduct was in complete harmony with Emerson's own views as they were beginning to take definite form in his mind at this time.

He questioned her further about her religion, and she unfolded to him her extreme doctrine of obedience, a doctrine which was to figure in Emerson's writings to the very last. The long passage in the *Journals* in which he discusses this doctrine is worth quoting in full in view of the use which he was later to make of it.

Pleasantly mingled with my sad thoughts the sublime religion of Miss Rotch yesterday. She was much disciplined, she said, in the years of Quaker dissension, and driven inward, driven home, to find an anchor, until she learned to have *no choice,* to acquiesce without understanding the reason when she found an obstruction to any particular course of acting. She objected to having this spiritual direction called an impression, or an intimation, or an oracle. It was none of them. It was so simple it could hardly be spoken of. It was long, long, before she could attain to anything satisfactory. She was in a state of great dreariness, but she had a friend, a woman, now deceased, who used to advise her to dwell patiently with this dreariness and absence, in the confidence that it was necessary to the sweeping away of all her dependence upon traditions, and that she would finally attain to something better. And when she attained a better state of mind, its beginnings were very, very, small. And now it is not anything to speak of. She designed to go to England with Mr. and Mrs. Farrar, and the plan was very pleasant, and she was making her preparations, and the time was fixed, when she conceived a reluctance to go for which she could not see any reason, but which continued; and she therefore suspended her purpose, and suffered them to depart without her. She said that she had seen reason to think it was best for her to have staid at home. But in obeying it, she never felt it of any importance that she should know now or at any time what the reasons were. But she should feel that it was presumption to press through this reluctance and choose for herself. I said it was not so much any particular power as a *healthful state of the mind;* to which she assented cordially. I said, it must produce a sublime tranquillity in view of the future,—this assurance of higher direction; and she assented.[74]

He goes on, speaking *in propia persona,* to find classical antecedents for the beliefs of the simple old Quakeress:

[73] Conway, *Emerson at Home and Abroad,* p. 69.
[74] *Journals,* III, 258-259.

Can you believe, Waldo Emerson, that you may relieve yourself of the perpetual perplexity of choosing, and by putting your ear close to the soul, learn always the true way? I cannot but remark how perfectly this agrees with the Daemon of Socrates, even in that story which I once thought anomalous, of the direction as to the choice of two roads; and with the grand unalterableness of Fichte's morality. Hold up this lamp and look back at the best passages of your life. Once there was choice in the mode, but obedience in the thing. In general there has been pretty quiet obedience *in the main,* but much recusancy *in the particular.*

"HAMLET. But thou wouldst not think how ill all's here about my heart,—but it is no matter.

"HORATIO. If your mind dislike anything, obey it."[75]

This doctrine made a lasting impression upon Emerson. Eight years later he still recalled Mary Rotch's words, for he made this note in his *Journal:*

Mary Rotch inclined to speak of the spirit negatively and instead of calling it a light, "an oracle," "a leading," she said, "When she would do that she should not, she found an objection."[76]

The first explicit appearance of this doctrine in his published writings (it is present, of course, by implication in "Self-Reliance") is to be found in "Spiritual Laws" in his first volume of essays:

We need only obey. There is guidance for each of us, and by lowly listening we shall hear the right word. . . .

I say, *do not choose;* but that is a figure of speech by which I would distinguish what is commonly called *choice* among men, and which is a partial act, the choice of the hands, of the eyes, of the appetites, and not a whole act of the man.[77]

Later on, as this teaching sank deeper into his consciousness, he saw it as the necessary bridge between self-reliance and the Over-Soul, and in the essay on "Worship" in *The Conduct of Life* it has become inextricably woven into the fabric of his thought:

And so I think that the last lesson of life, the choral song which rises from all elements and all angels, is a voluntary obedience, a necessitated

[75] *Journals,* III, 260.

[76] *Ibid.,* VI, 280. The negative function which Mary Rotch assigned to the Inner Light is not generally characteristic of Quaker belief. The more normal Quaker position is that the Light reveals truth and positively leads to action. Emerson, however, regularly follows Miss Rotch's negative definition. In his essay on "Swedenborg" (*Representative Men,* p. 140), he writes, "The illuminated Quakers explained their Light, not as somewhat that leads to any action, but it appears as an obstruction to anything unfit."

[77] *Essays, First Series,* pp. 139-140.

freedom. Man is made of the same atoms as the world is, and he shares the same impressions, predispositions, and destiny. When his mind is illuminated, when his heart is kind, he throws himself into the sublime order, and does, with knowledge, what the stones do by structure.[78]

As he grew older, the doctrine of complete acquiescence, which Mary Rotch had arrived at only after a long period of self-communion and inward struggle, became more and more acceptable to him as a rule of life. In "The Sovereignty of Ethics," printed four years before his death, in the *North American Review,* we find this passage:

Have you said to yourself ever: "I abdicate all choice, I see that it is not for me to interfere. I see that I have been one of the crowd; that I have been a pitiful person, because I have wished to be my own master, and to dress and order my whole way and system of living. I thought I managed it very well. I see that my neighbors think so. I have heard prayers, I have prayed even, but I have never until now dreamed that this undertaking the entire management of my own affairs was not commendable. I have never seen, until now, that it dwarfed me. I have not discovered, until this blessed ray flashed just now through my soul, that there dwelt any power in Nature that would relieve me of my load. But now I see."[79]

Finally, in "Greatness," one of his very last essays, he enunciated the doctrine once more, this time acknowledging its Quaker origin:

If you have ever known a good mind among the Quakers, you will have found that is the element of their faith. As they express it, it might be thus: "I do not pretend to any commandment or large revelation, but if at any time I form some plan, propose a journey or a course of conduct, I perhaps find a silent obstacle in my mind that I cannot account for. Very well,—I let it lie, thinking it may pass away, but if it do not pass away I yield to it, obey it. You ask me to describe it. I cannot describe it. It is not an oracle, nor an angel, nor a dream, nor a law; it is too simple to be described, it is but a grain of mustard-seed, but such as it is, it is something which the contradiction of all mankind could not shake and which the consent of all mankind could not confirm."[80]

This was not the only debt which Emerson owed to Mary Rotch. His ideas on the subject of immortality bear the impress of her ripe wisdom.

[78] *The Conduct of Life,* p. 240.
[79] *Lectures and Biographical Sketches,* pp. 196-197.
[80] *Letters and Social Aims,* pp. 309-310.

> My Reason [he wrote in his *Journals*] is well enough convinced of its immortality. It knows itself immortal. But it cannot persuade its down-looking brother, the Understanding, of the same. That fears for the cord that ties them, lest it break. Hence Miss Rotch affirms undoubtedly, "I shall live forever," and, on the other hand, does not much believe in her retaining Personality.[81]

This, essentially, was the final position which he reached in his essay on "Immortality," where he wrote:

> I confess that everything connected with our personality fails. Nature never spares the individual; we are always balked of a complete success: no prosperity is promised to our self-esteem. We have our indemnity only in the moral and intellectual reality to which we aspire. That is immortal, and we only through that.[82]

The Quakerism of Mary Rotch must therefore be taken into account in any discussion of the influences which contributed to the shaping of Emerson's intellectual viewpoint. Together with his reading in the literature of Quakerism and his early personal contact with the Quaker preacher Edward Stabler, it formed a significant strand in the background of ideas out of which his essays came.

There is no need to labor the point. I have no desire to exaggerate the importance of the Quaker influence. Nevertheless, this much can safely be asserted: that between 1827 and 1836, when the salient ideas which characterize the essays were in the germinal state, Emerson was strongly subject to the influence of Quaker thought through the three channels which I have enumerated and discussed. His receptive mind eagerly assimilated this new body of thought. It sank deep into his consciousness, and inevitably colored all his subsequent thinking. Although the period of direct contact was substantially over before the publication of his first book in 1836, the interest in Quakerism remained, indelibly engraved on his mind, and concretely embedded in his *Journals* where it could fertilize and nourish all his later speculations.

The doctrines of self-reliance and the Inner Light are, as Emerson himself was aware, only two figures of speech to express the same basic concept of individualism;[83] and reliance upon self is, in

[81] *Journals*, III, 398-399.

[82] *Letters and Social Aims*, pp. 342-343.

[83] The essential unity between the central faith of Quakerism and the individualism of Emerson comes out clearly in a passage from the *Journals* in which he records a con-

the end, reliance upon God as the Over-Soul made manifest in the individual consciousness. Emerson's "spiritual religion" is entirely at one with Quakerism in this respect. Religion for him, as for George Fox and Mary Rotch, was an intuitive and personal experience, completely divorced from traditional forms and authority.[84] The central conviction upon which Emerson's religious views were founded is admirably stated in a letter to Solomon Corner of Baltimore, written in 1842:

> I count these to be low, sleepy, dark ages of the Soul, only redeemed by the unceasing affirmation at the bottom of the heart—like the nightingale's song heard all night—that the powers of the Soul are commensurate with its needs, all experience to the contrary notwithstanding.[85]

"This way of thinking," he wrote in the same year, "falling . . . on prelatical times, made . . . Quakers; and falling on Unitarian and commercial times, makes the peculiar shades of Idealism which we know."[86]

---

versation with a Quaker acquaintance: "At Harrisburg, [last] April, I met W. L. Fisher. The good old Quaker believes in Individualism still: so do I. Fourierism seemed to him boys' play; and so indeed did money; though he frankly admitted how much time he had spent about it: but a vital power in man, identical with that which makes the grass grow, and the sweet breeze blow, and which should abolish slavery, and raise the pauper,—that he believes in against all experience. So we held sweet counsel together . . ." (*Journals*, VIII, 141-142). William Logan Fisher (1781-1862) was a leader among the Progressive Friends and a prominent anti-Sabbatarian writer.

[84] He liked the silent church before the service began better than any preaching ("Self-Reliance," *Essays, First Series*, p. 71). "It is not in the power of God," he said, "to make a communication of his will to a Calvinist. For to every inward revelation he holds up his silly book, and quotes chapter and verse against the Book-Maker and Man-Maker, against that which quotes not, but is and cometh. There is a light older than intellect, by which the intellect lives and works, always new, and which degrades every past and particular shining of itself. This light Calvinism denies, in its idolatry of a certain past shining" (*Journals*, VI, 377).

[85] *A Letter of Emerson*, ed. Willard Reed (Boston, 1934), p. 18.

[86] "The Transcendentalist," *Nature, Addresses and Lectures*, p. 339.

William James and Emerson

Frederic I. Carpenter

I

TO THE POPULAR mind, pragmatism has always seemed the exact opposite of transcendentalism. What could a crude philosophy of action hold in common with a refined spiritual idealism? Emphasizing this contrast, George Santayana suggested that "the genteel tradition in America philosophy" logically ended in Emerson, while William James marked the beginning of the more robust American way of thought. More academically, Professor Woodbridge Riley's textbook gave sanction to this interpretation, and specifically described pragmatism as "a recoil against transcendentalism." Always to the lay reader, and often to the professional philosopher, the pragmatism of William James has marked the beginning of a new intellectual movement, typical of America.

But of recent years the old picture painted all in black and white has come to seem false. The shrewd Yankee aspects of Emerson have stood out more clearly, while the religious and spiritualistic side of James has been emphasized. After all, Emerson's famous address on "The American Scholar" did something to stimulate the robust American philosophy. Both Henry James, Senior, and his son William, recognized the fact. Emerson and James were seeking, in different ways, to escape the shadow of the old, genteel tradition. Emerson had expressed the situation clearly in a letter to Henry James, Sr., in 1850: "I find or fancy (just as Wilkinson finds me guilty of Unitarianism) that you have not shed your last coat of Presbyterianism, but that a certain legendary and catechetical Jove glares at me sometimes, in your page."[1] If William James transformed this legendary Jove into a more impersonal "psychic energy," the basic substance remained the same. The most recent interpreter of American thought, Professor Harvey Gates Townsend, has gone so far as to assert that "William James . . . is the central figure of what should be called neo-transcendentalism in New England. Quite definitely in the line of descent from Emerson, he succeeded

[1] R. B. Perry, *The Thought and Character of William James* (Boston, 1935), I, 62.

to a remarkable degree in translating the aspirations of the older transcendentalism into the language of philosophy."[2]

The general relations of the James family to Emerson have been described before.[3] Henry James, Senior, first made the acquaintance of Emerson in 1842—the year in which William was born. He "named the boy William, and a few days later, brought his friend Ralph Waldo Emerson to admire and give his blessing to the little philosopher-to-be."[4] The friendship of the two men ripened steadily, until, in 1864, the James family finally took up its residence in Boston. Both fathers and children frequently visited one another; and Henry James, Senior, regaled the Emersons with excerpts from the letters of his elder sons, written from Europe. In 1872, he himself wrote and delivered "a short appreciation" of Emerson before the "Friday Evening Salon" of Mr. and Mrs. Fields—a paper afterwards printed in the *Atlantic*. Finally, in 1903, William James, then a professor of philosophy at Harvard, wrote his own laudatory address for the Emerson centenary at Concord, in which he too made his votive offering to the "beloved master."

These friendly relations are generally known. On the other hand, the philosophical books and letters of William James frequently expressed negative criticisms of Emerson, and of his philosophy. On occasions James was enthusiastic, on other occasions critical; but always the occasion influenced the expression of opinion. The question remains: What did James, in his private mind, really think of Emerson? Without attempting to summarize the known evidence, this paper will consider the question on the basis of certain unpublished material.

The philosophical library of William James, consisting of some three hundred books, has been preserved as a whole in the treasure room of Widener Library at Harvard. In this collection are included nine volumes by Emerson, and one about Emerson.[5] These volumes have been marked, annotated, carefully cross-referenced by James.

[2] H. G. Townsend, *Philosophical Ideas in the United States* (New York, 1934), p. 134.

[3] Cf. R. B. Perry, *op. cit.;* Austin Warren, *The Elder Henry James* (New York, 1934); C. H. Grattan, *The Three Jameses* (New York, 1932); and F. I. Carpenter, "Points of Comparison Between Emerson and William James," *New England Quarterly*, II, 458-474 (July, 1929).

[4] *Letters of William James*, ed. Henry James (Boston, 1920), I, 9.

[5] These volumes are: *Miscellanies: Nature and Addresses* (1868); *Essays: First Series* (1869); *Essays: Second Series* (new ed., 1889); *Essays: Second Series* (Centenary ed., 1904); *Representative Men* (1895); *The Conduct of Life* (1889); *Letters and Social Aims* (1883); *Lectures and Biographical Sketches* (1884); *Natural History of Intellect* (1893); and *Emerson in Concord*, by E. W. Emerson (1889).

They describe his enthusiasm for certain aspects of the Emersonian philosophy. And they also describe his disagreement with other aspects of it.

The first two volumes of Emerson's writings are inscribed: "William James, Scarboro, July 5, 1871." These have obviously been read many times, for they contain notes, references, and markings, entered successively in pencil, pen, and blue pencil. Two flyleaves at the end of each are scribbled with indexes, quotations, and comments of all varieties. Clearly these have been revised, altered, and added to on different occasions. Almost every page of the text is underlined or annotated in such a way as to make clear James's interest.

Of the other volumes, only one is inscribed. His copy of *Lectures and Biographical Sketches,* printed in 1884, bears the words: "William James, from his Wife, Quincy St., Cambridge, June, 1879 [*sic*]," on the first flyleaf. The remainder of the volumes may have been purchased later, at some time before the centenary address of 1903. Each of these contain about ten or twelve quotations and references entered on the flyleaves; and numerous marks along the margins of the text. The most striking fact which these reveal is that James literally read almost everything which Emerson wrote. Only a few of the essays at the end of *Natural History of Intellect* have not been marked. When James wrote his brother that "The reading of the divine Emerson, volume after volume, has done me a lot of good,"[6] he was not exaggerating the thoroughness of this reading.

But before considering James's comments in detail, it is important to recall that he may have read other of Emerson's works earlier, in the library of his father, that he certainly heard his father read some of them aloud, and that, from his birth to his marriage, as long as he lived under his father's roof, he was subject to the Emersonian influence. Thus in 1870, his father wrote:

My dear Emerson,—

Many thanks for *Society and Solitude,* of which I have read many chapters with hearty liking. But unfortunately just before the new volume arrived, we had got a handsomely bound copy of the new edition of the old essays, and I had been reading them aloud in the evening to Mama and Willy and Alice with such delectation on all sides, that it was vain to attempt renewing the experience.[7]

[6] *Letters of William James,* II, 190.

[7] R. B. Perry, *op. cit.,* I, 100.

The year after hearing his father read Emerson's essays aloud, William James acquired the first two volumes for his own library. His comments on these are significant.

II

In general, James's remarks upon Emerson's essays fall into three classes. The first includes passages which James considered typical of the author, or particularly revealing of "Emerson's singularity." These he usually indexed under the initials "R. W. E." But since he used many of these in the later composition of his centenary address without further comment, their interest is comparatively small.

The second group includes passages from Emerson which James considered "against my philosophy." For the most part he indexed these under such titles as "monism," "abstract unity," "the ONE," and "transcendental." Some of these reappear—often with his disapproving comments omitted—in *The Varieties of Religious Experience.* Sometimes these passages are mingled with other Emersonian passages of which he approved. They seem to have irritated him either because of their abstractness, their denial of "pluralism," or their statements of the transcendental doctrine of evil.

The third group of passages, which James wholeheartedly approved, seems the most interesting, the most various, and the most revealing. Under the title of "pragmatism" he indexed many paragraphs, usually containing the words "action" or "deeds." Related to these are other sections emphasizing "the present tense," and the word "to-day." Another group of marked passages celebrates "the common man," "the poor," and "the laborer"; and condemns the "puny, protected person." Still others describe "the creative I," "psychic energy," and "expansiveness" or power in general. Lastly, James underlined and approved many of Emerson's sentences for their "concrete style." All in all, since James's enthusiasms seem more important and more suggestive than his criticisms, we may consider them first.

The form in which James's comments are scribbled suggests that he first read Emerson's text for its general interest and stimulation, without specific reference to his own thought. Many passages were indexed, without comment. At some later date he returned to the text, noted that some of these passages were "against my philosophy," and added: "but see pp. —— for pragmatism." Then he again wrote: "pragmatism," in connection with other page references, formerly listed without specific comment. Although he carried out this procedure only for the first two volumes of Emerson's work, his comments are sufficiently numerous to be significant.

As might have been expected, the passages specifically "against my philosophy" appear in the chapter on "Idealism," in Emerson's *Nature;* while the neighboring chapters on "Discipline," and "Prospects" contain suggestions of "pragmatism." James underlined:[8] "Words are finite organs of the infinite mind. They cannot cover the dimensions of what is in truth. They break, chop, and impoverish it. An action is the perfection and publication of thought."[9] And he sidelined the whole peroration of *Nature,* beginning: "Nature is not fixed but fluid. Spirit alters, moulds, makes it. . . ." Particularly he underlined the phrase: "Build therefore your own world."

Most suggestive of "pragmatism," however, was the section on "Action," in "The American Scholar": "The great soul will be strong to live. . . . Thinking is a partial act. Let the grandeur of justice shine in his affairs."[10] "Colleges and books only copy the language which the field and work-yard made."[11] And James underlined: "As the world was plastic and fluid in the hands of God, so it is ever to so much of his attributes as we bring to it."[12] In "Literary Ethics," also, he underlined several pragmatic passages: "Let him [the man of letters] endeavor . . . to solve the problem of that life which is set before *him*. And this by punctual action, and not by promises or dreams . . . Feudalism and Orientalism had long enough thought it majestic to do nothing; the modern majesty consists in work."[13]

All these passages appealed to James as celebrating "pragmatism," or "the superiority of action." But he found these mixed with other passages which declared "the superiority of what is intellectualized." Therefore he indexed the two contrasting series of statements, and referred specifically to certain paragraphs which contained "both close together." On one page he underlined: "I do not see how any

[8] It is not always possible to state with assurance whether James's underlinings expressed approval or disapproval. One can only infer this from the context, and from his marginal comments.

[9] *Works* (Centenary ed.), I, 44-45. All page references have been corrected to refer to this standard edition.

[10] I, 99.

[11] I, 98. James cross-referenced this to the chapter on "Language," in *Nature.*

[12] I, 105.

[13] I, 178-179.

man can afford, for the sake of his nerves and his nap, to spare any action in which he can partake"; but also underlined the qualifying sentences: "The true scholar grudges every opportunity of action past by, as a loss of power. It is the raw material out of which the intellect moulds her splendid products."[14]

A similar set of sentences had been underlined and indexed five pages earlier. Obviously James considered Emerson's remarks ambiguous, if not contradictory. Which did Emerson consider superior —deeds or thoughts; actions or ideas? If the answer were "ideas," James called Emerson "transcendental"; if "actions," Emerson was "pragmatic." Throughout his life, James praised the pragmatic Emerson, but disapproved the transcendentalist.

It might be argued that Emerson was essentially a transcendentalist, because he commonly set ideas above actions. "Action is with the scholar subordinate, but it is essential," he wrote. Certainly he called himself an idealist, and certainly he emphasized ideas as the ultimate concern of the American Scholar. In this he disagreed with James, who emphasized particular acts. In a later essay on "Nominalist and Realist," Emerson definitely classed himself with the platonic realists. But was this attitude inconsistent with his incipient "pragmatism"?

The answer depends upon the definition of "pragmatism," and, for the moment, takes us beyond the philosophy of James. For pragmatism originated as a theory of ideas, in Peirce's historic essay: "How to Make Our Ideas Clear."[15] It declared that an idea, or conception, consisted simply in the sum total of its conceivable relations to practical experience: "The elements of every concept enter into logical thought at the gate of perception and make their exit at the gate of purposive action; and whatever cannot show its passports at both those gates is to be arrested as unauthorized by reason."[16] In general terms, pragmatism declared the doctrine of the necessary interrelation of ideas and active experience. We may adopt this broad definition, both because it was prior to the more specific definitions

[14] I, 95.

[15] *The Collected Papers of Charles Sanders Peirce* (Cambridge, Mass., 1931-1935), V, 248-271.

[16] *Ibid.*, V, 131. Since Peirce, "the grandfather of pragmatism," occupies a position midway between Emerson and James, both in history and, to some extent, in logic, occasional reference to his writings may help to clarify this discussion. The "gate of perception" is specified by all empirical philosophy; the "gate of purposive action" is more peculiar to pragmatism.

of James, and because it suggests the philosophic continuity between Emerson and James.

Pragmatism, then, declared ideas to be meaningless except as they related themselves to experience—to perception and to action. In this it contradicted the transcendentalism of the German philosophers who declared the dichotomy between ideas and actions. But the fact that pragmatism refused to admit the transcendence of ideas does not mean that it necessarily proclaimed the superiority of actions. As Peirce protested to James: "Pragmatism is correct doctrine only in so far as it is recognized that material action is the mere husk of ideas. The brute element exists, and must not be explained away, as Hegel seeks to do. But the end of thought is action only in so far as the end of action is another thought."[17]

Emerson, in as much as he repeatedly proclaimed the necessary interaction of thought and experience, was pragmatic, and James frequently recognized the fact. Thus he labeled as "pragmatism" Emerson's exhortation: "Let the scholar first learn the things. . . . Let him know how the thing stands; in the use of all means, and most in the reverence of the humble commerce and humble needs of life,—to hearken what *they* say, and so, by mutual reaction of thought and life, to make thought solid, and life wise."[18] "The mutual reaction of thought and life"—had not Emerson founded his thought upon this principle? In other words, he had described it as "the uses of nature," ascending from the use of nature as the brute material for experience, to the use of nature as the material for purposive action: "Build therefore your own world." "The secret of Emerson," as one of his best biographers has observed, "lies in the superlative value which he found in the unit of experience, the direct, momentary, individual act of consciousness."[19] And, as even the unsympathetic Santayana recognized: "he coveted truth, and returned to experience."[20]

Besides the broadly pragmatic passages which proclaimed the necessity of concrete observation and action to ideas, James clearly approved two related aspects of Emerson's thought—the first celebrating the importance of "to-day," and the second the importance

[17] R. B. Perry, *op. cit.*, II, 424-425. [18] *Works*, I, 180-181.
[19] O. W. Firkins, *Emerson* (Boston and New York, 1915), p. 297.
[20] *Winds of Doctrine* (New York, 1926), p. 197.

of common, manual labor. Under such titles as "now," "to-day," and "the present tense," he indexed many passages which appealed to him. And he underlined many more, for this doctrine was central to both men. From the first paragraph of Emerson's first book, which announced: "The sun shines to-day also," throughout his writings, the refrain recurred: "Give me insight into to-day, and you may have the antique and future worlds."

On the flyleaf of his volume of Emerson's essays, James quoted a phrase from "Self-Reliance": "roses; they exist with God to-day." In connection with this he cross-referenced a passage from "The Over-Soul," which developed the idea: "the soul that ascends to worship the great God is plain and true; dwells in the hour that now is, in the earnest experience of the common day,—by reason of the present moment and the mere trifle having become porous to thought and bibulous of the sea of light." In the midst of Emerson's discussion of the Over-Soul, clothed in mystical language, James found this nugget of pure ore. The occurrence was typical. James approved the foundation of Emerson's thinking—"the hour that now is," and "the experience of the common day." But he distrusted the sudden leaps which Emerson took from daily experience to the sea of light.

Both men began with today. Both celebrated its value, because of the experience which it offered, and of the implications which it suggested. But at this point the two diverged: Emerson emphasized the thoughts or insights which it suggested, James the actions. Another passage indexed by James suggests both the agreement and the difference:

> To-day is a king in disguise. To-day always looks mean to the thoughtless, in the face of an uniform experience that all good and great and happy actions are made up precisely of these blank to-days. Let us not be so deceived. Let us unmask the king as he passes. Let us not inhabit times of wonderful and various promise without divining their tendency.[21]

James sought to convert these daily experiences into the stuff of further actions. Emerson was content for the time to "divine their tendency." But both felt that their to-days pointed rather towards the future than the past.

[21] *Works*, I, 267.

Like his earlier essays, Emerson's essay on "Experience" emphasized this, and James marked it heavily, in both his editions of the work. Both times he noticed especially the paragraph beginning: "The mid-world is best. Nature, as we know her, is no saint"; and continuing: "If we will be strong with her strength we must not harbor such disconsolate consciences, borrowed too from the consciences of other nations. We must set up the strong present tense against all rumors of wrath, past or to come." For both men, "today" opened the gate from the prison of the past to the promised land of the future.

As in the address on "The American Scholar," the doctrine of "the present tense" supported Emerson's Americanism, and his democracy. Immediate empiricism frees the individual, and also the nation, from dependence upon the past. As James had applauded these doctrines, so he applauded their corollaries. In "The Young American" he underlined two sentences: "Here, here in America, is the home of man," and "Let us live in America, too thankful for our want of feudal institutions."[22]

Professor John Dewey has described Emerson as "The Philosopher of Democracy." Clearly, Emerson's recognition of the necessity of action, and his distrust of the past with its "feudal institutions," tallied with the democratic spirit of the new world. "The present" *was*, in a sense, "the common." The American scholar who acted in the present, asked "not for the great, the remote, the romantic," but embraced "the common, the familiar, the low." He did not seek protection nor privilege, but only life in "the mid-world," and travel on its highways of experience and thought. James also sought this spiritual democracy. Besides the passages already noticed, he indexed others on the democracy of the intellect.

Action is necessary, Emerson had said; and by action he meant hard work, day labor, manual toil. He praised poverty, and condemned the growth of an hereditary aristocracy. "Consider the difference between the first and second owner of property," he wrote. "Instead of the sense of power and fertility of resource in himself which the father had . . . we have now a puny, protected person, guarded by walls and curtains."[23] James approved this heartily, and marked also the further development of Emerson's thought: "I do

[22] I, 391, 394.

[23] I, 238-239.

not wish to overstate this doctrine of labor, or to insist that every man should be a farmer. . . . Neither would I shut my ears to the plea of the learned profession . . . that the amount of manual labor necessary for the maintenance of a family, indisposes and disqualifies for intellectual exertion. . . . But . . . every man ought to stand in primary relations with the work of the world; ought to do it himself. . . . The whole interest of history lies in the fortunes of the poor. . . . Every man ought to have the opportunity to conquer the world for himself."[24]

Repeatedly James marked passages such as this.[25] But the objections of "the learned professions," and of men like Hawthorne at Brook Farm, remained unanswered. Reading a later essay of Emerson's, James came upon a new statement and clarification of the earlier idea. Labor is necessary for the scholar: "Labor, iron labor, is for him." But the labor of brain does not differ essentially from the labor of brawn: "If you are a scholar, be that. The same laws hold for you as for the laborer. . . . Let the student mind his own charge; sedulously wait every morning for the news concerning the structure of the world which the spirit will give him. . . . Nature, when she adds difficulty, adds brain."[26]

James underlined all these passages, for he too was seeking to discover the true relations of physical and mental labor. He, too, sought "news" of the structure of the world. And, significantly, the development of his pragmatism closely paralleled the development of Emerson's thought. Both began with a somewhat naïve glorification of physical action, continued to emphasize the essential unity of physical and mental action, and finally pointed to the efficacy of the brain in helping to overcome the actual, physical difficulties of life.

III

In his reading of Emerson, James came upon many brilliant insights and suggestions valuable for the development of his own thought. But even in the midst of these "pragmatic" passages, he found much with which to disagree. He never read Emerson uncritically. Thus, in "The American Scholar," he commented upon

[24] I, 240-241.

[25] Cf. VI, 260-261: "He who is to be wise for many must not be protected. He must know the huts where poor men lie, and the chores which poor men do. The first-class minds, Aesop, Socrates, Cervantes, Shakespeare, Franklin, had the poor man's feeling and mortification." James underlined the passage.

[26] VIII, 310-312.

the sentence: "The discerning will read, in his Plato or Shakspeare, only that least part,—only the authentic utterances of the oracle;—all the rest he rejects, were it never so many times Plato's or Shakspeare's,"[27] and added in the margin: "true of R. W. E." Mixed with his frequent enthusiasm, he retained an acute perception of difference. Later in the same essay, he added the initials "R. W. E." beside another sentence: "If it were only for a vocabulary, the scholar would be covetous of action." Emerson, he felt, was something too much a "scholar."

This amounted to saying that Emerson was too much a transcendentalist. But just as James objected to certain aspects of Emerson's "pragmatism," so he approved much of his transcendentalism. In the *Essays: First Series* he doubly underlined the title of "The Over-Soul" in the Table of Contents, and marked numerous passages in the text of that essay. In the *Miscellanies: Nature and Addresses,* he read and marked "The Transcendentalist" exhaustively. Partly, of course, this was due to his specific interest in the subject matter of these essays. Many quotations from them reappear to illustrate his *Varieties of Religious Experience.* But James also accepted and sympathized with some of the transcendental teachings. Even when he criticized them, they often corresponded to elements of his own thought and faith.

Under such index headings as "Increase of psychic energy," and "the I creates its history," he referred to sentences such as: "The Transcendentalist . . . believes in the perpetual openness of the human mind to new influx of light and power. . . . You think me the child of my circumstances: I make my circumstance."[28] Or again: "Power dwells with cheerfulness; hope puts us in a working mood, whilst despair is no muse, and untunes the active powers."[29] Although James criticized Emerson's "optimism," and his "mysticism," a goodly portion of these qualities appeared in his own thought.

Similarly, Emerson often reminded James of others of his favorite authors. In the "Nominalist and Realist" essay, he wrote "Bergson," opposite the sentence: "It is the secret of the world that all things subsist and do not die, but only retire a little from sight." He felt that Emerson's doctrine of Compensation, with its larger attempt to apply the "high laws" of physics to the fields of ethics and

[27] I, 93. [28] I, 334-335. [29] VI, 265.

economics, suggested the thought of Ernst Mach. And finally, he indexed a particularly vivid passage from the volume of *Lectures and Biographical Sketches,* as: "for Hodgson." When to these marginalia are added the many quotations of James from Whitman and other followers of Emerson, the conviction grows that Emerson belonged naturally to James's family of favorite authors.

Even when he disagreed most sharply with Emerson's doctrines, James instinctively admired the vividness of his style. The strangely earthly and homely quality of the transcendentalist appealed to him perennially. Many of his index notes refer only to single, striking sentences. Often he underlined these in the text without listing them separately. In his centenary address he quoted some, merely to describe Emerson. But frequently he copied these phrases for their intrinsic interest, and sometimes absorbed them into his own later writing. For example, he liked: "the soul's mumps," "Crump is a better man," "pop-gun," "our affections are tents for a night," "so hot, my little Sir," "a mush of concession," "Time is slit and peddled into trifles and tatters," and others of the same type. Finally, he considered as a "motto for my book," the third paragraph of "Self-Reliance," ending: "And we are now men, . . . not minors and invalids in a protected corner, not cowards fleeing before a revolution, but guides, redeemers and benefactors, obeying the Almighty effort and advancing on Chaos and the Dark."

IV

Of course it is impossible wholly to separate the "abstract" transcendentalism which James disliked in Emerson, from the concrete, practical, and active moralism which he admired. He recognized clearly that the two co-existed, and indexed passages in the same essay as "for" and "against my philosophy"; as embodying alternately "specific emotion" and "abstract monism," and as praising alternately action, and thought. But he did attempt to make a sharp distinction between Emerson, the transcendental philosopher, and Emerson, the man of letters. Although we may question the justice of considering Emerson's rhapsodic mysticism as "philosophy," and his pragmatic moralism as "literature," James's distinction is clear, and his reasons for making it may be suggested.

First, Emerson had called himself a "transcendentalist," had written an essay on the subject, and had become associated with that "philosophic" sect, in the popular mind. Second, James was to discuss transcendental idealism as an important philosophic example of *The Varieties of Religious Experience,* and was to declare its logical inadequacy. Therefore it was natural for him to overlook, for the purposes of philosophic argument, the connections between transcendentalism and pragmatism. Finally, James possessed an instinctively receptive temperament which permitted him to choose what he liked, even when that was mixed with much that he did not like. By separating Emerson's "philosophic" transcendentalism from his "literary" pragmatism, James perhaps rationalized his instinctive preferences.

In an early chapter of his book, James described at length the peculiarly Emersonian variety of religious experience, and suggested his own mixed attitude towards it: "Modern transcendental idealism, Emersonianism, for instance, also seems to let God evaporate into abstract Ideality."[30] Here James's criticism seems wholly negative. But he goes on: "Not a deity *in concreto,* not a super-human person, but the immanent divinity in things . . . is the object of the transcendentalist cult." We begin to wonder whether James is not yearning towards the "legendary and catechetical Jove" of his father's writings. He continues: "In that address to the graduating class at Divinity College in 1838 which made Emerson famous, the frank expression of this worship of mere abstract laws was what made the scandal of the performance." In other words, the abstractness of Emerson's transcendentalism constituted both its power and its danger. In his copy of Emerson, James had underlined: "Beware when the great God lets loose a thinker on this planet." James clearly approved Emerson's celebration of the effective power of thought. But, after quoting two pages of the Divinity School Address in his book, he objected to the vagueness of Emerson's abstract over-soul: "It quivers on the boundary of these things, sometimes leaning one way, sometimes the other, to suit the literary rather than the philosophic need." To him, the transcendental over-soul was bad because it was vague, and literary. But it was also good, because it was effective: "Whatever it is, though, it is active. As much as if it were a God, we can trust it to protect all ideal interests, and keep the world's balance straight. The sentences in which Emerson, to the

[30] *The Varieties of Religious Experience* (New York, 1925), pp. 31 ff.

very end, gave utterance to this faith, are as fine as anything in literature."[31] And again James quoted samples of the Emersonian style.

These remarks of James are significant, and suggestive. They confirm his enthusiasm (which we have already described) for Emerson's active "pragmatism." And they suggest that his disapproval of Emerson's "transcendentalism" was caused not by any suspicion of its ultimate ideals, or ends; but, partly by the mere abstractness of those ideals, and partly by its failure to describe any method—other than that of intuitional self-reliance—by which those ideals might be realized. James's critical comments on Emerson's text fall into three groups: the first objecting to his abstract "monism" as such; the second critizing the primacy which he assigned to non-empirical intuition; and the third objecting to his transcendental view of evil.

In spite of his many objections to it, James felt instinctively, and described consciously, the significance of pure abstraction. In *The Varieties of Religious Experience,* he wrote: "All sorts of higher abstractions bring with them the same kind of impalpable appeal. Remember those passages from Emerson which I read at my last lecture. The whole universe of concrete objects, as we know them, swims, not only for such a transcendentalist writer, but for all of us, in a wider and higher universe of abstract ideas, that lend it its significance."[32] James was the son of his father, and a philosopher who did not deny his heritage. But he had grown to feel that mere abstraction was dangerous, and that the old emphasis should be changed. Specific ends and concrete acts should be preached to modern man.

In reading Emerson, James noted a recurrent emphasis upon "the ONE." In the essay on "Self-Reliance" he underlined: "the ultimate fact which we so quickly reach on this, as on every topic, the resolution of all into the ever-blessed ONE." And in "The Over-Soul" he again marked: "that Unity . . . the universal beauty, to which every part and particle is equally related; the eternal ONE." In whatever essay he found it, in whatever language he saw it described, he indexed the passage. His own phrases include: "the ONE," "Unity," "Monism," "intellectualizing," "the rationalist attitude," "absolute thought," "abstract unity," and other quotations and descriptions even more pungent and more specific. But for the most part, and

[31] *Ibid.,* p. 33.

[32] *Ibid.,* p. 56.

especially where these passages appeared in their natural context (as in "The Over-Soul," and "The Transcendentalist") he passed them by with a nod of recognition.

The essay on "The Method of Nature," however, stimulated James to strong, and explicit disagreement. In the Table of Contents, where he had underlined "The American Scholar" and "The Divinity School Address," he wrote opposite "The Method of Nature": "the weakest." With this warning, and also with the proviso that this essay is "weakest," only if extreme transcendentalism be a weakness, we may consider his comment.

First, James passed over Emerson's important introductory distinction: "I do not wish to look with sour aspect at the industrious manufacturing village. . . . But let me discriminate what is precious herein. There is in each of these works an act of invention, an intellectual step, or short series of steps, taken; that act or step is the spiritual act; all the rest is mere repetition of the same a thousand times."[33] Thus Emerson announced his intention of considering in this essay, only the acts of invention, or creative intuition—what C. S. Peirce was to call the work of "abductive" or creative thought.[34] This creative activity Emerson described, in somewhat technical language, as "ecstasy": "Nature can only be conceived as existing to a universal and not to a particular end . . . a work of *ecstasy,* to be represented by a circular movement, as intention might be signified by a straight line of definite length." This passage James underlined, ominously.

Shortly afterwards, James registered his specific objection to a similar statement that "nature . . . does not exist to any one or to any number of particular ends, but to numberless and endless benefit"; adding an exclamation mark in the margin, and an index reference: "the Thought, which Nature is, evaporates." On the next page he again exclaimed against making the distinction between: "the fact seen from the platform of action," and "from the platform of intellection." Indeed, for the next ten pages, James repeatedly marked similar passages, and indexed them as "intellectualism," "the abstract One," and "vagueness of the idea." Only in one passage (p. 210) did he believe that he had detected: "specific emotion here."

[33] I, 192.
[34] See C. S. Peirce, *Collected Papers,* V, 105 ff.

Finally, after Emerson had repeated once again: "the soul can be appeased not by a deed but by a tendency. . . . I say to you plainly that there is no end to which your practical faculty can aim, so sacred or large, that if pursued for itself, will not at last become carrion and an offense to the nostril."[35] James could contain himself no longer. Opposite Emerson's further question: "And what is Genius but a finer love, a love impersonal, a love of the flower and perfection of things . . . ?" James answered: "But there is no such flower, and love and genius both cleave to the particular objects which are precious because at the moment they seem unique."

Emerson repeatedly declared truth to be ideal, undefinable, and abstract; while James declared it to be specific, definable, and embodied in concrete objects. But, at the end, the two men agreed upon one and perhaps the most important question. Emerson phrased it: "If you ask, 'How can any rules be given for the attainment of gifts so sublime?' " and answered: "I shall only remark that . . . the one condition coupled with the gift of truth is its use. . . . The only way into nature is to enact our best insight. . . . Do what you know, and perception is converted into character." James underlined these pragmatic sentences. But the bad taste remained. He indexed the last of them under the title of: "his optimism."

James objected to abstraction, mysticism, and vagueness, in all its forms. But specifically he objected to that mystical individualism which denied the possibility of the guidance of action by means of communicable experience. One of the passages in "The Method of Nature" to which he had objected, concluded: "The imaginative faculty of the soul must be fed with objects immense and eternal. Your end should be one inapprehensible to the senses."[36] Did not this deny all empiricism?

Emerson's transcendence of sensuous experience disturbed James even more when it appeared in the essay on "Self-Reliance," for there it seemed to vitiate much that was best in the Emersonian gospel. The essay, it will be remembered, first described the need for self-reliance in eloquent language, which James copied. But it then based this reliance on personal intuition. "And now at last the

[35] I, 215-216. Compare all these passages with C. S. Peirce's chapter entitled "What Pragmatism Is," in his *Collected Papers,* Vol. V. Many of the Emersonian ideas to which James objected find repetition and clarification in Peirce.

[36] I, 216.

highest truth on this subject remains unsaid; probably cannot be said; for all that we say is the far-off remembering of the intuition. . . . When good is near you, when you have life in yourself, it is not by any known or accustomed way; you shall not discern the footprints of any other . . . the way, the thought, the good, shall be wholly strange and new. It shall exclude example and experience."[37] This angered James. On his first reading he called it: "The anaesthetic revelation," although he commonly used this phrase only to describe mystical trances induced by drugs, or other artificial means.[38] Then, on a second reading, he indexed the same passage as: "the tasteless water of souls."

"—It shall exclude experience. . . ." But had not Emerson himself celebrated "experience," many times? James explained Emerson's thought as: "sometimes leaning one way, sometimes the other, to suit the literary rather than the philosophic need." He separated Emerson's pragmatism, or empiricism from his transcendentalism, or intuitionalism. But are the two necessarily exclusive? Are they not rather complementary? Are they not different aspects of the same life-process? Emerson suggested this by distinguishing the inventive, creative, "spiritual act," from the routine, mechanical act. C. S. Peirce developed a similar distinction between "abductive" or intuitive thought, which originates ideas, and inductive and deductive thought which merely tests ideas: "Induction never can originate any idea whatever. No more can deduction. All the ideas of science come to it by way of Abduction."[39] He identified this intuitive "Abduction" with the scientific method of hypothetic inference. Later philosophers have confirmed his interpretations, using different terminology.[40] All have recognized that the creative, inventive mind works rather by intuition than by "example and experience."

Emerson's transcendentalism denied common experience when, and only when, it sought to describe the pure, creative act of consciousness—as, of course, it often did. Then it praised a "perfect self-reliance," as the only means of originating new ideas. It always, however, started from the more common, routine "uses of nature." And it always returned to experience, in order to enact its insights—

[37] II, 68.
[38] Cf. *The Varieties of Religious Experience*, pp. 387-393.
[39] *Collected Papers*, V, 90.
[40] Cf. Henri Poincaré, *Science and Hypothesis*, trans. G. B. Halsted (New York, 1905).

"to convert thought into truth." James, the experimentalist, approved the pragmatic action. James, the spiritualist, often sympathized with the transcendental enthusiasm for the conception of new ideas. But James, the moralist, felt instinctively the danger of too much uncontrolled transcendentalism. He distrusted the runaway intellect.

The practical dangers of transcendentalism have always appeared most clearly in its statements of the problems of evil, and James noted these statements frequently. The active man resists evil, obeys the moral code, and struggles against sin in all its forms. But the transcendentalist turns the other cheek. "Jesus Christ," as Emerson wrote, "was a minister of the pure reason." Few men, from the crucifixion to the present, have been willing thus to abandon the practical for the pure reason.

James did not oppose the transcendental morality as violently as might have been expected, but contented himself with noting it as he found it in Emerson's works. In "The Method of Nature," he condemned it together with its kindred ideas. Emerson had written: "Self-accusation, remorse, and the didactic morals of self-denial and strife with sin, are in the view we are constrained to take of the fact seen from the platform of action; but seen from the platform of intellection there is nothing but praise and wonder"[41]—to which James added a marginal exclamation. Similarly, in "The Transcendentalist," James indexed the admission that: "In action he [the transcendental moralist] easily incurs the charge of antinomianism by his avowal that he . . . may with safety not only neglect but even contravene every written commandment. . . . Jacobi, refusing all measure of right and wrong except the determinations of the private spirit, remarks that there is no crime but has sometimes been a virtue."[42]—and so James continued throughout his reading of Emerson's works. In "Self-Reliance," he noted Emerson's attack on "prayers, regrets, sympathies."[43] In *The Conduct of Life,* he indexed as "transcendental," the phrase: "every one of their vices being the excess or acridity of a virtue."[44] While even in the mystical conclusion to *Nature,* he had discerned a transcendental statement of the "scale of evil."

[41] I, 204.
[42] I, 336.
[43] II, 77-80.
[44] VI, 251.

The complex relationships between Emerson and William James have barely been outlined in this essay. The family relationships, the statements in James's letters, the comments and criticisms included in his books of philosophy, have been used only to suggest the background. Even his marginal comments on Emerson's writings have not been exhausted—those describing "Emerson's singularity" have largely been omitted.

Excluding James's merely descriptive comments, his marginal remarks on Emerson's ideas have seemed to fall into two classes. In the first, James praised Emerson's "pragmatism," his emphasis on the present tense and on immediate experience, and his democratic sympathy for the laborer and the poor. In the second, he objected to Emerson's abstract idealism, to his frequent preference of intuition to experience, and to his transcendental doctrine of evil. Between these two extremes, James found much that seemed suggestive and sympathetic, even when mixed with much that was distasteful.

The philosophic relationships involved in this interplay of ideas have been suggested in passing. Many of the "transcendental" passages to which James objected find development in the philosophy of Charles Sanders Peirce. Many even lie implicit in James's own thought. Few can be said to contradict the fundamental pragmatic principle of a perpetual "return to experience." Rather they emphasize one particular aspect of the principle. Emersonian "transcendentalism" clearly belongs to the intellectual heritage of William James and of the pragmatic movement of which he was a leader. A detailed study of the philosophic relationship of the two might make clear much that has seemed obscure in the history of modern thought.

Emerson and Cudworth:
Plastic Nature and Transcendental Art

Vivian C. Hopkins

I

RALPH CUDWORTH'S *The True Intellectual System of the Universe* (1678) deserves to be re-examined, as a shaping influence upon Emerson's concepts of nature and art.[1] Although Professor John Harrison some years ago indicated the importance of Cudworth's work in Emerson's thinking, the relationship has not been further studied.[2] Perhaps Emerson himself may be blamed for this neglect. In the *Journals* he describes Cudworth as "a dull writer," a "magazine of quotations," comparing him to a cow chewing the "cud" of the ancient sages. Had Emerson stopped to consider, he might have seen a similarity between Cudworth's career and his own. Emerson's "doubts" concerning the Lord's Supper might well have aroused his interest in Cudworth's treatise on the subject, in which Cudworth compared the Christian communion with the Hebrew passover, and concluded that the Christian rite was

[1] Ralph Cudworth (1617-1688), an eminent member of the group known as the Cambridge Platonists, held various country livings, was master of Christ's College, Cambridge, 1654-1662, and prebendary of Gloucester, 1678-1688. Though his *The True Intellectual System* . . . , 4 vols. (London, 1820) made use of extensive evidence from ancient atomism to prove the naturalness of theism and the reality of human freedom, it was attacked by orthodox divines as subversive to the Christian religion. Never a widely popular book, *The True Intellectual System* was first published in one volume (London, 1678), ed. Thomas Birch, with notes and dissertations from Dr. J. L. Mosheim's Latin translation of the work; in two volumes, London, 1743; reprinted in four volumes in London, 1820; had its first American edition, of two volumes, at Andover, 1837-1838; and was reprinted in London, in three volumes, in 1845. Emerson owned and used the London, 1820, edition.

[2] John S. Harrison, *The Teachers of Emerson* (New York, 1910). Professor Harrison showed the relation between Emerson's definition of art and Cudworth's "plastic nature" (pp. 188-190), and the connection between Emerson's application of gods' names to his poet, with Cudworth's listing of classic trinities (pp. 201-202), matters which will be more fully discussed in this article. Professor Kenneth Cameron has recently pointed out the need for a more complete analysis of the relation between Emerson and Cudworth, through the selections reprinted from Cudworth in his *Background of Emerson the Essayist* (Raleigh, N. C., 1945).

not a sacrifice, "but a feast upon a sacrifice." The "martyr" of *The Divinity School Address* should have felt some sympathy with the author of *The True Intellectual System*, whose purpose—to strengthen Christianity by finding its "seeds" in early atomic philosophers—called forth a storm of orthodox protest.[3]

Despite Emerson's failure to claim blood brotherhood with Cudworth, or even to recognize the controlling purpose of *The True Intellectual System*, there is no question of the fertilizing effect upon Emerson's thought of certain ideas which he first discovered in Cudworth's monumental work. Of course no student who has observed the confluence in Emerson's mind of such widely separated literary streams as, for example, Montaigne's *Essays* and the *Bhagvad-Gita*, will seek to interpret his thought in terms of a single source, or to assert that the mere establishment of a literary relation explains the ideas finally evolved by his highly original mind. On the other hand, not only does a rather startling resemblance appear between Emerson's concepts of nature and art and related statements in Cudworth, but the meaning of transcendental "nature" and "art" becomes clearer when examined in the light of *The True Intellectual System*.

In 1835, when Emerson makes the first *Journal* reference to Cudworth (III, 489), he says that Cudworth has fed "entirely on ancient bards and sages."[4] In January, 1836, when Emerson is completing *Nature*, he shows Cudworth's importance in his own speculation by terming him "an armory for a poet to furnish himself withal" (*Journals*, IV, 8). Clearly Emerson regards Cudworth as a kind of anthology embracing Plato, Aristotle, and the Neoplatonists.

Emerson showed some acquaintance with Plato as early as 1820, when he wrote the Bowdoin Prize Essay on "The Character of Socrates." A Latin edition of Plato bearing Emerson's autograph

[3] So judicious a critic as John Dryden states that Cudworth "raised such strong objections against the being of a God and providence, that many think he has not answered them" ("Dedication to Translation of Virgil, *Aeneid*," *Works*, London, 1730, II, 378).

[4] That Cudworth's influence upon Emerson may have been more subtle than he realized is indicated by his writing, immediately after the first casual reference to Cudworth: "I endeavor to announce the laws of the First Philosophy" (*Journals*, Boston, 1909-1914, III, 489).

It is interesting to notice that Cudworth's *The True Intellectual System* was one of three books (the other two: Carlyle's *Miscellanies* and Emerson's *Nature*) which Emerson recommended that the Dartmouth College Library purchase with his lecture fee in July, 1838 (*Letters*, ed. Ralph L. Rusk, New York, 1939, II, 144).

and the date 1822 (*Platonis Atheniensis*, Basileae, 1561) reveals little evidence of use, not a surprising fact in view of Emerson's preference for translations. During 1830 he was withdrawing from the Athenæum library the first three volumes of the Taylor-Sydenham edition of Plato, which he later bought for his own library[5] and in which he made copious notes. If we assume that Emerson's copy of the Taylor-Sydenham edition is that mentioned as a possible purchase from Charles Lane's library in 1844 (*Letters*, III, 257), we may be fairly certain that he owned these volumes by that date.[6] Independent reading in Plato, however, did not keep Emerson from looking to Cudworth for Platonic quotations; as late as 1845 Emerson says that "Cudworth is sometimes read without the Platonism, which would be like reading Theobald's Shakespeare, leaving out only what Shakespeare wrote" (*Journals*, VII, 95-96).

As we shall see, Cudworth's quotations from Aristotle enter into the concepts of "nature" and "art" which figure largely in Emerson's thought. Since Emerson never became a serious student of Aristotle, we need not consider the extension of his study from Cudworth to Aristotle himself.

The Neoplatonists, however, especially Plotinus, had a strong and decisive influence upon Emerson's thought, and Emerson first discovered direct quotations from Plotinus, Proclus, and Iamblichus in Cudworth. As early as 1830, of course, he had read condensed accounts of Neoplatonic philosophers in De Gérando's *Histoire comparée des systèmes de philosophie* (Paris, 1820) and was familiar with Coleridge's adaptation of Plotinian thought in *The Friend* and *Aids to Reflection* (*Letters*, I, 291), but undoubtedly it was Cudworth who provided him with the words and phrases of the Neoplatonists themselves. Emerson's direct knowledge of the Neoplatonists definitely postdates his reading in Plato. Had Emerson

[5] It is difficult to date accurately Emerson's acquisition of this five-volume edition of Plato's *Works*, tr. by Taylor and Sydenham (London, 1804), but it was probably acquired after 1842, since in 1836 he withdrew vol. IV from the Athenæum; in 1842 vol. V. In 1840 he mentions (*Journals*, V, 369) reading Plato's dialogue "The Politician" in Cousin (*Oeuvres complètes de Platon*, 13 vols., Paris, 1822-1840), which he probably would not have done if he had owned the Taylor-Sydenham edition at that time. Nor can the volume of selected works translated by Taylor (*Cratylus, Phaedo, Parmenides, Timaeus*, London, 1793), which Emerson also studied carefully, be given a more accurate acquisition date in Emerson's library.

[6] This seems like a reasonable conclusion; yet one must note that in 1845 Emerson was still withdrawing vols. I and IV of the Taylor-Sydenham edition from the Athenæum.

possessed Taylor's translation of Plotinus[7] in 1837, for example, he would hardly have gone to the trouble of translating Plotinus's comment on art from Goethe's German (*Journals*, IV, 218-221). Probably by 1840, when Plotinus is mentioned as a "spermatic" book and some quotations are introduced in the *Journals* (V, 508), it may be assumed that Emerson read Plotinus at first hand.[8] From 1835, when Cudworth is first mentioned in the *Journals*, until about 1840, Cudworth becomes the chief source for Emerson's knowledge of Neoplatonism, of which tradition Plotinus was the chief representative.

Even when Emerson turned to the works of the Neoplatonists themselves, he followed the lines of interest which he first discovered in Cudworth. The kind of notations which Emerson made in his copy of *The True Intellectual System* recur, with some additions, in his volumes of Plotinus, Proclus, and Iamblichus, as he acquired them.[9] References to Nature, to Love, to Intellect, to Orpheus, to Zoroastrian oracles indicate the phases of Neoplatonic thought which Cudworth laid open for Emerson, and which he followed into the works of these Neoplatonic writers when he came to study them at first hand. Here occurs the first reference I have found to the Sphinx, later to emerge in one of Emerson's finest poems.[10] Emer-

[7] The two sets of Plotinus in Emerson's library are both translated and edited by Thomas Taylor: *Five Books of Plotinus* (London, 1794) and *Select Works* (London, 1817).

[8] References in the *Letters* of this period are so brief as to be inconclusive (II, 195, 1839; 328, 1840). On the other hand, it is difficult to imagine that Emerson could have written "The Over-soul" without direct knowledge at least of Plotinus, and this essay was published in *Essays, First Series* (1841).

[9] As late as 1868 Emerson spoke of his surprise in discovering that his college classmate, Charles Upham, had read Cudworth for his "argument and theology," whereas Emerson had always sought in Cudworth "citations from Plato and the philosophers" (*Manuscript Journal NY*, p. 111).

Emerson's direct acquaintance with Proclus is easier to establish than that with Plotinus, since he writes from Nantasket in July, 1841 (*Letters*, II, 429-430) of Proclus as one of "three volumes new to me." The Proclus here mentioned is probably one of two works still in Emerson's library: *Commentaries of Proclus on the Timaeus of Plato*, tr. Taylor, 2 vols. (London, 1820); or *Six Books of Proclus*, tr. Taylor, 2 vols. (London, 1816). Emerson's copy of Iamblichus, *On the Mysteries of the Egyptians, Chaldeans, and Assyrians*, tr. Taylor (Chiswick, 1821), may have been acquired at the same time, but is not specifically mentioned in the *Letters* or *Journals*.

[10] Emerson marks the passage on the Sphinx, which describes it as no "imperfect and infant God," but "the president of men's speech concerning the gods, that is but imperfect, balbutient, and inarticulate; his finger upon his mouth being a symbol of silence and taciturnity" (Ralph Cudworth, *The True Intellectual System of the Universe . . .*, 4 vols., London, 1820, II, 117-118).

son's hunger for curious, strange information foreign to English culture was fed by such references as the Egyptian symbol of God as a crocodile, with a film over its eyes by which it saw without being seen,[11] and the representation of God sitting on a lotus tree above watery mud, showing God's transcendency over matter.[12] Empedocles's statement that the world was created from the opposing principles of "contention and friendship"[13] Emerson marks in his copy of Cudworth as "Affinity and repulsion, or polarity"—an early reference to one of Emerson's controlling ideas. In Cudworth also Emerson found frequent references to Orpheus, whose mysterious origin as the father of Greek myth fascinated Emerson by its combination of poetry and theology. Orpheus became for him (as for Alcott) the master symbolist.[14]

We may safely say that from 1835 to 1840 Cudworth represents for Emerson a reservoir of Neoplatonic thought from which he drew deep and satisfying draughts, and that Emerson's reading in the Neoplatonists themselves became a search for fuller explication of the ideas which he first found in Cudworth. Even in September of 1841, when Emerson undoubtedly knew some of the Neoplatonists at first hand, he was still associating them with Cudworth and other seventeenth-century authors, for he wrote to Mary Moody Emerson that no reviews came into his study—"Nothing but old Plotinus, Iamblichus, Mores, Cudworths, and Browns" (*Letters*, II, 451). To say that Cudworth was a major power in shaping Emerson's Platonic and Neoplatonic ideas is not of course to deny that other authors, such as Goethe and Coleridge, furnished him with occasional Greek inspiration, nor to minimize his direct acquaintance with Plotinus, Proclus, and Iamblichus after 1840. On the other hand, it is clear that Cudworth, through direct quotations from Greek authors, first introduced Emerson to the body of Platonic and Neoplatonic tradition, and that Cudworth was a continuing influence, since close parallels to Cudworth exist in "The Poet" (1844) as well as in *Nature* (1836). Without any pretension to the claim

[11] *Ibid.*, II, 156-157. [12] *Ibid.*, II, 159. [13] *Ibid.*, II, 268-269.

[14] The effect upon him of "the cyclus of orphic words" which he found in Cudworth and others Emerson describes: "I perceive myself addressed thoroughly. They do touch the intellect and cause a gush of emotion which we call the moral sublime" (*Journals*, IV, 154). In "The Poet" Emerson places Orpheus at the head of the list of men who "explore the double meaning," or "the quadruple or the centuple" meaning of every sensuous fact (*Works*, III, 4). Cf. Cudworth, *op. cit.*, II, 82.

that Cudworth is the "single" source of Emerson's Neoplatonism, one may affirm that Emerson's reading in Cudworth formed the mold for his apprehension of Neoplatonic thought.

II

The most important single idea which Emerson found in *The True Intellectual System* was that of the plastic nature, which strongly affected his own concepts of nature and art. Deriving his material from Aristotle and Plotinus, Cudworth states that the plastic nature is the deputy of Divine Mind, the energetic principle which imposes God's commands upon matter, the intelligible cause of the orderly, regular, and artificial frame of things in the universe.[15] Emerson's statement in *Nature* of the "Unity" which fashions the world owes something to Cudworth's plastic nature; Emerson's nature also is controlled by spirit, which acts easily within matter:

Emerson	*Cudworth*
Spirit creates; . . . behind nature, throughout nature, spirit is present; one and not compound; it does not act upon us *from without*; that is, in space and time, but spiritually, or through ourselves ("Nature," *Works*, I, 63-64). [Italics mine.]	[Nature operates] according to laws . . . prescribed to it by a perfect intellect . . . essentially depending upon a higher intellect (*True Int. System*, I, 370). The difference between nature and human art [is] that the latter is imperfect art, acting upon the matter *from without*, and at a distance; but the former is art itself, or perfect art, acting as an inward principle in it (*ibid.*, I, 335). [Italics mine.]

Developing the thesis that nature is controlled by spirit, Cudworth emphasizes nature's subserviency to God; Emerson's nature, equally humble, shows subordination to man:

Emerson	*Cudworth*
Nature is thoroughly mediate. It is made to serve. It receives the	Nature is not master of that consummate art and wisdom accord-

[15] Cudworth, *op. cit.*, I, 331. All the passages from Cudworth which are here compared with Emerson's statements have been marked by Emerson in his copy of *The True Intellectual System*.

dominion of man as meekly as the ass on which the Savior rode. It offers all its kingdoms to man as . . . raw material . . . (*Works*, I, 40).

ing to which it acts, but only a servant to it, and a drudging executioner of the dictates of it (*True Int. System*, I, 338).

Thus in the Emersonian universe man holds a higher position than in the Neoplatonic, since nature is shown as the servant, not of divine art, but of divinely-inspired man.

To compare Emerson's reading of earth with Cudworth's plastic nature also illuminates the distinction which Emerson makes between the two aspects of "nature." Lower-case "nature" (*natura naturata*), the material aspects, in so far as they are unchanged by man, is distinguished from "Nature" in upper case (*natura naturans*), the Spirit which passes through material objects and also through man's will.[16] Cudworth states the difference between the two aspects of nature by denoting the two controlling principles which atomic philosophers recognized in the universe:

Emerson

Nature, in its ministry to man, is not only the *material* [lower-case nature], but is also *the process and the result* [upper-case Nature] (*Works*, I, 13). [Italics mine.]

Cudworth

The one . . . passive matter, and the other active power, vigour, and virtue. . . . Passive matter and bulk, and self-activity or life. The former—τό πάσχον—that which suffers or receives. The latter—τό ποίουν—active principle (*True Int. System*, I, 120-121).

Clearly Emerson's distinction between passive matter (nature) and Active Spirit (Nature) closely resembles Cudworth's. Although Emerson sometimes shifts without warning from one sense of the term to the other, a clear perception of the two "natures" will help us to follow him even when he confuses them.

[16] The first, Emerson calls "the philosophical sense of nature," "not-me," including nature and art, all other men, and his own body ("Nature," *Works*, I, 4-5).

Coleridge of course also expresses this Plotinian distinction of two "natures," in *The Friend*, and Emerson could have found it in his copy (London, 1818), III, 166-167 n.: "The word Nature has been used in two senses, viz. actively and passively; energetic (forma formans), and material (forma formata)." Coleridge's emphasis here, however, differs from Emerson's; since Coleridge is concerned with the reflection of these two natures in a specific natural object, and the comparison of a natural object with a mathematical figure. Nor did Emerson mark this passage in Coleridge, though he was much interested in the definition of "Idea" which follows this passage, on p. 168.

The distinction has an important bearing upon Emerson's discussion of aesthetic creation. In the "second" essay on "Art," which I shall term the *Dial* essay to distinguish it from that published in *Essays, First Series* (1841),[17] Emerson again differentiates between "passive" and "active" nature, in relating nature to human art. Certain deductions, he says, must be made from the credit allowed an artist for his creation. Art's debt to material nature involves three areas: first, such elements as the stone in statues, language in poetry, physical sounds in strings; second, the pleasure an observer derives from a work of art because of its resemblance to a natural object, apart from the artist's design; third, the adventitious contribution of material nature to an object of art, as sunlight and clouds surrounding a temple.[18] Much as these material elements enhance the beauty of his creation, the artist may not be praised for them; simply by availing himself of nature's stone, sounds, and sky, he has automatically enriched his work.[19]

If material or passive nature does much for art, the active spirit of Nature can do even more. The Spirit, however, Emerson finds, will not serve the artist so automatically as material nature. To get in tune with the all-pervading Unity, the artist must make the moral effort of renouncing egotism, surrendering his will to the All.[20] Once this surrender is accomplished, the artist will find his work enriched by the Spirit of Nature far more than by her material things; his work will in fact acquire "a fixed place in the chain of being, as much as a plant or a crystal" ("Art," *Works*, VII, 50).

[17] The "first" essay on Art, published in *Essays, First Series*, was largely composed of the Lecture on Art, the third in the 1836 series. The "second" essay, though not published in a volume until 1870 (*Society and Solitude*), may be dated about four years later than the first, since it appeared in the *Dial* of Jan., 1841, and was probably written early in 1840. The fact that it contains some earlier material appears in Emerson's statement to Margaret Fuller, Dec., 1840: "You was [*sic*] very magnanimous to take the *poor obsolete* essay" (*Letters*, II, 372; italics mine).

[18] "Art," *Works*, VII, 45-47.

[19] The fact that these material aspects of nature are never worthless explains the value which Emerson places upon "poor pictures." Inferior though such uninspired productions are to the work of painters animated by Soul, they can give the observer something because of the natural shapes and colors which they inevitably possess. Thus in the Lecture on Art (1836) Emerson speaks of our debt "to poor pictures; that namely which nature paints."

[20] "In art that aims at beauty must the parts be subordinated to Ideal Nature, and everything individual abstracted, so that it shall be the production of the universal soul" ("Art," *Works*, VII, 48). Cf. "Art," *Works*, II, 352.

What, then, is the importance for the artist of this distinction between passive and active nature? First, he must understand the distinction; then he will make use of both aspects of nature, keeping always in mind the priority of Spirit over matter.

Emerson has somewhat complicated the question of art's relation to nature by also distinguishing two senses of the term *art*. In the essay *Nature* Emerson denotes art (lower case) as the material work, or artifact, and Art (upper case) as a Spirit that closely resembles active Nature.[21] The two senses of the term "art" are closely related to the two senses of "nature":

> Thus is Art [upper-case] a nature [lower-case] passed through the alembic of man. Thus in art [lower-case] does Nature [upper-case] work through the will of a man filled with the beauty of her first works (*Works*, I, 24).

In this passage I take the first sense of Art (upper case) to be man's spiritual intuition of beauty in the material aspects of nature. It is this spiritual aspect of Nature, discovered by the artist, which dominates his production, and without which he would be quite unable to create. Since, however, his finished work must shrink when compared with the magnitude of his intuition, his production is called art (lower case) to distinguish the material object from the intuition which inspired it.

The distinction between these two senses of the term "art" clarifies a passage in *Nature* where Emerson shows some scorn for artistic production:

> Art is applied to the mixture of his [man's] will with the same things [material objects], as in a house, a canal, a statue, a picture. But his operations taken together are so insignificant, a little chipping, baking, patching, and washing, that in an impression so grand as that of the world on the human mind, they do not vary the result (*Works*, I, 5).

If we keep in mind Emerson's distinction between the two senses of art—as material, and as spiritual—we shall more easily resolve the difficulty of the passage. Emerson's apparent belittling of the fine arts relates only to their material aspect, and then only in

[21] In the *Dial* essay Emerson also uses Art (upper-case) in a historic sense, as the Art of the ancient Romans (*Works*, VII, 38); and in the first essay on Art he employs it in a generic sense, comparing the world of art to "the kingdom of nature" (*Works*, II, 365).

comparison to the picture which "the anointed eye" perceives in eternity. By that transcendental standard, all of man's creative works must wither and fade away. It does not, however, deny their importance as landmarks on the highroad of human life. Furthermore, by stating that art represents the mixture of man's will with natural objects, Emerson does not really contradict his frequent insistence upon the artist's "submission" to the Divine. Rather, the emphasis is upon the material element of nature (*natura naturata*) which his art must dominate and shape to his controlling, "God-enlightened" purpose.

When we consider Emerson's definition of art in the *Dial* essay, we discover a close relation to Cudworth's comparison of plastic nature to human art and to the Divine mind. Contrasting plastic nature with human art, Cudworth finds plastic nature superior, since it acts as an "inner principle" within matter, without the human artist's need to deliberate or to revise.[22] Plastic nature is in turn surpassed by Divine art and wisdom, working merely as a servant of Divine power, not understanding its ends; its activity resembles the movements of a dancer, which do not comprehend the purpose directing them.[23] Besides the lack of comprehension, plastic nature is further inferior to Divine Art because it exists only as mixed with matter, while Divine Art exists as pure being.[24]

In Emerson's definition of art, the first element resembling Cudworth's plastic nature concerns the purpose which must inform good art:

Emerson	*Cudworth*
The conscious utterance of thought, by speech or action, *to any end*, is art. . . . Art is the spirit's voluntary use and combination of things to serve *its end* (*Works*, VII, 38). [Italics mine.]	It is absurd for men to think nothing done *for ends*, if they do not see that which moves to consult. . . . Nature may act artificially, orderly, methodically, *for the sake of ends*, though it never consult or deliberate (*True Int. System*, I, 334-5). [Italics mine.]

[22] Cudworth, *op. cit.*, I, 333-335. Cudworth cites Plotinus, *Ennead* 3, l. 8, Sec. 1, p. 344, *Oper.*, and Aristotle, *Phys.* l. 2, c. 8, p. 477, tom. 1, *Oper.*

[23] *Ibid.*, I, 337-340. Cudworth cites Aristotle, *Met.* l. 1, c. 1, p. 260, tom. IV, *Oper.*; and Plotinus, *Ennead* 4, l. 4, c. 13, p. 467; *Ennead* 2, l. 3, c. 17, p. 147, *Oper.*

[24] *Ibid.*, I, 336. A diagram of Cudworth's theory will show this gradation: Divine art—Plastic nature—Human art.

Both passages emphasize the *end* or *purpose* toward which activity is directed: Emerson, for human art; Cudworth, for plastic nature. An apparent difference arises in Emerson's use of the terms "conscious" and "voluntary" as opposed to Cudworth's emphasis on plastic nature's "unconsciousness." As we read further, however, we find that Emerson is not really indicating human will:

Emerson

The Will distinguishes it [art] as spiritual action. Relatively to themselves, the bee, the bird, the beaver, have no art; for what they do they do instinctively; but relatively to the Supreme Being, they have. And the same is true of all unconscious action; relative to the doer, it is instinct; relatively to the First Cause, it is Art (*Works*, VII, 38).

Cudworth

Nature is . . . a living stamp or signature of the Divine wisdom. . . . Nature is not master of that consummate art and wisdom according to which it acts, but only a servant to it. . . . As, for example, the bees in mellification, in framing their combs and hexagonial [*sic*] cells, the spiders in spinning their webs, the birds in building their nests. . . . (*True Int. System*, I, 342.)

Cudworth here affirms the "subserviency" of plastic nature, which does its work in the same way as bees, spiders, and birds. Emerson, speaking of human art, places the action of the artist on the same level as Cudworth's plastic nature, comparing him to an animal in executing the behests of a greater Will. To reread the "conscious utterance" of the first passage is to discover that by contrast with the material objects of nature, the artist is indeed "conscious," but in the controlling power of the First Cause he is unconscious as an animal. So far, Emerson's artist closely resembles Cudworth's plastic nature: his work involves shaping materials toward an end, which a higher Will has indicated to his consciousness.

Let us see what becomes of Cudworth's assertion concerning the superiority of plastic nature to human art, in Emerson's definition of art:

Emerson

In this sense, recognizing the Spirit which informs Nature, Plato rightly said, "Those things which

Cudworth

Imperfect human art imitates the perfect art of nature, which is really no other than the Divine art itself,

are said to be done by Nature are indeed done by Divine Art." Art, universally, is the spirit creative. It was defined by Aristotle, "The reason of the thing, without the matter" (*Works*, VII, 39).	as . . . Plato had declared . . . "Those things which are said to be done by Nature, are indeed done by Divine art."[25] Art is defined by Aristotle to be . . . "The reason of the thing without the matter"[26] (*True Int. System*, I, 336).

Emerson's use of Cudworth's idea here shows how cleverly he could twist a proposition to his own purpose while retaining the author's phrasing: Cudworth's analysis has stated the *inferiority* of human art to plastic nature, and Cudworth quotes Plato and Aristotle in support. Picking up Cudworth's quotations, Emerson has turned them into a statement about human art, attributing to human art not only the skill of Cudworth's plastic nature, but also some of the power of Divine art and wisdom.

That Emerson claimed the qualities of plastic nature for human art is further shown by a sentence in the *Dial* essay, omitted from the version in *Society and Solitude*, where the art of shipbuilding is termed "all of the ship but the wood."[27] This closely parallels Cudworth's statement about the working of plastic nature: "If the naupegical art, that is, the art of the shipwright, were in the timber itself operatively and effectually, it would then act just as nature doth."[28] If, Cudworth says, the builder could imagine his bricks and mortar flying together of their own accord, or the musician could conceive of beautiful sounds issuing automatically from an instrument, these human artists would then understand how plastic nature surpasses them in ease of working. Emerson's definition of shipbuilding as "all of the ship but the wood," together with his application to human art of Aristotle's definition of Divine Art, as "the reason of the thing without the matter," indicates that his conception of human art has absorbed the "working as an inner principle" in matter, which Cudworth reserved for plastic nature.

[25] Cudworth cites *The Sophist*, p. 168, *Oper.*

[26] Cudworth cites *De partib. animal.* lib. 1, cap. 1, p. 472, tom. II, *Oper.*

[27] In the *Dial* version this line followed directly after the quotation from Aristotle: "The reason of the thing without the matter," *Dial*, I, 368 (Jan., 1841).

[28] Cudworth, *op. cit.*, I, 332. Cudworth cites Aristotle, *Phys.* lib. 2, c. 8, p. 447, tom. I, *Oper.*

If the artist has a strong influx of divine spirit, Emerson asserts that he will find his materials yielding obediently to his touch:

> In proportion to his force, the artist will find in his work an outlet for his proper character. He must not be in any manner pinched or hindered by his material, but through his necessity of imparting himself the adamant will be wax in his hands ("Art," *Works*, II, 360).

To sum up the importance of Cudworth's plastic nature for Emerson's concepts of nature and art, one finds in Cudworth a clear statement of the control of nature by Spirit, which is integral to Emerson's theory, though Emerson considers nature as controlled by the "God-inspired" man rather than Cudworth's "nature, the servant of God." In Cudworth's quotations from Plotinus, Emerson could find the distinction between the two aspects of nature, as matter and as Spirit, which became central in his own philosophy, and which he postulated as a theorem of first importance for the artist. The similarity in phrasing between Cudworth's analysis of plastic nature and Emerson's definition of art shows that Emerson based his aesthetic theory on the classic and Neoplatonic ideas which he found in Cudworth.

To compare closely the first essay on "Art," which we have found to be composed in 1836, with the second or *Dial* essay, which we have dated approximately 1840,[29] is to discover the answer to the question Emerson asked in 1836 about the dilemma of modern art and literature. Fresh from his European experience of 1833, Emerson was concerned with the form of painting and sculpture, and with the effect of that form upon the observer.[30] He expressed the current romantic dissatisfaction with modern art which he had picked up from such writers as Goethe and Coleridge, as well as from his own experience, and he was groping toward a cure for the "modern sickness" when he said that the best art always springs from one "aboriginal Power," that art must aim at "the creation of man and nature," that art must somehow catch the living, moving, reproductive quality of nature.

In the *Dial* essay Emerson comes to grips with the problem pre-

[29] See n. 18, above.

[30] Some passages on the right method of viewing the plastic arts, included in the 1836 lecture on Art, and omitted from the version in *Essays, First Series,* appear in the *Journals.* See, for example, IV, 465-466 (1838); V, 199-200 (1839).

sented in the first essay, and the answer with which he emerges is based upon his reading in Cudworth. It amounts to the very simple assertion, reiterated throughout the essay, that the best art is always produced, not by the artist's own will, but by the Universal Spirit flowing through the artist's soul.[31] The important principle for the artist is that of submission; once he has learned the secret of "unconsciousness," his works may take their place in the universe along with nature's plants and crystals. If works of art must lack the power of organic reproduction which plants possess, they have the compensating capacity of spiritual reproduction.[32] One may say, of course, that this lesson of submission Emerson had long since learned in his religious experience; but it was in Cudworth that he found the idea related to art. The apparent contradiction of the "conscious-unconscious" artist is resolved by Cudworth's statement that he is conscious in relation to material things, but unconscious in relation to the Divine Will. Emerson allows an apparent degradation of the artist to the animal level, in order to demonstrate that his motive power, like that of Cudworth's plastic nature, springs from the Divine. In adapting Cudworth's ideas, Emerson of course shows his own creative use of literary material "consciously to serve his own ends" as a creative thinker, in appropriating for human art all the skilful working of plastic nature, which Cudworth reserved for Divine power. Human art in Emerson's interpretation becomes not a second remove from the Divine, but a deputy with Nature of the Divine will, strongly driven by the impulse to create new life. Thus, by turning Cudworth's phrases to his own uses, Emerson was able to state the method by which modern art and literature might be saved from destruction. Furthermore, in the Cudworthian

[31] Emerson adumbrates this idea in the 1836 lecture on Art, though he does not develop it there with the fulness or the emphasis which it receives in the *Dial* essay. In the lecture he says: "This instruction in which we gain in the beauty of our world from our own efforts to reproduce it is certainly not the result a [*sic*] conscious study on our part. It is the late discovery of many years and many trials: but the attempt to produce works arose from the instinct of creation which exists throughout the universe precisely measured by the degree of power that appears in any mind."

[32] That the arts still lack sufficient spiritual power to make them equal to nature is shown by Emerson's comparison of the effect upon man of nature and art; in nature, he says, "I stand in a thoroughfare"; while in art, "creation is driven into a corner" (*Works*, II, 364); and in the lecture on Art: "Art is a corner, nature a passage." Cf. Thoreau's use of the term, with opposite emphasis, in *Walden:* "to drive life into a corner" (*Works*, Boston, 1894-1895, II, 143).

distinction of the two aspects of nature: matter and spirit, Emerson perceived the method of dissolving what he considered the artificial barrier between the useful and the fine arts. Just as in nature matter may be analyzed apart from spirit, but not actually severed from it, so in the arts should matter and spirit be distinguishable, but mutually interdependent. If the fine arts can ground themselves strongly in the stones, sounds, and colors which are *natura naturata*, they will overcome their present "separation" from the world; if the useful arts can derive more inspiration from that Divine power, *natura naturans*, they will share with the fine arts the excellence of true beauty. In reaffirmation of Cudworth's importance for Emerson's theory of art, one has only to compare the questioning and inconclusive close of the first essay on art with the confident conclusion of the *Dial* essay, where Emerson insists that "beauty, truth, and goodness are not obsolete. . . . And that Eternal Spirit whose triple face they are, moulds from them forever . . . images to remind him of the Infinite and Fair" (*Works*, VII, 57).

III

To turn from Emerson's definition of art to his conception of the creative artist is to discover further illumination from *The True Intellectual System*. Man's position in the world, described by Emerson at the close of Nature, shows similarity in idea and phrasing to Cudworth's "orphic" quotations concerning the creation: the concept of an earlier period when man was in harmony with the World-spirit, including the hermaphroditic myth of God the Creator as both father and mother,[33] man's "fall from grace"—in a spiritual rather than a theological sense,[34] the theory of pre-existence,[35] and the statement of the way to recover that lost union of man with Spirit: through the intuitive perception of a purified soul.[36] So clearly did Emerson retain Cudworth's statement of intuition as a method of reaching truth that he used it, line for line, in a lecture given in London in 1848 on "Powers and Laws of Thought."[37] So

[33] *Works*, I, 71. Cf. Cudworth, *op. cit.*, I, 287; II, 90, 204.

[34] *Ibid.*, I, 71. Cf. Cudworth, *op. cit.*, I, 114. This particular quotation in Cudworth is not from Orpheus, but from Empedocles.

[35] *Ibid.*, I, 71. Cf. Cudworth, *op. cit.*, I, 113.

[36] *Ibid.*, I, 73-74, 76. Cf. Cudworth, *op. cit.*, I, 64, 114.

[37] "We have all of us by nature a certain divination and parturient vaticination in our

"We have all of us by nature . . . a certain divination, presage, and parturient

much for the relation of man in general to the natural world.

When Emerson considers the qualities of his favorite creative artist, the poet, he finds in him a representative man, surpassing all others in the perfect balance of his powers. For support of his belief in the poet's remarkable abilities, he looks to Cudworth's list of the Greek trinities, which Cudworth compares to the Christian:

Emerson

The Universe has three children, born at one time,[38] which reappear under different names in every system of thought, whether they be called cause, operation and effect;[39] or more poetically, Jove, Pluto, Neptune. . . .

These stand respectively for the love of truth, for the love of good, and for the love of beauty ("The Poet," *Works*, III, 6-7) or, theologically, the Father, the Spirit and the Son; but which we will call here

Cudworth

Jupiter, who, together with Neptune and Pluto, is said to have been the son of Saturn, was not the supreme Deity . . . but only the Aether, as Neptune was the sea, and Pluto the earth. All which are said to have been begotten by Chronos or Saturn. . . . These three, Jupiter, Neptune, and Pluto were not three really distinct substantial beings, but only so many names for the Supreme God (*True Int. System*, II, 473-474).

Plato here in *Cratylus* finds his trinity of Divine hypostases τ'αγαθόν, νοὺς, ψυχή,[40] in Uranus, Chronos and Zeus, or Coelus, Saturn and Jupiter (*True Int. System*, I, 531).

The Hebrews, placing the Holy

minds of some higher good and perfection than either power or knowledge. Knowledge is plainly to be preferred before power, as being that which guides and directs its blind force and impetus; but Aristotle declares that the origin of reason is not reason, but something better" ("Nat. Hist. of Intellect," *Works*, XII, 62).

The passage appears in the lecture (1848) in quotation marks, but these have been omitted by Emerson's editors.

vaticination in our minds of some higher good and perfection than either power or knowledge. Knowledge is plainly to be preferred before power, as being that which guides and directs its blind force and impetus; but Aristotle himself declares that there is . . . something better than reason and knowledge . . ." (Cudworth, *op. cit.*, I, 419-420).

[38] Cudworth does not say that all three were born at one time; merely that all were Saturn's children; possibly Emerson has picked up Saturn's other name, Chronos, and translated it "time."

[39] Cudworth has no parallel for the "cause, operation and effect" except that Saturn, father of the "triad," causes the others' existence.

[40] A more accurate translation of these terms would be: the good, Mind, and Soul.

the Knower, the Doer, and the Sayer.[41]	Ghost after the Father, and the Son in the third rank, [acknowledge] a holy and blessed Trinity . . . Plato enigmatically declareth the same things. . . . The Divine Scriptures in like manner rank the Holy Trinity of Father, Son, and Holy Ghost in the place or degree of a principle (*True Int. System*, III, 189).
Each is that which he is, essentially, so that he cannot be surmounted or analyzed, and each of these three has the power of the others latent in him and his own patent ("The Poet," *Works*, III, 7).	The word Saturn was Hetrurian . . . and . . . signifies hidden; so that by Saturn was meant the hidden principle of the universe, which containeth all things (*ibid.*, II, 460).

From a theological point of view, one can hardly overestimate Emerson's daring in applying to his poet the terms of the Christian as well as the Greek trinity. His assumption that the poet's creative activity earns him the right to the titles "Father, Son, and Holy Ghost" surely underlines his lofty conception of the poet—"in action, how like a god." Cudworth's connection of the Platonic triad with the Christian trinity gives Emerson an opportunity to relate poetry to the religious and moral world. At the same time, he distinguishes clearly here (as he does not always do elsewhere) between aesthetic and moral values. The Greek gods, in Cudworth's system, possess limited power over each others' domains, but have each of them one area for their main business: Saturn, the air; Neptune, the sea; Pluto, the earth. Like them, Emerson's poet has only a *latent* concern for the good and the true, which underlie his main interest—the beautiful.

Not only in making high claims for the poet, but in analyzing the poet's creative activity, Emerson draws on Cudworth. Compare

[41] Emerson's "Knower, Doer, and Sayer" finds no close parallel among Cudworth's trinities. Cudworth's citation from Numenius, of "the first of the three gods the father, the second of them the maker, and the third the work, or thing made" (*op. cit.*, III, 44), is not identical; nor is his analysis of Plato's hypostases, as "the first . . . all things unitively; the second, all things intellectually; and the third . . . all things animally;—that is, self-moveably, actively and productively" (*ibid.*, III, 106). Plato's third term is of course a *doer*.

Emerson, on poetic creation, with Plotinus (as quoted by Cudworth) on God's creation:

Emerson	*Cudworth*
The thought and the form are equal *in the order of time*, but in the order of *genesis* the thought is prior to the form ("The Poet," *Works*, III, 10).[42] [Italics mine.]	Mind or God was before the world, not as it existed before it *in time*, but because the world proceeded from it, and that was in *order of nature*,[43] first as the cause thereof, and its archetype . . . (*True Int. System*, I, 516-517, from Plotinus, *En.* 3, l. 2, c. 1). [Italics mine.]

Emerson's term "thought," indicating the poet's "spiritual" intuition for his work of art, closely parallels Plotinus's "intellectual principle" which causes the creation of the world. All poetic intuitions, according to Emerson's theory, resemble the "causing" intellect of God, in that they always exist in possibility—that is, no time can be established for their beginning any more than in the Plotinian system a time can be marked for the beginning of created things. Before the thought can be projected into form, however, Emerson asserts that the poet must "discover" it, just as Plotinus says that matter does not receive form until God causes it. This curious passage from "The Poet" when viewed in the light of its Plotinian ancestor, further underlines the "godlike" quality of Emerson's bard.

IV

One might conclude by likening Cudworth to a museum of ancient thought, from which Emerson selected such gems as he needed to fashion his concepts of nature, art, and the poetic genius. First attracted by the exotic quality of Cudworth's information, Emerson proceeded to a grasp of some more fundamental ideas of Plato, Aristotle, and Plotinus, which had been caught in the dragnet of *The True Intellectual System.* The clear distinction expressed by Cudworth between material and Spiritual nature became

[42] Compare a similar passage: "Thought is the seed of action; but action is as much its *second form* as thought is its *first*" ("Art," *Works*, VII, 38). Italics mine.

[43] Emerson may have used the term "genesis" instead of "nature" here because the passage from Plotinus, as well as another statement by Cudworth concerning the thought of later Platonists, had to do with the creation of the world.

in a sense the foundation-stone for Emerson's theory of art. Emerson's adaptation of Cudworth's material shows the original, sometimes perverse twist by which he passed others' ideas through the "polarized light" of his own imagination. The high claims which Cudworth makes for plastic nature over human art Emerson appropriates for his definition of art. By placing human art on a level with plastic nature, as a tool of the Divine Will, Emerson minimizes the artist's autonomous activity. Emerson's trust in the efficacy of inspiration for the creation of art leads, in fact, to the relative unimportance in his theory (as compared with that of Coleridge, for example) of the imaginative process. On the other hand, if the artist is a tool, he must also be considered a godlike creature, combining in one human shape the "three-in-one" of the Greeks as well as the Christians, sharing in his creative impulse the authoritative direction of the Divine Mind itself.

Emerson and the James Family

William T. Stafford

F. O. MATTHIESSEN has said that "the comments" of the James family "upon Emerson compose by themselves a chapter of American intellectual history."[1] Those comments are significant simply as near-contemporary evaluations of Emerson by three men of widely divergent tastes. That the Jameses were of one family, a father and two sons, does not lend conformity to their evaluations. The thesis of this study might therefore be stated as early evaluations of Emerson by a theologian, a philosopher, and an artist. On the other hand, these three men, Henry James, Sr., and his two sons, William and Henry, were of one family; and that fact cannot and should not be ignored.

C. Hartley Grattan pointed out a number of years ago that what the Jameses did, "individually and collectively, has long since become a part of the general stream of culture in the European-American world. Tendencies they initiated or gave impetus to have been taken up and further developed and sometimes redirected by later thinkers until it is well nigh impossible to see that the contemporary manifestation of that tendency is properly to be listed under the heading of a James bequest."[2] What has not been pointed out, however, is the fact that the Jameses did leave a bequest—in the form of an evaluation of Emerson—anticipating in many respects conclusions which scholarship has only recently caught up with. Nor, as far as I know, has it been pointed out that, although the three Jameses each saw Emerson only partially, taken as a unit, they saw him whole—according to Emerson's own definition of a whole man.

One calls the elder Henry James *theologian* only for want of a better term. One might call him a modified Swedenborgian, a supernaturalist, or even a socialist. Since, however, he did propound a theological system and since it was from a theological point of

[1] F. O. Matthiessen, *The James Family* (New York, 1947), p. 428.
[2] C. H. Grattan, *The Three Jameses: A Family of Minds* (New York, 1932), p. 358.

view that he interpreted and evaluated Emerson, theologian seems most appropriate for this particular study. William James is equally many-sided. He is claimed by both philosophy and psychology, but it is primarily as a philosopher that he was interested in Emerson. And Henry James, the novelist, was also an astute critic, a short-story writer, a biographer, a memoir writer, a dramatist, and a writer of travel books—in short, a man of letters—to equate his profession with that of the other members of his family. It was as a literary artist that he evaluated Emerson. And what was Emerson? To these three men, at any rate, he was three different things. Exactly what, it is the purpose of this study to disclose.

All three of the Jameses were contemporaries of Emerson and were personally acquainted with him. Henry James, Sr., born in 1811, was only seven years Emerson's junior, dying in 1882, the same year as Emerson. William James—born in 1842, the year after the publication of Emerson's *Essays, First Series* and the year of the death of Emerson's son Waldo[3]—died in 1910. The younger Henry James was born in 1843 and died a British citizen in 1916. Emerson lectured in New York on "The Times," March 3, 1842. Henry James, Sr., heard him, and with characteristic candor, wrote him a letter praising his lecture—with some reservations—and invited Emerson to come to see him.[4] Emerson did just that, and thus began a lifelong friendship that eventually encompassed all members of both families.

I

The elder Henry James was not really interested in Emerson the writer. He was interested in Emerson the man. This becomes manifest in the thirty-year correspondence of the two men, and James's two essays on his friend Emerson confirm it.[5] That the various studies of the relationship between these two men have not emphasized this obvious explanation of James's interpretation

[3] For the imaginative mind this might have some symbolical significance, for William James once intimated that he thought of himself as Emerson's "intellectual off-spring." See below, n. 59 and text.

[4] Matthiessen, *op. cit.*, pp. 39-40.

[5] The correspondence covered the years 1842-1872. James's first essay on Emerson, written *ca.* 1868, was first published in the *Atlantic Monthly*, XCIV, 740-745 (Dec., 1904). His second article, written in 1881, first appeared in *The Literary Remains of the Late Henry James* (Boston, 1884).

of Emerson is somewhat surprising,[6] for their correspondence moved in that direction from the very first letter.

A few months before the death of the elder James, James Elliot Cabot wrote to him requesting permission to quote from some of his letters to Emerson in the now famous *Memoir* Cabot was then preparing. James answered thus:

> I cannot flatter myself that any letter I ever wrote to Emerson is worth reading. . . . Emerson always kept one at such arm's length, tasting him and sipping him and trying him, to make sure that he was worthy of his somewhat prim and bloodless friendship, that it was fatiguing to write him letters. . . . I remember well what maidenly letters I used to receive from him, with so many tentative charms of expression in them that if he had been a woman one would have delighted in complimenting him. . . . It is painful to recollect now the silly hope that I had, along the early days of our acquaintance, that if I went on listening, something would be sure to drop from him that would show me an infallible way out of this perplexed world. For nothing ever came but epigrams; sometimes clever, sometimes not.[7]

Although it was written in illness and depression, James had some ground for his complaint. In reading the correspondence between the two, one inevitably concludes, as Professor Ralph Leslie Rusk did some years ago, that in comparison with James's, Emerson's letters "are prim, bloodless, and maidenly enough."[8] When James first met Emerson in 1842, however, his hopes were far from "silly." He was deeply moved and promptly said so to Emerson in an introductory letter. And in this very first letter is the germinal dichotomy upon which James interpreted Emerson for the rest of his life: on the one hand, he was slightly critical of what was to become his abiding objection to Emerson—Emerson's apparent indifference to intellect; on the other, he was obviously impressed with Emerson's sincerity of purpose, "that erect attitude of mind," which forecasts James's admiration of Emerson's personality and

[6] See William James, "Introductory Note," *Atlantic Monthly,* XCIV, 740 (Dec., 1904); Hansell Baugh, "Emerson and the Elder Henry James," *Bookman,* LXVIII, 320-322 (Nov., 1928); Grattan, *op. cit.;* Ann R. Burr (ed.), *Alice James: Her Brothers, Her Journal* (New York, 1934); Austin Warren, *The Elder Henry James* (New York, 1934); R. B. Perry, *The Thought and Character of William James* (Boston, 1935); and Matthiessen, *op. cit.*

[7] James Elliot Cabot, *A Memoir of Ralph Waldo Emerson* (New York, 1887), I, 358.

[8] R. L. Rusk (ed.), *The Letters of Ralph Waldo Emerson* (New York, 1939), I, xvi.

character.[9] A fascination with Emerson's personality coupled with an intrinsic distrust of his intuitive flights is, then, the anomaly with which their relationship begins.

The objection to Emerson's apparent distrust of intellect appears throughout their early correspondence. Although James's own theological system had not yet crystallized, he was already dialectical enough to consider his intellect "the necessary digestive apparatus" of his life. And in an undated letter of 1842, the year he met Emerson, James inquires if the same is not true for him—only, one adds, after candidly stating to Emerson that "you continually dishearten me by your apparent indifference . . . by the dishonor you seem to cast upon our intelligence, as if it stood much in our way."[10] This complaint, phrased in various ways, runs through all of their early correspondence, reaching its climax, perhaps, in a letter late in 1843 wherein James, in a well-known statement, good-naturedly expostulates over Emerson's determination not to "explain" or to "defend" his point of view. "Oh you man without a handle! shall one never be able to help himself out of you, according to his needs, and be dependent only upon your fitful tippings-up?"[11]

Concurrent with this objection, however, was a perplexing fascination with Emerson. His personality and character held forth a promise, it seemed to James, potentially capable of absolute perfection. Writing of this early fascination some thirty years later, James states: "What he mainly held to be true I could not help regarding as false, and what he mainly held to be false I regarded as true."[12] To James, Emerson's attraction was at first something ineffably personal, a sheer intuitive pull so persuasive as to become the dominant factor in James's interpretation of his friend. This personal charm was especially apparent in Emerson's lectures, and few have caught its potency quite so convincingly as James.

His demeanour upon the platform . . . was modesty itself; not the mere absence of display, but the presence of a positive personal grace. His

[9] "I do not value his substantive discoveries . . . half so highly as he values them, but . . . I chiefly value that erect attitude of mind about him which in God's universe undauntedly seeks the worthiest tidings of God, and calmly defies every mumbling phantom which would herein challenge its freedom" (Perry, *op. cit.*, I, 40).

[10] *Ibid.*, pp. 41-43.

[11] *Ibid.*, p. 51.

[12] Henry James, Sr., "Emerson," *Atlantic Monthly*, XCIV, 740.

deferential entrance upon the scene, his look of inquiry at the desk and the chair, his resolute rummaging among his embarrassed papers, the air of sudden recollection with which he would plunge into his pockets for what he must have known had never been put there, for his uncertainty and irresolution as he rose to speak, his deep relieved inspiration as he got well from under the burning glass of his auditor's eyes, and addressed himself at length to their docile ears instead: no maiden ever appealed more potently to your enamoured and admiring sympathy. And then when he looked over the heads of his audience into the dim mysterious distance, and his weird monotone began to reverberate in your bosom's depths, and his words flowed on, now with a river's volume, grand, majestic, free, and anon diminished themselves to the fitful cadence of a brook, impeded in its course, and returning in melodious coquetry upon itself, and you saw the clear eye eloquent with nature's purity, and beheld the musing countenance turned within, as it were, and hearkening to the rumour of a far-off but on-coming world: how intensely personal, how exquisitely characteristic, it all was.[13]

Warm and picturesque as is this description of Emerson's platform manner, James found in Emerson's personality a promise which his intellect did not fulfil.

James was later to fit this hope-frustration evaluation into his own theological system. Meanwhile, his friendship with Emerson continued. The latter, upon first meeting James, had written with enthusiasm about him to both his wife and Margaret Fuller.[14] And occasionally he good-naturedly rallied James for his criticisms—"the madness (is it?) you find in my logic. . . ."[15] He loaded James with introductions to his friends in Europe, including Carlyle,[16] depended upon him to arrange for lecture halls in New York,[17] sent Thoreau to visit him,[18] introduced him to his New England friends, and once at least invited him to deliver a paper on socialism before the Town and Country Club in Boston.[19] James in the meantime had focused and fixed his own theological system. Although he had overtly rejected Calvinism, he actually still retained a large

[13] *Ibid.*, p. 741.
[14] Rusk, *op. cit.*, III, 23, 30.
[15] Perry, *op. cit.*, I, 49.
[16] Charles E. Norton (ed.), *The Correspondence of Thomas Carlyle and Ralph Waldo Emerson, 1834-1872* (Boston, 1883-1884), II, 38.
[17] Rusk, *op. cit.*, IV, 184.
[18] F. B. Sanborn (ed.), *The Familiar Letters of H. D. Thoreau* (Boston, 1894), p. 95.
[19] Rusk, *op. cit.*, IV, 169.

residuum of that faith, so that when he met the writings of Swedenborg and Fourier, their teachings did not convert him so much as they confirmed and sustained him, "giving him a language, a systematic framework, and an organized support for the faith that was in him."[20] The elder James's system is perhaps best explained by his son William in an introductory note, published in 1904, to some differences between his father and Emerson:

My father was a theologian of the "twice-born" type, an out-and-out Lutheran, who believed that the moral law existed solely to fill us with loathing for the idea of our own merits, and to make us turn to God's grace as our only opportunity. But God's grace, in Mr. James' system, was not for the individual in isolation: the sphere of redemption was *Society.* In a Society organized divinely our natures will not be altered, but our spontaneities, because they will then work harmoniously, will all work innocently, and the Kingdom of Heaven will have come. With these ideas Mr. James was both fascinated and baffled by his friend Emerson. The personal graces of the man seemed to prefigure the coming millennium, but the resolute individualism of his thought, and the way in which his imagination rested on superior personages, and on heroic anecdotes about them, as if these were creation's ultimates, set my father's philosophy at defiance. For him no man was superior to another in the final plan. Emerson would listen, I fancy, as if charmed, to James' talk of the "divine natural Humanity," but he would never *subscribe;* and this, from one whose native gifts were so suggestive of that same Humanity, was disappointing. Emerson, in short, was "once-born" man; he lived in moral distinctions, and recognized no need of a redemptive process.[21]

Herein is clearly articulated James's fascination with all that Emerson's personality and character seemed to promise along with his disappointment at what was not forthcoming.

This dichotomy becomes even clearer—in that it points up their intrinsic antagonisms—when Emerson, on at least one occasion, deigns to criticize one of James's books, *Moralism and Christianity.* As might be expected, he objects to James's "argumentative style: every technical *For* and *Suppose* and *Therefore* alarms and extrudes me." Moreover, he fears that James has not quite shed his last coat of Presbyterianism. Finally, he is disconcerted by James's

[20] Perry, *op. cit.,* I, 20.

[21] William James, *op. cit.,* p. 740.

refusal to make authoritative statements, a necessity, Emerson feels, for "one broaching matters so vital and dear."[22] Obviously, Emerson's intuitive flights, his lack of a certain moral sternness, and the absolute certitude of his manner were the very qualities which so distressed James.

As James became even more socially conscious—now sure that man was not to be redeemed individually, but collectively *in society*—it was inevitable that he would become even less sympathetic toward Emerson. For example, in a letter to Edmund Tweedy in 1852 James says that although Emerson seems "much interested in my ideas . . . he thinks I am too far ahead." This, continues James, because "he has no faith in man, at least in progress. He does not imagine the possibility of 'hurrying up the cakes' on a large scale. Indeed, he denies that any cakes are baking upon any larger scale than that of the family griddle."[23] James, however, remained intimate with Emerson—if adamant in his particular objection—for in 1855 he was writing to him very warmly, indeed very perceptively, informing Emerson that the whole strain of his influence was "to translate patriotism into humanity, and make one feel one's country to be that which harbours only the best men." James, turning upon his old dichotomy, continues with obvious warmth to inform Emerson that he is "the best and most memorable" of men and that, whether "the computation begin from my heart or my head . . . your life is a very real divine performance . . . and a still fuller prophecy."[24]

James was beginning to place Emerson in his own scheme of things and was beginning to see in him an unconscious embodiment of the "divine natural Humanity," of the "New Jerusalem," in short, of the new social redemption of man. An increasing distrust of Emerson's ideas and intellect, his culture and science, was forcing James's attention back to Emerson the man, his character and his personality.

This growing distrust becomes more specific, but with no loss of percipience, in James's objections to particular Emersonian works. He was especially displeased with Emerson's *English Traits*. Unlike his son, the elder James could not abide the English exclusive-

[22] Perry, *op. cit.*, I, 62.
[23] *Ibid.*, p. 75.
[24] *Ibid.*, p. 80.

ness and complacency. In a letter to Edmund Tweedy from Paris in 1856 he states that Emerson's treatment of the English is grossly overdone:

They [the English] are an intensely vulgar race, high and low; and their qualities, good or evil, date not from any divine or diabolic *depths* whatever, but from most obvious and superficial causes. They are the abject slaves of routine, and no afflatus from above or below ever comes, apparently, to ruffle the surface of their self-complaced quietude. They are not worth studying. . . . They lack heart. Their love is clannish. They love all that wear their own livery, but they don't even *see* anyone outside of that boundary.[25]

James was, however, more pleased with *Representative Men,* for he perceived that Emerson honored great men for their human substance, their representativeness of finite traits. And James was aware that to Emerson they represented something more than they individually constituted.[26] Conversely, James said elsewhere that the little nobodies, "on the ground of their not exhibiting so dense an obscuration in their proper personality of the Divine glory . . . . let the Lord shine through them without an excessive clouding of his splendour," unlike some of "these pretentious somebodies," a "Plato or Emerson or Washington."[27] In James's system, no man was superior to another in the final plan, and the unpretentious, in this obvious exaggeration, more often reflected the divine than did the great. Finally, James felt that Emerson's *Society and Solitude,* though admirable, was inferior to Emerson's first two books of essays, a judgment which has met the agreement of posterity—perhaps for the reasons he gives: "The difference, of course, between the two series is only that between youth and age, or promise and fulfilment, the former leaving something to the imagination, the latter excluding it. The sunset is just as admirable in its way as the sunrise; but every one knows that the latter excites, and should excite, a very much more tender enthusiasm.[28]

In the years following the Civil War the intimacy between James and Emerson became noticeably cooler. Both men were getting old and both, one suspects, were becoming somewhat less

[25] *Ibid.,* pp. 122-123.

[26] James, Sr., *op. cit.,* p. 742.

[27] Warren, *op. cit.,* pp. 184-185.

[28] Perry, *op. cit.,* pp. 100-101.

tolerant of others' ideas. In a well-known letter of 1868 to his son William, who was then studying medicine in Berlin, James, in what perhaps is his most caustic evaluation of Emerson—and one of his most significant—reiterates his old dilemma: Emerson's inability to communicate intellectually, "his ignorance of everything above the senses," and his paradoxical fascination with Emerson's personality, "I love the man very much, he is such a born natural." In addition, however, he here also charges Emerson with no love of nature, but of being only a "police-spy upon it, chasing it into its hiding-places, and noting its subtlest features, for the purpose of reporting them to the public." James offers as proof of this Emerson's "intellectual offspring," in whom, says James, Emerson breeds no love of nature, but "only the love of imitating him and saying similar 'cute' things about nature and man."[29] Much more significant, however, is his caustic conclusion: "his books are to me wholly destitute of spiritual flavour, being at most carbonic acid gas and *water*."[30]

This acid judgment standing by itself seems, of course, mere impertinence. And, in part, possibly it is. In view, however, of James's lifelong distrust of Emerson's intellect, indifference to dialectic, and dependence upon intuition and inspiration, it is more likely that he hit directly upon his real feeling for Emerson. This is supported by the fact that in a calmer moment James had written Emerson (as early as 1849), stating clearly that "I never read you as an author at all. Your books are not literature, but life, and criticism always strikes me, therefore, as infinitely laughable when applied to you."[31] Finally, and perhaps most significant of all, this dismissal of Emerson's writings throws into still higher relief James's appreciation of Emerson the man. This appreciation James never lost, and with the single exception of a brief public disagreement over the intellectual worth of Fourier,[32] the two remained on intimate terms throughout their lives.

[29] See also *ibid.*, p. 91. Emerson himself records in his *Journal* as early as Oct., 1849, that "Nature pays no respect to those who pay any respect to her, was H. J.'s doctrine" (W. E. Forbes and W. E. Emerson, eds., *The Journals of Ralph Waldo Emerson*, Boston, 1909-1914, VIII, 63).

[30] Perry, *op. cit.*, pp. 96-97. For his son William's reaction to this letter, see below, n. 59 and text.

[31] Perry, *op. cit.*, p. 58.

[32] James had publicly questioned Emerson's understanding of Fourier when Emerson

James's first formal essay on Emerson, which was not published until 1904, has been interpolated into this examination of their correspondence, which ends in 1872 with James pertly requesting permission to read this paper—not to Emerson, but to his family and friends; for "you have too dainty a taste in literature for my wares, but to Mrs. Emerson, say, and Ellen and Elizabeth Hoar, or Miss Elizabeth Ripley. . . ." Emerson, apparently delighted, replies, setting a date convenient for his wife.[33]

More succinct than this essay, however, and an excellent supplement to the Jamesian interpretation of Emerson in this correspondence, is the brief essay written some nine years later (1881), the year before James died, and first published in *The Literary Remains of the Late Henry James*. The years had not softened James's basic objection to Emerson's indifference to intellect; nor, on the other hand, had they dispelled his fascination for Emerson's personality and character. Here, too, appears what does not appear in the correspondence, James's feeling that Emerson lacked a sense of evil—an opinion growing out of James's conviction that Emerson, as F. O. Matthiessen has pointed out, was in an arrested state of innocence, completely impervious, in the Blakean sense, to experience.[34]

In James's system, consciousness of self was consciousness of evil. To become aware of oneself as an individual was to experience evil. This is the necessary base upon which James fixed his belief in the redeemed form of man being a social form. The new man, the redeemed man, was to lose himself with self-consciousness and find himself in society. James begins this essay with the observation that Emerson did not have a consciousness, that being the secret of his fascination for men. He admits that Emerson did comprehend the outward or moral difference between good and evil. It is, however, the inner revelation of evil that is important, the revelation that makes itself apparent only when one becomes unchangeably evil in his own sight while his neighbor becomes unchangeably good in comparison. Emerson, James is convinced,

disparaged the socialist in his lecture "Greatness" at Boston, Nov. 16, 1868 (*ibid.*, pp. 98-99).

[33] *Ibid.*, pp. 101-102.

[34] Matthiessen, *op. cit.*, p. 428.

never had the impulse to break any of the ten commandments. He could not, *ergo,* have had a conviction of personal sin. James had such a sense, and, upon meeting Emerson, was at once overjoyed at meeting so much innocence and goodness, hoping therefrom to discover how one "got that way." To his amazement and chagrin, Emerson had no earthly idea how or that he was innocent. Emerson's superiority was personal or practical, "acquired by birth or genius," but by no means "intellectual."

Emerson thereby became to James—through his lack of consciousness—the embodiment of innocence. He came to symbolize for James the divine spirit. In a way, he was God. Innocence attaches itself in James's system only to what is universally unindividualized in our nature. It appropriates itself to individuals only in so far as they denude themselves of personality or self-consciousness. James concludes his essay with Christ's saying: "He that findeth his life shall lose it, and he that loseth his life for my sake shall find it,"[35] which may be roughly translated into the Jamesian system as "he who becomes aware of himself shall lose his innocence, and he who loses his innocence *in and for society* shall regain it." Emerson was never aware of his innocence; he therefore never lost it or found it. He was it.

It has been said of James that he was "one of the very few intellectual associates of Emerson who was not an Emersonian."[36] In any conventional sense, this is certainly true. On the other hand, his oblique insight illuminates a little-regarded aspect of Emerson which is peculiarly appropriate to Emerson's own point of view. To see divine attributes reflected in the personality and character of an individual whose ideas are meaningless and unintelligible is perhaps less magnanimous than penetrating. That James the theologian saw Emerson the man as a manifestion of God is a subtle tribute which is perhaps a juster evaluation than one might at first realize.

II

Henry James, Jr., the novelist, was also an astute Emersonian critic. An awareness of "the great Emerson's" presence in his father's household was one of his earliest and most memorable im-

[35] *Ibid.*, pp. 435-438, *passim.*

[36] Grattan, *op. cit.*, p. 102.

pressions. As he matured, the younger Henry James, like his father, felt that the evil and sin of the world was "a side of life to which Emerson's eyes were thickly bandaged."[37] Unlike his father, however, he did not find Emerson unintelligible. On the contrary, he was all too eager to "explain" him. And in his own inimitable manner, he laid bare the heart of Emerson's moral worth.

As early as 1867, in a letter to the elder Henry James, Emerson had written: "Thank your boy Harry for me for his good stories,"[38] in reference to some of the younger James's very earliest tales. And Henry James, during his first mature stay in Europe (1869), writes to his brother William from Rome upon learning that his father had been reading some of his letters to Emerson, "I am extremely glad you like my letters, and terribly agitated by the thought that Emerson likes them."[39] Much later, in his most advanced "manner," the younger James was to record an even earlier impression:

I "visualize" at any rate the winter of our back parlour at dusk and the great Emerson—I knew he was great, greater than any of our friends—sitting in it between my parents, before the lamps had been lighted, as a visitor consentingly housed only could have done, and affecting me the more as an apparition seriously and, I held, elegantly slim, benevolently aquiline, and commanding a tone alien, beautifully alien, to any we had roundabout, that he bent this benignity upon me by an invitation to draw nearer to him, off the hearth rug, and know myself as never yet, as I was not indeed to know myself again for years, in touch with the wonder of Boston.[40]

Henry James is not at all "agitated" ten years later when in his study of Hawthorne he is able to evaluate Emerson with more detachment. His earliest feeling that Emerson's tone was "alien, beautifully alien" to James's own New York environment did not blind him to the naturalness of Emerson's affinity with the Concord milieu: "The value and the importance of the individual, the duty of making the most of one's self, of living by one's own personal light and carrying out one's own disposition. . . . must have had great charm for people living in a society in which introspection, thanks to the want of other entertainment, played almost the part

[37] Matthiessen, *op. cit.*, p. 451. [38] Rusk, *op. cit.*, V, 514.
[39] Perry, *op. cit.*, I, 311.
[40] Henry James, *Notes of a Son and Brother* (London, 1914), p. 191.

of a social resource." On the other hand, Emerson's insistence upon sincerity, independence, and spontaneity was "a beautiful irony," reflected James, "upon the exquisite impudence of those institutions which claim to have appropriated the truth, and to dole it out in proportionate morsels, in exchange for a subscription."[41] Even this early (1879), however, James was not unaware of Emerson's limitations, for in what is perhaps one of his happiest critical phrases he found it not at all surprising that "Emerson, as a sort of spiritual sun-worshipper, could have attached but a moderate value to Hawthorne's cat-like faculty of seeing in the dark."[42]

James's next evaluation of Emerson, in the form of a review of the Carlyle-Emerson correspondence for the *Century* magazine in 1883, demonstrated his critical awareness of other Emersonian limitations. For example, James felt that in comparison with Carlyle's, Emerson's letters ran a poor second—analogous, perhaps, to the position of Emerson in the Emerson-James, Sr., correspondence. Whereas Carlyle "takes his place among the first . . . of all letter writers," Emerson "had not an abundant epistolary impulse. . . . His letters are less natural, more composed, have too studied a quaintness." He further felt that Emerson's "noble conception of good" was not properly balanced with a "definite conception of evil." James was not, on the other hand, blind to the value of both men. He realized that they both

> were men of the poetic quality, men of imagination; both were Puritans; both of them looked, instinctively, at the world, at life, as a great total, full of far-reaching relations; both of them set above everything else the importance of conduct—of what Carlyle called veracity and Emerson called harmony with the universe. Both of them had the desire, the passion, for something better—the reforming spirit, an interest in the destiny of mankind.[43]

The novelist, however, takes as a vehicle for his most considered and thorough evaluation of Emerson the publication of James Elliot Cabot's *A Memoir of Ralph Waldo Emerson*. James wrote the article in 1887 and republished it as the introductory

[41] Henry James, *Hawthorne* (London, 1902), pp. 84-85.
[42] *Ibid.*, p. 99.
[43] Henry James, "The Correspondence of Carlyle and Emerson," *Century*, XXVI (June, 1883), and 265-272, *passim*.

essay in the critical volume, *Partial Portraits,* the next year, 1888. He opens his essay with the regret that Cabot did not take the opportunity—especially since, to James's mind, Emerson's own life was in a way so pale—to reflect through Emerson his milieu. "I mean," he said, "greater reference to the social conditions in which Emerson moved, the company he lived in, the moral air he breathed." James takes it upon himself in this article to supply this deficiency. In typical Jamesian fashion, he insists that Emerson could not have been Emerson without his particular progenitors: "His ancestors had lived long . . . in the same corner of New England, and during that period had preached and studied and prayed and practiced. . . . A conscience like Emerson's could not have been turned off, as it were, from one generation to another." Many attempts, several refinements, were necessary. James was even more piqued by Cabot's only cursory attention to Emerson's contemporaries. James saw the period as representative and significant—"a subject bringing into play many odd figures, many human incongruities . . ." abounding "in illustration of the primitive New England character . . . during the time of its queer search for something to expend itself upon." His artistic imagination was particularly stimulated by Emerson's aunt, Mary Moody Emerson, who, to him, had a "kind of tormenting representative value," which, he says, "would have been an inspiration for a novelist."[44] Mrs. Ripley also interested him. And there are others upon whom James wished Cabot had expended more attention—such "as the imaginative, talkative, intelligent and finally Italianized and shipwrecked Margaret Fuller."[45]

James elsewhere disparages the idea that America has no respect for literary men. On the contrary, he says, "there is no country in which it is more readily admitted to be a distinction—*the* distinction: or in which so many persons have become eminent for showing it even in a slight degree." And James is here, it seems to this writer, more perceptive than Emerson. "In what other coun-

[44] "We want to see her from head to foot, with her frame and her background; having . . . an impression that she was a very remarkable specimen of the transatlantic Puritan stock, a spirit that would have dared the devil. . . . a grim intellectual virgin and daughter of a hundred ministers, with her local traditions and her combined love of Empire and speculation" (quoted in Matthiessen, *op. cit.,* pp. 444-445).

[45] *Ibid.,* pp. 439-445, *passim.*

try," James asked, "on sleety winter nights, would provincial and bucolic populations have gone forth in hundreds for the cold comfort of a literary discourse?" He points out that no scholar had ever been more revered in his lifetime than Emerson, and he called Emerson's funeral "a popular manifestation, the most striking I have ever seen provoked by the death of a man of letters." Emerson's relative indifference to the reform movements of his fellow Transcendentalists James characteristically (but not too naïvely), simply explains away as not being the sort of thing that Emerson was really interested in. And James lumps the *Dial,* Brook Farm, and Fruitlands (again not too naïvely) all together as a "Puritan carnival . . . the amusement of the leisure class."[46]

But what of Emerson the writer? What is James's evaluation of Emerson as a man of letters? James adhered throughout his career to the aesthetic dictum that style makes the man. And he did not feel that Emerson ever really found his proper form. Emerson "never really mastered the art of composition," he says in one instance. And the remark is intentionally if gently disparaging when he says that Emerson had but "one style, one manner, and he had it for everything—even for himself in his notes and journals." One is somewhat amused at James, himself probably the most periphrastic of all American writers, accusing Emerson of circumlocution, Emerson's habit of "hovering round and round an idea." James recognizes this, however, as part of Emerson's manner, "which was," he said, "to practice a kind of unusual passive hospitality," adding that "it was only because he was so deferential that he could be so detached."[47] James, however, could not subscribe to the Emersonian concept that talent was inferior to inspiration and could only conclude that Emerson was an exception to "the general rule that writings live in the last resort by their form." This exception is of no mean significance, however, for it indicates James's appreciation for Emerson's message, which he considered of such importance that a deficiency in style—"usually the bribe or toll-money on the journey to posterity"[48]—made his accomplishment all the more striking.

[46] *Ibid.*, pp. 447-448, 450.

[47] With this statement James indicates that he was not so blind to Emerson's aesthetic as some of his other remarks might lead one to suppose.

[48] Matthiessen, *op. cit.*, pp. 445-447, 452-453.

Early in his life, James, like his father, had remarked Emerson's personal magnetism. Emerson had, said James, "the equanimity of a result; nature had taken care of him and he had only to speak." Also like his father, James felt that Emerson's contemporaries should have perceived that Emerson himself was "the prayer and the sermon . . . in his own subtle insinuating way a sanctifier."[49] Unlike his father, however, he felt that it was Emerson's "great distinction and his special sign that he had a more vivid conception of the moral life than anyone else"; and Emerson's "ripe unconsciousness of evil" was to James also a distinction, for, as he says, "it is one of the most beautiful signs by which we know him." And James gets close to the heart of Emerson's genius when he recognizes it as a "genius for seeing character as a real and supreme thing."[50]

James is fascinated with Cabot's statement that Emerson thought Hawthorne's novels "not worthy of him" (i.e., not worthy of Hawthorne). James pounces on this situation, the sort of which he was so peculiarly fond, saying on the one hand, how "highly he [Emerson] must have esteemed the man of whose genius *The House of the Seven Gables* and *The Scarlet Letter* gave imperfectly the measure," and on the other, "how strange that he should not have been eager to read almost anything that such a gifted being might have let fall." James explains the antipathy by juxtaposing Hawthorne's penchant for "the evil and sin of the world" to Emerson's "little sense for the dark, the foul, the base."[51]

James concludes his essay with the remark that writers need continual re-evaluation and that Emerson continues to triumph over his biographer, for "he did something better than anyone else; he had a particular faculty, which has not been surpassed, for speaking to the soul in a voice of direction and authority. There have been many spiritual voices appealing, consoling, reassuring, exhorting, or even denouncing and terrifying, but none had had just that firmness and just that purity."[52]

[49] For the moral allegiance which Henry James owed to his father, see Quentin Anderson, "Henry James and the New Jerusalem," *Kenyon Review,* VIII, 515-566 (Autumn, 1946).

[50] Matthiessen, *op. cit.,* pp. 441-442.

[51] *Ibid.,* p. 452.

[52] *Ibid.*

Equally perceptive, moreover, are James's remarks on Emerson in his *The American Scene* (1907), the decision to write which, says Matthiessen, was as if James "had explicitly decided to be Emerson's 'transparent eyeball' and nothing else."[53] While examining New England for what he calls "the value of the Puritan residuum," James finds that in Boston the value is relatively low, little remaining from the age of Emerson but "business" and "Puritanism educated."[54] In Concord, however, he finds more:

I felt myself, on the spot, cast about a little for the right expression of it, and then lost any hesitation to say that, putting the three or four biggest cities aside, Concord, Massachusetts, had an identity more palpable to the mind, has nestled in other words more successfully beneath her narrow fold of the mantle of history, than any other American town. . . . "There are so many places, 'fifty times your size' which yet don't begin to have a fraction of your weight, or your character, or your intensity of presence and sweetness of tone, or your moral charm, or your pleasant appreciability, or, in short, of anything that is yours. . . . The country is lucky indeed to have you, in your sole and single felicity, for if it hadn't where in the world should we go, inane and unappeased, for that particular communication of which you have the secret?"[55]

The deficiency he had found in Cabot's *Memoir* many years earlier James herewith supplied, for he was only half-humorous when he called Concord the American Weimar and equated Emerson and Thoreau with Goethe and Schiller.[56]

Finally, one finds in James's *Notes of a Son and Brother* a remarkable passage, where in his most intricate and involved final manner, in reacting to his father's primary dissatisfaction with Emerson, James expresses a universal complaint not inappropriate, one suspects, to any idealism whatever:

[53] Matthiessen, *Henry James: The Major Phase* (New York, 1944), p. 107.
[54] Henry James, *The American Scene*, ed. W. H. Auden (New York, 1946), p. 241.
[55] *Ibid.*, pp. 256-257.
[56] "We may smile a little as we 'drag in' Weimar, but I confess myself, for my part, much more satisfied than not by our happy equivalent, 'in American money,' for Goethe and Schiller. The money is a potful in the second case as in the first, and if Goethe, in the one, represents the gold and Schiller the silver, I find (and quite putting aside any bimetallic prejudice) the same good relation in the other between Emerson and Thoreau. I open Emerson for the same benefit for which I open Goethe, the sense of moving in large intellectual space, and that of the gush, here and there, out of the rock, of the crystalline cupful, in wisdom and poetry, in Wahrheit and Dichtung . . ." (*ibid.*, p. 264).

Very marked, and above all very characteristic of my father, in this interesting relation [his father's relation with Emerson], which I may but so imperfectly illustrate, his constant appeal, his so inspired, yet so uninflamed, so irreducible and, as it were, inapplicable, friend for intellectual and, as he would have said, spiritual help of the immediate and the adjustable, the more concretely vital, kind, the kind translatable into terms of the real, the particular human terms of action and passion. "Oh you man without a handle . . ." [is] a remarkably felicitous expression, as it strikes me, of that difficulty often felt by the passionately-living of the earlier time, as they may be called, to draw down their noble philosopher's great over hanging heaven of universal and ethereal answers to the plane of their comparatively terrestrial and personal questions: the note of the answers and their great anticipatory spirit being somehow that they seemed to anticipate everything but the unaccommodating individual case.[57]

This passage, like James's other comments on Emerson, seems to the reader at first to be more James than Emerson. That it was an artist speaking throughout one never forgets. From his earliest impression of being in the presence of greatness through a growing critical awareness of Emerson's inability to see in the dark, the evaluation of the son, like that of the father, was almost uniquely acute. Not really blind to Emerson's aesthetic, though he complains of Emerson's lack of form, it is not as an artist that James judged Emerson; for what is Emerson's particular faculty if it is not speaking to the soul in a voice of direction and authority? Henry James the artist was not insensitive to Emerson the moral philosopher.

III

Neither Henry James the theologian nor his son the novelist, however, had the spiritual or the intellectual affinity with Emerson that William James the philosopher had. Like his father and his brother, William James knew Emerson personally, read his later books as they were published, and often visited the Emerson household. He was throughout his life enthusiastic about Emerson's writings, and he was to incorporate into his own philosophical system many Emersonian concepts: all while being aesthetically conscious of Emerson the artist.

[57] *Notes of a Son and Brother,* pp. 173-174.

As early as 1868, when he was only twenty-six years old, he intimates this affinity when, in a letter to his brother Henry about one of their father's more harsh diatribes against Emerson,[58] James writes: "I was very much amused by Father's account of Emerson, but I think Emerson probably has other 'intellectual offspring' than those wretched imitators, and has truly stirred up honest men who are far from advertising it by their mode of talking."[59] That James himself was one of those honest men who were truly stirred up was so little advertised indeed that scholarship did not catch up with that fact until about 1929.[60] And in one of his very earliest reviews, William James cites Emerson as evidence for the central idea of that review—his belief in "the teleological character of the mind"—which, says R. B. Perry, "may be said to be the germinal idea of James's psychology, epistemology, and philosophy of religion." James refers to this essay in his *The Will to Believe* with the remark that "the conceiving or theorizing faculty . . . functions *exclusively for the sake of ends* that . . . are set by our emotions and practical subjectivity."[61] It is Emerson's famous "Brahma" which James utilizes to point out that "teleology (had she a voice) would exclaim with Emerson:

"If the red slayer think he slays
Or if the slain think he is slain
They know not well the subtle ways
I keep, and pass, and turn again
* * * * * *
They reckon ill who leave me out;
When me they fly, I am the wings;
I am the doubter and the doubt," etc.[62]

How this poem *could* be interpreted as giving expression to the theorizing faculty is clear enough.

To utilize Emerson in this manner was both to evaluate and

[58] See above, n. 30 and text.
[59] Perry, *op. cit.*, p. 270.
[60] See Frederic I. Carpenter, "Points of Comparison between Emerson and William James," *New England Quarterly*, II, 458-474 (July, 1929). James and Emerson had been compared before this, but only briefly, as in John Macy's *The Spirit of American Literature* (New York, 1908), pp. 54-55, 302.
[61] R. B. Perry (ed.), *Collected Essays and Reviews* [of William James] (New York, 1920), p. 43, n. 1.
[62] *Ibid.*, p. 62.

interpret him. And in practically every major book William James wrote, Emerson was brought into play for either illustration or support. In his first book, the famous *Principles of Psychology* (1890), he touched upon the only recently evaluated Emerson aesthetic. James had been discussing the fascination of metaphors, how difficult, if not impossible, to explain or paraphrase them; for, "as Emerson says, 'they sweetly torment us with invitations to their inaccessible homes.' "[63] Elsewhere in the work, after affirming that "speaking generally, the more a conceived object *excites* us, the more reality it has," James again quotes Emerson: "There is a difference between one and another hour of life in their authority and subsequent effect. Our faith comes in moments. . . . Yet there is a depth in those brief moments which constrains us to ascribe more reality to them than to all other experiences."[64]

In James's second period, the period of his famous moral essays and transformation from psychology to philosophy, as one would expect, he used Emerson even more profusely. In his book *The Will to Believe* he quotes from him in support of his well-known plea for belief in a free will, since life thereby is more exciting and meaningful:

> "Look to thyself, O Universe
> Thou art better and not worse."[65]

And in *Human Immortality* James had been postulating the theory that consciousness is not necessarily self-creating, that is, it does not, as the idealists would have it, make itself aware of itself. The transmission theory, continues James, therefore "not only avoids in this way multiplying miracles, but it puts itself in touch with general idealistic philosophy better than the production theory does. It should always be reckoned a good thing when science and philosophy thus meet." James adds, in a footnote to this passage:

> The transmission-theory connects itself very naturally with the whole tendency of thought known as Transcendentalism. Emerson, for example, writes: "We lie in the lap of immense intelligence, which makes us receivers of its truth and organs of its activity. When we discern

[63] William James, *Principles of Psychology* (New York, 1923), I, 582.
[64] *Ibid.*, II, 307.
[65] William James, *The Will to Believe* (New York, 1897), p. 175.

justice, when we discern truth, we do nothing of ourselves, but allow a passage of its beams."

Not to accuse Emerson of pluralism, however, James adds that for his purpose (i.e., James's purpose), many might do as well as one as long as they should "transcend *our* minds . . . —thus come from *something* mental that pre-exists, and is larger than themselves."[66] There is a Jamesian passage in *Talks to Teachers* which, while not Emerson, sounds enough like him to make apparent James's kinship. Here James is pointing to the significance of life if one would only allow his "responsive sensibilities" to function. "We are," he said,

> trained to seek the choice, the rare, the exquisite exclusively, and to overlook the common. We are stuffed with abstract conceptions, and glib with verbalities and verbosities; and in the culture of these higher functions the peculiar sources of joy conected with our simpler functions dry up, and we grow stone-blind and insensible to life's more elementary and general goods and joys.[67]

He had previously said that it is not "occasion and experience," but the "capacity of the soul to be grasped, to have its life-currents absorbed by what is given." And he quotes Emerson to explicate: " 'Crossing a bare common . . . in snow puddles, at twilight, under a clouded sky, without having in my thoughts any occurrence of special good fortune, I have enjoyed a perfect exhilaration, I am glad to the brink of fear.' "[68]

In James's philosophical period, especially in his well-known *Varieties of Religious Experience,* the use of Emerson had not diminished. In his very definition of religion—"the feelings, acts, and experiences of individual men in their solitude, so far as they apprehend themselves to stand in relation to whatever they may consider the divine"—it is Emerson he uses to explicate the key word *divine.* This, says James, is

[66] William James, *Human Immortality* (Boston, 1900), p. 58, n. 5.

[67] William James, *Talks to Teachers* (New York, 1920), p. 257. For other Emerson-like passages and correspondences, see Frederic Carpenter, *op. cit.;* Irwin Edman, "For a New World," *New Republic,* CVIII, 224-228 (Feb. 15, 1943); Eduard C. Lindeman, "Emerson's Pragmatic Mood," *American Scholar,* XVI, 57-64 (Winter, 1947); and Matthiessen, *The James Family,* pp. 432-433.

[68] William James, *Talks to Teachers,* p. 257.

> . . . the Emersonian religion. The universe has a divine soul of order, which soul is moral, being also the soul within the soul of man. But whether this soul of the universe be a mere quality like the eye's brilliancy or the skin's softness, or whether it be a self-conscious life like the eye's seeing or the skin's feeling, is a decision that never unmistakably appears in Emerson's pages. It quivers on the boundary of these things, sometimes leaning one way, sometimes the other, to suit the literary rather than the philosophic need. Whatever it is, though, it is active. As much as if it were a God, we can trust it to protect all ideal interests and keep the world's balance straight.

James goes on to say that this type of religion is as much "religion" as any other kind; and although James certainly utilized Emerson's philosophy, he already intimates that his final judgment of Emerson will not be a judgment of the philosophical Emerson but of the literary or artistic Emerson. Even here James can state that the later utterances of this Emersonian faith "are as fine as anything in literature."[69]

In this same book is his famous criticism of Transcendentalism, the last half of which is too often left unquoted. James certainly states that "modern transcendental idealism, Emersonianism, for instance . . . seems to let God evaporate into abstract Ideality." He added, however, and this has been ignored far too often: "Not a deity *in concreto,* not a superhuman person, but the immanent divinity in things, the essentially spiritual structure of the universe, is the object of the transcendentalist cult." James's attitude here is hardly derogatory, and when he adds that the "frank expression of this worship of mere abstract laws was what made the scandal of the performance,"[70] it clearly leans in the other direction.

In his demonstration of the relativeness of any sort of spiritual conversion, however, James reveals an attitude toward Emerson not dissimilar to that of his father. James apparently is somewhat piqued at Emerson's characteristic disdain for those who "resist" their native impulses. Emerson had written: "When we see a soul

[69] William James, *The Varieties of Religious Experience* (New York, 1902), pp. 31-34.

[70] *Ibid.,* p. 32. In 1903, in a letter to Henry W. Rankin, James states: "I see in the temper of friendliness of such a man as you for such writings as Emerson's and mine (*magnus comp. parvo*) a foretaste of the day when the abstract essentials of belief will be the basis of communion more than the particular forms and concrete doctrines in which they articulate themselves" (*The Letters of William James,* ed. his son Henry, Boston, 1920, II, 196-197).

whose acts are regal, graceful and pleasant as a rose, we must thank God that such things can be and are, and not turn sourly on the Angel and say: Grump is a better man, with a grunting resistance to all his native devils." True enough, James adds, yet: "Grump may really be the better Grump, for his inner discords and second birth; and your once-born 'regal' character [Emerson?] may fall far short of what he individually might be had he only some Grump-like capacity for compunction over his own peculiar diabolisms, graceful and pleasant and invariably gentlemanly as these may be."[71]

Finally, it is again Emerson he utilizes in pointing to the abhorrence of ritualistic minds for the "formless spaciousness" of the Transcendentalists, who, on their part, abhor the "toy-shop furniture, tapes and tinsels, costume and mumbling and mummery" of the ritualists. He paraphrases Emerson and remarks that "Luther . . . would have cut off his right hand rather than nail his theses to the door at Wittenberg, if he had supposed that they were to lead to the pale negations of Boston Unitarianism."[72] The point that James had been making here was that one must have his own religious experience in order to gain any meaningfulness from it at all. Religious experience cannot come, as it were, secondhand.

In 1903 James was invited to deliver a fifteen-minute address at the Emerson centenary at Concord. In preparation he characteristically reread all of Emerson.[73] On May 3, he writes to his brother Henry:

The reading of the divine Emerson, volume after volume, has done me a lot of good, and, strange to say, has thrown a strong practical light on my path. The incorruptible way in which he followed his own vocation, of seeing such truths as the Universal Soul vouchsafed to him from day to day and month to month, and reporting them in the right literary form, and thereafter kept his limits absolutely, refusing to be intangled with irrelevances however urging and tempting, knowing both

[71] *The Varieties of Religious Experience*, pp. 234-235, n. 1. For a similar judgment by his father, see above, n. 34 and text.

[72] *Varieties of Religious Experience*, p. 324.

[73] James writes to Theodore Flournoy on April 30, 1903: "I am neither writing nor lecturing, and reading nothing heavy, only Emerson's works again (divine things, some of them!) in order to make a fifteen-minute address about him on his centennial birthday" (*Letters of William James*, II, 187).

his strength and its limits, and clinging unchangeably to the rural environment which he once for all found to be most propitious, seems to me to be a moral lesson to all men who have any genius, however small, to foster.[74]

James began his lecture by remarking that death is pathetic in that it so often leaves only "the phantom of an idea"[75] about a man. That is, one's insignificances are so great in comparison with one's sometime distinctions, that it is indeed a joyous occasion when one finds a figure whose significance is so distinct that no such abridgment is necessary. He thought Emerson to be such a figure.

It was not, however, Emerson's individuality, but the harmonious combination of his gifts that pleased William James. No one, James adds, knew his genius so well or stayed so unfailingly within his own limitations, meaning by this, loyalty to one's own form, one's own capabilities. Follow your own form and you will discover the truth. But, James adds—and this is extremely significant—such thoughts, that is, thoughts within your own form, unless expressed in the right words, are often trivial, if not trite. And here William James is perhaps more keen than either his father or his brother, for he quickly recognized that Emerson saw the inseparability of thought and expression, recognized that for Emerson they were one. In one word, says James, Emerson was artist—"an artist whose medium was verbal and who wrought in spiritual material."[76]

It was his conscientious attention, James continues, to his own duty—"the duty of spiritual seeing and reporting"—which sometimes made him appear provokingly remote. But, says James, we, on the other hand, must give unqualified approval to that report. We must approve his action. James found Emerson's insight and creed best summed up in the famous passage:

> "So near is grandeur to our dust
> So near is God to man."

For in individual fact is found universal reason. To be true to God is to be true to ourselves.[77]

[74] *Ibid.*, II, p. 190.
[75] Matthiessen, *The James Family*, p. 453.
[76] *Ibid.*, p. 454. [77] *Ibid.*, p. 455.

William James reasons that if the absolute thus appears out of the fact, there is something mandatory about assessing an original relation to the universe. Emerson's most characteristic note, to William James, is his belief in the sacredness of life at first hand. On the other hand, he feels that his most passionate, "his hottest persuasion," was that we should not discover truth through conformity, through others' eyes. This independence electrified Emerson's generation and was, said James, "the soul of his message." In another passage that could have easily been Emerson himself, James says: "The present man is the aboriginal reality, the Institution is derivative, and the past man is irrelevant and obliterate for present issues."[78] It was throughout, then, Emerson's independence and usefulness—his self-reliant, pragmatic artistry—that seem to have appealed to America's leading pragmatist.

James affirms Emerson's belief in being truthful to one's own consciousness. Nothing can harm a man, echoes James, who does his appointed duty, for he "balances the universe, balances as much by keeping small when he is small as by being great and spreading when he is great." He also praises the absence of vanity and pretense, which was, to James, another prime Emersonian concept. "Character infallibly proclaims itself." The same indefeasible right, to be exactly what one is, if one only be authentic, spreads from persons to things and from things to time and place. If reality is not here today available to the individual, it is nowhere.[79]

James then radically departs from the evaluation of his father and brother[80] and extracts the core of Emerson's significance. James readily admits that to find divinity everywhere easily leads one to an optimism of the sentimental type. But, James expostulates, Emerson had a sense of difference that excluded him from this school. "Emerson's optimism," says James, "had nothing in common with that indiscriminate hurrahing for the Universe with which Walt Whitman has made us familiar." To be sure, the individual fact and moment reveal a divine spark—but only upon certain conditions: (1) they must be sincere, authentic, archetypal; (2) they must be connected with the Moral Sentiment; and (3) they must in

[78] *Ibid.*, pp. 455-456. [79] *Ibid.*

[80] He did agree with them in feeling that Emerson had "too little understanding of the morbid side of life" (*Letters of William James*, II, 197).

some way be symbolic of the Universe. What fulfils these requirements is difficult to say, but, says James, Emerson knew, and knew well. *It is his genius*—the genius of the artist—for Emerson could see the squalor of the individual fact while simultaneously seeing its universal significance.[81]

This, then, James concludes, somewhat anticlimactically, is Emerson's revelation: "The point of any pen can be an epitome of reality: the commonest person's act, if genuinely activated, can lay hold on eternity . . . and it is for this truth, given to no previous literary artist to express in such a penetratingly persuasive tone, that posterity will reckon him a prophet."[82]

The preponderant bulk of the remainder of James's comments on Emerson expressed more and more an awareness of Emerson the artist rather than Emerson the philosopher. In fact, his own reaction to the centenary was primarily an aesthetic one. He actually described that reaction as "the most harmoniously aesthetic or aesthetically harmonious thing," effecting "that rarely realized marriage of reality with ideality, that usually only occurs in fiction and poetry."[83]

In 1905, in a letter to Dickinson S. Miller, James had been discussing Santayana's *The Life of Reason,* which had just been published. He immediately recognized its kinship with Emerson, while being fully aware of the differences, especially the artistic differences.

The book is Emerson's first rival and successor, but how different the reader's feeling! The same things in Emerson's mouth would sound entirely different. E. receptive, expansive, as if handling life through a wide funnel with a great indraught; S. as if through a pin-point orifice that emits his cooling spray outward over the universe like a nose-disinfectant from an "atomizer."[84]

[81] Matthiessen, *The James Family,* p. 458.

[82] *Ibid.*

[83] "The weather, the beauty of the village, the charming old meeting-house, the descendants of the grand old man in such profusion, the mixture of Concord and Boston heads, so many of them of our own circle, the allusions to great thoughts and things, and the old-time New England rusticity and rurality, the silver polls and ancient voice of the *vieille garde* who did the orating (including this 'yer child), all made a matchless combination, took one back to one's childhood. . ." (*The Letters of William James,* II, 194).

[84] *Ibid.,* II, 234-235.

And to W. C. Brownell in 1909 only a year before James's death, apropos of the former's essay on Emerson in his *American Prose Masters,* it was again as artist that James wrote of Emerson:

Emerson evidently had no capacity whatever for metaphysic argument, but he found that certain transcendentalist and Platonic phrases *named* beautifully that *side* of the universe which for his soul (with its golden singing sense that the vulgar immediate is as naught relatively to the high and noble, gleeful and consoling life behind it) was all important. So he abounded in monistic metaphysical talk which the very next pages belied. I see no great harm in the literary inconsistency. The monistic formulas do express a genuine direction in things, though it be to a great extent only ideals. His dogmatic expression of them never led him to *suppress the facts* they ignored, so no harm was done.[85]

And in James's very last book, *Some Problems of Philosophy,* published the year after his death, James is still a great utilizer of Emerson. Herein James explains that for the rationalists conceptual knowledge is a "self-sufficing revelation," which, for them, admits of a diviner world—"the world of universal rather than that of perishing fact, of essential qualities, immutable relations, external principles of truth and right." It is Emerson he quotes in order to clarify this appeal: " 'Generalization is always a new influx of divinity into the mind: hence the thrill that attends it.' "[86] And elsewhere in the book, while demonstrating how "life's value deepens when we translate percepts into ideas," pointing out that the "translation appears far more than the original's equivalent," he again quotes Emerson to support and explicate: "Each man sees over his own experience a certain stain of error, whilst that of other men looks fair and ideal. . . . Everything is beautiful seen from the point of view of the intellect, or as Truth, but all is sour if seen as experience. Details are melancholy; the plan is seemly and noble."[87]

William James deeply respected Emerson, and that respect rewarded itself in a more lively and penetrating insight into Emerson's significance than that demonstrated by either his father or his

[85] *The Thought and Character of William James,* I, 144.
[86] William James, *Some Problems of Philosophy,* ed. H. M. Kallen and Henry James (New York, 1928), pp. 56-57.
[87] *Ibid.,* pp. 72-73 n. 1.

brother. Some aspects of Emerson's thought that would appeal to William James one could easily guess—his independence, his self-reliance, his artistic perceptiveness of the significant. That he would see him primarily as an artist is more speculative, and that he would justify Emerson's idealism on artistic grounds is still less predictable. In addition to this basic aesthetic appreciation, however, James utilized Emerson.[88] Were Emerson to disappear from our literary consciousness, a goodly portion of his thought would survive in James's writings. Indeed, the term "Pragmatic Mysticism," first applied to Emerson's philosophy by Henry D. Gray some years ago[89] and still widely current, was in both theory and practice anticipated by James himself.[90] What James owed to Emerson's style is too obvious to be remarked upon. Ultimately, however, for William James the philosopher, it was Emerson the artist.

IV

Admittedly, then, each of the Jameses saw Emerson only partially. And the pattern of that partiality must now be so apparent that one hesitates to articulate it. The fact that to a theologian Emerson was a divine manifestation; to an artist, primarily a moral philosopher; and to a philosopher, the supreme artist is so pat and definite that one is instinctively suspicious of the formulation. Indeed, both Emerson and the Jameses are much too elusive to be restricted to any such inflexible pattern. On the other hand, Emerson himself states in his essay "The Poet" that

> the Universe has three children, born at one time, which reappear under different names in every system of thought, whether they be called cause, operation, and effect; or more poetically, Jove, Pluto, Neptune; or, theologically, the Father, the Spirit, and the Son; but which we will call here the Knower, the Doer, and the Sayer. These stand respectively for the love of truth, for the love of good, and for the love of beauty. These three are equal. Each is that which he is, essentially, so that he

[88] For a highly significant and informative article on the marginalia and marked passages in James's copies of Emerson's books, see Frederic I. Carpenter, "William James and Emerson," *American Literature,* XI, 39-57 (March, 1939).

[89] Henry D. Gray, *Emerson* . . . (Stanford, Calif., 1917), p. 14.

[90] In 1910 James, in an essay on Benjamin Paul Blood, significantly calls him "a Pluralistic Mystic." Even more significant, however, is the fact that in this essay James adds: "There are passages in Blood that sound like a well-known essay by Emerson" (*Memories and Studies,* ed. his son Henry, New York, 1912, p. 391 n. 1.).

cannot be surmounted or analyzed, and each of these three has the power of the others latent in him and his own, patent.[91]

For the James family, collectively, Emerson therefore comes to represent a whole man; for the James family, individually, in so far as he represents respectively the love of truth, the love of good, and the love of beauty, Emerson is also a whole man: for "these three are equal . . . and each has the power of the other latent in him. . . ."[92]

[91] *The Complete Works of Ralph Waldo Emerson,* ed. E. W. Emerson (Boston, 1903-1904), III, 7.

[92] I wish to express my appreciation to Dean Herman E. Spivey of the University of Kentucky for valuable editorial suggestions.

The Riddle of Emerson's "Sphinx"

Thomas R. Whitaker

I

SINCE the time when Francis Bowen declared that "The Sphinx" appropriately opened a volume containing "the most prosaic and unintelligible stuff" he had ever encountered,[1] critics have generally categorized and dismissed the poem as "typical" and "obscure." Even the more respectful critics who have seen in it one of Emerson's "most Emersonian ideas" or "the most condensed of his great affirmations,"[2] have not been able to agree upon precisely what affirmation or idea it contains. In recent decades, partly because of its obscurity, partly because of the undeniable awkwardness and banality of many of its lines, "The Sphinx" has received little attention. Most recently Frederic I. Carpenter has simply dismissed it by saying that " 'Each and All' and 'Brahma' deal with the same idea more clearly and effectively."[3]

It is a mistake, I think, to allow "The Sphinx" to slip off into critical limbo in this fashion. It was Emerson's favorite poem—and for good reason: it reflects in miniature the full scope of his thought and literary method. But if we are to see how it does so, we must first solve its riddle. It is clear, of course, that the Sphinx demands an explanation for the Fall of Man, which she presents in typically romantic symbolism as a fall from the integrity of Nature.[4] And it is clear that the answering "poet" asserts that Love is the First Cause and that man is necessarily imperfect merely because of his infinite perfectibility. But a double riddle remains: Who is the Sphinx? And does the "poet" answer her successfully?

[1] "Nine New Poets," *North American Review*, LXIV, 407 (April, 1847).

[2] Ralph L. Rusk, *The Life of Ralph Waldo Emerson* (New York, 1949), p. 313; George E. Woodberry, *Ralph Waldo Emerson* (New York, 1907), p. 172.

[3] *Emerson Handbook* (New York, 1953), p. 82. Carpenter once called it "Emerson's most typical poem" (*Ralph Waldo Emerson: Representative Selections*, New York, 1934, p. 450).

[4] For parallel prose statements of this symbolic fall, see *The Complete Works of Ralph Waldo Emerson* (Boston, 1903-1904), I, 65, and II, 78.

The most usual answers to this double riddle have been presented anew in Ralph L. Rusk's *Life of Emerson.* According to Mr. Rusk, the Sphinx is a human faculty, "man's inquiring spirit,"[5] and the poet answers her successfully. The Sphinx's analysis is superficial; the evil of the world properly dissolves before the "penetrating glance" of the poet-seer, who easily discovers "love, the unifying force, operating . . . just below the surface."[6] The poem thus seems to dramatize an easy Emersonian optimism, like that present in the version of the fable that appears in Emerson's essay on "History." Life, Emerson writes, is "an endless flight of winged facts or events . . . all putting questions to the human spirit. Those men who cannot answer by a superior wisdom these facts or questions of time, serve them." But if a man "remains fast by the soul and sees the principle, then the facts fall aptly and supple into their places; they know their master and the meanest of them glorifies him."[7] The Sphinx is vanquished. And, with much oversimplification, Emerson himself once apparently supported such an interpretation of his poem. The meaning of "The Sphinx," he wrote in 1859, is this:

The perception of identity unites all things and explains one by another, and the most rare and strange is equally facile as the most common. But if the mind live only in particulars, and see only differences (wanting the power to see the whole—all in each), then the world addresses to this mind a question it cannot answer, and each new fact tears it in pieces, and it is vanquished by the distracting variety.[8]

Does this not settle the question? We have an Emersonian interpretation apparently sanctioned by Emerson himself; and so, as George Woodberry thought, the poem turns out to be "less difficult than it appears."[9]

[5] Rusk, *op. cit.,* p. 313. Thoreau (*The Journal of Henry D. Thoreau,* Boston, 1906, I, 229) called the Sphinx "man's insatiable and questioning spirit"; Charles Malloy ("The Poems of Emerson: The Sphinx," *Arena,* XXXI, 501, May, 1904), man's "intellect"; and John S. Harrison (*The Teachers of Emerson,* New York, 1910, p. 232), man's "phantasy or imagination."

[6] Rusk, *op. cit.,* p. 314. The poet's success had been emphasized by William T. Harris ("Ralph Waldo Emerson," *Atlantic Monthly,* L, 245-246, Aug., 1882), Charles Malloy ("Emerson's Sphinx," *Arena,* XVII, 411, Feb., 1897, and "The Poems of Emerson: The Sphinx," *Arena,* XXXI, 274, March, 1904), George Woodberry (*op. cit.,* p. 171), and John S. Harrison (*op. cit.,* pp. 230-235). Frederic I. Carpenter (*Emerson Handbook,* p. 82 n.) apparently accepts Rusk's discussion.

[7] *Complete Works,* II, 32-33.

[8] *Ibid.,* IX, 412.

[9] Woodberry, *op. cit.,* p. 172.

Unfortunately, the simplicity is itself illusory, and appears only if we ignore the Sphinx's retort to the poet, and deny the coherence and dramatic point of the entire conclusion:

> The old Sphinx bit her thick lip,—
> Said, "Who taught thee me to name?
> I am thy spirit, yoke-fellow;
> Of thine eye I am eyebeam.
>
> "Thou art the unanswered question;
> Couldst see thy proper eye,
> Always it asketh, asketh;
> And each answer is a lie.
> So take thy quest through nature,
> It through thousand natures ply;
> Ask on, thou clothed eternity;
> Time is the false reply."
>
> Uprose the merry Sphinx,
> And crouched no more in stone;
> She melted into purple cloud,
> She silvered in the moon;
> She spired into a yellow flame;
> She flowered in blossoms red;
> She flowed into a foaming wave:
> She stood Monadnoc's head.
>
> Thorough a thousand voices
> Spoke the universal dame;
> "Who telleth one of my meanings
> Is master of all I am."[10]

Harris, Harrison, and Rusk completely ignore this retort, which, if taken seriously, overthrows their interpretation of the poem. Far from endorsing a facile optimism, the Sphinx holds that the question is still "unanswered" and *"each* answer is a lie":

> "Ask on, thou clothed eternity;
> Time is the false reply."

Woodberry notes these lines as one of Emerson's "great affirmations,"[11] but does not see that it is an affirmation inconsistent with

[10] All quotations from "The Sphinx" follow the text in *Complete Works,* IX, 20-25.

[11] Woodberry, *op. cit.,* p. 172. Charles Malloy sees the Sphinx's retort as indicating man's inability to comprehend the "soul," but does not relate this to the poet's answer, which he considers successful (*Arena,* XVII, 413-414, and XXXI, 501). His discussion is suggestive but incoherent.

the poet's "victory": his confidence that he has penetrated beneath the "pictures of time" is baseless, for as a "clothed eternity," a noumenal subject immersed in the phenomenal world, he can never himself describe the noumenal. Nor can we dismiss this as the false retort of the defeated "inquiring spirit," who rankles under the sting of the poet's words. The Sphinx is irritated when she begins her speech, not because her riddle has been solved (if defeated, why does she so soon become "merry"?), but because the poet has brashly derided her:

> "Rue, myrrh and cummin for the Sphinx,
> Her muddy eyes to clear!"

She is nettled by such presumption in a "man-child" who does not even know who she is:

> . . . "Who taught thee me to name?
> I am thy spirit, yoke-fellow;
> Of thine eye I am eyebeam."

Should we then echo the poet's presumption by dismissing her as simply "man's inquiring spirit"? Is she not more complex than that? Does man's inquiring spirit *become* cloud, moon, flame, blossoms, wave, and mountain?

In answering this question, Mr. Rusk would have us accept a quite arbitrary and meaningless departure from the established symbolic drama of the poem: "With her mission obviously at an end, the inquiring spirit, now reverting to genuine Sphinxhood, wrapped herself up in the altered garment of the ancient myth and faded away, becoming indistinguishable from the pleasing aspects of nature. . . ."[12] The answer which Harrison offers is subtler. He holds that the poet (whom he interprets as intellect) has successfully answered the Sphinx (phantasy or imagination): that is, the intellect has comprehended "the dark essence of phantasy." The Sphinx's transformations symbolize the fact that "phantasy when intellect functions properly is elevated and shines with a light imparted by intellect"; in so doing, it "uses things as symbols, thus translating earthly things into a higher power."[13] But this interpretation relies excessively upon an external source[14] and lacks

[12] Rusk, *op. cit.*, p. 314.
[13] Harrison, *op. cit.*, pp. 234-235.
[14] A marked passage in Emerson's copy of Taylor's *Select Works of Plotinus*. Because of the variety of Emerson's treatments of this myth (which we shall note later) there is no necessary force in his marking this passage.

sufficiently close relation to the Sphinx's riddle: in answering that particular riddle the intellect is not in Harrison's sense comprehending "the dark essence of phantasy." And, even if the Sphinx's identity with natural objects clearly meant that she was using them as symbols, what relation would such use have to her riddle? Finally, Harrison must not only ignore the Sphinx's retort but also smooth over the incoherence between her transformations and the sudden appearance of the "universal dame," whom he identifies with Nature. Because Nature "had originally asked the question," because the Sphinx "got it from her," the poem "properly ends with the sanction which Nature gives to the truth that the Poet has spoken."[15] But "the great mother" had been genuinely alarmed over the problem of her wayward man-child; can she now sanction the answer, as though she had been posing a mere riddle? And in any case, nowhere does the Sphinx say she got her question from "the great mother"; she quoted the great mother's question as a dramatic rendering of her own riddle, which she had called "my secret."

Clearly such interpretations raise more questions than they answer, and require us to accept the poem as being woefully abrupt and incoherent. However, if we read the poem's conclusion without presuppositions about the validity of the poet's answer or the identity of the Sphinx, its unity is perfectly clear. Irritated by the poet's presumption, the Sphinx rebukes him for addressing and criticizing her, points out his ignorance of her identity, and proceeds, by a natural transition, to taunt him with having failed to answer her riddle. During this retort, her momentary pique passes; she is merry, obviously, because she has the better of the poet. And as if to demonstrate further his presumption in naming her, she rises and, like a veritable Proteus, enters into many natural forms. Thus in context the phrase "universal dame" clearly refers to the Sphinx herself, who has just been referred to by six parallel pronouns, and who has just convincingly demonstrated her universality. And her final taunt—

> "Who telleth one of my meanings
> Is master of all I am"

—states a fact that her transformations have symbolized.

[15] Harrison, *op. cit.*, p. 235.

Surely the Sphinx is the One who animates both the poet (himself the "unanswered question") and "the great mother" (the maternal aspect of Nature). She might well have added to her taunt, for the benefit of the poet and later critics:

> They know not well the subtle ways
> I keep, and pass, and turn again.

For she is here both the doubter and the doubt—and also, as we shall see later, the hymn the Brahmin sings.[16] Thus her actions themselves validate her retort to the poet. And indeed, the poet might have foreseen his failure to solve the Sphinx's riddle, for it was implicit in part of her own answer:

> "To vision profounder,
> Man's spirit must dive;
> His aye-rolling orb
> At no goal will arrive. . . ."

Because he forgets that his own vision is subject to this irony of inclusive circles, and because he forgets his own warning that "Pride ruined the angels," he is properly rebuked by the symbol of the Infinite, who points out that, should he take his quest through a thousand natures, time would still condition and falsify his reply.

As Thoreau saw in 1841, "The Sphinx" dramatizes, not a superficial Emersonian optimism, but an ultimate skepticism concerning man's ability to comprehend the Infinite. The poet, he said, shows "great presumption"; it is wisdom "to suspect time's reply, because we would not degrade one of God's meanings to be intelligible to us." We "career toward" Truth eternally, "not fearing to pass any goal of truth in our haste"; but in "the annihilation of ages alone" is the Sphinx's secret revealed.[17]

[16] "Brahma," *Complete Works,* IX, 195. In herself the Sphinx is not, as Harrison maintains (*op. cit.,* pp. 232-233), "perplexed" by her own question. She is "drowsy" and "broods on the world"; but as Thoreau noted (*Journal,* I, 229), this is "the mood in which the Sphinx bestirs herself in us," for when "we are awake to the real world, we are asleep to the actual," and hence "Menu says that the 'supreme omnipresent intelligence' is 'a spirit which can only be conceived by a mind slumbering.'" However, Thoreau did not follow out the implications of his own remark, and see the Sphinx as the omnipresent intelligence, and its drowsiness as its self-contemplation.

[17] Thoreau, *Journal,* I, 236, 230. William S. Kennedy, in the only other commentary treating the poem as skeptical, used terms more closely suggesting Emerson's philosophical interests: the poet, a "fragment of the Infinite Soul," is "swathed about with maya, or nature," and "cannot understand the Noumenon, the real. Only the Boundless . . . can comprehend itself" ("Clews to Emerson's Mystic Verse," *American Author,* II, 205-206, June, 1903). Frederic I. Carpenter (*Emerson and Asia,* Cambridge, Mass.,

Such a reading of the poem not only accords with the internal evidence, but also receives more support from the context of Emerson's work than does the usual interpretation. In Emerson's journals the very first reference to the Sphinx establishes the pattern. In 1826 he quoted from Mme de Staël: "The aenigma of ourselves swallows up, like the Sphinx, thousands of systems which pretend to the glory of having guessed its meaning."[18] And he countered his optimistic treatment of the myth in "History" with a very different treatment in the second essay on "Nature." There is throughout nature, he wrote, "something mocking, something that leads us on and on, but arrives nowhere; keeps no faith with us." To the poet, nature is as elusive as the mocking protean Sphinx: each natural object is but "a far-off reflection and echo of the triumph that has passed by and is now at its glancing splendour and heyday, perchance in the neighboring fields, or, if you stand in the field, then in the adjacent woods."

> To the intelligent, nature converts itself into a vast promise, and will not be rashly explained. . . . Many and many an Oedipus arrives; he has the whole mystery teeming in his brain. Alas! the same sorcery has spoiled his skill; no syllable can he shape on his lips.[19]

As the Sphinx claims in this poem, the poet is "the unanswered question," and yet "each answer is a lie."

Again, Emerson defended Plato's inability "to dispose of nature—which will not be disposed of." "No power of genius has ever yet had the smallest success in explaining existence. The perfect enigma remains."[20] And the essay "Nominalist and Realist" is exactly parallel in structure to "The Sphinx": first Emerson defends the realist's description of unity and law under the various "pictures of time"; then, echoing the Sphinx's retort and transformations, he declares that the belief that "life will be simpler when we live at the centre and flout the surfaces" is "flat rebellion."

> Nature will not be Buddhist: she resents generalizing, and insults the Philosopher in every moment with a million of fresh particulars. . . . She will not remain orbed in a thought, but rushes into persons; and

1930, pp. 127-128) and Stephen E. Whicher (*Freedom and Fate*, Philadelphia, 1953, p. 91) may possibly imply a similar reading.

[18] *The Journals of Ralph Waldo Emerson*, ed. E. W. Emerson and W. E. Forbes (Boston, 1909-1914), II, 121.

[19] *Complete Works*, III, 189-190, 192, 193-194. Cf. the conclusion to "Adirondacs" (*ibid.*, IX, 194), which also indicates that not even "one riddle of the Sphinx" is guessed.

[20] *Ibid.*, VI, 78.

when each person . . . would conquer all things to his poor crotchet, she raises up against him another person, and by many persons incarnates again a sort of whole.[21]

Even Emerson's own frequent conviction of "Love at the centre" was, he admitted, such a realist's "poor crochet": merely the "emphatic symbol" by which "Jesus and the moderns" have attempted to represent the ineffable First Cause, which, like the Sphinx, "refuses to be named."[22]

So the Sphinx mocks us, "leads us on and on, but arrives nowhere." Emerson would have us good-naturedly admit that we may be the sport of her illusions,[23] and because the poet in "The Sphinx" fails to make that admission, the poem demonstrates to him that "Yoganidra, the goddess of illusion, Proteus, or Momus, or Gylfi's Mocking,—for the Power has many names,—is . . . stronger than Apollo."[24] In some moods Emerson agreed with the humorist who maintained "that the attributes of God were two,—power and risibility, and that it was the duty of every pious man to keep up the comedy."[25] Certainly in "The Sphinx" he seems to do just that, giving the last word, not to the poet-seer who believes that God is Love, but to the powerful and merry Sphinx. We seem to be left with the reflection proper to the philosophy of "Circles" and "Illusions": "All is riddle, and the key to a riddle is another riddle."[26]

II

Around the poet's mystic circle of love, usually accepted as the horizon of this poem, we have drawn another circle, that of the mocking, riddling Sphinx. But there are further circles, in infinite regression, yet leading paradoxically to an infinite affirmation. For "The Sphinx" is typical of Emerson's work in moving from a seemingly radical skepticism toward a genuinely radical (if ambiguous) affirmation. And in doing so, it is also typical in embodying Emerson's effort to cope dialectically and symbolically with the antinomy of the Many and the One.

First of all, the poet's defeat in "The Sphinx" is not in any simple sense Emerson's defeat. What the poet sees but fails to apply to himself, Emerson sees in his essays with frequent self-irony: "Our life is an apprenticeship to the truth that round every circle another

[21] *Ibid.*, III, 235-236. [22] *Ibid.*, III, 72-73. [23] See *ibid.*, VI, 317, 319.
[24] *Ibid.*, VI, 313. [25] *Ibid.*, VI, 314-315. [26] *Ibid.*, VI, 313.

can be drawn; that there is no end in nature, but every end is a beginning; that there is always another dawn risen on mid-noon, and under every deep a lower deep opens."[27] Therefore Emerson admits, after making an assertion, "I am a fragment, and this is a fragment of me. . . . I gossip for my hour concerning the eternal politics."[28] In this, as he thought, Emerson was following Plato, whose "circumspection never forsook him" even in his highest transcendental flights[29]; and thus the dialectic Emerson saw in Plato's work informs his own.[30]

"The Sphinx" itself embodies this dialectic, which Emerson calls the conversational game of circles:

> The man finishes his story—how good! how final! . . . Lo! on the other side rises also a man and draws a circle around the circle we had just pronounced the outline of the sphere.[31]

"The idealism of Berkeley," Emerson had written, "is only a crude statement of the idealism of Jesus, and that again is a crude statement of the fact that all nature is the rapid efflux of goodness executing and organizing itself."[32] This is the poet's position in "The Sphinx"; but the poem encloses even this utterance in an infinity of circles, carrying the self-critical dialectic to the ultimate, as the Absolute itself rises up against the speaker. However, the poet is not simply a proud fool; though his vision is transcended, his pride is a temporary necessity, for a "man can only speak so long as he does not feel his speech to be partial and inadequate. . . . As soon as he is released from the instinctive and particular and sees its partiality, he shuts his mouth in disgust."[33]

This theory of vigorous dialectic, of course, partly explains, and for Emerson partly justified, his many overstatements and contradictions. "No sentence will hold the whole truth," he declared, "and the only way in which we can be just, is by giving ourselves the lie." No utterance of the discursive Understanding, that is,

[27] *Ibid.*, II, 301.

[28] *Ibid.*, III, 83.

[29] *Ibid.*, IV, 58.

[30] See William T. Harris, "The Dialectic Unity of Emerson's Prose," *Journal of Speculative Philosophy*, XVIII, 195-202 (April, 1884). Ironically, Harris failed to see the dialectic unity of "The Sphinx" (see "Ralph Waldo Emerson," *Atlantic Monthly*, L, 245-246, Aug., 1882). See also Sherman Paul, *Emerson's Angle of Vision* (Cambridge, Mass., 1952), pp. 113 ff., and Charles Feidelson, *Symbolism and American Literature* (Chicago, 1953), pp. 158-159.

[31] *Complete Works*, II, 304-305.

[32] *Ibid.*, II, 309-310.

[33] *Ibid.*, III, 189.

can transcend the antinomies: "All the universe over, there is but one thing, this old Two-Face, creator-creature, mind-matter, right-wrong, of which any proposition may be affirmed or denied."[34] This is virtually the skeptic philosophy of "fluxions and mobility," which holds that "We are golden averages, volitant stabilities, compensated or periodic errors, houses founded on the sea."[35] But this philosophy is Emerson's only while he remains in the realm of the Understanding. He may transcend it intuitively, through Reason, and express his perception symbolically and paradoxically. And that is precisely what happens in "The Sphinx."

Despite the Sphinx's victory, the conclusion of the poem is strikingly affirmative in point of view, tone, and content. It focuses not upon the defeated poet but upon the victorious Sphinx—upon transformations presented as fascinating and beautiful, light and merry. (The playful note in "universal dame" was more glaringly evident in two lines of the first version: "She hopped into the baby's eyes,/She hopped into the moon."[36]) Emerson's attitude seems typically ambivalent: though sympathizing partly with the poet, as with all men in their inevitable defeat by the enigma of Nature, he also rejoices that Nature transcends human understanding. In part, his joy grows from his love of freedom. He rejoices in seeing thought beyond thought, heaven beyond heaven, because he believes that "every thought is also a prison, every heaven is also a prison."[37] Hence his satisfaction when each new speaker in a conversation "emancipates us from the oppression of the last speaker," or when Nature eludes such mystics as Swedenborg: "The slippery Proteus is not so easily caught. . . . Nature avenges herself speedily on the hard pedantry that would chain her waves."[38] The "free spirit" is at home in the flux of Nature, amid the metamorphoses of the Sphinx; he "sympathizes not only with the actual form, but with the power or possible forms. . . . Hence the shudder of joy with which in a clear moment we recognize the metamorphosis, because it is always a conquest, a surprise from the heart of things."[39]

But Emerson rejoices in the Sphinx's conquest also because it

[34] *Ibid.*, III, 245. The theory of the microcosm further justified self-contradiction. See *Journals*, V, 326-327.

[35] *Complete Works*, IV, 160-161.

[36] *Dial*, I, 350 (Jan., 1841).

[37] *Complete Works*, III, 33.

[38] *Ibid.*, II, 310; IV, 121.

[39] *Ibid.*, VIII, 71.

demonstrates her infinite power, and he has faith in man's potential access to that power. In the second essay on "Nature," the passage (quoted earlier) describing Oedipus' continual defeat modulates into an affirmation of that faith:

> We cannot bandy words with Nature. . . . If we measure our individual forces against hers we may easily feel as if we were the sport of an insuperable destiny. But if, instead of identifying ourselves with the work, we feel that the soul of the Workman streams through us, we shall find the peace of the morning dwelling first in our hearts, and the fathomless powers of gravity and chemistry, and over them, of life, preexisting within us in their highest form.[40]

And the verse which opens this essay presents the same transcendence of the Sphinx's riddle:

> The rounded world is fair to see,
> Nine times folded in mystery:
> Though baffled seers cannot impart
> The secret of its laboring heart,
> Throb thine with Nature's throbbing breast,
> And all is clear from east to west. . . .[41]

Although "The Sphinx" presents no such explicit affirmation, it does contain a symbolic equivalent. The defeated poet-seer gives way not only to the Sphinx but also to Emerson himself, attempting the task of the true Poet, who knows that "the quality of the imagination is to flow, and not to freeze," and that "all symbols are fluxional."[42]

> Ever the Rock of Ages melts
> Into the mineral air[43]

—and the Sphinx cannot remain frozen as Love, the symbol of one religion:

> Uprose the merry Sphinx,
> And crouched no more in stone;
> She melted into purple cloud,
> She silvered in the moon;
> She spired into a yellow flame;
> She flowered in blossoms red;
> She flowed into a foaming wave:
> She stood Monadnoc's head.

[40] *Ibid.*, III, 194.
[41] *Ibid.*, III, 167.
[42] *Ibid.*, III, 34.
[43] *Ibid.*, IX, 355.

Where the mystic was foiled, the true Poet succeeds: he "sees through the flowing vest the firm nature, and can declare it"—but since Nature is "no literalist," since she never gave us power to make "direct strokes" against her, he must declare it symbolically, obliquely, in a series of glancing blows.[44] Because his symbols dramatize the fusion of the One and the Many, we "stand before the secret of the world, there where Being passes into appearance and Unity into Variety."[45] This is the miracle of Poetry, and indeed, the "one miracle, the perpetual fact of Being and Becoming, the ceaseless saliency, the transit from the Vast to the particular, which miracle, one and the same, has for its most universal name the word God."[46]

Emerson the Poet can have this vision only because mind and universe correspond: only because the Sphinx is the object of the Poet's vision and also, as she says, his spirit and his eyebeam. She is "the act of seeing and the thing seen, the seer and the spectacle, the subject and the object."[47] Therefore her transformations in external nature also dramatize the fundamental law of perception, containing itself the mystery of Unity and Variety:

> this incessant movement and progression which all things partake could never become sensible to us but by contrast to some principle of fixture or stability in the soul. Whilst the eternal generation of circles proceeds, the eternal generator abides. That central life is somewhat superior to creation, superior to knowledge and thought, and contains all its circles.[48]

In perceiving and symbolizing this "secret of the world" Emerson transcends the Sphinx's riddle and establishes harmony with the First Cause. For the "condition of true naming, on the poet's part, is his resigning himself to the divine *aura* which breathes through forms, and accompanying that."[49] This is "proper creation"; it is "the working of the Original Cause through the instruments he has already made"[50]—and in this sense the Sphinx is, like Brahma, her own hymn. Thus "The Sphinx," viewed as Emerson's poetic creation, is a symbolic affirmation of faith, dramatizing the

[44] *Ibid.*, III, 37; IV, 121; III, 49-50.
[45] *Ibid.*, III, 14.
[46] *Journals*, VI, 124.
[47] *Complete Works*, II, 269.
[48] *Ibid.*, III, 318.
[49] *Ibid.*, III, 26.
[50] *Ibid.*, I, 31. It is, of course, the operation of Coleridge's primary Imagination, which "sees all things in one" (*Table Talk and Omniana*, Oxford ed., London, 1917, p. 309) and is "a repetition in the finite mind of the eternal act of creation in the infinite I AM" (*Complete Works of S. T. Coleridge*, ed. Shedd, New York, 1853, III, 363). (All passages I quote from Coleridge have been cited by Kenneth Cameron in his valuable chapter "Emerson's Coleridge," in *Emerson the Essayist*, Raleigh, N. C., 1945.)

thought of the verse which opens "Nature": throbbing with Nature's throbbing breast, Emerson perceives the secret which the baffled seer cannot impart. As he wrote in his journal:

It pains me never that I cannot give you an accurate answer to the question, What is God? What is the operation we call Providence? and the like. There lies the answer: there it exists, present, omnipresent to you, to me. . . .[51]

The victory is thus Emerson's as well as the Sphinx's: "Horsed on the Proteus," he rides "to power/And to endurance."[52] For that reason, although the Sphinx counters the poet's too simple assertion of "Love at the centre,/Heart-heaving alway" with her own mocking demonstration of Multiplicity, that demonstration itself resolves into a forceful affirmation of its implicit Unity. Though ever the Rock of Ages melts into the mineral air, ever it returns to stone: "She stood Monadnoc's head." Monadnoc here, as in Emerson's poem about it, is the "grand affirmer of the present tense," the "Firm ensign of the fatal Being"—Coleridge's "infinite I AM."[53]

We have seen how the dialectic of circles appropriate to the Understanding is transcended by the direct intuition and symbolic expression of the One-in-Many. But the last stanza of the poem raises a further problem, for there Emerson abandons purely symbolic expression and has the Sphinx utter a direct statement not only taunting the poet but affirming Emerson's own belief that "there is no fact in nature which does not carry the whole sense of nature."[54] Paradoxically, the poem affirms the correspondence of every part to the whole, and yet maintains that Nature's meaning (or even one of her meanings) has not been guessed. Vacillating between confident insight and complete bafflement, haunted by a sense of barely glimpsed intelligibility, Emerson was drawn to just this position. "Why hear I the same sense from countless differing voices," he asked, echoing the conclusion of this poem, "and read *one never quite expressed fact* in endless picture language?"[55] But the paradox, as he saw it, was not just a compromise between ignorance and faith; it was the mystery of being as revealed to the Aeolian harp of Reason, "that intuition of things," in Coleridge's phrase, "which arises when we possess ourselves, as one with the

[51] *Journals,* VI, 246.
[52] *Complete Works,* VI, 308.
[53] *Ibid.,* IX, 73. Cf. Exodus 3:14, and John 8:58.
[54] *Complete Works,* III, 17.
[55] *Ibid.,* IV, 118 (my italics).

whole,"[56] or, in Emerson's phrase, which arises when we throb "with Nature's throbbing breast." According to Coleridge, the mystery in every form of existence appears to the Understanding (in time) as an infinite chain of cause and effect and (in space) as an infinite law of action and reaction; but when "freed from the *phaenomena* of time and space, and seen in the depth of real being," it "reveals itself to the pure reason as the actual immanence or in-being of all in each."[57]

The Reason, therefore, seeing all in each, can present that perception either symbolically in the Sphinx's transformations (through the forms of the Imagination), or else paradoxically in her utterance (for truth reduced to the forms of the Understanding appears as paradox).[58] And we can now see that Emerson's own interpretation of "The Sphinx" is most probably an oversimplified account, not of the usual reading of the poem, but of the reading offered here. The Reason's "power to see the whole—all in each," is implicit in the conclusion. It is the "poet" who is "vanquished by the distracting variety" (note that Emerson stresses this defeat, the poem's explicit subject), but he is vanquished not because he lives "only in particulars" but because his vision of the whole is rigid and partial: he loses "the infinite in the striving after the one," and is to that extent captive to the Understanding.[59] The Reason, remaining true to both the One and the Infinite, must hold that all is in each, and yet that no one of the universal dame's meanings has been guessed:

> Are we struck with admiration at beholding the cope of heaven imaged in a dewdrop? The least of the *animalculae* to which that drop would be an ocean, contains in itself an infinite problem of which God omnipresent is the only solution.[60]

"The Sphinx" dramatizes the belief that man's nature contains just such an infinite problem, with just that solution. Emerson himself had asked: "Whence this fact that the natural history of man has never been written? . . . Whence, but because God inhabits

[56] Coleridge, *Complete Works,* II, 469.

[57] *Ibid.,* I, 450. Cf. Emerson (*Complete Works,* VI, 319): "What seems the *succession* of thought is only the distribution of wholes into causal series"; the "intellect sees that every atom carries the whole of nature."

[58] See Coleridge, *Complete Works,* I, 252 n.

[59] Emerson, *Complete Works,* IX, 412; Coleridge, *Complete Works,* I, 456.

[60] Coleridge, *Complete Works,* I, 450.

man and cannot be known but by God?"[61] And in "The Sphinx," his expanding circles lead finally to the paradox quoted by Coleridge as one of the truths of Reason: "God is a circle, the centre of which is everywhere, and circumference nowhere."[62] Though all is riddle, we are led to the final, affirmative riddle: *"Omnia exeunt in mysterium."*[63]

Nor is such a "solution" of the Sphinx's riddle inconsistent with the frequently oversimplified optimism of Emerson's *Nature.* "Undoubtedly," Emerson had written with disconcerting assurance, "we have no questions to ask which are unanswerable. . . . Every man's condition is a solution in hieroglyphic to those inquiries he would put." But that solution is not translatable into discursive terms: the "absolute Ens" has "innumerable sides," and its central Unity, the unity of the Sphinx, is "the unspeakable but intelligible and practicable meaning of the world."

> That essence refuses to be recorded in propositions, but when man has worshipped him intellectually, the noblest ministry of nature is to stand as the apparition of God. It is the organ through which the universal spirit speaks to the individual, and strives to lead back the individual to it.[64]

These sentences foreshadow the poet's failure, in "The Sphinx," to describe the First Cause, and Emerson's own success in implicitly representing it through natural symbols. And already, in his journal, Emerson had related this function of nature to the riddle of the Sphinx. "There sits the Sphinx from age to age . . . ," he had written, "and every wise man that comes by has a crack with her." One such was the Swedenborgian Oegger: "Why the world exists, and that it exists for a language or medium whereby God may speak to man, this is his query, this his answer."[65] But unlike Oegger, Emerson saw the symbols of this language as fluxional and transitive, leading not to any clear proposition but to an intuition of the ineffable One-in-Many.

[61] *Journals,* V, 151.

[62] Coleridge, *Complete Works,* I, 252 n.

[63] *Ibid.,* I, 195. Christopher Cranch's poem "The Riddle," published in the same number of the *Dial* (I, 383-384, Jan., 1841), comes to the same conclusion. Indeed, it seems almost a simplified version of "The Sphinx," so close is it in both theme and dramatic detail.

[64] Emerson, *Complete Works,* I, 3-4, 44, 47, 61-62.

[65] *Journals,* II, 525 (1835).

III

Emerson quite properly opened his *Poems* with "The Sphinx," for, like the microcosm he believed every utterance to be, it reflects the full reach of his thought. It embodies the dialectic of circles in discursive expression, transcended by the intuition, and the symbolical and paradoxical expression, of the One-in-Many; and it therefore presents Emerson's characteristic "volitant stability," a "house founded on the sea"—but also upon a faith in an infinity of supporting depths beneath: "If my bark sink, 'tis to another sea."[66] Thus his skeptical mind found rest only in the Infinite; or, as he preferred to put it, thus "the spiritualist finds himself driven to express his faith by a series of skepticisms."[67] The poem also embodies the Emersonian movement from a vision of man's Fall (the problem of moral evil in an apparently dualistic universe) to a vision of man's "inevitable" rise (a solution in ethical monism), and on to an enacted harmony with the Sphinx (an aesthetic and religious, but amoral, transcendence of monism and dualism). It therefore presents Emerson's dilemma when confronted with the conflict he necessarily saw between God's ethical will and His enigmatic creative will. Characteristically, he avoided this antinomy either, like the poet in "The Sphinx," by hastily absolutizing the ethical will, or, in more complex moods, by throbbing with the enigmatic creative will—and thus identifying instinct and intuition, living "from the Devil" if need be,[68] and, horsed on the Proteus, riding to power and endurance.

Far from being merely an ineffective treatment of the idea expressed in "Each and All" and "Brahma," "The Sphinx" encompasses those poems, and thus partly escapes Charles Feidelson's criticism of the "facile harmony" of Emerson's symbolism; for like the ideal symbolic work that Mr. Feidelson opposes to Emerson's, it is saved from indeterminacy "by the struggle to melt and reorder accepted distinctions," and its world is "built up by the continuous interplay between real opposition—the compulsion toward moral choice—and real harmony—the compulsion toward moral indifference."[69] Of course, it is true that Emerson's "totally poetic universe"—with all in each—deprives him of "any brake on the trans-

[66] *Complete Works,* IV, 161, 186.
[67] *Ibid.,* IV, 181.
[68] *Ibid.,* II, 2.
[69] Charles Feidelson, *Symbolism and American Literature,* pp. 123, 150, 218.

mutation of form."[70] (That fact lies behind the *detailed* weakness in "The Sphinx.") But Emerson did not simply write in accordance with his developed vision; he also dramatized its development. "The Sphinx" is one passage in what Mr. Feidelson himself admirably describes as "a continuous monologue in which the genesis of symbolism is enacted over and over,"[71] and the process of enactment provides its form. We remain dissatisfied not only because of the imprecision, banality, and awkwardness of phrasing, but also because of the rather facile dramatic progression. Never did Emerson sufficiently resist the progress of his vision.

However, contrary to Mr. Feidelson's statement, Emerson did think to exploit "the tension between opposite meanings in paradox and the tension between logical paradox and its literary resolution."[72] He admired Plato's mind, which held the synthesis of the antinomies, "the upper and under side of the medal of Jove," and here he imitates that Platonic quality. He "cannot forgive in himself a partiality, but is resolved that the two poles of his thought shall appear in his statement." Aware that great art is such by synthesis and that the artist's "strength is transitional, alternating," he balances dialectically the problem, the answer of his partial self, and the ultimate symbolical and paradoxical answer—and so also balances the method of thought, which "seeks to know unity in unity," with that of poetry, "which seeks to show it by variety."[73]

"A believer in Unity, a seer of Unity, I yet behold two."[74] That classical problem was Emerson's great theme. In essay after essay he turned the medal of Jove, showing the unity of the Chaos, the contradictions of the Universe. "Life is a pitching of this penny, —heads or tails. We never tire of this game, because there is still a slight shudder of astonishment at the exhibition of the other face, at the contrast of the two faces."[75] In "The Sphinx" that "old Two-Face"[76] rises up to cause another shudder of astonishment and joy—at both the contrast and the identity.

[70] *Ibid.*, p. 150.
[71] *Ibid.*, p. 123.
[72] *Ibid.*, p. 122.
[73] Emerson, *Complete Works*, IV, 55-56.
[74] *Journals*, IV, 248.
[75] *Complete Works*, IV, 149.
[76] *Ibid.*, III, 245.

Emerson on Plato: The Fire's Center

Ray Benoit

THE IDEALISTS DISMISS EMERSON as a pragmatist and the pragmatists dismiss him as an idealist. It is safe to say that one is wrong, but it is safer to say that both are right. Newton Arvin's remark that Emerson is "a polarized, a contradictory, writer"[1] echoes Robert Pollock's statement that he "resists easy classification."[2] Yet he has been classified, and all too readily classified, but what does the reader do when he discovers that two exactly opposite philosophies claim him, and not as a minor, second-rate spokesman, at that, but indeed as a great forerunner of their respective heresies? He brushes him off as a befuddled thinker, sincere but befuddled. It only depends on how you choose your quotations, as William James was well aware when he chose his.[3] Here is Emerson, then: what he offers with his right hand, an emphasis on the vertical otherworldly, his left hand withdraws with an emphasis on the horizontal worldly. For every step forward there seems to be one backward for, as F. O. Matthiessen points out (and our attitude has not changed significantly since the *American Renaissance*), "He did not want his idealism to be divorced from the material facts of his age."[4]

Emerson foresaw, as he did so many other things, how the modern student would reply: "And thus, O circular philosopher, I hear some reader exclaim. . . ."[5] "Which did Emerson consider superior," asks Frederic Carpenter, "deeds or thoughts; actions or ideas?"[6] Didn't Melville spot the same polarity in *The Confidence-*

[1] "The House of Pain: Emerson and the Tragic Sense," *Hudson Review*, XII, 51 (Spring, 1959).

[2] "A Reappraisal of Emerson," *Thought*, XXXII, 86 (Spring, 1957).

[3] "All these passages appealed to James as celebrating 'pragmatism,' or 'the superiority of action.' But he found these mixed with other passages which declared 'the superiority of what is intellectualized.' Therefore he indexed the two contrasting series of statements, and referred specifically to certain paragraphs which contained 'both close together' "; Frederic I. Carpenter, "William James and Emerson," *American Literature*, XI, 43 (March, 1939).

[4] New York, 1941, p. 11.

[5] *The Complete Works of Ralph Waldo Emerson* (Boston, 1903-1904), II, 317; hereafter references are in the text.

[6] "William James and Emerson," p. 44.

Man? "And moonshiny as it in theory may be, yet a very practical philosophy it turns out in effect."[7] This view, as many critics confess, has conditioned our response against Emerson. There is the attack from Yvor Winters in *Maule's Curse*:

Emerson's guiding spirit was, in effect, instinct and personal whim, which, in his terms, became identical with the Divine Imperative, but which, in practice, amounted to a kind of benevolent if not invariably beneficent sentimentalism. The religious experience for Emerson was a kind of good-natured self-indulgence.[8]

And then there is the less damning, but in its way perhaps the more cutting, remark of Perry Miller: "Fortunately," speaking of all the transcendentalists, "no one is compelled to take them seriously."[9]

But we should take them seriously. I think the reason that we have more or less shelved Emerson is that we have not really bothered to try to come to grips with him. When we read him we discover a structural and thematic curve and it is just in this circularity, I believe, that the answer to the problem in Emerson is to be found. "Sometimes the world seemed to him to have independent material existence, colored and interpreted by mind," Stuart Brown wrote, "and sometimes it seemed to him wholly dependent and ideal. He never could entirely make up his mind."[10] What I wish to show is that this inconsistency (and all others it implies: time-eternity, subject-object, individual-society) is a logical inconsistency and that it stems from his contact with Plato; that Emerson did in fact make up his mind but with a difference, a difference which is one of the more significant philosophic shifts. Briefly: by interpreting Plato, he chose neither spirit nor matter but viewed each as aspects of a ground of being, if you will, higher than both. For this reason he is a pragmatist and an idealist without, strictly speaking, being either one. It is his answer to that dilemma posed by George Ripley in the *Dial*:

Spiritualism and materialism both have their foundation in our nature, and both will exist and exert their influence. Shall they exist as antagonist principles? Is the bosom of Humanity to be eternally torn by these two contending factions? . . . Here then is the mission of the

[7] New York, 1955, p. 261.

[8] Norfolk, Conn., 1938, p. 126.

[9] "From Edwards to Emerson," *Interpretations of American Literature*, ed. Charles Feidelson and Paul Brodtkorb (New York, 1959), p. 115.

[10] "Emerson's Platonism," *New England Quarterly*, XVIII, 336 (Sept., 1945).

present. We are to reconcile spirit and matter. . . . Nothing else remains for us to do. Stand still we cannot. To go back is equally impossible.[11]

It is important to notice from this statement that Ripley is not advocating idealism, for to advocate one side of the opposition can scarcely be called a reconciliation. If we object that the idealists do not deny the reality of matter, affirming it as a manifestation or phenomenon of spirit, it can be argued that neither do the materialists deny the reality of spirit, affirming it as a development or phenomenon of matter. "Emerson knew only too well," Robert Pollock wrote in *Thought*, "that reality resists every attempt to reduce it to an undifferentiated whole such as is to be found in a materialistic or spiritualistic monism."[12] The "mission of the present" was to find a third principle under which both could be subsumed. In his essay on Plato, Emerson called it a "union of impossibilities." In view of this I think Charles Feidelson is right when he says that Emerson's originality "consisted in trying to take his stand precisely at the gateway through which these movements pass";[13] "each extreme was tacitly conditioned by a third view in which both became partial."[14]

If we are prone to regard this monistic dualism, or dualistic monism, as a contradiction, then we should keep two things in mind: (1) the question is not so much what do we think now but what did Emerson think then; we must get that straight first; and (2) "contradiction itself," Stuart Brown happily phrases, "is sometimes only the logical name for mystery."[15] On the contrary, it seems to me that comparatively recent books—notably, Pierre Teilhard de Chardin's *The Phenomenon of Man*—are stating in longhand what the shorthand of Emerson has led us to misconstrue and therefore reject as the ravings of a crackpot. George Santayana's statement is probably correct finally:

If we ask ourselves what was Emerson's relation to the scientific and religious movements of his time, and what place he may claim in the history of opinion, we must answer that he belonged very little to the past, very little to the present, and almost wholly to that abstract

[11] Quoted in Charles Feidelson, Jr., *Symbolism and American Literature* (Chicago, 1959), p. 115.

[12] "A Reappraisal of Emerson," p. 104.

[13] *Symbolism and American Literature*, p. 127.

[14] *Ibid.*, p. 124.

[15] "Emerson's Platonism," p. 339.

sphere into which mystical or philosophic aspiration has carried a few men in all ages.[16]

Mystic or philosophic is right when applied to Emerson's conclusion, but the conflict of which monistic dualism is his resolution was the dilemma of the age, and perhaps Santayana is a little too hasty in removing him from any historic milieu. Before entering into an examination of Emerson's essay "Plato; Or the Philosopher," it will help to review romanticism, a movement which, like Emerson himself, too often has been caricatured by an easy acceptance of the popular image.

I

Modern criticism has made great advances in the study of romanticism, but an important aspect of it has been overlooked because it is the slipperiest to handle. The breakthrough made by Coleridge and Wordsworth has been labeled pantheistic because their fusion of matter and spirit has been taken as an identification, whereas their deepest thought implies, it seems to me, rather a mutual harmony of those opposites in a higher third realm where the opposition ceases though neither item is reduced to the other. The tension stated so well by them has become peculiarly ours, and their resolution has too, but because that comes so close to being downright ineffable we seem to have overlooked it, just as we have spotted the tension in Emerson only to have missed, more often than not, the really significant conclusion he reached.

A glance at Keats's "Ode on a Grecian Urn" will tie down what I mean, and will exemplify just why it is that spirit by itself is as insufficient as matter by itself, and that we need both at the same time, however contradictory, from the standpoint of these writers, English and American, to be happy. The central conflict in Keats's poem is a scenic one between permanence and change. The poet sees that both have their value, for what permanence lacks (for instance, "Bold lover, never, never, canst thou kiss") change possesses (the realization of the kiss), and vice versa, for once the kiss is realized the very overness of the experience must follow ("That leaves a heart high-sorrowful and cloy'd"). The trick is to get these together, and Keats, after playing each against the other, arrives at the dramatic resolution of the conflict: "Beauty

[16] *Interpretations of Poetry and Religion* (New York, 1957), p. 231.

is truth, truth beauty." This famous crux might be clarified if we substitute for the terms of the resolution the items which have been in conflict throughout the poem. The ending would then read: "Change is permanence, permanence change." Now Keats here could be interpreted in exactly the way we have grown accustomed to seeing Emerson. Keats desires change; therefore he is an experimental pragmatist. Keats desires permanence; therefore he is an idealist. Both are possible but both are wrong, or rather only half right. Keats desires change (matter), yes, but without permanence (spirit), no; he desires permanence (spirit), yes, but without change (matter), no: since he wants both he places them in a third realm where neither will cancel the other out. It is not this way here, he says, but it is somewhere: "that is all / Ye know on earth, and all ye need to know."[17]

Emerson's problem was the same. He wrote in "Experience" that "Our love of the real draws us to permanence, but health of body consists in circulation, and sanity of mind in variety or facility of association. We need change of objects" (III, 55). And later in the essay: "I know that the world I converse with in the city and in the farms is not the world I *think*. I observe that difference, and shall observe it. One day I shall know the value and law of this discrepance" (III, 84-85).

So: the polarity is between matter or materialism on the one hand and spirit or idealism on the other. Unifying them without sacrificing the properties of either is the romantic calculus. Matter is good because it has what spirit lacks and possesses the desired quality only because it does lack what is associated with spirit (permanence); and spirit is good because it has what matter lacks and is good only because it does lack what is associated with matter (change). We are faced with the dilemma that what makes each desirable is precisely what makes each inadequate by itself: their opposition to each other. Any synthesis of them is then distinctly mystical. Keats's and Emerson's are such syntheses.

There is more to this than meets the eye. On the surface it looks like only wishful thinking, having your cake and eating it too, but we begin to think twice when we learn that such a stream of thought was implicit in Plato himself, and that, in fact, almost two thousand years of philosophy—and literature—have in one way or another

[17] Cf. his "Bright Star" sonnet.

dealt with the same problem. In the romantic era a solution was forthcoming. An essential ambiguity in Plato's *Timaeus* was spotlighted, and Emerson found "the value and law of this discrepance."

II

Plato for so long has been misrepresented that only constant radio commercials over three years' time could erase the little brain pocket of idealism we have stuffed him into. Emerson knew that a man "who could see two sides of a thing" was no more of an idealist than he was a materialist. Hegel, Fichte, and Kant were the idealists, and somewhere along the line Plato was made an honorary member of the group with very high standing indeed. This was bound to happen because of a literary trope in the *Republic*. Emerson's Plato, however, was not the philosopher the Germans found in the *Republic,* but the Plato of the *Timaeus*, and that Plato is anything but an idealist. If one does not understand the *Timaeus,* he can never understand Emerson; the relation seems to me this close. But if the dialogue is grasped then Emerson's entire position, so strange, willy-nilly, here and there, contradictory, and incoherent before, suddenly becomes clear—movingly, thrillingly clear.

Only once in his essay on Plato does it sound as though Emerson is not describing himself: Socrates "can drink, too; has the strongest head in Athens; and after leaving the whole party under the table, goes away as if nothing had happened, to begin new dialogues with somebody that is sober. In short, he was what our country-people call 'an old one'" (IV, 71). This is not Emerson's poet who "should be tipsy with water," and Emerson is hardly "an old one," but the difference ends right there.

The essay does, however, reel back and forth between two opposite poles: the one and the many, spirit and matter. In other words, it is a first-class example of what we expect in Emerson—inconsistency and contradiction. Except, that is, for one thing: here we discover the logic behind it as we do not in other essays, or, if we do, not so clearly. The reason is that Emerson found Plato a monistic dualist; he found him believing that spirit and matter have an existence independent of each other, i.e., one is not a refinement of the other, but hinting at a higher ground in which they are reconciled into a bipolar unity. Plato's movement, like Emerson's, is what we saw in Keats's ode: there is permanence (spirit) and there is change (matter); somewhere they come together and we can enjoy the benefits of each, although here and now they would seem to cancel each other out. I suggested earlier that this was not just wishful thinking, that the attitude, as Emerson said, is "somewhat better than whim at least." We can now discover why.

In any copy of the *Timaeus* one passage might be set off in capitals or by italic type, for its influence on subsequent thought is nearly incalculable. It is this passage which Emerson chooses to quote; the rest of the essay revolves around it as does Emerson's philosophy itself:

> Let us declare the cause which led the Supreme Ordainer to produce and compose the universe. He was good; and he who is good has no kind of envy. Exempt from envy, he wished that all things should be as much as possible like himself. Whosoever, taught by wise men, shall admit this as the prime cause of the origin and foundation of the world, will be in the truth. (IV, 56-57)

If we can unravel that, we can understand Emerson.

Luckily, it has already been done for us. Arthur Lovejoy's book *The Great Chain of Being* is entirely devoted to the ramifications of this passage.[18] The explication of Plato, from which his examination proceeds, can be summarized as follows:

(a) If God is perfect then it is impossible that he could be jealous of anything less perfect, but if this is so then
(b) he requires by this necessity of his own nature, by this very perfect completion, that there be things less perfect, less complete, and therefore
(c) the world and its diversity paradoxically complete God, and we are logically faced with an empirical infinity, an absolute immersed in the relative.

This sounds like syntactic high jinks to the modern reader, a sort of verbal abracadabra, but Mr. Lovejoy has demonstrated conclusively the pervasive influence which this ambiguity of "two-Gods-in-One, of a divine completion which was yet *not* complete in itself," has had down the centuries. Somehow, because of his very completeness, God is incomplete: he requires the world. Since

[18] Cambridge, Mass., 1957; see pp. 49-50 for the statement of departure which follows here in summary.

God requires material things and does not have anything material in his nature, being pure spirit, there must be a higher ground of which both matter and spirit are attributes. We should begin to smell the tracks of Emerson's inconsistency, his shifting back and forth with an emphasis first on spirit and then on matter. Following Plato's speculation he is postulating a third realm beyond both and containing both. The American dream of enjoying the many and the one at the same time, the ideal and the real, has a chance of coming true. Emerson also, American par excellence, wanted both and spotted a chance to have them, with Plato, of all people, to back him up. Mr. Gray writes most cogently on this point that

just as we are driven from Materialism by the need to take account of the appearance of something forever different from matter, so we are driven from the deeper but still inadequate conception of evolving spirit, in order to give any reality or independence to the individual. And thus is Emerson driven to his final theory of the identity of subject and object in "a substance older and deeper that either mind or matter." . . . We must find this Reality to be essentially One, yet to include in itself both spirit and nature, and to have therefore a reality as great as theirs and a potency as effective in producing a world of actual spirit and of actual nature.[19]

This reality, in Emerson's phrase, is "the union of impossibilities" or "the marriage of thoughts and things."

That Emerson saw in Plato what Mr. Lovejoy has shown us is there cannot be doubted. First there is the fact that he quoted the same passage, which would not be significant by itself except that Emerson goes on and describes Plato's philosophy in such a way as to prove he did have that passage especially in mind and was fully aware of its implications. The tone of the essay is one of complete approval and affirmation in which Emerson clearly allies himself with the Greek. In Plato "a balanced soul was born, perceptive of the two elements"; his argument, Emerson tells us, is "self-poised and spherical"; he saw the "upper and the under side of the medal of Jove," and

imbibed the idea of one Deity, in which all things are absorbed. The unity of Asia and the detail of Europe; the infinitude of the Asiatic soul and the defining, result-loving, machine-making, surface-seeking,

[19] *Emerson: A Statement of New England Transcendentalism as Expressed in the Philosophy of Its Chief Exponent* (Palo Alto, 1917), p. 51.

opera-going Europe,—Plato came to join, and, by contact, to enhance the energy of each. (IV, 53-54)

There is one remark which urges the polarity we find throughout Emerson and re-states what Ripley had called "the mission of the present"; but more than this it develops A and B of the formula above:

> All philosophy, of East and West, has the same centripetence. Urged by an opposite necessity, the mind returns from the one to that which is not one, but other or many; from cause to effect; and affirms the necessary existence of variety, the self-existence of both, as each is involved in the other. These strictly-blended elements it is the problem of thought to separate and to reconcile. (IV, 48)

That is to arrive at C, at a philosophy of dualistic monism, of "Two-Gods-in-One."

Emerson found the same duality in the *Timaeus* and he saw the reconciliation that Plato was leading to. In "Works and Days" he calls it a "mid-plain," and we can place special emphasis on the passage in which it occurs, for just previous to it Emerson had written that "the scholar must look for the right hour for Plato's *Timaeus*":

> This miracle is hurled into every beggar's hands. The blue sky is a covering for a market and for the cherubim and seraphim. The sky is the varnish or glory with which the Artist has washed the whole work,—the verge or confines of matter and spirit. Nature could no farther go. Could our happiest dream come to pass in solid fact,—could a power open our eyes to behold "millions of spiritual creatures walk the earth",—I believe I should find that mid-plain on which they move floored beneath and arched above with the same web of blue depth which weaves itself over me now, as I trudge the streets on my affairs. (VII, 171)

Explicit is the dichotomy and the desire for union—not one into the other but both into a third of "spiritual creatures" and "solid fact"; both into a dualism which is nevertheless monistic, a oneness of two. That this is what he means is clear from a journal entry on May 26, 1839. Though he is speaking of man's relationship to nature, this is the vibration of a higher conclusion to a lower level; the meaning is the same though the terms are different: "If, as Hedge thinks, I overlook great facts in stating the absolute laws of the soul; if, as he seems to represent it, the world is not a dualism, is not a bipolar unity, but is two, is *Me* and It, then is there the alien, the unknown, and all we have believed and chanted out of our deep instinctive hope is a pretty dream."[20]

In beginning his book, F. O. Matthiessen rightly says that "the problem that confronts us in dealing with Emerson is the hardest we shall have to meet, because of his inveterate habit of stating things in opposites." Matthiessen goes on to say, however, that the "representative man whom he most revered was Plato. For Plato had been able to bridge the gap between the many and the One, society and solitude."[21] Emerson's essay on Plato seems to me the key to that "inveterate habit of stating things in opposites." From the apex of the triangle, that "substance older and deeper than either mind or matter," which Plato implies, Emerson can look down with equal favor upon ascetic withdrawal and business know-how, upon the left angle of material progress and upon the right angle of spiritual development. "A believer in Unity, a seer of Unity, I yet behold two."[22] He can plug materialism in "Self-Reliance" and "Experience" while insisting upon its opposite in "The Transcendentalist" and "Nature," or he can combine the two and work both ends against each other, as in "Circles." It doesn't make any difference. The simultaneous superiority of action and "what is intellectualized," in James's terms, is possible because both are part and parcel of the same ground; though opposite on the triangle, both lines eventually converge and mingle at the same point.

> Each new step we take in thought reconciles twenty seemingly discordant facts, as expressions of one law. Aristotle and Plato are reckoned the respective heads of two schools. A wise man will see that Aristotle platonizes. By going one step farther back in thought, discordant opinions are reconciled by being seen to be two extremes of one principle . . . . (II, 308)

We have started off on the wrong foot with Emerson, or rather on two wrong feet. He is not an idealist. He is not a materialist. He does not dissolve matter into spirit nor does he dismiss spirit into matter. Neither idealists nor materialists have understood the Emersonian principle that only the whole truth could be true at all.

[20] *Journals of Ralph Waldo Emerson,* ed. Edward Waldo Emerson and Waldo Emerson Forbes (Boston, 1909-1914), V, 206.

[21] *American Renaissance,* p. 3.

[22] *Journals,* IV, 248.

In *The Shaping of the Modern Mind,* Crane Brinton speaks of the "eternal contrast, the eternal tension, so strong in Western culture, between this world and the next, the real and the ideal, the practical and the desirable."[23] This is especially the American tension, and it finds its loudest drumbeater for both sides in Emerson. Floyd Stovall's description of the typical American fits Emerson snugly:

> His very egotism is heartening because it is naive, as if it were but the measure of his pride in his humanity. Beyond question, he is a materialist; yet in his heart of hearts he is also a perfectionist and an idealist. He who would understand America must resolve this contradiction.[24]

It is true. We keep asking ourselves with Thoreau, "Shall I go to heaven or a-fishing?"[25] We find in ourselves "an instinct toward a higher, or, as it is named, spiritual life, as do most men, and another toward a primitive rank and savage one," and again with Thoreau, we "reverence them both."[26] It was these two fish that Thoreau tried to catch with one hook at Walden. We do not believe him when he says that he did. We are caught between hating what is not spiritual and loving all that is most delicious of earth. We cannot stand the effervescence of heaven or the tediousness of the world; so we talk of Moby Dick, the great symbol, who is a little bit of each and not wholly either. Moby Dick: who can swim, dive, rinse, and roll (because in time and in a real ocean), but everlastingly (because in timelessness and spacelessness).

Melville was not so far away from Emerson and Thoreau as he thought he was. He would have found in Emerson, had he looked closely enough, the same solution to his problem that Emerson found to his in Plato: there is no reason for being alarmed that if you choose one, the earth (real), you automatically lose the other, heaven (the ideal), and vice versa; you can have both, change and permanence, because they are together in a third realm. Emerson did not deny the material any more than Melville denied the spiritual. Both were trying to save each from confiscation by the other. They represent two horns of the same problem but we have

[23] New York, 1959, p. 241.
[24] *American Idealism* (Norman, Okla., 1943), p. 4
[25] *The Writings of Henry David Thoreau* (Boston, 1893), II, 349.
[26] *Ibid.,* p. 327.

forgotten that they were after the same conclusion: " 'Beauty is truth, truth beauty,'—that is all / Ye know on earth, and all ye need to know."

This was the theme of the time and has continued to haunt American literature ever since. If we want to understand America and resolve this contradiction, we would do well to begin with Emerson's essay on Plato. There the two streams branch out, the ideal and the real, but they branch out from a common source, the fire's center, which gives both equal meaning.

Transcendentalism and Psychotherapy: Another Look at Emerson

William E. Bridges

WRITING HOME FROM PROVIDENCE, RHODE ISLAND, where he was lecturing in the winter of 1840, Emerson told his mother,

> You must know I am reckoned here a Transcendentalist, and what that beast is, all persons in Providence have a great appetite to know: So I am carried duly about from house to house, and all the young persons ask me, when the Lecture is coming upon the great subject. In vain I disclaim all knowledge of that sect of Lidian's,—it is still expected I shall break out with the New Light in the next discourse. I have read here my essay on the Age, the one on Home, one on Love, & one on Politics,—These seem all to be regarded as mere screens and subterfuges while this dread Transcendentalism is still kept back. They have various definitions of the word current here. One man, of whom I have been told in good earnest defined it as "Operations on the Teeth". . . .[1]

Now, this is a heartening story, for though I have often found Transcendentalism confusing, I have never found it *that* confusing. More my style is "our accomplished Mrs. B" who liked to define Transcendentalism, according to Emerson's journal, "with a wave of her hand [and the words], *A little beyond*."[2] For coverage, that definition is hard to beat—although just *what* it is beyond and exactly what lies beyond whatever it is that is on this side, well, these are things that are still in doubt.

What I would like to do in the following essay is to suggest that Emerson's thought can very fruitfully be considered in the light of several related systems of modern psychotherapy and of psychologically oriented theology. On a superficial level, of course,

[1] *The Letters of Ralph Waldo Emerson*, ed. Ralph L. Rusk (New York, 1939), II, 266. (Hereafter called *Letters*.)

[2] *The Journals and Miscellaneous Notebooks of Ralph Waldo Emerson*, ed. William Gilman *et al.*, Vol. V, ed. Merton M. Sealts, Jr. (Cambridge, Mass., 1965), p. 218. (Hereafter called *JMN*. No attempt has been made in quoting from this source to indicate Emerson's revisions or the editorial symbols.)

it has always been realized that the reading of "Self-Reliance" had a vaguely therapeutic effect on the discouraged and self-doubting. But that Emerson provides his audience with something approximating a system for analyzing modern man's psychic dislocations and a coherent set of therapeutic counsels for meeting them has not been sufficiently appreciated. And so in this essay, I should like to consider him, not as the heir to the Protestant tradition and a student of Platonists, the various Oriental scriptures, and his own European contemporaries, but as a forerunner of those who concern themselves with the potentialities of, and the dangers to, selfhood: psychotherapists like Carl Rogers, Erich Fromm, and Frederick Perls, and theologians like Martin Buber and Paul Tillich.

I

It is ironical that Emerson is purported to be too optimistic and idealistic for modern tastes, for he constantly reiterated his low opinion of the men he saw about him: "Respect a man! assuredly," he wrote in his journal, "but in general only as the potential God. . . . Now he is only a scrap, an ort, an end & in his actual being no more worthy of your veneration than the poor lunatic."[3] The difficulty was, he told a Boston audience in 1837, that

> men do not imagine that they are anything more than fringes and tassels to the institutions into which they are born. They take the law from things; they serve their property, their trade or profession; books; other men; some religious dogma; some political party or school of opinion that has been palmed on them; and bow the back & the knee & the soul to their own creation. . . .[4]

For one who is reputed to be too lofty for facts (Hawthorne called him "the mystic, stretching his hand out of cloud-land, in vain search for something real"),[5] Emerson reveals a surprisingly acute sense of the psychological dynamics of modern society. In *English Traits*, for example, he foreshadows modern social theory with his comments on machine work: ". . . it is found that the machine unmans the user. What he gains in making cloth, he loses in

[3] *JMN*, Vol. IV, ed. Alfred R. Ferguson, p. 335.

[4] "Human Culture," *The Early Lectures of Ralph Waldo Emerson*, Vol. II, ed. Stephen Whicher, Robert Spiller, and Wallace Williams (Cambridge, Mass., 1964), p. 218.

[5] Nathaniel Hawthorne, *The American Notebooks*, ed. Randall Stewart (New Haven, 1932), p. 157.

general power. . . . The incessant repetition of the same hand-work dwarfs the man, robs him of his strength, wit and versatility, to make a pin polisher, a buckle-maker, or any other specialty."[6] It was not only the machine worker, moreover, who was unmanned by his function in the prevailing economic order, for Emerson pointed out in an earlier essay that "the common experience is that the man fits himself as well as he can to the customary details of that work or trade he falls into, and tends it as a dog turns a spit. Then is he a part of the machine he moves; the man is lost."[7] As he announced near the beginning of "The American Scholar," socio-economic means were increasingly becoming ends in themselves, and "man is thus metamorphosed into a thing."[8]

The process by which the individual became thus depersonalized was characterized by what Emerson liked to call "Otherism." By this term he meant man's tendency to project his own positive qualities into others and to esteem them there as he cannot esteem them within himself. "The very sentiment I expressed yesterday without heed," he mused in his journal, "shall sound memorable to me tomorrow if I hear it from another."[9] In the light of subsequent social psychology, it is interesting that this particular journal entry begins, "I see plainly the charm which belongs to Alienation or Otherism," for in many ways Emerson's "Otherism" is very like "alienation" as Erich Fromm uses the term. Compare, for example, these two passages, the first from Fromm's *The Sane Society* and the second from Emerson's "Self-Reliance":

Man does not experience himself as the active bearer of his own powers and richness, but as an impoverished "thing," dependent on powers outside of himself, unto whom he has projected his living substance. . . . [Man's] whole creation . . . stands over and above him. He does not feel himself as a creator and center, but as the servant of a Golem which his hands have built.[10]

The man in the street, finding no worth in himself which corresponds to the force which built a tower or sculptured a marble god, feels poor

[6] *The Complete Works of Ralph Waldo Emerson* (Centenary Edition), ed. E. W. Emerson (Boston, 1903–1904), V, 166-167. (Hereafter called *Works*.)

[7] "Spiritual Laws," *Works*, II, 142.

[8] *Works*, I, 83.

[9] *JMN*, V, 254. See also p. 162.

[10] (Greenwich, Conn., 1965), pp. 114-115. The whole section entitled "Alienation" (pp. 111-137) should be read with Emerson in mind.

when he looks on these. To him a palace, a statue, or a costly book have an alien and forbidding air . . . and seem to say like that, "Who are you, Sir?"[11]

It is particularly in his early lectures that he analyzes the psychological effects of the social forces of his era, and there the picture that he draws clearly foreshadows the now-familiar patterns of life in the mass society. In "The Present Age" he writes that

we have lost all reverence for the state. It is merely our boarding house. We have lost all reverence for the Church; it is also republican. We call a spade, a spade. We have great contempt for the superstitions and nonsense which blinded the eyes of all foregoing generations. But we pay a great price for this freedom. The old faith is gone; the new loiters on the way. The world looks very bare and cold. We have lost our Hope. . . . Out of this measuring and decorum and prudence what refreshment can ever issue? . . . I have heard that no man sees his face in the glass without a melancholy emotion.[12]

Emerson saw the degree to which his society had managed to "demythify" life, as political and religious entities become mere associations, and the breaking of taboos leaves things simply as *things*; and he also saw the other side of the resulting liberation, the side on which the person was simply delivered into a new and terrifying emptiness.

In a slightly later "Lecture on the Times" Emerson described more precisely the "disease" that beset his age: "our torment is Unbelief, the Uncertainty as to what we ought to do; the distrust of the value of what we do."[13] And behind this doubt lay the person's estrangement from himself, the experience of himself as an alien that Emerson caught so graphically in the little Kafkaesque fable that he recorded in his journal in the spring of 1838:

There was a simple man [who] grew so suddenly rich that, coming one day into his own stately door & hall in a reverie, he felt on his mind the accustomed burden of fear that now he should see a great person, & was making up his mouth to ask firmly if —— was at home, when he bethought himself, Who is ——? who is it I should ask for? & on second thought, he saw it was his own house, & he was ——.[14]

[11] *Works*, II, 61-62.
[12] *Early Lectures*, p. 169.
[13] *Works*, I, 282.
[14] *JMN*, V, 460.

It was not simply work that estranged man from himself, for the whole cultural style of his day seemed to Emerson inimical to self-possession. There was, for instance, the increasing importance of urban life and the improvement in transport and communication, all of which served to homogenize the population. Together with the destruction of hereditary elites and the substitution of popular opinion as the organ of official taste and policy, these things put the individual in a position that Emerson believed to be historically unique. On the positive side, the situation gave "every man an opportunity to win respect by his behavior" instead of his birth. But unfortunately the very same circumstances

> force every man to respect the opinion of multitudes where once it was sufficient to consult the good will of a few. In the multitudes of modern society and in the domestic life which has taken the place of the camp or the public table of the ancient communities, opportunity of intimate acquaintance with each citizen is not afforded; so that decorum answers to the eye of the public the purpose of virtue and wisdom.[15]

This diction is traditional, but the line of analysis is not. The picture it draws of modern man reminds one of Riesman's other-directed man with the internal "radar screen" who forever scans the social horizon for signals by which to steer. Emerson's "decorum" refers not to manners but to behavior that is shaped to meet the expectations of others or the person's own preconception (itself the product of others' past expectations) of what he ought to do in such and such a situation.

The situation that produces decorum is, in Emerson's lexicon, "society"—a term that refers as much to the orientation toward others as it does to their actual presence. "Not insulation of place, but independence of spirit" provides a break with "society."[16] Yet this independence of spirit was always treated by Emerson as well-nigh impossible to achieve in others' presence, and that led him to argue that the real person came across more authentically in writing than in conversation: "Instead of the old verse, 'Speak that I may know thee,'" he wrote his brother Charles, "I write, 'Speak that I may suspect thee; write, that I may *know* thee.'"[17] So obvious did

[15] "The Present Age," *Early Lectures*, p. 162.
[16] *Works*, I, 174.
[17] *Letters*, I, 191.

this equation of "society" and "decorum" seem to Emerson that he told one of his early audiences, "If a man lived alone it is plain he could never act foolishly, never with affectation, but always he would be in earnest. It is with Society that Seeming comes in."[18]

As "society" is the mental framework and social situation producing "decorum," so that other-directed form of behavior is the hallmark of the state of personal inauthenticity that he called "seeming." "Decorum," he believed, made people "not false in a few particulars, authors of a few lies, but false in all particulars. Their every truth is not quite true. Their two is not the real two, their four not the real four. . . ."[19]

"Seeming" ran so deep, he went on to say, that "we know not where to begin to set [such persons] right." Yet setting right the victims of "seeming" is Emerson's basic purpose as a lecturer and an essayist, and his work is an interlocking system of exhortations to this end. For "society," he said again and again, man must substitute *solitude*; in place of "decorum" he must develop *virtue*; and instead of "seeming," man must *be*. Behind these paired terms stands a single conceptual dualism: the contrast between alienation and self-recovery. (The latter term, like the former, is his own; in *Nature* he speaks of living as being a process of "continual self-recovery.")[20]

Self-recovery is not the recovery of a thing—a self—although it is difficult not to speak of it in these terms. Rather it is the re-opening of the lines of inner communication so that the person can once again respond authentically and openly to life around him. Like the modern-day Gestalt therapists, who have demonstrated so startlingly modern man's inability to respond to experience as a natural and total organism, Emerson spoke of our difficulties in knowing and saying what we feel as signs of a tragic loss of human power. It was only the poets (who were only complete persons, not specially talented ones) who retained what should be the universal capacity to respond. "Too feeble fall the impressions of nature on us to make us artists," he wrote in "The Poet": "Every touch should thrill. Every man should be so much an artist that he could

[18] "Being and Seeming," *Early Lectures*, p. 296.

[19] *Works*, II, 55.

[20] *Works*, I, 66.

report in conversation what had befallen him. Yet, in our experience, the rays or appulses have sufficient force to arrive at the senses, but not enough to reach the quick and compel the reproduction of them in speech."[21] More concrete than these generalizations were the instructions to himself that he recorded in his journal in 1835, instructions that can profitably be compared to the "here and now I am aware . . ." exercises that appear throughout the first section of *Gestalt Therapy* by Perls, Hefferline, and Goodman.[22] "Keep your eye & ear open to all impressions," writes Emerson, "but deepen no impression by effort, but take the opinion of the Genius within, what ought to be retained by you & what rejected by you. Keep, that is, the upright position. Resign yourself to your thoughts, & then every object will make that mark, that modification on your character which it ought."[23] This radical and total receptiveness has response as its natural sequel, and it is the basic state from which meaning could issue into the person's life. To speak of it as "mystical," however, is to tag it with a term that brings with it too many alien associations in the minds of most modern, Western readers. It would be more satisfactory to think of the state Emerson is urging as one of total "presence," wherein the whole person confronts his environment without conceptualizing it or otherwise distorting it into preconceived patterns. The whole person is "present," in that none of him is held back and hidden, and since the experience is unconceptualized and so unrelated to causes and effects, it is also "present" in the sense of being an expanse of pure awareness, unconnected to time-past and time-future.

Emerson's day (like our own) viewed a preoccupation with the present as being tantamount to selfish hedonism. Both the secular and the religious sectors of nineteenth-century American society were oriented toward a future in which present hopes could be materialized and present evils eradicated. Even today it seems to many of his readers that Emerson is playing some sort of a word game when he urges man to "set up the strong present tense" and not to "wander from the present, which is infinite, to a future

[21] *Works*, III, 6.
[22] (New York, n.d.), pp. 2-115 *passim*.
[23] *JMN*, V, 6-7.

which would be finite."[24] Far from playing with incongruities, however, Emerson is urging man to consider the present as a continuous state of being rather than as the dividing line between a past full of causes and an effect-laden future. He is reminding man that past and future are mental constructs, and that they are only incorporated into the human mind by learning; the child learns to remember the past and to calculate the possibilities of the future. The child develops (to use Emerson's term) the Understanding, and as he wrote his friend Hedge, without the Understanding "there could not be either porridge or politics."[25] But the Understanding has a tendency to overwhelm man's direct response to the here-and-now and to displace into past and future the highest potentials of presentness. "We say Paradise was; Adam fell; the Golden Age; & the like. We mean man is not as he ought to be; but our way of painting this is on Time, and we say Was."[26] A few months before, he had written in the same journal pages, "The Understanding, listening to reason, on one side, which saith *It is*, & to the senses, on the other side, which say *It is not*, takes middle ground & declares, *It will be*."[27] The mind did this in response to the threat of living in a world of absolute presence, but in so doing it blocked man's natural access to the world of ultimate values—a world which was not a lost paradise or a future heaven, but right there in the here-and-now.

One of the most important advantages of the natural landscape was its uninvolvement with the sequential framework in which purpose and regret robbed man of an independent present in which a person could live. So it is that he describes nature as a setting in which the person's attention is "absorbed by new pictures and by thoughts fast succeeding each other, until by degrees the recollection of home was crowded out of the mind, all memory obliterated by the tyranny of the present. . . ."[28] This too is the burden of one of his most famous passages, the "transparent eyeball" statement in *Nature*: "In the woods we return to reason and faith. . . . Standing on the bare ground,—my head bathed by the blithe air and up-

[24] *Works*, III, 64, and II, 284.
[25] *Letters*, II, 29.
[26] *JMN*, V, 371.
[27] *JMN*, V, 273.
[28] "Nature," *Works*, III, 170.

lifted into infinite space,—all mean egotism vanishes. I become a transparent eyeball; I am nothing; I see all." In the original journal entry from which this metaphorical description of total awareness and absolute openness to experience was taken, he had added that thereupon "the mind integrates itself again. The attention, which had been distracted into parts, is reunited, reinsphered. The whole of nature addresses itself to the whole man. We are reassured. It is more than a medicine. It is health."[29] The therapeutic terms are significant, as is the fact that the previously quoted description of how nature absorbs the attention is immediately followed by the sentence, "These enchantments are medicinal, they sober and heal us."[30]

As here used, "health" was not a state existing within the person but between the person and the elements of his experience. Emerson sometimes wondered, in fact, whether there was anything very significant to be said about an individual taken out of his relational context: "Do you not see," he asked himself, "that a man is a bundle of relations, that his entire strength consists not in his properties but in his innumerable relations?"[31] This matter of relation—of warped actual relation between person and experience and of potential healthy relation—is at the very heart of Emerson's thought. The center of the Emersonian program of self-therapy is the appeal to detach oneself from the old and damaging relation to experience and to fashion a new relation: to stop existing behind a protective screen of conceptualizations and to begin living in a state of full presence. In his appeals of this sort, however, Emerson confused his own issues somewhat by using terms inconsistently. Whenever he wished to contrast the person's direct presence with the indirect relation that the Understanding provided, he was likely to use "personal" and "individual" as positive terms; but when he wanted to contrast the experience of direct presence with what actual individuals mistakenly believed to be life, he used "personal" and "individual" very differently—witness his advice in *Nature* to be "resolute to detach every object from personal relations" and his description of the artist's power (in "The Poet") as that of bringing us

[29] *JMN*, V, 19.

[30] "Nature," *Works*, III, 170.

[31] *JMN*, V, 266. See also "Beauty," *Works*, VI, 281, where he writes, "The bird is not in its ounces and inches, but in its relations to Nature."

out of "that jail-yard of individual relations in which [we are] enclosed."[32]

In using these terms negatively, Emerson is calling on men to stop assigning persons and objects specious "identities" that are, in fact, no more than projections from the viewers' own self-systems. Instead, he calls upon men to begin the radical and ongoing process of seeing objects-in-themselves and to experience thereby an environment that is absolutely discontinuous with the self, an environment made up of unique entities that are not objects-in-a-classification-system nor anything that we can already have known through others' descriptions. "Whilst I read the poets, I think that nothing new can be said about morning and evening," he told his Dartmouth College audience in 1838,

> but when I see the daybreak I am not reminded of these Homeric, or Shakespearian, or Miltonic, or Chaucerian pictures. No, but I feel perhaps the pain of an alien world; a world not yet subdued by the thought; or I am cheered by the moist, warm, glittering, budding, melodious hour, that takes down the narrow walls of my soul, and extends its life and pulsation to the very horizon.[33]

Since this terrible and wonderful world of the here and now is not the familiar world picture that we carry in our heads, it is "impersonal." But in another sense it is totally personal, for it can be confronted only directly through one set of senses and realized through them in one mind. So, balancing his warnings that experience must be detached from "personal relation" to be made real is his equally unqualified demand that the person put himself back into the very center of his world. One finds this latter demand throughout his writing, most personally stated at the critical time that he was reaching his decision to move to Concord. At that time he wrote of his resolve to work "as I project in highest most farsighted hours," adding, "Well, & what do you project? Nothing less than to look at every object in its relation to Myself."[34]

A paradox, to be sure, but his message was no more than that to gain a new world, the person must lose an old one. Yet his terms really do set up a block to comprehension, as it is confusing

[32] *Works*, I, 74, and III, 28.
[33] *Works*, I, 168.
[34] *JMN*, IV, 272.

to find this prophet of "individualism" writing in his journal, "that which is individual and remains individual in my experience is of no value."[35] Such data were useless because their validity was limited to the particular interpersonal context from which they were derived and to what he called the "biographical Ego"[36] that was an adjustment to it. Trusting and cultivating *that* ego was just the opposite of what Emerson was urging, and although he never met this linguistic difficulty head on, he commented on a similar problem when he wrote that the word "subjective . . . is made to cover two things, a good and a bad."[37]

One of the ironies of Emerson's reputation is that the kind of individualism he dismissed as worthless should so often have been understood to be his prescription for man's ills. But an even deeper irony is that in defending him against the misconception that self-reliance meant narrow selfishness, his champions have all too often twisted his intent in the opposite direction. Thus, in distinguishing Emerson's message from what his enemies claimed it to be, Frothingham wrote that "by 'self-culture' . . . [Emerson] meant the culture of that nobler self which includes heart, and conscience, sympathy, spirituality" and other altruistic qualities.[38] Even in the usually very reliable *Emerson Handbook* by Carpenter we find that "the 'self' to be relied on is the higher 'self' which is governed by principles rather than by circumstances. . . . The 'Self' of the essay ["Self-Reliance"] is the 'soul' or conscience, which communicates directly with the 'Over-Soul' or God."[39] The difficulty with these statements is that the concepts of a *nobler* and a *higher* self obscure the issue by making "self" a kind of Platonic ideal toward which actual men struggle. The problem here is that Emerson meant "self" to refer to the realm of psychology, not philosophy, and that he conceived of man's task as that of realizing fully the person he already was rather than as that of striving to transform himself into an ideal person that he ought to be.

The rejection of the principle of oughtness and the indorsement

[35] *The Journals of Ralph Waldo Emerson*, ed. E. W. Emerson and W. E. Forbes (Boston, 1909–1914), V, 36. (Hereafter called *Journals.*)

[36] *Journals*, VIII, 79.

[37] *Journals*, V, 347.

[38] Octavius B. Frothingham, *Transcendentalism in New England: A History*, Introduction by Sydney E. Ahlstrom (New York, 1959), p. 150.

[39] Frederic Ives Carpenter, *Emerson Handbook* (New York, 1953), p. 59.

of realizing the self as it already exists is memorably summarized in the words of his brother, Charles, that Emerson copied into one of his notebooks after the young man's death:

> I have a dread of [—] say rather an antipathy to [—] whatever is imitative in states of mind as well as in action. The moment I say to myself I *ought* to feel thus & so life loses its sweetness [and] the soul her vigor & truth. I can only recover my genuine self by stopping short—refraining from every effort to shape my thought after a Form & giving it boundless freedom & horizon.[40]

With Charles, the condition of estrangement from his "genuine self" was only temporary, for he found that when he released his mind from the hold of some notion of what he "ought to feel," it brought him back again to himself and "after oscillation more or less protracted as the mind has been more or less forcibly pushed from its place I fall again into my orbit & recognize myself. . . ." In those less aware than Charles of the need for self-recovery, the alienation could lead to the state described by Emerson in his vignette of the acquaintance who "resembled a nest of Indian boxes, one after the other, each a new puzzle, & when you come to the last there's nothing in it." Far from being unique, this person seemed to Emerson really very typical of the modern predicament, and he wrote that "so [it is] with each man, a splendid barricade of circumstances, . . . name . . . professional character, . . . manners & speech but go behind all these & the Man [—] the self—is a poor, shrunken, distorted, imperceptible thing."[41]

The point is that the idea of self-reliance does not refer so much to the person's reliance on himself as it does to his reliance on his self—and on the *self* as many modern humanistic or existential psychotherapists use the term. This movement within contemporary psychology and psychiatry sees man quite differently from the way in which he is described by the Freudians and behaviorists, but in ways that often recall Emerson. To illustrate these parallels, here are some section headings from the introductory section of Carl Rogers's *On Becoming a Person*, where this great American psychologist summarizes his conclusions from his decades as a therapist: "I find I am more effective when I can listen acceptantly

[40] *JMN*, Vol. VI, ed. Ralph H. Orth, p. 267.
[41] *JMN*, IV, 51.

to myself, and can be myself"; "I can trust my experience"; "Evaluation by others is not a guide for me"; "Experience is, for me, the highest authority"; "I enjoy discovering order in experience"; "What is most personal is most general"; "It has been my experience that persons have a basically positive direction."[42]

In both Emerson and Rogers the way in which the person makes his own evaluations and sets his own course is by a process that transcends rationalistic calculation. Emerson, for example, wrote,

> I say *do not choose*; but that is a figure of speech by which I would distinguish what is commonly called *choice* among men, and which is a partial act, the choice of the hands, of the eyes, of the appetites, and not a whole act of the man. But that which I call right or goodness, is the choice of my constitution.[43]

Compare that statement to Rogers's description of the direction taken by the person as he responds to therapy:

> The person increasingly discovers that his own organism is trustworthy, that it is a suitable instrument for discovering the most satisfying behavior in each immediate situation. . . . To the extent that this person is open to all of his experience, he has access to all the available data in the situation, on which to base his behavior. He has knowledge of his own feelings and impulses, which are often complex and contradictory. . . . He is better able to permit his total organism, his conscious thought participating, to consider, weigh and balance each stimulus, need, and demand, and its relative weight and intensity.[44]

In the light of the widespread belief that Emerson is naively optimistic in his evaluations of individual power, it is important to notice several elements in these two defenses of the self as a reliable guide. First, they do not indorse "intuition" as opposed to "rationality," if these terms are taken as designating different elements in the person. Rather, both Emerson and Rogers speak for a total awareness of self-in-situation instead of the narrower focus on and objectification of the situation per se. Second, neither man suggests any mysterious inner organ of insight—only the resources of the whole person acting with as little screening out of experience as possible. Third, although both men sometimes argue tactically that

[42] Carl R. Rogers, *On Becoming a Person* (Boston, 1961), pp. 16-27 *passim*.
[43] "Spiritual Laws," *Works*, II, 140.
[44] Rogers, p. 118.

the person will always be led aright when thus oriented to experience, what each man actually assumes is that real openness simply assures continued contact with the situation and one's own feelings, and so makes readjustments continuously possible.

Both men associate external concepts of oughtness with the tendency to screen out potentially important elements in experience, and so both reject them as aids. Neither man would argue that many particular "oughts" are not true, but only that their use categorizes experience and patterns it mechanically in such a fashion that trustworthy patterns inherent in the experience are destroyed. Emerson's statement of his faith in such patterns is the more succinct: "Every man's condition is a solution in hieroglyphic to those inquiries he would put"; and again, "Let me record day by day my honest thought without prospect or retrospect, and I cannot doubt, it will be found symmetrical, though I mean it not and see it not."[45] On his part, Rogers quotes approvingly the following summary that a patient made of his progress toward self-recovery:

> You know, it seems as if all the energy that went into holding the arbitrary pattern [of my life] together was quite unnecessary—a waste. You think you have to make the pattern yourself; but there are so many pieces, and it's so hard to see where they fit. . . . Then you discover that left to themselves the jumbled pieces fall quite naturally into their own places, and a living pattern emerges without any effort at all on your part. Your job is just to discover it. . . . You must let your own experience tell you its own meaning; the minute you tell it what it means, you are at war with yourself.[46]

The "meaning" and the "pattern" here referred to are dynamic ones rather than static answers to the person's difficulties. To Rogers, in fact, it is a willingness to give up such fixed positions that is a critical stage of self-recovery, and he writes that "the individual seems to become more content to be a *process* rather than a *product*."[47] Emerson too believes in the dynamic character of life, and he argues that this is lost when response is frozen and fixed as data that are organized in the memory. In his journal he reflected that "the truest state of mind, rested in, becomes false. Thought is

[45] *Works*, I, 4, and II, 58.
[46] Rogers, p. 114.
[47] Rogers, p. 122.

the mana that cannot be stored. It will be sour if kept, & tomorrow must be gathered anew."[48]

In these terms, Transcendentalism is an appeal to alienated man to recover and trust his own responses to experience—to take a stance toward that experience that is one of total confrontation and total awareness. In his attempt to bring into full consciousness "my honest thought without prospect or retrospect," Emerson meant to bring to his experience the same degree of presence that he found wonderful in natural objects. "These roses under my window make no reference to former roses or to better ones," he wrote in "Self-Reliance":

> they are for what they are; they exist with God today. There is no time to them. There is simply the rose. It is perfect in every moment of its existence. Before a leaf bud has burst, its whole life acts; in the full-blown flower there is no more; in the leafless root there is no less. Its nature is satisfied and it satisfies nature in all moments alike. But man postpones or remembers; he does not live in the present, but with reverted eye laments the past, or heedless of the riches that surround him, stands on tiptoe to foresee the future. He cannot be happy and strong until he too lives with nature in the present, above time.[49]

The quality of the natural object that most attracted Emerson was what he sometimes termed its "self-existency"—that quality that made him point out that "with sublime propriety God is described as saying, I AM."[50]

When his concern for the self-existency of true Being was combined with his fear of the mental state he called Society and the inauthenticity he called Seeming, Emerson could deliver himself of proclamations about our need for independence of each other that are very hard to take: "We should meet each morning as from foreign countries, and, spending the day together, should depart at night, as into foreign countries. In all things I would have the island of man inviolate. Let us sit apart as the gods, talking from peak to peak all round Olympus. No degree of affection need invade this region."[51] Whenever he could afford to abandon this tacti-

[48] *JMN*, V, 38.
[49] "Self-Reliance," *Works*, II, 67.
[50] "Spiritual Laws," *Works*, II, 160.
[51] "Manners," *Works*, III, 137.

cal position of defending man's need for independence from others' expectations, his tone changed. Such was the case when, after revising his essay on Love, he was dissatisfied with the result because it said less than he felt: he was, he suggested in his journal, "cold at the surface only as a sort of guard and compensation for the fluid tenderness" in his heart; then, as if not quite satisfied with the logic of that, he added, "in silence we must wrap much of our life, because it is too fine for speech, because also we cannot explain it to others, and because somewhat we cannot yet understand." But then, after that groping after reasons, he comes to the point and acknowledges his fear that the kinds of human relationships he seeks are not actually available to him. "We do not live as angels," he writes sadly,

> eager to introduce each other to new perfections in our brothers and sisters, and frankly avowing our delight in each new trait of character, . . . but that which passes for love in the world gets official, and instead of embracing, hates all the divine traits that dare to appear in other persons. A better and holier society will mend this selfish cowardice, and we shall have brave ties of affection, not petrified by law, not dated or ordained by law to last for one year, for five years, or for life; but drawing their date, like all friendship, from itself only.[52]

This is, actually, no more than the simple corollary of the concept of life-as-process, for that view of living demands that persons allow one another to function openly in the ongoing relation of self to experience and without trying to tie one another to patterns of predictability: only when one can allow another to be himself by being his self can a relationship foster growth.

But most of what passed in Emerson's day for constructive human relationships were anything but the encounters between complete persons in which the meeting of self with self confirmed and strengthened each. Rather, as in our own day, they tended to be relations between two self-interested individuals, each surrounded by a conceptual field into which others were fitted as objects with a purpose. Much that has been written on Emerson has failed to appreciate the implications of this situation, partly because it is too often assumed that his thought really has no roots in the socio-psychic realities of his age; and thus frequently it is assumed that

[52] *Journals*, V, 411-412.

he urged independence, isolation, and self-containment as ends in themselves. In fact, however, Emerson meant to urge them upon his readers as means and not ends—as necessities in response to a social situation encouraging self-estrangement rather than as ideals in themselves. And that is why his journals show him to have been frequently depressed with the actuality of aloneness, although out of context these reactions might seem to contradict the optimism of his faith in self-reliance. Under the heading "Society an imperfect union," he wrote:

> Is it not pathetic that the action of men on men is so partial? We never touch but at points. The most that I can have or be to my fellow man, is it the reading of his book, or the hearing of his project in conversation? I approach some Carlyle with desire and joy. I am led on from month to month with an expectation of some total embrace & oneness with a noble mind, & learn at least that it is only so feeble & remote & hiant action as reading a Mirabeau or a Diderot paper, & a few the like. This is all that can be looked for. More we shall not be to each other. Baulked soul![53]

In "The American Scholar" he made the same point by quoting the Swiss educator Johann Heinrich Pestalozzi, who had written, "I learned that no man in God's wide earth is either willing or able to help any other man." To that Emerson added simply, "Help must come from the bosom alone."[54]

Emerson's tone here is one of resignation, and he evidently believes himself to be facing squarely the real nature of things. What Emerson hoped was that the person might capitalize on his inevitable aloneness by turning inward and finding there the strength to Be amid the social encouragements of Seeming. That hope was what William Henry Channing referred to when he listed at mid-century the central "maxims" of Transcendentalism: "Trust, dare, and be. . . . All that your fellows can claim or need is that you should become, in fact, your highest self."[55] Insofar as Transcendentalism went beyond self-therapy, it did so in the severely limited manner suggested by Channing: first, you can help others only by being yourself and encouraging them thereby to be themselves;

[53] *JMN*, V, 328.
[54] *Works*, I, 113.
[55] Perry Miller, ed., *The American Transcendentalists* (Garden City, N. Y., 1957), p. 37.

second, you can be yourself only by being your self. This trust in the potentialities of Being, that leads the person to "dare" to Be, foreshadows the ideas of Paul Tillich, and the whole Transcendental endeavor prefigures the positions taken in our day by Martin Buber, who has written:

He who really knows how far our generation has lost the way of true freedom, of free giving between I and Thou, must himself, by virtue of the demand implicit in every great knowledge of this kind, practise directness—even if he were the only man on earth who did it—and not depart from it until scoffers are struck with fear, and hear in his voice the voice of their own suppressed longings.[56]

This "directness," this speaking out of the person who really *is*, provides Buber's starting point and corresponds to Emerson's doctrine of self-reliance. But Buber makes it very clear that this confrontation of the other is not in any sense an imposition of one's ways on that other. On the contrary, he writes that

the chief presupposition for the rise of genuine dialogue is that each should regard his partner as the very one he is. I become aware of him, aware that he is different, essentially different from myself, in the definite, unique way which is peculiar to him, and I accept whom I thus see, so that in full earnestness I can direct what I say to him as the person he is.[57]

This "acceptance of otherness," as he terms it elsewhere,[58] is a reminder that human relations of a profound sort have nothing to do with a merging or a blending of identities and that, on the contrary, relation depends on separateness. That is what Emerson meant when he wrote in "Friendship":

I hate, where I looked for a manly furtherance or at least a manly resistance, to find a mush of concession. Better be a nettle in the side of your friend than his echo. The condition which high friendship demands is the ability to do without it. . . . There must be very two, before there can be very one.[59]

The experiential vision that Emerson sought was of a world made up of unique entities, each of which awaited, and in fact de-

[56] Martin Buber, *The Knowledge of Man* (New York, 1965), p. 79.
[57] Buber, p. 79.
[58] Buber, p. 69.
[59] *Works*, II, 208-209.

manded, his attention and full awareness. The person's environment would then live in his response to it, a response that provides him with his own "original relation" to it. Every element in that experience must acquire for the person a significance which, for lack of a better term, we may call "symbolic." But the symbol corresponds to a way of knowing and not to the resulting knowledge, to the experience of encounter and not to the remembered event. This was the distinction he made between the mystic and the poet, wherein he argued that the former discovers a symbolic relation and then fixes its significance for all time, whereas the poet realizes that "all symbols are fluxional; all language is vehicular and transitive, and is good, as ferries and horses are, for conveyance, not as farms and houses are, for homestead."[60] The poet is, one must remember, simply the complete and self-recovered person; and so his is only everyone's potential openness to experience whereby time is transcended in a state of pure presence—a state better described in images of motion than in those of rest, for "life is a progress, and not a station."[61]

From the beginning, this aspect of Emerson's thought has seemed irresponsible to many of his readers, for an abandonment to the flux of experience is incompatible with conventional notions of social responsibility. Yet as Emerson himself pointed out, responsibility is by no means a simple idea. "You may fulfill your round of duties by clearing yourself in the *direct*, or in the *reflex* way," he wrote. The latter, by fulfilling everyone's expectations, is really endless, for it forces you to decide "whether you have satisfied your relations to father, mother, cousin, neighbor, town, cat and dog—whether any of these can upbraid you."[62] But in that the direct way was the inner obligation to respond, it was certainly no easier; in fact he had to admit in private that he was not really capable of it except at moments:

Should I obey an irregular impulse and establish every new relation that my fancy prompted with the men and women I see, I should not be followed by my faculties; they would play me false in making good their very suggestions. They delight in inceptions, but they warrant

[60] "The Poet," *Works*, III, 34.
[61] "Compensation," *Works*, II, 122.
[62] "Self-Reliance," *Works*, II, 74.

nothing else. I see very well the beauty of sincerity, and tend that way, but if I should obey the impulse so far as to say to my fashionable acquaintance, "You are a coxcomb,—I dislike your manners—I pray you avoid my sight"—I should not serve him or me, and still less the truth; I should act quite unworthy of the truth, for I could not carry out the declaration with a sustained, even-minded frankness or love, which alone could save such a speech from rant and absurdity.[63]

Is this honesty or self-deception? I think that it is the former, but whatever one decides, it is clear that trusting the dictates of the self and living out their consequences is neither an easy escape from responsibility nor a cover for common selfishness.

Furthermore, Emerson does not claim that the life of open response is possible as a constant way of life. "It is not the intention of Nature that we live by general views," he reminds his readers in "Nominalist and Realist":

We fetch fire and water, run about all day among the shops and markets, and get our clothes and shoes made and mended, and are victims of these details; and once in a fortnight we arrive perhaps at a rational moment [i.e., a moment of living by Reason]. If we were not thus infatuated, if we saw the real from hour to hour, we should not be here to write and to read, but should have been burned or frozen long ago.[64]

Emerson was convinced, moreover, that little "was gained by manipular attempts to realize the world of thought,"[65] for such attempts could succeed only at the cost of converting a process into a product and a relation into a concept. But if he thus found the dualism of time and presence inevitable, he also found it frustrating, and his journals are full of complaints over the difficulty and infrequency of his own escapes from "the painful kingdom of time and place" to the regenerative communication with "this Me of Me" which was the self.[66]

Increasingly he came to see the key to meaningful life as being the idea and practice of alternation: "Solitude is nought and society is nought," he wrote in the late thirties. "Alternate them and the

[63] *Journals*, V, 114.
[64] *Works*, III, 237.
[65] "Experience," *Works*, III, 85.
[66] "Love," *Works*, II, 171, and *JMN*, V, 337.

good of each is seen. . . . Undulation, alternation is the condition of progress, of life."[67] More than a decade later he expanded on this idea in his essay "Fate":

> One key, one solution to the mysteries of the human condition, one solution to the old knots of fate, freedom, and foreknowledge exists; the propounding of the double consciousness. A man must ride alternately on the horses of his private and his public nature, as the equestrians in the circus throw themselves nimbly from horse to horse, or plant one foot on the back of one and the other foot on the back of the other.[68]

If one reads this as a claim that a person sometimes needs to be with others and sometimes needs to be alone, it is very trivial; and if it is taken as a commentary on the relation between ideals and actualities, it makes little sense. But if it is seen as a statement about two frames of mind and two orientations to experience, it makes more sense than most of Emerson's contemporaries were making out of a similar plight. Nor have we, faced with very similar problems, done so much better that we can afford the luxury of viewing Emerson as one of that splendid company of currently irrelevant literary masters.

For as I have tried herein to show, Transcendentalism provides a still impressive analysis of the psychic strains of life in a mass society and a collection of prescriptions that can best be understood as a system of self-therapy. In the present essay I have been able to suggest only some of the parallels that exist between Emerson's thought and the writing of modern students of self-estrangement, but I think that they are enough to make it clear that beneath the surface of a traditional vocabulary Emerson was at work on matters that still vitally concern us and that his ideas foreshadow in their main outlines work that was not even begun until decades after his death.

[67] *Journals*, IV, 473.
[68] *Works*, VI, 47.

Henry Miller, Emerson, and the Divided Self

Paul R. Jackson

IN HENRY MILLER's *Tropic of Cancer* an Emersonian epigraph announces the romanticized autobiography that would become the staple of Miller's art. "These novels," Emerson asserts, "will give way, by and by, to diaries or autobiographies—captivating books, if only a man knew how to choose among what he calls his experiences that which is really his experiences, and how to record truth truly."[1] Along with Whitman—"In Whitman the whole American scene comes to life, her past and her future, her birth and her death"—Emerson stands as a clear, if surprising, link to those traditions of American writing that produced the prophetic autobiographer that Miller became.[2] Moreover, the extent of his early interest in Emerson is indicated by the selection of an epigraph, not from one of the standard Emerson essays, but from the *Journals* themselves, suggesting a familiarity with the New England transcendentalist somewhat at odds with Miller's reputation as shouting, American vulgarian. Indeed Miller's preoccupation with Emerson in *Tropic of Cancer* is attested by a second quotation from the *Journals*, this one a comic appropriation of an 1847 entry. " 'Life,' said Emerson, 'consists in what a man is thinking all day.' If that be so, then my life is nothing but a big intestine. I not only think about food all day, but I dream about it at night" (p. 69).[3]

While Whitman has remained a perennial constant in Miller's literary enthusiasms, Emerson recurs only as a supportive figure in the Americanism that marks the volumes of a writing career that spans at least three decades and that binds the literary expatriate to the artistic roots of his own country. Yet Miller returns to Emerson often enough to suggest an attachment more significant than one would at first suppose. As late as 1957 in *The Books in My Life,*

[1] The epigraph is from an 1841 entry, *Journals of Ralph Waldo Emerson*, ed. Edward Waldo Emerson and Waldo Emerson Forbes (Boston, 1909–1914), V, 516. All quotations from the *Journals* are from this edition.

[2] *Tropic of Cancer* (New York, 1961), pp. 239–240. All quotations are from this edition.

[3] See *Journals*, VII, 319.

Miller listed *Representative Men* as one of the hundred books that influenced him most.[4] Whitman, Emerson, and Thoreau are noted in a list of "specific influences" (p. 124), and Miller laments the passing of excited interest in writers like Maeterlinck and Emerson, with their "inspiring references to great figures of the past." "Their spiritual pabulum is suspect nowadays. Domage! The truth is, we really have no great authors to turn to these days—if we are in search of eternal verities. We have surrendered to the flux" (p. 129). Emerson remains an old favorite, a literary source to be returned to with enthusiasm. "I mentioned Emerson. Never in my life have I met anyone who did not agree that Emerson is an inspiring writer. One may not accept his thought in toto, but one comes away from a reading of him purified, so to say, and exalted. He takes you to the heights, he gives you wings. He is daring, very daring. In our days he would be muzzled, I am certain" (p. 184).[5] "The great influences," Miller wrote to Lawrence Durrell in 1949, "were Nietzsche, Spengler, yes, Emerson, Herbert Spencer (!), Thoreau, Whitman—and Elie Faure."[6] And to Anais Nin he reported: "I wanted to raise Waldo Emerson to the skies, just to prove to the world that once there had been a great American—but more than that, because I once had been greatly influenced by him, he was bound up with a whole side of me that I consider my better side."[7]

Miller's indebtedness to general Romantic and Transcendental modes of thought emerges in his prophetic announcements, often with the cadences of a speaking voice reminiscent of that of Emerson himself. In *Sexus*, the first volume of *The Rosy Crucifixion* trilogy, for example, Miller proclaims the correspondence of the human and the divine: "The great joy of the artist is to become

[4] *The Books in My Life* (New York, no date), p. 318. All quotations are from this edition.

[5] In writing about Thomas Merton, Miller has commented: "Like Emerson and Nietzsche, he is a real radical." *Writer and Critic: A Correspondence with Henry Miller*, ed. William A. Gordon (Baton Rouge, La., 1968), p. 48. Many of Miller's later comments on Emerson emphasize his criticism of American culture. So in the essay "Henry David Thoreau" in *Stand Still Like the Hummingbird* (New York, 1962), pp. 111–118, and in the preface to that book, p. viii.

[6] *Lawrence Durrell and Henry Miller: A Private Correspondence*, ed. George Wickes (New York, 1963), p. 261. Miller is given to such lists of influences; Emerson appears in a similar passage in "An Open Letter to Surrealists Everywhere," and again in "Autobiographical Note," both in *The Cosmological Eye* (New York, 1939), pp. 188, 370.

[7] *Henry Miller: Letters to Anais Nin*, ed. Gunther Stuhlmann (New York, 1965), p. 58.

aware of a higher order of things, to recognize by the compulsive and spontaneous manipulation of his own impulses the resemblance between human creation and what is called 'divine' creation."[8] The ultimate is everywhere visible: "It is not necessary to die in order to come at last face to face with reality. Reality is here and now, everywhere gleaming through every reflection that meets the eye" (p. 425). "We are all part of creation, all kings, all poets, all musicians; we have only to open up, only to discover what is already there" (p. 35). Emerson's emphasis on intuitive understanding with its resultant reliance on childhood experience, dream, and vision is constantly echoed. "As a child it was impossible to penetrate the secret of that joy which comes from a sense of superiority. That extra sense, which enables one to participate and at the same time to observe one's participation, appeared to me to be the normal endowment of every one" (p. 24). Turning his back on an expiring cultural past, Miller can proclaim in perfect Emersonian tones, "My face is always set toward the future" (p. 33). Finally, the ecstatic merging of the emancipated individual with divine process is dependent, with the insistence of a contemporary Emerson, on self-reliance: "The world would only begin to get something of value from me the moment I stopped being a serious member of society and became—*myself!* The State, the nation, the united nations of the world, were nothing but one great aggregation of individuals who repeated the mistakes of their forefathers" (p. 261).

But while Miller's interest in Emerson does seem to issue in such varied and wide parallelism, he has been especially intrigued by a complex of Emersonian ideas concerned with the artistic necessity of using autobiographical fact, the relation of fiction to life and the difficulty of understanding the mystery of selfhood basic to autobiographical fiction. In *The Books in My Life*, Miller again chooses a quotation from Emerson, this time from "The American Scholar," as one of the five epigraphs for the book. " 'When the artist has exhausted his materials, when the fancy no longer paints, when thoughts are no longer apprehended, and books are a weariness—he has always the resource *to live.*' " Such elevating of life over books clearly reinforces Miller's own impulse, announced on numerous occasions, to give up writing altogether. "The act of dreaming when wide awake," he says in *Sexus*, "will be in the

[8] *Sexus* (New York, 1965), p. 270. All quotations are from this edition.

power of every man one day. Long before that books will cease to exist, for when men are wide awake *and* dreaming their powers of communication (with one another and with the spirit that moves all men) will be so enhanced as to make writing seem like the harsh and raucous squawks of an idiot" (p. 28). The supreme imperative is to live; books may indeed constrict that essential.

Nevertheless, Miller has gone on writing and living the literary life, and he has been most preoccupied with the recording and understanding of autobiographical fact. That preoccupation has involved the necessity of knowing, in Emerson's words, "how to choose . . . that which is really his experiences." Indeed, Miller returned to *Cancer*'s epigraph in *The Books in My Life* in a passage commenting on the difficulty of expressing personal truth, of revealing the various selves in inevitable and constant competition.

> The autobiographical novel, which Emerson predicted would grow in importance with time, has replaced the great confessions. It is not a mixture of truth and fiction, this genre of literature, but an expansion and deepening of truth. It is more authentic, more veridical, than the diary. It is not the flimsy truth of facts which the authors of these autobiographical novels offer but the truth of emotion, reflection and understanding, truth digested and assimilated. The being revealing himself does so on all levels simultaneously. (p. 169)

The emphasis in this passage falls clearly on the "deepening" of autobiographical fact as it includes the essential truth that comes from the simultaneous revelation of all the levels of selfhood. Rejecting by implication the vitality of traditional fictional modes as well as the validity of unembellished confessional writing, Miller here announces a literary form that, whatever its sources in Romantic thought, constitutes for him a new departure for the contemporary novel.[9] The imaginative projection of autobiographical fact, especially the emotional life basic to biographical externals, will be the stuff of fiction. Neither fictionalist nor confessor, Miller would use the assimilated facts of his own experience in a mode that would bring together life and art in intimate association.

Throughout his career, Miller has been drawn to autobi-

[9] In *Writer and Critic*, p. 65, Miller again distinguishes his autobiographical writing from other forms: "All the backward and forward jumps have pertinence, from standpoint of 'true' autobiographical narrative, which, incidentally, bears no relation to Diaries or Confessions or Biographies."

ographical writers of all sorts, and letters, diaries and confessions rank high in those books to which he has enthusiastically responded. Louis-Ferdinand Céline's *Journey to the End of the Night* was an early favorite in the thirties, and the list of books that influenced him most in the appendix of *The Books in My Life* emphasizes the biographical genres. Autobiography is represented by those of Cellini and Herbert Spencer, the diary by the anonymous *Diary of a Lost One* and Nijinsky's. Abelard's *The Story of My Misfortunes*, Chesterton's *St. Francis of Assisi*, Gide's *Dostoievski*, and Plutarch's *Lives* all further indicate the fundamental direction of Miller's literary interest. More immediately, his enthusiasm for the diaries of Anais Nin has been constant and public since the publication of *Un etre étoilique* in 1937. While the effects of many of these books may be traced in Miller's writing, Emerson clearly provided a basic clue to the autobiographical romance Miller made his own peculiar province. In Emerson's *Journals* and essays, Miller found that the divided self of the visionary seer in his long journey of emancipation into life was his subject.

The completeness with which Miller has been willing to confront Emerson's simultaneous levels of selfhood is nowhere better underscored than in one direct borrowing from Emerson's *Journals* in *Sexus*. This long autobiographical romance records the trying years of the 1920's; it begins with the turmoil of Miller's first marriage to the Maude of the romances and his initial meeting with Mona, the fictionalized second wife, chronicles his escape from employment with the telegraph company, his early attempts to begin writing, and ends on the night of his second marriage. At the close a life stretches before him that is to be marked by the ambiguities of the trilogy's title. Through the process of personal crucifixion paradoxically will come the new life.

Sexus ends with two parallel fantasies, the first taking place in a burlesque theater on the night of Miller's marriage to Mona. Watching the show unfold and allowing his mind to play with elements of his own predicament, Miller begins to fantasize about the death of a young soapbox orator he names Osmanli.[10] A "dark, sleek chap, nattily attired," Osmanli is "disguised as a boulevardier, a flaneur, a Beau Brummel." With all the appearance of success, he sports a

[10] The Osmanli episode in *Sexus* appears on pages 606–614. It is immediately followed by the second fantasy, pages 614–634.

roll of money, is suave and nonchalant, well read, has a taste for good music and has found that his love for words allows him to sway men. But his real aim is "to spread poison, malice, slander"; he is a "man without country, without principle, without faith, without scruples." In the fantasy, Osmanli stands on the steps of the Hotel Astor about to address the crowd and to create the confusion which as "a servant of Beelzebub" and a "free-wheeling ego" he finds it easy to do.

Yet this diabolically successful orator is a man of illusion. Priding himself on his freedom, he has no close friends of any kind. Moreover, his ability to sustain himself without love is incomplete; the series of masks behind which he has retreated has left an empty man who is now driven toward suicide. His thoughts of self-destruction bubble up from a self he is unable to recognize, a "hidden being" he has spent a life denying. Propelled by this essential self, Osmanli finds himself driven on down a street and, after discarding his money and possessions and presumably reaching his basic self, he is accidentally killed by a police bullet. In standard literary fashion, he thinks back over his life at the moment of his death.

In the flashback, Osmanli is deserted by his wife, who tells him she had never loved him. The effect of her declaration is to make Osmanli feel that for the first time he is free. And to test that freedom in the desperado fashion Miller loves, he cuts off the dog's head, rapes the maid, and leaves to commit a "few murders." And so began the life of the free-wheeling Beelzebub. But now at the moment of his death, Osmanli realizes that he had never finally been free. "To begin with, he had never chopped the dog's head off, otherwise it would not now be barking with joy." He is in fact a man who has denied his own vision and who has submerged his own vital self, living out a lie of heroic strength. "His flight . . . had brought him face to face with the bright image of horror reflected in the shield of self-protection. . . . He had reached his own identity in death."

Osmanli, of course, is a projection of Miller himself, a fantasized image of the autobiographical hero as he enters on a rocky, second marriage. "When Osmanli fell face forward on the sidewalk he was merely enacting a scene out of my life in advance. Let us jump a few years—into the pot of horror." The second fantasy explains the first, as Miller now dramatizes himself without the disguise of Osmanli. Married to Mona, he is living in a cellar with his wife and one of her female friends. Although Miller tries to rage against such inappropriate arrangements, he is soon reduced to the status of a pet dog. Escape fails and the hero returns to a life of emasculation and loveless manipulation. As domestic dog he is taken by his mistress to a dog show where he wins first prize. His reward is a knuckle bone "encircled by a gold wedding ring." With the ring appropriately mounted on his penis, the dog-Miller is carried off whimpering while the maternal wife comforts him. " 'Woof woof! Woof woof!' I barked. 'Woof! Woof, woof, woof.' "

The two fantasies complement each other. The dog-life significantly presents the reality of an emasculated existence with the very woman who is to free Miller from the shackles of a debilitating first marriage. It thus explains both the suicidal urge and the real illusion that govern Osmanli's sense of freedom in the first fantasy. While Osmanli acts with firm, if illusory, heroism in cutting off the dog's head, it seems clear that Miller is suggesting his own identification with the dog; at Osmanli's death the dog is still there to bark. The whole carries Miller's recognition that freedom was not to be gained simply by leaving wives or marrying them. In fact the two fantasies dramatize the discrepancy between the young Miller's expectations of his role in life and the honest awareness that freedom was still to be achieved.

It seems likely that Osmanli is Miller's version of Emerson's Osman, the alter ego who appears throughout the *Journals* and in the essay on "Manners." The change in his name presumably suggests a "manly" version of the ideal man Emerson secretly defined over so many years, a more masculine projection than that of the author Miller found at once "daring" and the writer of "pabulum." A comparison of Osman and Osmanli makes clear the hopes Miller entertained for himself as a young man and substantiates the technique that is basic to his art—the simultaneous projection of himself as heroic paradigm and the honest admission of the personal failures that marked much of his early adulthood.

Osman, the *Journals* tell us, was not especially noteworthy in youth. Underwitted while his brothers were ambitious, it is only at age thirty-five that he becomes known for his wisdom (V, 431–433; VI, 20). Since he has been so undistinguished, there is no need to hide anything from him; every man honestly reveals himself to him without a mask (V, 432). In his relations with others, Osman remains interested in the "rude self" beneath the mask, and although a remarkable man in middle age, "he was never interrupted by success" (V, 481; VI, 20). He is not interested in fine people but only in "highway experience"—he is a "poor and simple man," and "poor man's poet" (V, 431, 481). He prides himself on his "good constitution," believes in the vital force and self-denial (V, 563–564). He is a man of bold and free speech; a man of broad humanity who draws all sufferers to him.[11] At times he seems in his simplicity, Emerson says, to be a dog (V, 432). Rejecting all mercantile values, he emphasizes the reality of what a man is and what he communicates (VII, 260). He is well liked and sympathizes with the "sad angels who on this planet of ours are striking work and crying, O for something worthy to do!" He argues that we are all near the sublime (VI, 50). "Seemed to me that I had the keeping of a secret too great to be confided to one man; that a divine man dwelt near me in a hollow tree" (VI, 137).

Certain elements of this portrait would surely appeal to Miller. In a book detailing its author's late arrival on the literary scene—Miller was in his early thirties during the period dramatized here—Osman's neglected youth and the obscurity of his early adulthood closely parallel Miller's account of his own early years. In important ways a "poor man's poet" himself, generally preferring the responses of average men to professional critics, Miller has also taken pride in his simple ability to listen, a trait, we are told, that causes people to reveal the honest reality beneath their masks. Miller's concern with his own health, his broad humanity, and his ability to remain the same in spite of fame are all characteristics attested in his books or by friends. A writer of "bold and free speech," he too has argued for the closeness of divinity, the unimportance of mercantile values, and the crucial significance of communication in defining a man. Like Osman, he has been interested in the "rude self" and in "highway experience." In short, there is much in Emerson's portrait of Osman that corresponds to Miller's estimate of himself, at least with the "better side" he confessed to Anais Nin Emerson invoked. If he was a dog, he was also, in aspiration at least, many of the things Emerson hoped for himself.

[11] See "Manners," in *The Complete Works of Ralph Waldo Emerson*, ed. Edward Waldo Emerson (Boston, 1903), III, 154.

There are, however, at least two essential differences between Osman and Osmanli, and Miller's fantasy creature is not the simple alter ego that his Emersonian counterpart had been. While Emerson's Osman is a "poor and simple man," without any touch of the violent, Osmanli is a desperado of action—in fantasy he cuts off the dog's head, rapes the maid, and spends a life promoting anarchy. Moreover, he is disguised as a dandy, "a boulevardier, a flaneur, a Beau Brummel." Both changes suggest the real pressures to which Miller felt himself subject in the twenties and the intensity with which he had to respond. The autobiographical hero of Miller's romances is generally conceived as a comic but nonetheless serious man of forceful, especially sexual, action. While other men vacillate in their responses toward women, Miller can depict himself as assured and bold. The final scene of *Cancer*, for example, shows a frightened and timid Fillmore, one of that group of closely knit expatriate males, confessing to a confident Miller all his sad affair with the tyrannous Ginette. "Look here, Fillmore, what is it you'd *really* like to do?" asks the assured and knowledgeable hero (p. 309). And helping Fillmore retreat to America is an act parallel to the sexual heroics of the forceful Millerian hero responding to women throughout the books. "I'm a desperado of love," the very American Miller announces at the beginning of *Sexus*, "a scalper, a slayer. I'm insatiable; I eat hair, dirty wax, dry blood clots, anything and everything you call yours" (p. 14). And generally with just such comic gusto he shoulders his way through ranks of threatening women.

Yet such heroics are undercut by the dramatization of himself as henpecked husband and canine lover. Hesitant and reluctant, Miller emancipated himself slowly and with the utmost difficulty. "People often think of me as an adventurous fellow," he confesses in *Tropic of Capricorn*. "Nothing could be farther from the truth. My adventures were always endured rather than undertaken. I am of the very essence of that proud, boastful Nordic people who have never had the least sense of adventure."[12] Osmanli, the forceful emancipator, is in fact a perfect projection of the ideal actor Miller, at the time, felt himself incapable of being. Himself a dog bound to an ambiguous mate in Mona, he could neither decapitate a dog nor rape a maid.

[12] *Tropic of Capricorn* (New York, 1961), p. 11.

Similarly, Osmanli's dandyism functions as a parallel projection. The son of middle-class Brooklyn parents, Miller spent enough years as down-and-outer to dream of the amenities of the rich. Speaking of an attractively heroic friend in *Cancer*, Miller could remark: "I liked the way Collins moved against this background of literature continuously; it was like a millionaire who never stepped out of his Rolls Royce" (p. 203). And at the end of the book the sight of a French poodle riding in a taxi propels Miller to emulation. Spending all his newly acquired money on a taxi ride through the Bois, he remarks: "Inside me things were running smoother than any Rolls Royce ever ran. It was just like velvet inside" (p. 317). "Be a stevedore in the daytime and a Beau Brummel in the nighttime," Miller advises in *Capricorn* (p. 295). The self-assurance of the rich in fact merges with the assertiveness of the desperado to form a composite of the forceful, calm hero often comically expressing Miller's own aspirations.

But Osmanli is not a simple character of wish fulfillment, any more than he is a one-dimensional alter ego. He dramatizes a strength that, no matter how attractive, Miller felt was fictitious in himself, and he is presented as a hollow man, a straw hero who has to come to terms with his own hidden self. Beneath his ostentatiousness, Osmanli is essentially the kind of empty, trapped human being Miller evidently felt himself to be in the twenties. Bound and visionless, Osmanli is merely the mockery of heroic strength. Like the watch and money that he discards as he runs down the street, his outer self is mere sham, and behind the glibness of the words he finds it so easy to manipulate is a personal vacuum that turns words into empty gesture. Until emancipation is complete, freedom remains a fiction, strength an illusion. For Miller the hollowness of his life as he looked forward to it is symbolized by a dying man learning at the last moment that dogs were still there to bark in spite of his own futile acts.

By borrowing Emerson's own creation, Miller followed the direction the earlier American had indicated. If novels were to give way to autobiography, the personal statement would have to express the complexity of what it is to be human at any given time. For Miller in the twenties, his humanity involved the combination of competing hopes of forceful action and acknowledged fears that actions without selfhood would result at best in comic emptiness. Emerson's Osman eventually flowers into a wise and famous man; Miller's Osmanli dies the product of a freak accident, a parallel to the domestic dog who can only win blue ribbons for a demanding mistress. For Miller, the autobiographical novel has been indeed the vehicle with which he has presented "the truth of emotions, reflection and understanding, truth digested and assimilated." Emerson's secret Osman suggested the possibilities for dramatizing the simultaneous levels of being Miller felt in his own divided self.

Spelling Time: The Reader in Emerson's "Circles"

David M. Wyatt

> In stripping time of its illusions, in seeking to find what is the heart of the day, we come to the quality of the moment, and drop the duration altogether.—"Works and Days"

FOR EMERSON the effect of his place in time has everything to do with the timing of effects in his prose. As the self-proclaimed originator of a tradition, he cannot help hoping to activate in his reader a sense of being at the beginning—in the first presence—of things. To the question "What will we have?" he swiftly answers "This only—a good timing of things."[1] Because Emerson is so concerned with giving his own measure to time, the documents which fully register this project are the finished ones. The Journals never engage time through a form which tests the human power to account for it even as it is being dismissed. As a source of our sense of the man they remain invaluable; as a realization of his will resisting the element it must work in, they tell us little.[2] Emerson's greatest temptation—to risk becoming nothing by trying to be All—knows no bounds in the Journals, as it finds nothing formal there to oppose it. Works always *in medias res,* they risk neither the arbitrariness of a beginning nor the curtailment of an end. It is rather while constructing performances addressed to an audience that Emerson does attend to the timing of effects within a limited stretch of discourse. While composing *Nature* Emerson distinguishes between the demands of private thought and public saying: "that statement only is fit to be made public which you have got at in attempting to satisfy your own curiosity. For himself, a man only

[1] *The Journals and Miscellaneous Notebooks of Ralph Waldo Emerson,* ed. Ralph H. Orth and Alfred R. Ferguson (Cambridge, Mass., 1971), IX, 303. Hereafter *JMN* in the text.

[2] Jonathan Bishop forwards this claim: "The key is still to be looked for in the familiar texts. No one who grasps a part of Emerson's meaning there should find himself seriously altering his view through a study of the antecedent or secondary material," *Emerson on the Soul* (Cambridge, Mass., 1964), p. 7.

wants to know how a thing is; it is for other people that he wants to know what may be said about it" (*JMN,* IV, 52). Only when Emerson risks descent into a public form which, according to its own laws, must end, does he ever make a beginning.

The decision to write in sentences constitutes Emerson's primary submission to form. Within them (rather than the poetic line) he fights his battle against time. Meanwhile he embeds his sentences within a structure—the essay—continually struggling to make of its parts a whole. "Unity" hardly results. The tension between his sentences and the structure they compound never resolves itself into that marvelous and mythic entity, "organic form," which "shapes, as it developes, itself from within."[3] While this may seem a critical failure, it simply reflects Emerson's practical insight into the limited workings of language. With Coleridge he can endlessly dilate upon the mind as "essentially *vital,*" while recognizing that "all objects"—even works of art— (as objects) are "essentially fixed and dead."[4] He understands that the vital power in his mind must submit to connection with and activation of power in his audience through the wholly mediate form of words. So he argues in 1835:

> There is every degree of remoteness from the line of things in the line of words. By & by comes a word true & closely embracing the thing. That is not Latin nor English nor any language, but *thought.* The aim of the author is not to tell truth—that he cannot do, but to suggest it. He has only approximated it himself, & hence his cumbrous embarrassed speech: he uses many words, hoping that one, if not another, will bring you as near to the fact as he is. (*JMN,* V, 51)

With the "line of words" Emerson always falls knowingly, if reluctantly, into step.

The decision to write in order to be read thus becomes for Emerson an acceptance of limitation, a descent into time. He values form, including literary form, insofar as it permits a release of power. He knows that "there is no action of any physical organism [even less an essay] that remotely approaches the power of the human mind to reverse and recast *itself,* constantly to reaffirm or to cancel its own precedent action, in whole or in part."[5] To preserve this

[3] Coleridge, *Essays and Lectures on Shakespeare.*

[4] Coleridge, *Biographia Literaria,* Chapter 13.

[5] William Wimsatt, "Organic Form: Some Questions about a Metaphor," in *Romanticism: Vistas, Instances, Continuities,* ed. David Thorburn and Geoffrey Hartman (Ithaca, N.Y., 1973), p. 22.

power it is necessary to appeal as directly as possible to the reader's consciousness through (rather than to) the work. While lacking the esemplastic nature of its source, the work which results need not remain inert. It consists of a discontinuous or veiled structure which reading can enliven. "This is that law," Emerson argues in "Spiritual Laws," "whereby a work of art, of whatever kind, sets us in the same state of mind wherein the artist was when he made it." The unique resource which Romantic theorists reserve for the imaginative artist Emerson presumes and develops in his audience. Our active involvement in the form as proceeding is intentionally provoked by the entire American symbolist tradition. Its works, often noticeably incomplete in themselves, inspire the trust that they can, should, and will be by us completed. It becomes difficult to speak of such works, especially Emerson's, as anything but pretexts for events, for direct transactions between the soul of the author and the soul of the reader.

Trans action—the exchange of power from one mind to another—this is the essential experience of Emerson's essays. The best ask us to make our own way, to answer the question with which "Experience" begins: "Where do we find ourselves?" This way typically resolves into a "stairway of surprise" ("Merlin"), a perambulation through "a series of which we do not know the extremes" ("Experience"). "Step by step we scale this mysterious ladder; the steps are actions, the new prospect is power" ("Circles"). As we emerge onto the landings which such essays periodically provide it is ourselves in the act of becoming capable readers we are always finding. Jonathan Bishop has given us this Emerson of the verb. His book's central noun—"soul"—continually resolves into a procedure—"active soul." And acting proves more definitive of his version of Emerson than being soul-ful. For the soul lives in change: "metamorphosis of circumstances into consciousness is the consummation of the Soul's great act."[6] Bishop attempts to define the "Soul," and succeeds; I would like to define further the definer. For, as Bishop admits, it is Emerson's reader *as reader* who best realizes and preserves the meaning of the word "Soul." "It must mean the mind of the reader understanding what is before it, following some verbal action upon the page. This literary action is all that an author can be sure he will

[6] Bishop, p. 23.

share with his reader."[7] As a prospectus for Emerson criticism, this will prove definitive. In following the verbal action of "Circles," we can discover ourselves becoming active souls. We are processed by a structure aspiring at once to closure and continuity. While reading "Circles" we enjoy a sense of resolved being and unstayed becoming. The patterns we spell while moving through the essay grant simultaneous access to "the quality of the moment" and to "duration" and so illuminate the temporal dimensions whose usually alternating interchange forms the tension sending up Emerson's work.

Emerson concentrates "Circles" into a microcosm of itself in its first sentence: "The eye is the first circle; the horizon which it forms is the second; and throughout nature this primary figure is repeated without end." The immediate impression conveyed here is one of compression, authority, wholeness. In no other essay are we asked to admit and condense so much at the outset, to "scan the profile of the sphere" in miniature before reading through its more "copious sense." We feel that something—maybe everything—has been said, that what remains to be read may dilate upon, but will not diverge from, the senses this unit circumscribes. Yet the essay's primary "analogy"—"that every action admits of being outdone"—quickly intrudes to counsel against acceptance of finality, sphericity, closure. Fundamentally at odds with itself, "Circles" addresses a reader no less capable of balancing opposing rhythms and claims.

This first sentence has in fact already engaged us with the argument, or "analogy," its apparent formal roundedness opposes. Composed of three stages of statement, each stage absorbs and enlarges—"outdoes"—the preceding. The eye moves through larger and larger arenas. The semicolons create a pause rather than a stay, permitting the reader, without marked delay, to move unhindered from one circumscription to the next. And the sentence ends with a denial of the very closure it enacts and describes—with an admission that the formal entities it defines proliferate "without end." Thus endlessness intrudes into a semantic unit seemingly committed to its opposite. For the sentence contains an abundance of fixities and definites: "eye," "circle," "horizon," "figure." Predication merely brings them into relation, not into activity. Of all these nouns only the "eye"

[7] Bishop, p. 24.

"forms." Such passivity can suggest a world more static than "self-evolving." As for the propositional form of the sentence, it can be read as casting these entities into discrete, logical steps, steps as additive as they are supersessive. So we are also led into an orderly, reflexive universe, one with "primary" and secondary figures, one governed by repetition. The extent of this repetition—it is endless—can be interpreted as always confirming, rather than ever-opening, the confines of this world. Reading this sentence, we cannot help wavering between the conflicting experiences at once offered by it.

Are we to be exposed then to a static or a developing essay? To both, as the paragraph goes on to demonstrate. "We are all our lifetime reading the copious sense of this first of forms." Even more gracefully than in his opening sentence, Emerson here confounds the dimensions of our project. This sentence first sentences us to an unvarying task, a spending of "all our lifetime." But the task assigned, we quickly discover, is "reading," the pursuit of the evanescence of meaning itself. The object of this constantly inconstant attention is next admitted to be a multiplicity: "copious sense." But such historical variety derives from a singular priority, from a "first" which has developed into "forms." We emerge from such an interval alerted to the presence of the one within the many, to the possibility of recovering during history ("our lifetime") a sense of originality (apprehending the "first"). In such a context the reader has no choice but too many options.

But before proceeding to multiply our options, the essay deflects us into the memory of another one. The reader is addressed as if he had just finished "Compensation." "One moral we have already deduced in considering the circular or compensatory character of every human action." We are meant to turn aside here, for the last time, into a consideration of this companion piece. In each of his essays Emerson seeks a fitting style through which, as James Cox argues, the character of his thought can "eventuate."[8] In "Compensation" he typically casts his sentences into antitheses. They become in that context the formal vehicles the experience of which embodies the principle they deduce. The essay's larger structure also betrays a compensatory pattern. Its second movement asks us to balance the "affirmative" force of "Being" against the indifferency of all action

[8] James M. Cox, "Emerson and Hawthorne: Trust and Doubt," *Virginia Quarterly Review*, XLV (Winter, 1969), 93.

argued in the first. The reversion to "Compensation" at the beginning of "Circles" alerts us to the deconstruction of the former mode about to be carried out. "Circles" renders simultaneous the this and the that, the More and the Less between which the earlier essay had us alternate. "The radical tragedy of nature seems to be the distinction of More and Less"; this is the imbalance which "Compensation" mechanically seeks to redress. "Circles" converts this seeming tragedy into an outright comedy by denying from the outset the experience of a certain distinction between more and less, completion and beginning, arrest and motion. The allusion to the former essay thus functions as proof of the "analogy" now being traced. As a literal re-vision of "Compensation," "Circles" demonstrates that "every action"—especially outmoded literary action—"admits of being outdone."

But Emerson jettisons more than the mode of an earlier essay here. The period leading up to the composition of this work had been dominated, in Harold Bloom's phrase, by the "three anti-influence orations-essays of 1837–1840."[9] This prolonged struggle with his relation to the thoughts and acts of forebears finds relief in "Circles." Emerson discovers through the essay an original style, one which acknowledges and incorporates the forces he had wished, especially in *Nature,* to exclude. These are the forces of history and continuity. "His revolt," Stephen Whicher argues, "had been designed to cut the traces that bound him to history and bring him to live, not in the kingdom of time, but in direct contact with the divine life beyond and above time."[10] His compromise, in "Circles," is to evolve a style which eventuates in a reading experience both continuous and arrested, one with a developing memory of itself (a history), and one continually fulfilling itself in single moments.

Thus "Circles" simultaneously spells and dispells time. Standing midway between the full acknowledgment of duration in "Experience" and the early expansion into the moment won in *Nature,* it fuses the prevailing temporal mode of each essay. It is at once a pulsation and an artery. More pointedly, it flows and stays its flow throughout. Its sentences repeatedly ask us to complete, while at the same time to extend, a syntactic and argumentative motion, as if to

[9] Harold Bloom, "The Freshness of Transformation or Emerson on Influence," *American Transcendental Quarterly,* No. 21 (Winter, 1974), 58.

[10] Stephen E. Whicher, *Freedom and Fate* (Philadelphia, 1953), p. 98.

enact the basic pattern which is its subject: spiraling and staying. We can experience this double pattern at work in the following: "There are no fixtures in nature. The universe is fluid and volatile. Permanence is but a word of degrees. Our globe seen by God is a transparent law, not a mass of facts. The law dissolves the fact and holds it fluid." One could go on; there is no need to. Here each sentence seems to forget its dependence on those around it. This epigrammatic "shower of bullets" ("Montaigne") strikes us at first as though unsubordinated to a single argumentative source. The curt propositional thrust of each sentence gets abruptly stayed by each period. The temporary arrest any period naturally provides is so marked here as to fix each proposition into separate, momentous intervals. Syntax and punctuation create a rhythm suggestive of a world of isolated facts. Meanwhile, the paragraph's argument—for fluidity—attempts to cohere into an eddy of implication, one which strains against the consistently stayed rhythm which bears it. The infinitely repellant particles of Emerson's diction are negated or qualified into locutions that keep dissolving hard distinctions. "Fixtures," "Permanence," and "facts" surface only to be denied existence or stability. Those terms allowed to stand—"degrees," "transparent," "fluid"—suggest a flowing interconnectedness. As the connections within each sentence emerge, attention strains to dissolve its steps into a more fluid motion. But to see through (render "transparent") the isolated status of these sentences to their underlying unity is to adopt "God's" perspective, to operate through the knowledge of a "law" presently unavailable to us. In the tension *between* fixity and flowing we have our being. The combined effects of this passage render up not a portable subject, but an acute knowledge of the limits and powers of an attention operating in time.

In "Circles" Emerson's prose dissolves successive distinctions between spiraling and staying. We may stop with each sentence, or follow out the paragraph's ongoing movement. Reading becomes an experience of single, separate moments as "Step by step we scale the mysterious ladder" of this prose. At the same time, it moves through a duration like the "life of man," through a "self-evolving circle, which, from a ring imperceptibly small, rushes on all sides outwards to new and larger circles, and that without end." This doubleness of experience accounts for the overpowering sense of freedom, of choice between two modes of being which surrounds us while reading "Circles." Its title is only half a title: "Circles" also describes "Spirals." We remain free to metamorphose between the perfected circle of timelessness, of a completed thought, and the ongoing spiral of time, of Man Thinking. But such a choice becomes a burden: to be at once in time and out of it may be more freedom than we can bear.

The doubleness of this achievement in the essay's opening we have already deduced. What larger patterns are generated by reading the essay as a whole? It is one of Emerson's shortest. Memory of the essay as it is being read is thereby encouraged. It is not surprising therefore that we proceed by way of repetition. As each "new generalization" meets its echo the reader discovers that to advance he must remember. Emerson admits that in "my daily work I incline to repeat my old steps." This inclination sends up the steps which compose the essay. The will to choose a "straight path" continually revealing new perspectives is chastened into a spiraling course.

The essay proper begins with two propositions to be repeated almost verbatim. "There are no fixtures in nature" and "Permanence is but a word of degrees" soon find echo in "Permanence is a word of degrees" and "There are no fixtures to men." Such recurrences are the fixtures of the essay. They provide a permanent path of reference, a staying of the outrunning argument. While each paragraph counsels against limitation and fixity, these "old steps" hold a steady sound. As the argument proceeds, the repetitions abide. Thus "Fear not the new generalization" encourages abandonment of the old, only to deliver us over to a rehearsal—of the phrase itself—in "all are at the mercy of a new generalization." The frequent restatement of the essay itself argues for the difficulty of advancing a vision wholly new. This is acknowledged in "Yet is that statement approximate also, and not final," an acceptance of limited verbal resources which itself bears repeating and revision: "There is no virtue which is final; all are initial." Perhaps Emerson's unwillingness to have us settle into one path issues most succinctly in "I unsettle all things." But the will to undo is shadowed even here by the urge to re-do: "People wish to be settled; only as far as they are unsettled is there any hope for them." Through such repetitions the reader is stayed and gathered in again, as his progression curves into a circumlocution.

If the repetitions arrest the shoves given by the argument, the reverse is also true. The effect of a return can be, as we have seen, to create a sense of timelessness, of being still in the presence of an unchanged truth. Or it can create a sense of connection with and dependence upon the past, a sense of historical awareness. The essay's repetitions have such a bipolar effect. Any attempt to describe one pole of this effect cannot escape implying the other. What is true of the essay's repetitive structure is also true of its argument. I have characterized it as urging newness, a continuous present, discontinuity. But a continuous argument against continuity acquires a history of its own. As its author acknowledges, he shall one day "wonder who he was that wrote so many continuous pages." The point to be made is that on every level of its realization "Circles" involves us in contradiction. It employs form in order to attack form.[11] Its sentences can be read as a "plenteous stopping at little stations" ("Powers and Laws of Thought"). But they also can be taken as nudges forward on the "self-evolving circle" of discovery. We negotiate in "Circles" an "at once" world, one which plunges us into "incessant movement and progression" even while manifesting a "principle of fixture or stability."

The image of man generated by "Circles" is consequently of a figure still *and* moving. The linearity of the writing process receives much more elaboration than in *Nature,* and through the same metaphor employed so frugally there: walking. Statements and thoughts are imaged not as transcendental leaps but as a horizontal series of moves, "step by step," through the essay's prose. Intellectual pursuits here depend upon strolling. "Each new step we take in thought reconciles twenty seeming discordant facts." The steps may be forward, or "farther back"; the point is that insight is to be found along the way. For this walker—and his reader—temporality resolves into an "anxiety that melts / In becoming, like miles under the pilgrim feet."[12]

At the same time "Circles" induces a motionless heroism: "Valor consists in the power of self-recovery, so that a man cannot have his flank turned, cannot be out-generaled, but put him where you will, he stands." Character also serves which only stands and looks. The

[11] Carolyn Porter, in "Form and Process in American Literature," unpublished dissertation, Rice University, 1973, p. 72, argues that "Circles" "illustrates Emerson's increased awareness of the need for form as well as his reduced ambitions toward final form."

[12] John Ashbery, "The Task" in *The Double Dream of Spring* (New York, 1970), p. 13.

need for a vantage point "to command a view" tempts one into such arrest. Rather than submit to the passage of time, "Character makes an overpowering present." But the will to stand in a moment of our own making may be doomed as we continually discover that "this surface on which we stand is not fixed, but sliding." The axis of vision cannot be coincident with the axis of things until both are stilled.

The very context which creates such contradictions—the essay—apprises us of itself as the platform from which they can be resolved. Literature here recommends "Literature" as a "point outside of our hodiernal circle through which a new one may be described. The use of literature is to afford us a platform whence we may command a view of our present life, a purchase by which we may move it." Here the context in which we are "present" speaks out to us to recommend itself as something on which we might stand to move, or view, the world. In what sense can an experience we are having be conceived as a platform or lever? Can we extricate ourselves from immersion in the essay being read to consider it as an "it"? Again "Circles" attempts to double our experience, asking us to read it and to read *about* it. We must move—walk—through it in order to conceive of staying to use—stand on—it. We must be here in order to think of being *on* here. So Emerson fulfills his theory of complementarity: "a sentence causes us to see ourselves. I be & see my being, at the same time" (*JMN,* V, 278). This is the essay's ultimate confounding of its reader's singleness—to urge the necessity of our absence while we are still in the essay's presence.

In "Circles" motion and arrest, duration and the moment, all become dimensions of power *and* loss. In motion we can scale the mysterious ladder on which "the steps are actions" and "the new prospect is power," or we can too quickly bypass "that central life somewhat superior to creation."[13] Arrest can "confer a sort of omnipresence and omnipotence which has nothing of duration," or it can "solidify and hem in the life." But the experience of the essay recommends a paradoxical combination of both dimensions, a life in an "overpowering present," but a present on the move. This

[13] Todd M. Lieber, in *Endless Experiments* (Columbus, Ohio, 1973), pp. 27–28, elaborates the complementarity inherent in Emerson's experience of motion: "Emerson, however, recognizes two very different types of motion. These may be differentiated by calling the first, which involves a sense of the constant presence of divinity and yields continual affirmation, *process,* and the second, *flux,* to denote an aimless, purposeless, unachieving drift."

precarious and "sliding" nick of time neither Emerson nor his reader can forever isolate from the influence and anxieties of the past and future. For in reading the later "Experience" we find ourselves in a "series of which we do not know the extremes," rather than in the ever "new position of the advancing man." The moving bead reveals itself as part of a string of beads. Our horizon begins to expand, and as the visible distance increases from our beginning and our end, so too recedes the presence of memory and hope.

Any center or present occupied in "Circles" is superseded and must be continually reimagined. As attention to this process of redefinition frees us from the gravity of any and each new-found center, our career is given over to "freeplay" rather than to a fixed locus. Jacques Derrida describes the movement from *Nature* through "Circles" as a "decentering." This rupture of his traditional notions of structure and metaphysics is the "central" event in Emerson's career. It occurs to his readers most dramatically while negotiating "Circles." As its every circle devolves into a spiral, its every center permanently shifts. Derrida argues that whenever belief in a fixed transcendental center collapses, it becomes "necessary to begin to think that there was no center, that the center could not be thought in the form of a being-present, that the center had no natural locus, that it was not a fixed locus but a function, a sort of nonlocus in which an infinite number of sign-substitutions came into play. This moment was that in which language invaded the universal problematic."[14] This records the death of the circle. Emerson's "Circles" asks us to pursue and deny its lost heart. In "Experience" we eventually give up any hope of capture, consigning ourselves simply to the disciplines of pursuit.

Emerson never fully abandons, however, the nostalgia for a sustaining center, for a solitary moment of stay. It is impossible for him to do so, for he pursues his project by way of terms evocative of the very centeredness and timelessness he comes to know better than to seek. Bloom claims that "Emerson had come to prophecy not a de-centering, as Neitzsche had, and as Derrida and de Man are brilliantly accomplishing, but a peculiarly American *re-centering*."[15]

[14] Jacques Derrida, "Structure, Sign and Play in the Discourse of the Human Sciences" in *The Structuralist Controversy*, ed. Richard Macksey and Eugenio Donato (Baltimore, 1970), p. 249.

[15] Harold Bloom, *A Map of Misreading* (New York, 1975), p. 176.

That this re-centering ends in what Bloom calls the "transparency of solipsism" is a claim we should accept and lament, since such a restoration of meaning is won only at the cost of its being common to more than one center. Knowing this, Emerson finds himself drawn down, in "Experience," into the limitations of a continual and communal dialectic. Certainly the old superhuman language of presence persists in reappearing as he speaks of "Godhead": "though not in energy, yet by presence, this magazine of substance cannot be otherwise than felt." Yet the will and power to re-present such experience for the reader, rather than simply to invoke it, the essay fully chastens. This most concessive, least arresting essay demands and creates in its audience more self-reliance than does *Nature* by asking it to relinquish belief in, if not the use of, the traditional language of divination upon which that seemingly original essay finally relies. The first answer "Experience" gives—that there is no *arche* and no *telos*—destroys the limits *Nature* strives to define (if only for the liberated self) and calls the soul into time without beginning or end. To find ourselves in a series of which we do not know the extremes is disorienting: to "believe that it has none" is to accept responsibility for discovering whatever form the series affords. As it develops, "Experience" becomes Emerson's most structuring essay. It structures the reader's power to recognize, to interrogate—to accept the absence of—structures in an ongoing duration. Although he warns, near the end of "Experience," that "We must be very suspicious of the deceptions of the element of time," it is into this element that an aging Emerson, no longer able to come to the quality of the moment, increasingly delivers his reader.

Children of the Fire: Charles Ives on Emerson and Art

David B. Robinson

THE IMPACT of the Transcendental writers upon Charles Ives has long been acknowledged in passing but seldom recognized as a pervasive element in his compositions or, indeed, as the ground of his whole view of musical expression. Ives himself is not responsible for this oversight, for in conversation, interviews, and published writings he repeatedly identified Emerson and Thoreau as his intellectual forebears; many writers, however, have regarded the Concord tradition as simply one among the innumerable components of his highly idiosyncratic music.[1] The list of titles which refer explicitly to this tradition is imposing: one song based upon an Emersonian text ("Duty") and another entitled "Thoreau"; an Emerson piano concerto (unfinished); the *Second Pianoforte Sonata,* subtitled "Concord, Mass., 1840–1860," with four movements called, respectively, "Emerson," "Hawthorne," "The Alcotts," and "Thoreau"; and the book-length *Essays Before a Sonata,* designed to accompany the previous work. The prose *Essays,* Ives's most extensive statement of his musical principles and, consequently, the starting-point for this article, is in effect a defense of the Transcendental attitude toward art as Ives interpreted it and applied it to his music. Not only does it reveal the extent of Ives's indebtedness to his fellow New Englanders, but it suggests that Ivesian musical techniques often suspected of being mere jokes or aberrations are actually carefully calculated pro-

[1] More critics are beginning to take Ives's Transcendental beliefs seriously. One is Alfred F. Rosa, in his article "Charles Ives: Music, Transcendentalism, and Politics," *New England Quarterly,* XLIV (Sept., 1971), 433–444. Rosa understands the intimate connection between the Concord philosophers and Ives's theory and practice of his art; however, in this brief article, which also deals with Ives's equally idiosyncratic political outlook, he has space only to touch upon a few of the most general correspondences, such as the idea of organic form. Rosalie S. Perry's book *Charles Ives and the American Mind* (Kent, Ohio, 1974) includes a chapter entitled "Ives and the Transcendental Tradition," which deals primarily with the Transcendental idea of music as a method of "communicating with one's own thoughts" and the implications of this view for Ives's conception of structure. A good overview of Ives's musical accomplishments which emphasizes his philosophical position is the chapter "Realism and Transcendentalism: Charles Ives as American Hero," in Wilfrid Mellers's *Music in a New Found Land* (New York, 1975, reprint), pp. 38–64.

cedures which embody Transcendental ideas in a beautiful and original manner.

Essays Before a Sonata began as a program-note for the *Second Pianoforte Sonata,* and grew into a one-hundred-page meditation on the Transcendentalists, religion, politics, the course of Western civilization, and the nature and purpose of art. It was the product of an array of motives: the original intention (to provide Ives's thoughts about the men to whom he had dedicated the sonata); an intention announced in the introduction (to deal with the validity of "program music");[2] and the implicit aim of justifying Ives's music to a recalcitrant public. The complete prose work and the sonata were eventually published separately in 1920, but in subsequent editions of the score Ives included excerpts from *Essays* as prefaces to each movement. The sonata itself was written between 1909 and 1915, and although *Essays* was not assembled and edited until 1918, the year of Ives's convalescence from a severe heart attack, we can be sure he had worked at it sporadically for many years. In fact, the "Emerson" chapter of *Essays* may go back as far as an article Ives submitted to a literary magazine at Yale,[3] and the book as a whole, sprinkled with quotations from treatises on the philosophy of art as well as from works by and about the Transcendentalists, suggests a long-term interest in aesthetic questions.

The book is divided into six major sections, the four which correspond to the sonata movements ("Emerson," "Hawthorne," "The Alcotts," "Thoreau") being rounded out by a prologue and an epilogue. The prose of these chapters is analogous to Ives's musical style: both include abrupt shifts of mood, moments of eloquence offset by moments of incoherence, nostalgia, Yankee humor, and

[2] Willi Apel and Ralph T. Daniel, in the *Harvard Brief Dictionary of Music* (New York, 1965), define "program music" as "music inspired by and suggestive of an extra-musical idea which is usually indicated in the title and sometimes further explained in a preface or additional remarks" (pp. 233–234). A familiar example is Berlioz's *Symphonie fantastique.*

[3] Ives had certainly begun reading the Concord writers by the time he entered Yale. Henry and Sidney Cowell, in their pioneering biography *Charles Ives and His Music* (New York, 1969, reprint), report Ives's comment that the Yale article was "promptly handed back" by the editors of the literary magazine (p. 36). The role of Transcendental ideas in Ives's life, as distinct from his art, is a whole topic in itself, and anyone interested in the subject is best referred to the Cowells' study, which despite its faults (its examination of several compositions is perfunctory) is still the best introduction to Ives. See also Frank R. Rossiter's thorough new biography, *Charles Ives and His America* (New York, 1975), *passim.*

startling juxtapositions (the same Ives paragraph may allude to Plotinus and to a baseball game).

The Transcendentalist of central importance to the book is Emerson. He is not the only Concord writer whose aesthetic views Ives found acceptable, but his remarks constitute a unified artistic doctrine as Thoreau's observations, say, do not. The Transcendentalists as a group, with their commitment to individual expression and nonconformity, gave Ives the moral support he needed simply to persevere at composition, while Emerson formulated the principles that gave his music its special character.

However, the "Emerson" chapter of *Essays,* the longest of the four "writers" chapters, concerns itself only obliquely with Emerson's aesthetic notions; instead, it is an attempt to explain the magnetism of his character. Ives believes the secret of Emerson's greatness is his personality, his spiritual restlessness, rather than his ideas: "Though a great poet and prophet, he is greater, possibly, as an invader of the unknown—America's deepest explorer of the spiritual immensities;" he understands from "the inevitable struggle of the soul's uprise" that " 'every ultimate fact is only the first of a new series.' "[4] He is not a reformer, but a regenerator, above all creeds, content to awaken his listeners to their own capabilities.

Yet in the epilogue Emersonian precepts are unleashed to bark Ives's enemies up a tree. Ives begins the chapter with some melancholy thoughts about the transience of a musician's fame. Is it the fate of every composer to be lionized in one age, forgotten in the next? But certain musicians, notably Bach and Beethoven, seem to ride out the tides of fashion. To explain their survival, Ives asks us to assume that one may detect intuitively in music a strong or weak moral fiber. He outlines a dualism in art consisting of a higher principle, "substance" ("reality, quality, spirit"), and a lower, "manner" ("form, quantity"). "Substance in a human-art-quality suggests the body of a conviction which has its birth in the spiritual consciousness, whose youth is nourished in the moral consciousness, and whose maturity as a result of all this growth is then represented in a mental image" (*Essays,* p. 75). The spiritual content is expressed, given shape, by "manner." "Substance," unlike "manner,"

[4] Charles Ives, *Essays Before a Sonata, The Majority, and Other Writings,* ed. Howard Boatwright (New York, 1970, reprint), pp. 11–12. Subsequent references to the work will appear in the text as "*Essays,*" followed by the page number.

is connected with character, and it is the predominance of "substance" in the music of Bach that elevates it above that of Wagner, whom Ives considers merely a superior technician. Not only can "substance"—i.e., moral strength—be conveyed by music, but it is the only important quality that music embodies.

This is familiar terrain: all the signposts point to Emerson. Ives's "substance," translated into the terms of Emerson's "The Poet," is "Genius" as distinct from "Talent." According to Emerson, all men may eventually be drawn to contemplation of the Good, but the poet is entrusted with the Promethean faculty of kindling the divine fire within them. The creative spirit which animates him is the organic principle of nature operating on a higher plane. His essential quality is not logical thought, but an openness to experience, an ear cocked to melodies too rarefied for ordinary men. The gift of receptiveness (i.e., "inspiration") separates the man of "Genius" from the man of "Talent," just as the work itself may be "organic" or "mechanical." Emerson writes, "For it is not metres, but a metre-making argument that makes a poem,—a thought so passionate and alive that like the spirit of a plant or an animal it has an architecture of its own, and adorns nature with a new thing."[5] He continues, "Talent may frolic and juggle; Genius realizes and adds," and his complaint about contemporary poetry is "Our poets are men of talents who sing, and not the children of music" ("The Poet," III, 9).

Moreover, Emerson, like Ives, blurs the distinction between aesthetic and moral value. As he explains in "Nature," natural beauty is but the shadow of eternal Beauty, which is identical with Truth and the Good: "God is the All-Fair" ("Nature," I, 24). Art, which is in turn the symbol or epitome of natural forms, thus seeks to represent this eternal Truth, as well; and since truth is its object, the creation of beauty in a work of art is, in the broadest sense, a moral act. "All high beauty has a moral element in it, and I find the antique sculpture as ethical as Marcus Antoninus . . ." ("Beauty," VI, 306). The genuine work inspires an audience with its "radiation of human character": "Art should exhilarate, and throw down the

[5] Ralph Waldo Emerson, "The Poet," in *The Complete Works of Ralph Waldo Emerson*, Centenary Edition (Boston, 1903–1904), III, pp. 9–10. All subsequent references to this standard edition will appear in the text, in the following form: specific essay title, volume, and page.

walls of circumstance on every side, awakening in the beholder the same sense of universal relation and power which the work evinced in the artist, and its highest effect is to make new artists" ("Art," II, 363). It has not come into full bloom "if it is not practical and moral . . . if it do[es] not make the poor and uncultivated feel that it addresses them with a voice of lofty cheer" ("Art," p. 363).

Ives takes these words very literally; speaking of the composer who succumbs to a desire merely to please the public, he says, "Do not the muscles of his clientele become flabbier and flabbier until they give way altogether and find refuge only in a seasoned opera-box—where they can see without thinking? (*Essays,* p. 98). He finds moral strength in unfashionable places—a revival meeting, for instance—and his music is deliberately rugged and uncompromising, so that the ears may not "lie back in an easy chair" (*Essays,* p. 97). A memo about the "Thanksgiving" movement of his "Holidays" Symphony sets forth his rationale for "difficult" music and asserts the mutual dependence of art and life:

Dissonances . . . had a good excuse for being, and in the final analysis a religious excuse, because in the stern outward life of the old settlers, pioneers, and Puritans there was a life generally of inward beauty, but with a rather harsh exterior. And the Puritan "no compromise" with mellow colors and bodily ease gives a natural reason for trying tonal and uneven off-counterpoints and combinations which would be and sound of sterner things—which single minor or major triads or German-made counterpoint did not (it seemed to me) come up to. This music must, before all else, be something removed from physical comfort.[6]

Yet these principles seem inadequate to explain some of Ives's odder musical practices. Granted that such dissonances and rhythms, however annoying to Ives's contemporaries, can be justified on reputable artistic grounds, what about the jokes and eccentricities in his music—hymns that go flat as if sung by an unlettered congregation, or the impertinent snatches of familiar song which pop up in the middle of a violin sonata? Has such a composer the right to brand the work of his fellow artists "trivial"?

Ives accepts another Emersonian article of faith: "The vocabulary

[6] The term "memo" refers to one of fifty-six miscellaneous prose writings—comments upon Ives's own work, replies to critics, and autobiographical sketches written from 1931 on—collected and edited by John Kirkpatrick in *Charles E. Ives: Memos* (New York, 1972). The page reference here is 130.

of an omniscient man would embrace words and images excluded from polite conversation. . . . Small and mean things serve as well as great symbols" ("The Poet," III, 17). His music, as his attachment to gospel and folk tunes makes clear, is a footnote to that important chapter in the history of taste in which the commonplace became a central subject of serious art—the new trend celebrated by Emerson in "The American Scholar." "The literature of the poor, the feelings of the child, the philosophy of the street, the meaning of household life, are the topics of the time. It is a great stride. It is a sign—is it not?—of new vigor when the extremities are made active, when currents of warm life run into the hands and the feet" ("Scholar," I, 111).

Ives comes late in this tradition, working in a medium less receptive than literature to the influence of vernacular. His accomplishment amounts to a sudden expansion of the musical lexicon, rather than a substitution of one language for another. His purpose is not to disown the great musicians of the past (insofar as he can be said to have any musical progenitors, they are Bach, Beethoven, and Brahms), but to remind American composers, in an era dominated by the European sensibility, to be faithful to their native heritage. Emerson had declared in 1837, "We have listened too long to the courtly muses of Europe" ("American Scholar," I, 114); in 1915 Ives gazed upon an America that still sent promising musicians to be educated in France, and imported its conductors from Germany.[7]

Ives is not fiercely chauvinistic about his art (he remarks in *Essays,* pp. 78–79, "a true love of country is likely to be so big that it will embrace the virtue one sees in other countries"), but he realizes the universal may best be reached through the particular, and the particular is as appropriately a New England locale as anything else. Besides, he feels, America prides itself on its diversity, its willingness to be the melting pot for all nationalities; why should not American music reflect this inclusiveness? The hymn

[7] The musical taste against which Ives was rebelling may be judged from a brief account of the prize-winning opera *Mona,* by Ives's composition teacher, Horatio Parker. Parker's friend Brian Hooker wrote the libretto, ". . . the tale of Mona, princess of Britain in the days of the invasion, torn between her love for the son of the Roman governor and her hatred of the Roman conquerors. . . . It has telling moments—Mona's narrative of her dream, the love duet, the prelude to the third act, the orchestral passage that follows Mona's killing of her lover." This descripion is from John Tasker Howard's *Our American Music* (New York, 1965, reprint), pp. 318–319.

tune, the sentimental song, ragtime, the popular march—all are valid expressions of the American spirit, and deserve a place in its music. A larger musical vocabulary allows greater variety and forcefulness of expression, too, even if the "words" are those "below" the standard of normal conversation. Thus Ives's "dictionary," unlike that of most other composers of his day, includes quotations which, at their best, are concise and vivid in the manner of the best literary examples.

Quotation is, in fact, a very remarkable feature of Ives's music, and since it not only is largely misunderstood, but serves as additional evidence of Ives's debt to Emerson, it is worth discussing at length. This habit of Ives's is much more complex than is commonly imagined. Quotations pervade his output from beginning to end (even a bit of doggerel that Ives composed at age fourteen, "Slow March," contains a tag from Handel's *Saul*), and proliferate in some of his greatest triumphs: *Three Places in New England,* the *Symphony No. 2,* the two piano sonatas. It is one thing which makes his music instantly recognizable and which gives his critics innumerable opportunities for condescension. As his biographer Henry Cowell has written, "Quotation has been a literary device for generations: at least one book of Chaucer's is as complete a tissue of allusion as the works of Joyce and T.S. Eliot in the 20th century. But music has frowned on it, and quotation from other composers has as a rule been unconscious."[8]

However, Ives was not intimidated by tradition so long as he had Emerson's authority for support. A little-known essay of Emerson's, "Quotation and Originality," invokes the "wisdom of humanity" as a rationale for quotation. All of us, he declares, are quoters in one province of life or another; we continually quote our parents, ancient sages, and neighbors, in word and act. "We quote not only books and proverbs, but arts, sciences, religion, customs and laws; nay, we quote temples and houses, tables and chairs by imitation" ("Quotation," VIII, 178–179). Almost every great writer has had a precursor: "Read in Plato and you shall find Christian dogmas, and not only so, but stumble on our evangelical

[8] Cowell, *Ives,* p. 9. But for a convincing demonstration of Ives's success in using hymn-tune quotations as a structural principle, see Dennis Marshall's article "Charles Ives's Quotations: Manner or Substance?" (*Perspectives of New Music,* Spring-Summer, 1968, 45–56). The article focuses upon the *First Pianoforte Sonata.*

phrases. Hegel pre-exists in Proclus, and, long before, in Heraclitus and Parmenides" (p. 180). These examples assure us that "borrowing is often honest enough, and comes of magnanimity and stoutness" (p. 183); furthermore, since it belongs to all men capable of perceiving it, "truth is the property of no individual" (p. 192). With these words in mind, Ives had no compunction about appropriating other men's melodies, and even techniques from other arts, for his own compositions. Once one has accepted Emerson's premise that the true and the beautiful are but different features of the All-Fair, one can justify borrowing on the loftiest philosophical grounds.

Composers before Ives had occasionally borrowed familiar tunes for their music—Haydn and Dvořák, for example, frequently incorporated folk melodies into symphonies or chamber music. But their interest in these melodies was, as a rule, purely musical (the tune had interesting harmonic or rhythmic properties), whereas Ives includes quotations which are funny and apparently gratuitous, or which stir up associations outside music altogether. One reason for the humorous examples is their accessibility to the educated and uneducated, casual listener and critic alike; the effect of crude, knee-slapping humor is often exactly what Ives intends. He believes that a certain kind of humor which cuts across social levels is ideally suited to "democratic" music, and his commitment to inclusiveness allows him to disregard the objection of bad taste. On a less elevated plane, he has the Yankee's pleasure in watching pomposity (even his own) take a pratfall. The comedy is thus doubly motivated; on the one hand is a mystical element ("humor is of the emotional, and the approaching spiritual," he writes in *Essays,* p. 87); but, like Emerson, he "would write on the lintels of the door-post, 'Whim,' " ("Self-Reliance," II, 51), and if we are startled to hear "Columbia, the Gem of the Ocean" wink out of the "Hawthorne" section of the *Second Pianoforte Sonata,* we should realize that we are not the only ones who are amused.

Ives's non-musical references are usually more elusive. His compositions regularly display clusters of extra-musical allusion which, without being exactly "programmatic" (i.e., evocative of a scene or action), are significant parts of the work but puzzling to those who do not understand Ives's unusual approach to art.

Fearing that Ives will be accused of composing mere "program music," Henry Cowell insists, "Ultimately the music stands independent of any literary or other extra-musical connection" (*Ives and His Music,* p. 147). But the next paragraph of his study, about Ives's curious decision to print the words to a hymn which appears in an entirely instrumental score, indicates the importance of the non-musical associations: "The presentation of the words recalls his father's practice of playing a fine hymn tune on the French horn, before a congregation each of whom was repeating the familiar words silently to himself; this was still deeply moving to Ives in retrospect" (p. 148). In other words, it is an autobiographical reference, a technique quite familiar in literature but unusual in music. Ives himself remarked that such references in his music are often signs of a mystical conception. One extraordinary memo concerns the origin of a quotation in the *Second Orchestral Set.* The morning after the *Lusitania* had sunk (May 8, 1915), Ives had gone to his insurance office in downtown New York. The tension in his office was almost palpable, though few people actually spoke of the disaster. After work, Ives took the Third Avenue elevated train at Hanover Square Station:

As I came on the platform, there was quite a crowd waiting for the trains, which had been blocked lower down, and while waiting there, a hand-organ or hurdy-gurdy was playing in the street below. Some workmen sitting on the side of the tracks began to whistle the tune, and others began to sing or hum the refrain. A workman with a shovel over his shoulder came on the platform and joined in the chorus, and the next man, a Wall Street banker with white spats and a cane, joined in it, and finally it seemed to me that everybody was singing this tune, and they didn't seem to be singing in fun, but as a natural outlet for what their feelings had been going through all day long. There was a feeling of dignity all through this. The hand organ man seemed to sense this and wheeled the organ nearer the platform and kept it up fortissimo (and the chorus sounded out as though every man in New York must be joining in it). Then the first train came in and everybody crowded in, and the song gradually died out, but the effect on the crowd still showed. . . .[9]

Ives notes that the tune was none other than the refrain to the old gospel hymn, "In the Sweet Bye and Bye"; the third movement of the Orchestral Set thus incorporates the hymn in an attempt to re-create a moment of spiritual unity. In *Essays* (p. 33), Ives speaks of

[9] *Ives: Memos,* pp. 92–93.

"the being willing to be leveled toward the infinite"; when Emerson uses similar language to describe "a certain wisdom of humanity . . . which our ordinary education labors to silence and obstruct," he is referring to the "Over-Soul" (II, 277). The musical instance recalls Emerson's statement that art must "awaken . . . in the beholder the same sense of universal relation and power which the work evinced in the artist" ("Art," II, 363), and it reflects Ives's belief that eventually music will develop into "a language so transcendent that its heights and depths will be common to all mankind" (*Essays,* p. 8). What more impressive testimony to the power of music than the communal singing in which the individual is lifted out of himself into a new consciousness of unity with others? This is why hymns, especially, have for Ives the associations of what Emerson called "thought above the will of the writer" ("Compensation," II, 108). Ives is aware that the old gospel and revival tunes did not spring full-blown from a collective unconscious, but he feels they have been sanctified by their appeal to generation after generation—winnowed out, by the passage of time, from the pretentious, the weak, and the spurious. "The man 'born down to Babbitt's Corners' may find a deep appeal in the simple but acute Gospel hymns of the New England 'camp meetin' of a generation or so ago. He finds in them—some of them—a vigor, a depth of feeling, a natural-soil rhythm, a sincerity—emphatic but inartistic—which, in spite of a vociferous sentimentality, carries him nearer the 'Christ of the people' than does the *Te Deum* of the greatest cathedral" (*Essays,* p. 80).

The familiarity of the hymn likewise gives Ives the opportunity to demonstrate the Emersonian proposition, "The invariable mark of wisdom is to see the miraculous in the common" ("Nature," I, 74). Sometimes an entire musical unit may be controlled by this idea. The second movement of the *Fourth Violin Sonata,* for instance, is based upon the refrain of "Jesus Loves Me." Now, the tour de force of weaving a magnificent sonata movement from a rather silly theme is not new—one recalls the second movement of Beethoven's "Appassionata." However, Beethoven *begins* his piece with the theme and gradually transforms it into a sumptuous musical line. Ives's procedure is the reverse. He presents us with a melodic line in which we glimpse, from time to time, fragments of the quoted hymn-tune, or its outline, but it is not until the end of the movement that the tune's refrain emerges, so to speak, from its cocoon. Ives expects us to identify this lowliest of hymns as the basis of the movement, and his dramatic coup has yet another motivation: it exemplifies what Henry Cowell, in his discussion of Ives's *Second Pianoforte Sonata,* has called "the concept of diversity drawing toward unity as its culmination" (*Ives and His Music,* p. 192). The analogy Ives implies is that the music progresses from complexity to simplicity, reducing all to its essence, just as the soul ascends from the confusion of earthly forms until the veil of the senses drops away and it stands in contemplation of the One. The movement is a masterpiece of Emersonian art—not only does it possess the "certain cosmical quality, or . . . power to suggest relation to the whole world" ("Beauty," VI, 303) which Emerson identifies as the hallmark of great art, but it achieves that quality with the humblest of materials.

This example is far from unique in Ives's music—one might choose instead the third movement of the *First Pianoforte Sonata,* in which the skein of melody is unwound to reveal "What a Friend We Have in Jesus"—and it illustrates Ives's habit of conceiving a work in philosophical as well as musical terms. Occasionally he explicitly fastens a meaning to a particular motif. The famous four-note opening theme of Beethoven's *Fifth Symphony* is subjected, in the *Second Pianoforte Sonata* ("Concord"), to all sorts of intricate permutations, from an exposition thick with countervailing themes to final isolation, both in the "Emerson" movement and in the sonata as a whole. Ives writes of the *Fifth Symphony* "oracle" as follows: "We would place its translation above the relentlessness of fate knocking at the door, above the greater human message of destiny, and strive to bring it toward the spiritual message of Emerson's revelations, even to the 'common-heart' of Concord—the soul of humanity knocking at the door of the divine mysteries, radiant in the faith that it *will* be opened—and the human become the divine!" (*Essays,* p. 36).

But the structure of a work must evolve from a germinating theme or idea; a variation form may be appropriate for one movement of a sonata, a modified sonata-allegro for another, as Ives's practice indicates. This determination to consider form anew with each composition, the distinction between "manner" and "substance," the contempt for structural "unity" effortlessly achieved ("unity is too easily accepted as analogous to form; and form . . . to custom; and custom to habit"—*Essays,* p. 98), reveals Ives's thoroughgoing commitment to the ideal of organic development in Emerson's sense, even to the notion of artistic design mirroring a cosmic principle (as the *Violin Sonata No. 4* suggests). Only when a composer cannot, as Emerson says, "connect his thought with the proper symbol" ("Nature," I, 29) does he resort to outmoded forms which sacrifice originality to clarity, for " 'Nature loves analogy and hates repetition' " (*Essays,* p. 22). Tacitly acknowledging Emerson's complaint that "men seem to have lost the perception of the instant dependence of form upon soul" ("The Poet," III, 3), Ives continues, "To Emerson, unity and the over-soul, or the common-heart, are synonymous. Unity is at least nearer to these than to solid geometry, though geometry may be all unity" (*Essays,* p. 99).

Ives's reflections on his own music show how deeply the organic analogy affected his thought. Emerson's doctrine emphasizes flow, the sense that motion has been arrested only for a moment. The idea of process dominates his conception of spirit, and he identifies growth and decay as its counterparts in nature. Art being in turn an "abstract" of the natural world, "nothing interests us which is stark or bounded, but only what streams with life, what is in act or endeavor to reach somewhat beyond" ("Beauty," VI, 292); in "Nature" Emerson quotes with approval Madame de Stael's definition of architecture: "frozen music" ("Nature," I, 43). Similarly, Ives was pleased to discover that the *Second Pianoforte Sonata* ("Concord") was continually growing in his imagination. "It may have something to do with the feeling I have about Emerson, for every time I read him I seem to get a new angle of thought and feeling and experience from him. . . . Some of the passages now played haven't been written out . . . and I don't know as I ever shall write them out, as it may take away the daily pleasure of playing this music and seeing it grow and feeling it is not finished" (*Memos,* pp. 79–80).

So far Emerson's and Ives's conceptions of organic form seem to be, for all practical purposes, identical. In one important respect, however, their views are at odds. Emerson deduces the principle of economy from the proposition that nature is the standard of excellence for art. "It is a rule of the largest application, true in a plant, true in a loaf of bread, that in the construction of any fabric or organism any real increase of fitness to its end is an increase of beauty" ("Beauty," VI, 296). Transferred to art, the principle demands that there be no superfluous parts, that everything contribute to the total design. Now, aside from a few scattered observations in *Essays,* Ives says little in his prose about nature per se; he seems to accept the Emersonian identity of nature and spirit, and he agrees that natural laws are applicable to art. But no one would accept "economical" as an accurate description of Ives's work in general, and, furthermore, Ives might consider the term a dubious compliment at best. Emerson requires the artist always to reduce the welter of natural forms to a single clear and coherent design, while Ives, though continually conscious of pattern (as any artist must be), wishes to reproduce moments of incoherence and excess as well—"nature" in its prodigal aspect. A man devoted to Emerson's ideal will insist his music be performed exactly as written, since each note is the only proper one in the context; Ives, on the contrary, was content if the performer understood and conveyed the underlying feeling of the score, whether or not the execution was flawless. His judgment upon Emerson, that the latter was more concerned with perception than expression, is intended as praise ("substance" being superior to "manner"), and sums up his own attitude toward art.

The whimsical Ives style, so often rough-hewn, appears to be a long way from beauty "which is simple; which has no superfluous parts; . . . which is the mean of many extremes" ("Beauty," VI, 289)—the rather chill perfection Emerson asks us to admire. Yet the Emerson who wrote to Whitman, "I am not blind to the worth of the wonderful gifts of 'Leaves of Grass.' I find it the most extraordinary piece of wit & wisdom that America has yet contributed,"[10] would likely have regarded Ives, too, as an example of the mind he described in "Experience": "When I converse with a profound mind. . . . I do not at once arrive at satisfactions . . . but I am first apprised of my vicinity to a new and excellent region of life" (III, 71).

[10] Ralph Waldo Emerson, letter to Walt Whitman, reprinted in Walt Whitman, *The Correspondence,* ed. Edwin Haviland Miller (New York, 1961), I, 41.

Convers Francis and Emerson

Joel Myerson

THE LIFE OF CONVERS FRANCIS shows the difficulty of being "intellectually radical" while remaining "ecclesiastically conservative" at the time when Transcendentalism was making its mark upon New England Unitarianism.[1] Francis had been in both worlds, from moderator of the Transcendental Club in 1836 to a Harvard Divinity School professorship in 1842, and had, in William R. Hutchison's words, "from the start combined [his] radical idealism with a deep awareness of the historical dimension of Christian experience."[2] Because of his "all-sided" view,[3] Francis's impressions of the time and its people are valuable. Although most of his manuscripts are apparently lost, we are fortunate to have preserved a series of extracts from his journal dealing with Ralph Waldo Emerson, here edited for the first time.[4] In these entries, spanning nearly thirty years, we can see how one of Emerson's more interesting and important contemporaries viewed him.

Francis was born on November 9, 1795, at West Cambridge, Massachusetts.[5] The fifth of six children, he moved with his family to Medford in 1800, where his father established himself as a baker. Francis showed an interest in literature and was prepared at a local academy in 1811 for entrance to Harvard. Upon his graduation from the College in 1815, he studied for the divinity and preached

[1] Frederic Henry Hedge, "Destinies of Ecclesiastical Religion," *Christian Examiner*, LXXXII (Jan., 1867), 12. While Hedge is talking about himself, the phrase fits Francis equally well.

[2] *The Transcendentalist Ministers* (New Haven, Conn., 1959), p. 189.

[3] Octavius Brooks Frothingham, *Boston Unitarianism 1820–1850* (New York, 1890), p. 186.

[4] I am grateful to the Boston Public Library and the Harvard College Library for permission to quote from manuscripts in their possession. Eleanor M. Tilton kindly helped me to locate the Francis material in the Ralph Waldo Emerson Memorial Association collection at the Houghton Library.

[5] Biographical information is from John Weiss, *Discourse Occasioned by the Death of Convers Francis* (Cambridge, Mass., 1863); William Newell, "Memoir of the Rev. Convers Francis," *Proceedings of the Massachusetts Historical Society*, VIII (March, 1865), 233–253; and Mosetta I. Vaughan, *Sketch of the Life and Work of Convers Francis* ([Watertown, Mass.], 1944).

his first sermon in 1818.[6] His ordination on June 23, 1819, represented an auspicious beginning to his career: among those who helped were President Kirkland of Harvard, the Reverend Ezra Ripley of Concord, Emerson's step-grandfather, and his son, the Reverend Samuel Ripley of Waltham, and John Gorham Palfrey. Francis was installed at Watertown at the excellent salary of $1,000 per year. On May 15, 1822, he married Abby Bradford Allyn and by 1834 they had had four children, two of whom died in infancy. Francis took time from his pastoral duties to write for the religious periodicals and to publish *An Historical Sketch of Watertown* in 1830 and the *Life of John Eliot,* apostle to the Indians, for Jared Sparks's Library of American Biography in 1836. In 1842 he left Watertown to become Parkman Professor of Pulpit Eloquence and the Pastoral Care at the Harvard Divinity School, a post he held until his death on April 7, 1863.

Francis's early religious beliefs found sympathy with the personalized religion espoused by the Transcendentalists. As a youth he had complained of the "Bibliolatry of almost all theology," which had removed "the *human* element" from the Bible.[7] In May, 1832, he favorably reviewed Alexander Crombie's *Natural Theology* in the *Christian Examiner* and his sympathy for the principle that "the human soul is a particle of the Divine Mind" greatly "enheartened" the young ministers who were becoming known as Transcendentalists.[8] By 1836, the "Annus Mirabilis" of Transcendentalism, he saw that "the spiritualists are taking the field in force." Francis had always felt that there would be a rift between the conservative followers of Locke's sensational philosophy and the more radical disciples of the spiritual or transcendental philosophy of Kant and Coleridge, and he believed the latter "have the most of truth."[9] His pamphlet *Christianity as a Purely Internal System* was apparently ranked by the Transcendentalists with George Ripley's favor-

[6] At this time there was no formal Divinity School; Francis and others studying for the divinity took whatever courses were voluntarily offered by the existing College faculty. Francis was awarded a divinity degree in 1837.

[7] Quoted in Weiss, *Francis,* p. 15.

[8] *The Transcendentalists: An Anthology,* ed. Perry Miller (Cambridge, Mass., 1950), pp. 63–64.

[9] He also foresaw that "it will take them some time to ripen, and meanwhile they will be laughed at, perhaps, for things that will appear visionary and crude" (journal entry, Weiss, *Francis,* pp. 28–29).

able review of James Martineau's *Rationale of Religious Inquiry* in the *Christian Examiner* and Orestes A. Brownson's *New Views of Christianity, Society, and the Church* as among the most encouraging publications of 1836.[10] In that year he was invited to become a member of the Transcendental Club; as the eldest member he was made moderator for the discussions and he attended at least half of its thirty meetings over the next four years.[11]

Francis made friends among the Transcendentalists. His wife attended Margaret Fuller's "Conversations" and had earlier schooled Bronson Alcott's wife.[12] Alcott considered Francis "one of our most worthy and feasible ministers," whose "influence with the sensible and moderate" made him "an admirable balance-wheel to keep all movements in fit order."[13] He also formed a close friendship with Frederic Henry Hedge, minister at Bangor, Maine, who, like Francis, tended towards a mediatory position as the Unitarian controversy with Transcendentalism developed.[14] But Francis's most important friendships were with Theodore Parker and Emerson.

In April, 1832, Parker, then a twenty-one year old schoolmaster, showed up at Francis's house in Watertown and announced: "I am told that you welcome young people, and I am come to ask if you will be kind to me and help me. . . . I long for books, and I long to know how to study."[15] Francis gave Parker access to his excellent library, helped him to enter the Harvard Divinity School in 1834, and had the pleasure of preaching the sermon at his ordination in 1837. The two continued close friends and Parker was a major factor in deciding Francis to take the Harvard professorship in 1842.[16]

[10] Miller, *The Transcendentalists*, p. 63.

[11] See Myerson, "A Calendar of Transcendental Club Meetings," *American Literature*, XLIV (May, 1972), 197–207.

[12] Emerson to Fuller, Nov. 14, 1839, *The Letters of Ralph Waldo Emerson*, ed. Ralph L. Rusk (New York, 1939), II, 234: hereafter cited as *L*; F. B. Sanborn and William T. Harris, *A. Bronson Alcott: His Life and Philosophy* (Boston, 1893), I, 111.

[13] Week XVIII, May, Alcott, "Journal for 1837," p. 328, Houghton Library: the dating by weeks is Alcott's; Alcott to Emerson, May 24, 1837, *The Letters of A. Bronson Alcott*, ed. Richard L. Herrnstadt (Ames, Ia., 1969), p. 33.

[14] For the career of Hedge, who founded the Transcendental Club in 1836 but renounced the Transcendentalists by 1840, see Myerson, "Frederic Henry Hedge and the Failure of Transcendentalism," *Harvard Library Bulletin*, XXIII (Oct., 1975), 396–410.

[15] Weiss, *Francis*, p. 67.

[16] As late as 1842, Parker kept "a page in my journal entitled '*Questions to ask Dr Francis*' " (Parker to Francis, Nov. 21, 1840, Boston Public Library).

Emerson had known Francis since at least 1819, when he took note of Francis's moving to Watertown, and he once preached for Francis there.[17] Francis liked Emerson and often defended him against critics, as once, when a lady was mourning "Emerson's insanity," he replied, "Madam, I wish I were half as sane."[18] Emerson made sure that Francis received a copy of *Nature* upon publication and enlisted his aid in editing Carlyle's writings.[19] Francis had exchanged friendly letters with Emerson on Goethe and German literature,[20] and in 1835 Emerson described him to Carlyle as one of the American "scholars and Spiritualists" who "love you dearly, and will work heartily in your behalf."[21] In 1837 Francis helped circulate Emerson's prospectus for his edition of *The History of the French Revolution* and the next year this "noblehearted man" provided his own copies of the *Foreign Review,* containing Carlyle's contributions, for Emerson's edition of *Critical and Miscellaneous Essays.*[22]

However, Francis never approached the social radicalism of Parker or the intellectual radicalism of Emerson, and the circumstances surrounding his taking the Parkman professorship at the Divinity School help to explain why.

Francis was probably offered the Parkman chair because, in the words of O. B. Frothingham, he was the "best man" for it "at a time when in an unsectarian school it was exceedingly desirable that the professors should harmonize all tendencies; for with a strong sympathy with 'transcendentalism,' as it was then called, he had been . . . a man in whom all the churches had confidence."[23] Frothingham was right; both liberals and conservatives applauded the choice. Parker rejoiced and urged Francis to accept, saying that the "young men at the [Divinity] School . . . are much gratified with the arrangement," as were "the intellectual and the liberal party

[17] Emerson to William Emerson, Feb. 14, 15, 20, *L,* I, 78; Nov. 5, 1831, *The Journals and Miscellaneous Notebooks of Ralph Waldo Emerson,* ed. William H. Gilman et al. (Cambridge, Mass., 1960–), III, 304: hereafter cited as *JMN.*

[18] Mrs. Samuel Ripley to Mary Moody Emerson, Sept. 4, 1833, George Willis Cooke, *Ralph Waldo Emerson* (Boston, 1881), p. 33.

[19] Ca. Dec. 6, 1836, *JMN,* V, 264.

[20] See Francis to Emerson, April 21, 1837, Houghton Library, and Emerson to Francis, April 24, 1837, *L,* II, 71–72.

[21] April 30, *The Correspondence of Emerson and Carlyle,* ed. Joseph Slater (New York, 1964), p. 125: hereafter cited as *CEC.*

[22] *L,* II, 99; Emerson to Carlyle, Aug. 6, 1838, *CEC,* p. 191.

[23] *Recollections and Impressions 1822–1890* (New York, 1891), p. 27.

of the clergy."[24] To Parker, Francis bore the proper "relation to *the times*" for the post, and after he began teaching, Parker reported the news he heard "that the School already wears a new aspect, as it has a new soul; that you stimulate the dull and correct the erratic, and set right such as have prejudices inclining to narrowness, if not bigotry."[25] Hedge, too, was cheered by Francis's taking the professorship, but, worrying that, if "the principle of dissent from existing institutions, & belief continues to spread at the rate it has done for the last two years, the entire *Clerus* . . . will be ousted in ten years," he gave this advice: "I perceive that there are new considerations & new responsibilities incident to your new position, which must necessarily affect, in some degree, the tone of your intercourse with old associates, & especially with those who have incurred the stigma of transcendental & heretical tendencies. . . . There is a rigid, cautious, circumspect, conservative *tang* in the very air of Cambridge which no one, who has resided there for any considerable time can escape."[26]

Hedge, not Parker, was the more astute, and proof came when the Boston Association of Unitarian ministers, following the publication of Parker's controversial *A Discourse on the Transient and Permanent in Christianity* (1841) and *A Discourse of Matters Pertaining to Religion* (1842), effectively prohibited its members from exchanging pulpits with him. Francis, too, "in consequence of the advice which he received from persons connected with the College," recalled an exchange.[27] Francis's defection must have hurt Parker the most. Francis had complained of the "civil prosecution" which had attended the delivery of the discourse on Christianity and, after the *Discourse of Religion* was published, had thought it "abominable" that Parker "should be treated unkindly by Unitarians, whose doctrine is individual freedom."[28] Francis's past friendship and his support of the abolition movement, partially as a result of his sister Lydia Maria Child's vigorous antislavery activities, led Parker to believe Francis would not now submit to the Unitarian majority.

[24] June 24, 1842, Weiss, *Francis,* pp. 37–38.

[25] July 2, Sept. 26, 1842, Weiss, *Francis,* pp. 38–39.

[26] February 14, 1843, Ronald Vale Wells, *Three Christian Transcendentalists* (New York, 1943), p. 205.

[27] Weiss, *Francis,* p. 71.

[28] June 13, 1841, June 25, 1842, Weiss, *Francis,* pp. 69–70.

But Parker did not realize, as one of Francis's biographers did, that "he remained the pastor of souls, not the crusader, and held his people together."[29] And although Francis considered Parker generally to be "more and more pious every time I see him," the publication of his book, with a spirit Francis found "bad, derisive, sarcastic, arrogant,—contemptuous of what the wise and good hold sacred," was disruptive and therefore bad.[30] Like Hedge, he feared the consequences of "the *practical* dissent of the time" and his refusal to exchange with Parker was rooted in this.[31] Or in Perry Miller's words, "Intellectually capable of understanding the new ideas, and apparently of embracing them, he fell away when the social hazards became too great."[32]

Against such a background, Francis's journal entries on Emerson take on added value. Francis himself shifted position regarding the Transcendentalists; did he also do so concerning Emerson? The following extracts, made by Francis's daughter at the request of Edward Emerson for use in James Elliot Cabot's 1887 biography of his father, will show.[33]

"Extracts from the Journal of C. Francis"

11 August 1835. Went with Mr. Hedge to Concord to attend association meeting at Dr. Ripley's; much good talk there: R. W. Emerson there. I found that Mr. H. and Mr. E. were not, as I was, disappointed in Coleridge's Table Talk; they saw little or nothing to be blamed in it; talked much of Coleridge.[34]

[29] Vaughan, *Francis,* p. 15. Or as Frothingham recalls, Francis "said once that he who defies public opinion, like the man who spit in the wind, spits in his own face" (*Boston Unitarianism,* p. 188).

[30] Dec. 11, 1841, June 25, 1842, Weiss, *Francis,* pp. 33, 70.

[31] Hedge to Francis, Feb. 14, 1843, Myerson, "Hedge," p. 409. Yet but a few months before taking up the Parkman professorship, Francis had complained of the "folly, as well as wickedness, of the *odium theologicum,*" which might condemn his own sermons of "the horrible crime of transcendentalism!" (July 23, 1842, Weiss, *Francis,* p. 34).

[32] *The Transcendentalists,* p. 63.

[33] In transcribing Miss Francis's copy of her father's journal (Houghton Library bMS Am 1280.F8471MAA.1835) I have regularized all punctuation and date lines, corrected obvious spelling and punctuation errors, expanded ampersands and abbreviations, and substituted correct dates where she has obviously miscopied the year. The transcriptions of Francis's Greek are often unclear; the text followed here is that in the Loeb Classical Library. My extensive search has failed to uncover the present location of Francis's entire journal.

[34] Probably the Unitarian association met at the home of the Reverend Ezra Ripley of Concord. Emerson had recommended *Specimens of the Table Talk of the Late Samuel Taylor Coleridge* to his brother William on July 27, 1835; the volume, with Emerson's

19 September 1836. Attended a meeting of several gentlemen at Mr. George Ripley's house. The object of the meeting was to form a sort of society for the discussion of great subjects in theology, philosophy, and literature.—We want more freedom of thought and expression, they say, than can be found in any of the present meetings of the day; we want congenial spirits to talk without fear or reserve on all topics.[35]

3 October 1836. Went to Boston and attended the meeting mentioned a fortnight ago. It was at Mr. Alcott's; present, Mr. A., Mr. Emerson, Brownson, Ripley, Hedge, Clarke, Bartol, and myself. It was an interesting meeting and the discussion edifying: the question,—why has our country hitherto failed to produce the highest order of genius, especially in the fine arts? The remarks of Alcott, Emerson, Ripley, and Hedge were admirable.[36]

16 January 1837. Dined at Mr. T.'s, whose daughter told me of the meetings for conversation at Mr. Alcott's school-room, and how gloriously he talked.[37] Mr. T. said his daughter was one of a knot of *transcendental* young ladies, to which she replied, she did not know the meaning of that, but she loved to hear Mr. Emerson lecture, and Mr. Alcott talk. I commend her taste.[38]

8 February 1837. Read Mr. Waldo Emerson's exquisite article on Michael Angelo in the North American Review.[39] Was ever a mind cast in a finer mould, than E.'s? He seems to have already anticipated the purity of the spiritual state.

16 February 1837. Went to Boston in the evening to hear one of Mr. Emerson's course of lectures. The subject was "Ethics." It was distin-

notes, is still in his library (*L,* I, 448; Walter Harding, *Emerson's Library,* Charlottesville, 1967, p. 64).

35 Francis was one of eleven men who attended this, the second, meeting of the Transcendental Club; for further information on this and other meetings, see Myerson, "A Calendar of Transcendental Club Meetings." Ripley was minister at Purchase Street in Boston and would later organize the Brook Farm community.

36 Present at the third meeting of the Transcendental Club were Alcott, a self-educated schoolteacher currently running his innovative Temple School in Boston; Orestes A. Brownson, a vigorous reformer who would begin the *Boston Quarterly Review* two years later; James Freeman Clarke, then preaching in Louisville and editing the liberal *Western Messenger*; and Cyrus A. Bartol, a Boston minister.

37 The first volume of Alcott's *Conversations with Children on the Gospels* had been published in late December, 1836, and was being vilified by the Boston press for its unorthodox and frank discussions of religion; see Sanborn and Harris, *Alcott,* I, 211–220.

38 Alcott later noted in his journal that Francis had read the *Conversations* with "great pleasure" (Week XVIII, May, "Journal for 1837," p. 327).

39 "Catalogue of One Hundred Drawings by Michael Angelo," *North American Review,* XLIV (January, 1837), 1–16.

guished by all his usual peculiarities of beautiful thought and expression. There is a charm about this man's mind and his compositions, which I know not how to explain, except by saying that it is the charm of hearty truthfulness and the simplicity of a pure, far seeing soul. His style is too fragmentary and sententious. It wants the requisite words or phrases of connection and transition from one thought to another; but has unequalled precision and beauty in single sentences. This defect, and his habit of expressing a common truth in some uncommon (is it not sometimes slightly fantastic?) way of his own, are the reasons perhaps that it is so difficult to retain and carry away what he says. I find that his beautiful things are *slippery,* and will not stay in my mind. Sometimes there is a homely familiarity in his illustrations, which is not a little amusing. Among other things he said this evening, that young persons were apt to have a diseased love of speculating on questions, which the mind in a pure and healthy state of action does not care enough about to recognize at all,—such as original sin, the origin of evil, etc. These things, he said, were "the mumps, measles and whooping-cough of the soul."[40]

30 April 1837. Exchanged with R. W. Emerson, preached at E[ast]. Lexington, where Mr. E. has care of the pulpit.[41]

29 May 1837. Went to George Ripley's, where I found a pleasant company, assembled by notice, consisting of Mr. Hedge, Stetson, Brownson, R. W. Emerson, Alcott, G. Ripley, Bartol, Dwight, Putnam, and Osgood. We had much social and philosophical talk; discussed several topics,—as what is the essence of *religion* as distinct from morality,—what are the features of the present time as to religion, etc. R. W. Emerson defined religion to be "the emotion of shuddering delight and awe from the perception of the infinite." Others said it was a "sentiment," others "a faith of reason." Yet, I think, when we came to explain, we all pretty nearly agreed.[42]

[40] "Ethics," the tenth lecture in Emerson's "The Philosophy of History" series, was delivered at the Masonic Temple, Boston, on February 16. Unless otherwise noted, all of Emerson's Boston lectures which Francis attended were delivered at the Masonic Temple. Francis is thinking of this passage: "Some young people are diseased with speculations, for example, the theological problems of original sin, origin of evil, predestination and the like. . . . These are the mumps and measles and whooping coughs of the soul" (*The Early Lectures of Ralph Waldo Emerson,* ed. Stephen E. Whicher, Robert E. Spiller, Wallace E. Williams [Cambridge, Mass., 1959–1972], II, 143, 145: hereafter cited as *EL*).

[41] Emerson apparently was in charge of supplying the pulpit at East Lexington; see his letters to Hedge, May 5, 1837, *L,* II, 73, and to J. S. Dwight, June 3, 1837, *L,* II, 79, and June 24, 1839, Stanley T. Williams, "Unpublished Letters of Emerson," *Journal of English and Germanic Philology,* XXVI (Oct., 1927), 476.

[42] This was the sixth meeting of the Transcendental Club. Not previously identified are Caleb Stetson, minister at Medford; John S. Dwight, an itinerant preacher who had

6 December 1837. To Boston, to hear Mr. Emerson's lecture. It was the first of his course this winter on Human Culture and was occupied in a general explanation of the nature, means, extent, etc. of Culture.[43] Like all the lectures, sermons, and writings of Mr. E., it was a rich strain of music from the upper air. The fault is that of too quick and easy *generalisation,* —the natural fault of a mind that dwells habitually on ideas and principles. But every sentence in it was a gem of thought. His description of the *ideal,* the universal aspiration towards the *better,* was admirable, and, what some of his statements are not, it was clear. He was perpetually opening such rich, lofty, far reaching veins of thought, that we sat breathless, as it were, and the mind ached with pleasure in following him. The commonness and quaintness of some of his illustrations threw a peculiar coloring of homely wisdom over parts of the lecture, which yet blended finely with the elevated spirituality of the whole. Nothing surprises me more than the inexhaustible beauties of Mr. E.'s style; you listen, expecting that, as in other men's writing, so in his an ordinary sentence will occur at least now and then; but it never comes; *every* sentence is a perfect one, showing the unconscious *artist,* as the most trifling turns in a fine statue show the master hand of the true sculptor. To hear Mr. E. and to see the varying expressions of his heavenly countenance, while truth radiates from him, rather than is uttered by him, seems like breathing a better atmosphere than that of the world. "Largior hic campos aether et lumine vestit. Purpureo, solemque suum, sua sidera norunt."[44]

13 December 1837. Went to Boston. Went to hear Mr. Emerson's lecture, the second in the course. It was on that part of Culture, which relates to the *hand,* "the doctrine of the hands," as he called it, including the forms of mechanical ingenuity and industry as manifestations, or promoters of the general human culture, etc.[45] It was less philosophical, less *transcendental* (as the talk of the day would say), than the first lecture; it was full of all pithy, quaint, humorous, and serio-comical remarks and illustrations, abounding in truth and wisdom. I suppose *practical men* (as they are called) must have liked it better than most of Mr. E.'s lectures.

3 January 1838. In the evening went to Boston and heard another of Mr.

---

graduated from the Harvard Divinity School in 1836; George Putnam, minister at Roxbury; and Samuel Osgood, a recent Divinity School graduate.

[43] The "Introductory" lecture in Emerson's "Human Culture" series was delivered on December 6 (*EL*, II, 213).

[44] "Here an ampler ether clothes the meads with roseate light, and they know their own sun, and stars of their own" (*Aeneid,* Book VI, ll. 640–641, *Virgil,* trans. H. Rushton Fairclough, rev. ed. [Cambridge, Mass., 1965], I, 550–551).

[45] "Doctrine of the Hands," the second lecture in Emerson's "Human Culture" series, was delivered on December 13 (*EL*, II, 230).

Emerson's admirable lectures; it was on the Culture of the Social Nature, full of his genius and beauty of manner, which appears frequently like originality, when the thought itself is not new.[46]

10 January 1838. Went to Boston—left the party to attend Mr. Emerson's lecture, which was on the *heart* as signifying *intellectual integrity*,—i.e. that we must do things *from the heart*, we must *be*, and not *seem*.[47] It was full of his rich moral eloquence, striking down deep into the truth which underlies all outside things. But after the lecture, I had some debate with him for saying that Walter Scott sometimes was not *real*, but acted the fine gentleman. The *spiritual* men, I find, are not disposed to do justice to Scott, because he lived so in the phenomenal, the outward; they will not allow him to be a *true man*, because he was not what they require. But why was not his development as true, hearty and real, as if he had been a spiritualist? It had as much reality, though it was different. I hold Scott to have been as true a *man* as Coleridge.[48]

6 February 1838. Went to Boston to attend Mr. Emerson's lecture. It was the last in the course, and was a most delightful survey or recapitulation of some of the principles of Human Culture.[49] I suppose every one present was sad to think it was the last: it was like a beautiful strain of music which one would fain have continued indefinitely. I could not but think of Milton's exquisite description, for I felt as his Adam felt:

> "The angel ended, and in Adam's ear"
> (quoted from this line down, to)
> "With glory attributed to the high Creator."
> (Par[adise]. Lost. Bk. VIII. 1–13.)

Mr. Emerson in this course of lectures has spoken of high things, and spoken of them as one filled with the pure inspiration of truth.

14 February 1838. Went to Cambridge to hear Mr. E., who is to repeat his lectures there. Heard the lecture on the "doctrine of the hands," man's

[46] "The Heart," the fifth lecture in Emerson's "Human Culture" series, was delivered on January 3 (*EL*, II, 278).

[47] "Being and Seeming," the sixth lecture in Emerson's "Human Culture" series, was delivered on January 10. Repeated at Concord on May 16, it was retitled "Intellectual Integrity" (*EL*, II, 295).

[48] In the lecture Emerson had stated that "Scott aspired to be known for a fine gentleman," and because of this: "Scott seems to me not to have been a great poet but to have had one talent, a sort of *clairvoyance*, so that no man died to him but whatever he knew of the history of a house or a hamlet or a glen instantly reproduced the ghosts of the departed in form and habit as when they lived. . . ." In short, Scott had a "reverence for great men" which "betrays always our deep sympathy with the real" (*EL*, II, 307).

[49] "General Views," the tenth and final lecture in Emerson's "Human Culture" series, was delivered on February 7 (*EL*, II, 357).

double-speeders, as he called them,—the culture arising from labor. We had heard it before in Boston; but it was as fresh and beautiful as ever.[50]

22 February 1838. To Cambridge to hear Mr. Emerson's lecture. It was on the culture of the *intellect,*—what the intellect is, how it grows and what *we can do* for it. The lecture, on the whole, I think superior to any I have heard from Mr. E., more methodical, and coherent,—at the same time full of lofty and far reaching views. The two practical directions to the student, have a room to yourself, and keep a journal.[51]

8 March 1838. To Cambridge to hear Mr. Emerson's lecture;—it was on *the heart,* or the affections, the social nature,—full to overflowing of beauty and truth; he closed with a description of a family of young, intelligent boys, struggling for education, and acquiring culture, amidst the rough training of poverty and hardship; nothing could exceed it for power of truth, and for felicitous sketching.[52]

15 March 1838. To Cambridge to hear Mr. Emerson's lecture; it was the second part on the Affections, a noble and beautiful thing. I had heard it before in Boston.[53]

22 March 1838. Went to Cambridge and heard Mr. Emerson's lecture on the heroic: it was grand in accordance with the subject,—alluded to Lovejoy and the Alton murder.[54]

28 March 1838. Went to hear Mr. Emerson's lecture on the culture of the

[50] This is Emerson's lecture, "Doctrine of the Hands." According to the editors of *EL,* this was probably repeated at Framingham on February 21 (II, 230). Both *EL* and Eleanor M. Tilton place Emerson in Framingham on February 14 delivering the "Introductory" lecture to his "Human Culture" series; neither reports Emerson's delivering the "Hands" lecture in his Cambridge series. If Emerson did deliver his Cambridge lectures on Thursday, as most in that series were, Francis would have heard him on the fifteenth, an open date in Tilton's schedule (II, 213; "Emerson's Lecture Schedule—1837–1838—Revised," *Harvard Library Bulletin,* XXI [Oct., 1973], 397).

[51] "The Head," the third lecture in Emerson's "Human Culture" series, was delivered on February 22 (Tilton, "Emerson's Lecture Schedule," p. 397). Emerson's "two practical directions to the student" which Francis recalls were "sit alone" and "keep a journal" (*EL,* II, 261).

[52] "The Heart" was delivered on March 8 (Tilton, "Emerson's Lecture Schedule," p. 397).

[53] "Being and Seeming" was delivered on March 15 (Tilton, "Emerson's Lecture Schedule," p. 397).

[54] "Heroism," the eighth lecture in Emerson's "Human Culture" series, was delivered on March 22 (Tilton, "Emerson's Lecture Schedule," p. 397). The abolitionist editor Elijah P. Lovejoy of Alton, Illinois, had been murdered by a mob on November 7, 1837. To Emerson, "brave Lovejoy" had died "for the rights of free speech and opinion, and died when it was better not to live." Francis himself thought the murder "an atrocity," and in a sermon expressed his "indignation at the outrage" (*EL,* II, 327, 338; journal entry, Nov. 30, 1837, Weiss, *Francis,* p. 56).

moral sentiment, *the holy* in man.[55] This is the lecture, which, when delivered in Boston, alarmed some people not a little, as certain parts of it were supposed to deny the personality of the Deity and to border close upon atheism. Strange what interpretations are sometimes put upon the words of a man, who is unique and original in thought and expression! So far from this lecture containing anything like atheism, it seemed to me a noble strain of fervent, lofty, philosophical piety. It was, like its topic, *holy*. The only idea of personality in the Deity, which he impugned, was, I think, the vulgar idea, which considers God as occupying space:—the personality which consists in a *will* and *consciousness* (and what other personality can there be?) he seemed to me to express or take for granted, though, it is true, some of his incidental expressions might look differently. I thought that in one passage of the lecture he seemed to take away the distinct, individual existence of man, as a conscious being, after death, and resolve him into the All, the Divine Soul: but my impression is probably erroneous. I wish exceedingly to see Mr. E. in private and hear him expound these matters more with all the sweet charm of his delightful conversation.[56] After return from Cambridge, read and wrote, but not much; my head and heart were too full of Mr. E.'s lecture for that.

29 March 1838. Went to C[ambridge]. with Miss M. to hear Mr. Emerson. It was the last lecture of the course, and that was the only sad thing about it: it gave a view of the obstacles to culture, the excitements to it, a noble conclusion to a noble course of wisdom and philosophical eloquence.[57]

10 September 1838. Took tea at——, a family belonging to the straitest sect of Boston conservatism. I found they had been taught by——to abhor and abominate R. W. Emerson as a sort of mad dog: and when I defended that pure and angelic spirit and told them he was full of piety and truthfulness (as he is, no man more so), they laughed at me with amazement,—for no such sounds had penetrated their *clique* before.

22 September 1838. Returned to Mr. Emerson's, and spent the night. There was abundance of good talk, which I hardly know how to report. What a pure, noble, loving, far-reaching spirit is Mr. E.! When we were alone, he talked of his Discourse at the Divinity School, and of the obloquy it had

[55] "Holiness," the ninth lecture in Emerson's "Human Culture" series, was delivered on March 28 (Tilton, "Emerson's Lecture Schedule," p. 398).

[56] Francis was apparently mistaken in his favorable impression, for Ellis Gray Loring, who talked with Emerson about the lecture the next day, felt "He carries idealism to the Extreme, Consequently if there is a God, he is God. God & he are one" (Tilton, "Emerson's Lecture Schedule," pp. 390–391).

[57] "General Views" was delivered on March 29, concluding the Cambridge series (Tilton, "Emerson's Lecture Schedule," p. 398).

brought upon him: he is perfectly quiet amidst the storm; to my objections and remarks he gave the most candid replies, though we could not agree upon some points: the more I see of this beautiful spirit, the more I revere and love him; such a calm, steady, simple soul, always looking for truth and living in wisdom, and in love for man, and goodness, I have never met. Mr. E. is not a philosopher, so called, not a logic-man, not one whose vocation it is to state processes of argument; he is a *seer* who reports in sweet and significant words what he sees; he looks into the infinite of truth, and records what there passes before his vision: if you see it as he does, you will recognise him for a gifted teacher; if not, there is little or nothing to be said about it and you will go elsewhere for truth: but do not brand him with the names of *visionary,* or *fanatic,* or *pretender*: he is no such thing,—he is a true, godful man, though in his love of the ideal he disregards too much the actual.

23 September 1838. In the morning at Mr. E.'s, we talked chiefly on matters of natural science, where Mr. Russell was continually giving us information and excellent remarks.[58] I laughed heartily at a quotation made by Mr. E. in his arch, quiet way; Mr. R. had told us of a naturalist, who spent much time and pains in investigating the habits and nature of the *louse* on *the cod-fish*; "O star eyed science" said Mr. E. "hast thou wandered there?"

9 January 1839. Then wife and I rode to Boston, to hear Mr. Emerson's lecture. It was on Genius.[59] Never before have I been so much delighted and excited even by this most delightful and exciting of all lecturers. It was a strain of inspiration, at once lofty and sweet, throughout. It was a burst of that power, of which it treated. I was reminded of the oft quoted line about Longinus,—"And is himself the great sublime he draws." Mr. E. gives one such a succession of the best things in condensed sentences, that we can scarcely *remember* any of them. He has not, like common writers, any of those dry, sandy spots, indifferent passages,—where we can rest for a few moments, and think of and remember the good things. Hence it is so difficult to give an account to others of what he says.

23 January 1839. We (i.e. my wife and I, W. White and Miss Meriam) set off for Boston to hear Mr. Emerson.[60] The lecture was on the Tragedy

[58] The naturalist John Lewis Russell was spending a "good woodland day or two" with Emerson when Francis visited Concord (Sept. 25, *JMN,* VII, 86).

[59] "Genius," the fifth lecture in Emerson's "Human Life" series, was delivered on January 9 (*EL,* III, 68).

[60] "Tho' I have not quoted always the *party* that went to hear the lectures, there were always a number of young people who went with my father—as well as my mother generally." (Abby Francis's note.)

of Life,—full of good thoughts, finely said, and of wisdom happily expressed,—perhaps not so striking, however, either for originality or beauty, as some of Mr. E.'s lectures. The idea of Fate was well described and dwelt upon,—how it is the idea of childish or savage life and is outgrown in the progress of refinement, being dispelled by reflection: its difference from philosophical necessity, which is optimism etc. Of the sadness occasioned by death he said, we have nothing to do with our own death,—we have only to do with living: the death of others saddens us, yet why should it? Sorrow, he said, after all belongs to the lower part of our nature, and is an element of weakness. Composure is the wise man's element etc.[61]

30 January 1839. To hear Mr. Emerson's lecture. It was on the *Comic* of Human Life.[62] It gave me on the whole but little satisfaction; the philosophy seemed not quite sound, and the illustrations and anecdotes were not so piquant and striking as his usually are. One, whose thoughts are usually so rich and beautiful, can afford to fail once in a while: it is rare indeed with him.

16 March 1839. We heard Mr. Emerson lecture at the Rumford Institute; it was one of the winter's course delivered in Boston. "The Protest,"—a most admirable exhibition of the disposition in young and ardent minds, in asserting their freedom, to protest against existing things. I have scarcely heard anything from E. which I liked so well. The instances of Michael Angelo and Columbus finely set forth.[63]

2 February 1840. W. came in this evening: told me among other things, that his aunt, Mrs.—— wished that Waldo Emerson had been among the lost in the steam-boat Lexington;[64] he is such a pestilent man!!

12 February 1840. With Sarah Clarke, Mary Channing, wife, and Mrs. Bartol went to hear Mr. Emerson's lecture. It was the last of his course,—on "Tendencies" with reference to the present Age; full of his good things, especially some keen remarks on the common foolish notions about

[61] "Tragedy," the seventh lecture in Emerson's "Human Life" series, was delivered on January 23 (*EL*, III, 103).

[62] "Comedy," the eighth lecture in Emerson's "Human Life" series, was delivered on January 30 (*EL*, III, 121).

[63] Emerson apparently repeated his lecture, "The Protest," the sixth in his "Human Life" series, at the Rumford Institute, Waltham, on March 16; no such lecture is recorded in *EL* or by William Charvat, *Emerson's American Lecture Engagements* (New York, 1961). For the "instances of Michael Angelo and Columbus," see *EL*, III, 100–101.

[64] The steamboat *Lexington* was destroyed by fire in Long Island Sound on January 13, 1840, with great loss of life (*L*, II, 250).

consistency; said this consistency was "the hobgoblin of little minds." There was more humor in this lecture than usual.[65]

7 November 1840. Spent the night at Mr. Emerson's. We talked till a late hour; he read me extracts of letters from Mr. Carlyle about Heraud, Landor, and others,—very amusing and striking from C.'s peculiar style of writing.[66] In conversation somehow I cannot get very nigh to Mr. Emerson: but after all, is not every person, by nature of the case, *insular, alone,* as to the intellect? do people ever come together, except through the affections? I suspect not.

31 March 1841. Among other reading, finished today Emerson's Essays, a most remarkable book.[67] It contains more closely packed thought, than anything I have read this long time. The style is altogether *suo more*, the most felicitous choice of words, so that every sentence is loaded with meaning and you cannot spare a word any more than you can spare a stone from the masonry of a compact, solid wall. Emerson's illustrations are arguments; they are not patched, or laid on the composition, but grow up from within it, as parts of its essential structure. There is in his mode of writing a constant use of figurative or allusive words, so that his sentences oftener suggest than tell his meaning; and this, I think, is the main cause of the alleged obscurity of his writings. The quaint familiarity, and the frequent allusion to the personal peculiarities or feelings of the author, without egotism, sometimes remind me of the manner of Montaigne, who, I know, is a favorite author with Mr. E. There will doubtless be a great outcry from some quarters about the sentiments expressed in these Essays, and with some of them certainly I can by no means agree. But nothing can be more disgusting than this ill-natured clamor of passion and ignorance. It is of little consequence whether you agree with Mr. E. or not: he is the most *suggestive* writer we have and stirs the reader's mind more than any other,—and that is a great merit, worth all the smooth proprieties, and approved commonplaces in the world.

26 November 1841. Went to Waltham, took tea, and heard Mr. Emerson

[65] "Tendencies," the tenth and final lecture in Emerson's "The Present Age" series, was delivered in Boston on February 12 (*EL*, III, 302). Emerson's famous "A foolish consistency is the hobgoblin of little minds" appears in *EL*, III, 310. Sarah Clarke was James Freeman Clarke's sister; Mary Channing was the daughter of the famous Unitarian minister, William Ellery Channing.

[66] For Carlyle's description of John A. Heraud, editor of the English *Monthly Magazine,* and the essayist Walter Savage Landor, see his letters to Emerson of April 1 and September 26, 1840, *CEC*, pp. 264–265, 281.

[67] Emerson's *Essays* [*First Series*] was advertised for sale on March 20 (*Boston Daily Advertiser*, p. 2). Emerson sent a copy to Francis one day earlier (*JMN*, VII, 546).

lecture on Poetry.[68] It had all his usual beauties, especially his magic felicity of style,—and some of his usual defects. How difficult it is to grasp and retain the nameless charm of that man's writing.

28 December 1841. Am reading the new volume of Emerson's Essays: how nobly and beautifully he speaks out from a world, which seems to be all his own! such an exquisite master of English expression is nowhere else to be found. I have tried in vain to analyse his mind: does it not defy analysis?

22 May 1847. From Athenæus we learn that the Rhodians were accustomed to welcome the arrival of the swallow in the Spring with a solemn song, beginning as follows:

> ἦλθ', ἦλθε χελιδὼν καλᾱ̀ς ὥρας
> ἄγουσα, καὶ καλοὺς ἐνιαυτούς,
> ἐπὶ γαστέρα λευκά, κἠπὶ νῶτα μέλαινα, &c.

"The swallow is come! is come! with her plumage white on the belly and black on the back, the herald of fair seasons and happy years" etc. (*Deipnosoph,* lib. VIII. cap. 15).[69]—O blessed nature, what are all the agonies of our studies by the side of thee! mere foolishness.—I love the sacred words, even better, when I remember that, as our *poet* (the ποιητής [poet] by way of eminence among us) has said,—

> "Out of the heart of nature rolled
> The burdens of the Bible old."[70]

15 January 1848. I am glad to see an article in Blackwood about Mr. Emerson, which does that great and good mind so much justice, though still the writer by no means understands Mr. E. or knows how to estimate him fully. The comparison of some of E.'s sentences to the quaint and rich ones of Sir Thomas Browne seems to me just and happy.[71]

5 August 1848. Today went to Concord to see R. W. Emerson, who has

[68] Emerson may have first delivered his lecture "The Poet," the third in his "The Times" series, at Concord on November 3, 1841, as "Nature and the Powers of the Poet." The lecture Francis heard was definitely read in Boston on December 16 (*EL,* III, 347). Neither *EL* nor Charvat, *Emerson's American Lectures,* note its delivery on November 26.

[69] See Book VIII, c. 60, *The Deipnosophists or Banquet of the Learned of Athenæus,* trans. C. D. Yonge (London, 1854), II, 567.

[70] "The Problem," ll. 13–14, *The Complete Works of Ralph Waldo Emerson,* ed. Edward Waldo Emerson (Boston, 1903–1904), IX, 6–7.

[71] The unidentified writer in *Blackwood's Edinburgh Magazine* said that Emerson, like Browne, "sometimes startles us by a *curiosity* of reflection, fitted to suggest and kindle thought, although to a dry logician it may seem a mere futility, or the idle play of imagination" ("Emerson," LXII [Dec., 1847], 646).

lately returned from England.[72] A charming conversation of two hours with him. The presence and the words of such a man are a quickening refreshment amidst the platitudes and the lies of the οἱ πολλοί [the masses] one meets with. He told me much in his charming way, of the men and things of London, of Milnes, Macaulay, etc., but especially of Carlyle, of whom he gave graphic descriptions.[73] He said that the authorship and literature of Carlyle were only accidental appendages to his strong, burly, earnest, intense soul, which was made for action rather than for writing; he was, E. said, "a great iron triphammer with an Eolian harp for an accompaniment,"—"he works great iron machinery to play his piano" etc.[74] E. went to Oxford, and was highly pleased with the scholars he found there;[75] he thought well of the institution of fellowships as means of promoting a general and spreading intellectual culture.

3 February 1849. Mr. Emerson is lecturing in Boston and my wife goes to hear him:[76] it is, I understand, the same sweet and lofty strain of intellectual and spiritual music, as ever, but how hard it is for any one, who hears and is charmed while he hears, to give an account of it! This comes inevitably from the character of Mr. E.'s genius: but I do not wonder that some think his lectures to be moonshine, because they cannot analyse them, or remember their parts: this is their mistake, but a natural one, for even his admirers are sometimes inclined to say of his fascinating words, in the language of Cowper—

> "Like quicksilver, the rhetoric they display
> Shines as it runs, but grasped at slips away."[77]

1 September 1849. I am reading again parts of Plato's Phædrus. In Plato's remarkable description of the man, whose soul is conversant with the divine reality of things (τὸ ὄν), is there not something applicable, without

72 Emerson had visited England and France from October, 1847, through July, 1848.

73 Richard Monckton Milnes had been introduced to Emerson's writings by Carlyle and had written an appreciative article on him in the March, 1840, *Westminister Review*; Thomas Babington Macaulay was a well-known English prose writer. Emerson had met both men while in London.

74 Emerson used the "triphammer" phrase in his journals of October 30, 1847, and 1852–1853; it was later printed in his "Impressions of Thomas Carlyle in 1848" (*JMN*, X, 179, 541; *Scribner's Magazine*, XXII [May, 1881], 89).

75 For Emerson's opinion of Oxford, see "Universities," *English Traits* (Boston, 1856), pp. 200–214.

76 According to Charvat, Emerson delivered the fourth lecture in his "Mind and Manners in the Nineteenth Century" series, repeated from a series given in England the previous year, at the Freeman Chapel, Boston, on February 5, 1849 (*Emerson's American Lectures*, p. 23; see *L*, IV, 80, 129, for possible topics).

77 "The Progress of Error," ll. 21–22, *The Poems of William Cowper* (New York, 1840), p. 30.

any arrogant assumption, to such a man as R. W. Emerson (I mention Mr. E. rather as representative of a class, than as individual)?—

> ἐξιστάμενος δὲ τῶν ἀνθρωπίνων σπουδασμάτων καὶ πρὸς τῷ θείῳ γιγνόμενος, νουθετεῖται μὲν ὑπὸ τῶν πολλῶν ὡς παρακινῶν, ἐνθουσιάζων δὲ λέληθεν τοὺς πολλούς.[78]

27 January 1855. Thursday evening, heard R. W. Emerson's lecture in the course on Slavery:[79] it was characteristic of him, of course,—for all he writes is so; admirable in parts, wise and true in all,—yet not well adapted on the whole for popular impression, though there was some hearty applause:—what a deep power sometimes wells out from his face!

28 July 1855. Went with Mrs. R. to R. W. Emerson's and had an altogether charming time of it. His brother, Wm. Emerson from N. York, was there. R. W. E. talked a good deal of Thomas Carlyle with whom he corresponds, and of Miss Bacon of New Haven.[80] He read a letter from the former, most characteristic and amusing, in which C. complains, in his own quaint way, of his disappointment about Frederick the Great, of whom he is making a book, and who turns out, he says, to be no hero to him.[81]

10 April 1858. Wednesday went with my wife to hear R. W. Emerson's lecture in Boston. Many years ago that strain of the poet-philosopher fell upon my ear often, and it always brought a charm with it. Now, after a long interval, heard again, it seemed just the same thing. The subject was "Self-possession," and I think there was no idea which I had not found in his lectures from 15 to 20 years ago, and the very words were about

[78] "But, as he forgets earthly interests and is rapt in the divine, the vulgar deem him mad, and rebuke him; they do not see that he is inspired" (*The Dialogues of Plato,* trans. B. Jowett, 4th ed. [Oxford, 1953], III, 156).

[79] According to Charvat, Emerson gave a lecture on slavery at the Tremont Temple, Boston, for the Massachusetts Anti-Slavery Society on January 25 (*Emerson's American Lectures,* p. 30).

[80] Delia Bacon's *The Philosophy of the Plays of Shakspere Unfolded,* published in 1857 with an introduction by Nathaniel Hawthorne, attempted to show Francis Bacon's authorship of Shakespeare's plays. Emerson had given her a letter of introduction to Carlyle when she left for England to do research and helped her to find a publisher. Carlyle thought "truly there can [be] no madder enterprise than her present one." She died in a mental institution in 1859. A copy of her book is still in Emerson's library (May 12, 1853, April 8, 1854, *CEC,* pp. 487–488, 502; Harding, *Emerson's Library,* p. 19).

[81] Carlyle wrote Emerson on May 13 he was discovering that Frederick "does not rise into the empyrean region," for his life was "the most dislocated, unmanagably incoherent, altogether dusty, barren and beggarly production of the modern Muses" (*CEC,* pp. 505–506).

the same.[82] The old topics, subjectiveness and individuality,—we create all that we see,—we are lords of all that is. I had hoped to find by this time something else; but, I doubt, Mr. E. never gets or has got beyond the old thought, however good that may be. The fault of his manner of discussing a subject seems to be that he never makes any progress in the subject itself: he empties before you a box or bag of jewels as he goes on, which you may take and make the most you can of; but you find no progress in the subject, no opening out, expanding, motion outwards,—but instead thereof standing still and giving the utterance that comes at the moment. He might as well begin anywhere else and end anywhere else, as where he does begin and end. The mind of the hearer has not the satisfaction of moving steadily on till the consummation is effected,—sweeping forward till the march of thought is brought to its natural close.

2 October 1858. Cattle-fairs and Agricultural shows are now the order of the day all over our Commonwealth. There was one at Concord, at which Mr. Emerson delivered the address, marked with his usual felicity of thought and expression:—it is quite noticeable what a *practical* man he is,—just what people generally think he is *not*.[83] I wish I had the privilege of seeing him more than I am ever likely to do in a world where every man has his own peculiar work, which drives him to the wall.

August 1859. On Wednesday I went to Concord, spent the night at Mrs. Ripley's: called in the evening at Mr. Emerson's, who talked charmingly, among other things, "what great things this time has done for us in giving us two such works as Carlyle's Frederick, Tennyson's new poem, the "Idylls of the King," said he.[84]

August 1862. At Mr. Emerson's, Mrs. Ripley and I met a room full of most pleasant and high company. Mr. E. himself,—his brother William with his lovely wife,—Channing, Elisabeth Peabody, etc.[85] Emerson talked with me (charmingly, as he always does) about the late Homeric contro-

82 "Self-Possession," the sixth lecture in Emerson's "Intellectual Science" or "Mental Philosophy" series, was delivered at the Freeman Place Chapel, Boston, on April 7 (Charvat, *Emerson's American Lectures*, p. 34).

83 Emerson delivered an address on "Man with the Hoe" at the Middlesex County Fair, Concord, on September 29 (Charvat, *Emerson's American Lectures*, p. 34).

84 Emerson called Carlyle's *History of Frederick the Second* "infinitely the wittiest book that ever was written." Tennyson's *Idylls of the King* showed "a supreme social culture, a perfect insight, and the possession of all the weapons and all the functions of a man." Copies of both works are still in Emerson's library (May, 1859, *The Journals of Ralph Waldo Emerson*, ed. Edward Waldo Emerson and Waldo Emerson Forbes, Boston, 1909–1914, IX, 195, 207; Harding, *Emerson's Library*, pp. 51, 269).

85 Not previously identified are Mrs. Samuel Ripley, wife of the minister at Waltham; Ellery Channing, poet and friend of Emerson and Thoreau; Elizabeth Palmer Peabody, reformer and long-time friend of Emerson.

versy, or discussion about the principles of translation as applied to the Iliad, between Matthew Arnold and F. W. Newman.[86] This was altogether a very bright evening.

3 January 1863. Read in the Eclectic Review a long, elaborate, would be philosophical article on R. W. Emerson, which interested me as coming from an English critic, and representing English thought about one whom *we* have known from his boyhood all the way from his growth up to fame.[87]

[86] Emerson had called Arnold's *On Translating Homer: Last Words* "the most amiable of books" when he read it upon publication in 1862. Arnold's work takes Francis Newman to task for the pedantic literalness of his diction and for the use of ballad metre in his recent translation of Homer. Arnold's book is still in Emerson's library (letter to Edward Emerson, June 12, *L*, V, 279; see William Robbins, *The Newman Brothers*, London, 1966, pp. 170–172; Harding, *Emerson's Library*, p. 15).

[87] "Emerson—The Conduct of Life," *Eclectic Review*, n.s. III (Nov., 1862), 363–409, favorably reviewed all Emerson's writings.

Emerson and Antinomianism: The Legacy of the Sermons

Wesley T. Mott

I

Ever since Andrews Norton characterized Transcendentalism as "the latest form of infidelity," Ralph Waldo Emerson's place in American thought has been a matter of dispute. The prevailing opinion, usually supported by selective reading of the bold, exuberant addresses and essays of the 1830's and 1840's, is that Emerson's intensely mystical piety and his antiauthoritarianism are rooted in a native Antinomian tradition.[1] But some scholars posit a very different Emerson—temperate, balanced, even conservative—an image that stands uneasily beside the portrait of the Transcendental rebel against religious formalism and social evils.[2] Crucial for understanding the sources of these seemingly contradictory elements are Emerson's long-neglected sermons, which to a remarkable degree shaped his later thought. As a minister Emerson tried to evoke a total commitment to Spirit and grace; at the same time, he cultivated a complex view of the spiritual life that implicitly confronted the dangers of Antinomianism. Finally, the habits of thought that led Emerson to resign his pulpit owe less to Antinomian antiformalism than to orthodox Puritan concepts of the Spirit. The sermons and their

Author's note: I am grateful to Professor Norman Pettit of Boston University for many suggestions in the preparation of this article.

1 See Perry Miller's influential "From Edwards to Emerson," *The New England Quarterly,* XIII (Dec., 1940), 589–617; rpt. in *Errand into the Wilderness* (New York, 1956), pp. 184–203. Miller was not the first to identify the strain of Protestant extremism in Emerson. Emerson's early biographer James Elliot Cabot saw that Transcendentalism belonged to the New England tradition of "various outbursts of religious enthusiasm overflowing the boundaries of accredited doctrine," in *A Memoir of Ralph Waldo Emerson* (New York, 1887), I, 253. Vernon L. Parrington believed that Transcendentalism heralded the release of "mystical aspirations" that Puritanism had "repressed," in *Main Currents in American Thought* (New York, 1930), II, 379.

2 See, for example, John Lydenberg's review of Edward Wagenknecht's *Ralph Waldo Emerson: Portrait of a Balanced Soul* and Jeffrey L. Duncan's *The Power and Form of Emerson's Thought,* in *American Literature,* XLVII (March, 1975), 121–123.

legacy reveal that Emerson's place in the Puritan tradition is even more central than has been supposed.

Emerson was reared in the twilight of New England Puritanism. His ancestor the Reverend Peter Bulkeley had founded Concord in 1635; his step-grandfather, the Reverend Ezra Ripley, and his Aunt Mary held to strict Reformed doctrine, for which young Waldo had respect and, later, occasional nostalgia. His father, William, was minister of First Church in Boston, church of John Winthrop and John Cotton. When from 1829 to 1832 Waldo served as minister to the church of the Mathers, Second Church in Boston, he was carrying on a family tradition. Undoubtedly he grew to chafe against the restrictions of duties and doctrine; but his ministry is all too often misconceived as a mere incubation period during which he outgrew the security of Aunt Mary's anachronistic notions and prepared to burst forth a full-blown Transcendentalist in the mid-1830's. In fact, Emerson took his sermons seriously and examined with great care both contemporary and perennial theological issues. Many of the sermons he continued to deliver as late as 1839; others, quickly abandoned, were crucial steps in his Puritan evolution toward Transcendentalism.

Recent Puritan scholarship has taught us the folly of viewing "the New England orthodoxy" or "Antinomianism" as a monolithic entity. But Larzer Ziff has given us a useful definition of Puritanism that transcends the historical period he speaks of: "the Anglo-American Christian tradition . . . exists in a tension between legalism and antinomianism." Puritanism, he goes on, "is not the antinomian pole itself but the political movement which, in the late sixteenth and early seventeenth centuries, brought into being institutions which adjusted the tension in favor of that pole."[3] In New England, where those institutions were given freest rein and where the dangers of Antinomianism were most fully realized, Puritans had continually to readjust that tension to prevent their experiment from vaporizing into an Antinomian denial of all things temporal. Indeed, in terms of both the inner life and church polity, "New England Puritanism" became the process of tension itself, whereby the heart, thirsting for the Spirit, made its necessary accommodations with the world.

[3] Larzer Ziff, "The Literary Consequences of Puritanism," *ELH*, XXX (Sept. 1963), 293.

The Synod that tried the Antinomian heresies of 1636–1638 arrived at firm doctrinal definitions—useful touchstones for the modern scholar—of just what Antinomianism is in terms of the nature of Spirit, human faculties, use of Scripture, and the relationship of individual to community. But the Puritans embraced many paradoxes. John Cotton, who came perilously close to being seduced into Anne Hutchinson's camp, went on to become the great apologist for the New England Way. Thomas Shepard, among the leading opponents of Hutchinson, hungered for assurance of salvation with an intensity that suggests emotional and spiritual needs in common with those who had drifted into heresy.

Such intensity and ambivalence became the trademark of subsequent Puritan revivals in New England. Jonathan Edwards, the champion of the Great Awakening of the 1730's and 1740's, took pains to warn his parishioners that conversion is not a wild, giddy liberation but a divine burden; indeed, genuine conversion had to be distinguished from mere emotional excitement or imagination. The saints, he declared, must not rest on their laurels, for conversion does not guarantee perpetual assurance. And in his Funeral Sermon for David Brainerd, Edwards praised his friend for decrying "enthusiasm" and "Antinomianism," and their attendant evil, Separatism. A century later Emerson grappled anew with traditional Puritan tensions. His entire career, from minister to sage, is a continual attempt to adjust and readjust inspiration to the demands of the world, to maintain a creative interplay between spiritual hunger and the constraints of the human constitution and social obligations.

II

Emerson brought to the ministry a conventional but genuine belief in original sin. His early journals and letters to Aunt Mary are filled with musings about the inadequacy of human nature and the problem of belief. Mere nature was no vehicle of divine insight at this stage of his life. Bothered by the problems of the "Origin of Evil" and skepticism, Emerson wrote to Aunt Mary on October 16, 1823, that he had found a solution in the sermons of Dr. Channing. Channing was preaching that "Revelation was as much a part of the order of things as any other event in the Universe."[4] Emerson added in his journal that Channing "considered God's word to be the only expounder of his works, & that Nature had always been found insufficient to teach men the great doctrines which Revelation inculcated."[5] Channing had naturalized Revelation while asserting the infinite superiority of Scripture over Nature. Emerson found Channing's example helpful in positing a tentative solution to his craving for spiritual assurance. But he continued to vacillate between doubt and certainty. He wrote in 1826: "It is not certain that God exists but that he does not is a most bewildering & improbable chimera" (*J*, II, 340. The degree of Emerson's doubt is evidenced by the fact that he struck out "wild" as the third adjective modifying "chimera").

Young Emerson pondered the nature of the spiritual life as had Puritans before him. His desire for assurance is hedged about on all sides by Puritan fears that he might be misled by his own enthusiasm. In his College Theme Book he acknowledges the benefits of enthusiasm for scriptural promises; but it is another matter to be deceived by "false raptures." A man cannot be a vehicle for pure Spirit; rather, he must accept "the necessity & finite nature of the human constitution, which will not admit of any expansion of ideas proportionate to the truth" (*J*, I, 193). As a minister Emerson well understood the terror of finite man contemplating his inadequacy. His descriptions of anxiety resemble those of seventeenth-century divines: "First, he feels that an indefinable evil hangs over him . . . his soul is oppressed with *fear*. Its active powers are paralyzed, its affections cramped, and all its energy directed to an anxious exploring of ways of escape, a way of atonement. . . . Fear makes the spirit passive." He warns, however, that one must not take the "rigid" way out by fleeing to the easy security of an inscrutable authority any more than one should deny one's sin and turn to the "licentiousness" of liberalism. Emerson's middle way is not compromise; it is a classic New England Puritan's readjustment of the counterclaims of legalism and Antinomianism. For Emerson, as for those who opposed Antinomianism in the 1630's, the successful Christian learns to rejoice "with trembling," to acknowledge "the weight of his sins" and "his

[4] *The Letters of Ralph Waldo Emerson*, ed. Ralph L. Rusk (New York, 1939), I, 137–139. Cited hereafter in the text as *Letters*.

[5] *The Journals and Miscellaneous Notebooks of Ralph Waldo Emerson*, ed. William H. Gilman et al. (Cambridge, Mass., 1960–), II, 160–161. Cited hereafter in the text as *J*.

occasional backslidings," without being broken by them; "though he is cast down he is not destroyed."[6]

Instead of opting for the passivity of Antinomian assurance, Emerson suggests ways in which a man can detect divine workings in his soul; but he condenses or eliminates the difficult steps by which earlier Puritans had measured growth in assurance of salvation. Throughout the sermons he proclaims the efficacy of reason. God does not reveal Himself through extraordinary events. He operates through natural, reliable means that "the heart" can perceive immediately. Experience and observation become one with assurance, for to know God does not require "time & preparation."[7] Like Jonathan Edwards, Emerson believes that the Book of Nature, read purely, unfolds and confirms the word of God. In Sermon No. 43, for example, he declares, "All that is beautiful is only a revelation . . . of that which is fairer"; and "Thro every image of poetry of art of science" man "worships" the Source of all beauty. Not content with easy correspondences, he insists in Sermon No. 121 that a man is obligated to will, to choose between body and spirit. He anticipates his concept of "compensation" when he warns that, even though Heaven and Hell are not literal, Judgment is. A man must therefore expand his spiritual capacity here and now: "The wants are spiritual, & so must the objects be."[8]

In Pauline terms he says that a man can *know* only what he *is*. For the prepared and receptive man, "Faith"—"the perception of spiritual things"—is its own evidence of divinity. To have such insight does not put a man above the Law. Living according to the Ten Commandments prepares a man for "spiritual discernment," which confirms and fulfills the laws of the prophets. For Antinomians, faith

[6] *Young Emerson Speaks*, ed. Arthur C. McGiffert, Jr. (Boston, 1938), pp. 83–84, 87. Cited hereafter in the text as *YES*. Orthodox Puritans had a higher toleration of spiritual anxiety than had Anne Hutchinson and her followers; indeed, the Synod of 1636–38 declared "sweet doubts" to be a part of preparation for grace. *The Antinomian Controversy, 1636–1638: A Documentary History*, ed. David D. Hall (Middletown, Conn., 1968), p. 224. I have modernized spelling and punctuation of all Puritan documents in this paper.

[7] Sermon No. 23, bMS Am 1280.215, Houghton Library, Harvard University. Quotations from Emerson's manuscript sermons are used by permission of the Harvard College Library and the Ralph Waldo Emerson Memorial Association. Manuscript sermons are cited hereafter in the text by number.

[8] Emerson's belief that the mind yearns instinctively for the Spirit resembles that of his ancestor Bulkeley: "Similitude breeds content. The soul is a spirit, and desires spiritual things." *The Gospel-Covenant; or the Covenant of Grace Opened*, 2nd edn. (London, 1651), p. 195.

had been an unnecessary preliminary to seizure; but for Emerson the preliminaries were themselves assurances. He did not need, as Anne Hutchinson did, sudden, absolute certainty effected without man's participation. Instead he found adequate comfort in the *growth* of "the spiritual faculty," which in transcending the natural senses transcended fear and death; for "A stronger and stronger word of assurance comes from the undeceiving inward Monitor" (*YES,* p. 202).

We can see in Emerson's notion of innate assurance the budding of his familiar concept of self-reliance. As a minister, however, he was not attempting to inflate man's inherent worth; he was insisting, as had the first American Puritans, that longing for the Spirit must not obliterate the role of the soul's faculties in preparing for salvation.[9] Retaining his youthful sense of man's finiteness, he reminded his parishioners in Sermon No. 123 of the moral and religious "limits of self-reliance." You can judge the truth, he said, of a "proposition the terms of which you understand"; but in trusting oneself *"the origin of self must be perceived"* lest one become a "bundle of errors & sins."[10] Yet God cannot make a man "perceive truth," he went on to say, "except by the use of his own faculties." New England Puritans from Hooker to Edwards confronted the Hutchinsonian argument that the influx of divine light destroys, or works above, human faculties. God *works through* the faculties, they countered; and they embraced the paradox that, although man must prepare for grace, it is Christ who is the worker in our salvation. So Emerson warns in Sermon No. 43 that we should not misjudge the cause of man's turning to God in adversity: "it seems to me it is the triumph of man, it is not man, it is God in the soul." He could admit in Sermon No. 73 that there is an unsettling lack of precision in "the Christian Revelation whose greatest value must always be reckoned the assurance it gives of the immortality of the human soul." But he added that fur-

[9] John Winthrop recorded the first "Error" of the Antinomians: "In the conversion of a sinner, which is saving and gracious, the faculties of the soul, and workings thereof, in things pertaining to God, are destroyed and made to cease." The Synod proclaimed that Scripture "speaketh of the faculties of the soul (as the understanding and the will) not as destroyed in conversion, but as changed, *Luk*. 24.45" (Hall, p. 219).

[10] Compare Emerson's "The Father is in me—I in the Father. Yet the Father is greater than I" (*YES,* p. 200) with Thomas Hooker's "The child holds the father, because the father holds him. So we hold God, because he holds us" (*The Soul's Ingrafting into Christ,* London, 1637, p. 3).

ther knowledge of "the next life" is withheld because it would "probably unfit us for the duties of this." "We have in our own minds," he declared, "intimations sufficiently clear for the direction of our conduct." It was in keeping with Emerson's honest view of human nature that he could hold in balance and creative tension both his need for assurance and the means for achieving evidence thereof.

Emerson spelled out the limits of self-reliance for another reason. He knew that Antinomians had courted slothfulness because they denied the efficacy of human endeavor, but that Unitarians were often charged with a different kind of "laxity": by stressing the "mercy" of God, contemporary Calvinists thought, Unitarians had lost the constraint, the ballast, for "a godly life." Indeed, Emerson declares in Sermon No. 43, it would be better to return to Calvinist doctrine, to "put a bridle on the heart," than to live loosely. He goes on to say, however, that "this laxity does not belong to true Christianity, but to bad men." He stresses that, although knowing God is sweet, Christianity is demanding and requires continual vigilance and obedience to a higher power. Ultimately, the efficacy of a man's deeds are attributable to the indwelling God, Who becomes "a principle of action."

By involving human faculties in the search for assurance, Emerson confronted the most threatening ethical implication of Antinomianism—that without the "witness of the Spirit," all of a man's "gifts and graces" and "contributions, &c. would prove but legal, and would vanish" (Hall, p. 263). Was a man absolved, then, from obedience to law and from good behavior? Thomas Shepard spoke for all orthodox Puritans when he demanded that a man must make an effort even though works are not inherently saving: "Thy good duties though they cannot save thee, yet thy bad works will damn thee. Thou art therefore not to cast off the duties, but thy resting in these duties."[11] For the Puritans it followed that, if a man is obliged to make an effort with his spiritual faculties, he must also, in a godly way, exert control over the material world. Culture and success, properly viewed, were both indexes of a man's spiritual estate and social restraints upon unbridled "natural men" in Christian communities. In mercantile nineteenth-century Boston, Emerson found men grossly overevaluating one another's respectability by standards of "wealth &

[11] *The Sincere Convert* (London, 1640), p. 258.

power." To do so, he charged, is to "judge . . . according to the flesh" (Sermon No. 5). But he was not opposed in principle to nurturing and using the world. The savagery of primitive islanders encountered by explorers proves, he said in Sermon No. 57, that "depravity was not the fruit of refinement, but was planted wherever the seed of man was sown." Just as the Puritans had permitted proper use of creatures for man's benefit, Emerson declares that "security of Property" and "dominion over the material world" are God-given imperatives to structure moral and godly societies.

Like a scrupulous Puritan, Emerson saw the danger of exalting the efficacy of human conduct. Always distrustful of reformers, he accuses liberal Unitarians of serving their egos rather than the needy with charity. The "overweening conceit" that often accompanies good deeds is futile; for God "explores the heart & the motive" that prompted the deed (Sermon No. 19). Like Edwards, Emerson understood that some acts can be performed "alike by those who feel & by those who do not feel their obligation"; indeed, "Decency & calculation may be proxies for self devotion & love" (Sermon No. 26).

Like Thomas Shepard, however, Emerson does not recoil from charity or recommend passivity. In Sermon No. 48 he interprets the history of Christianity as a continual debate between those who consider religion to be "a *system of belief*" and those who consider it "a *practical system*." Typically, Emerson settles for neither extreme. He argues that the only "index by which it is possible to determine your progress in goodness" is "good works." Like orthodox Puritans, he defines good works not simply as "any partial or outward or ostentatious activity" but also as inner movement by the *"will"* and *"conscience."* He implicitly criticizes the Antinomian attitude when he observes ironically: "If we are capable of a momentary glow of pious feeling, we think we are nothing less than martyrs. But our experience may show us that these feelings are very subject to ebb & to flow." Man, he goes on to say, is a creature of both "Reason & Affection." As such, man's works give continuity to his life; they are a preparation completed by "Faith." A man is therefore obliged to behave ethically. Though deeds are not intrinsically saving, as Emerson says in Sermon No. 81, a man's "character" is manifested in deeds and so recognized by good men and by God. Man's need to foster good works is not so much an Arminian assessment of human worth as a reminder that man cannot soar to spiritual perfection; he needs earthly signs to measure his growth.[12]

As a minister Emerson developed a dialectic of Pauline grace and human effort that expressed in the nineteenth century much of the seventeenth-century frame of mind. Of paramount importance both for Emerson and the Puritans was divine light; nature and man were fallen and could be reborn only through the saving power of Spirit. But Emerson shared with those Puritans who resisted Antinomian helplessness before Spirit the conviction that man must use the world as a passage to heaven. A man could not save himself by his own acts; but he must be able to detect in the workings of his mind the seeds of regeneration; and society must for a principle of order be able to judge men by their conduct. Young Emerson was more conservative than many of his fellow Unitarians in calling for a renewed awareness of the need for conversion by spiritual means. He was more liberal than Calvinists of his day in reviving the Puritan paradox that grace must be earned.

III

Emerson's analysis of the private spiritual life and its ethical obligations is ineluctably linked with an intense patriotism, a conviction that redemption in America is a corporate concern. Enthusiasts and Antinomians had always concluded from the doctrines of original sin and free grace that only the assurance of election, privately received, could satisfy the soul's longing. Other men, the mere clay of an imperfect world, were of little account in the drama of the soul's redemption. But Antinomianism was anathema on these shores largely because it denied that New England could be New Jerusalem; it denied the significance of historical, communal destiny.

Visible sainthood was for seventeenth-century Puritan congregations a means both to maintain social structure and to guarantee that the churches of New England should be a reasonably accurate reflection of the invisible church of the elect, whose members were known only to God. The forging of strong bonds with other Christians was part of the godly man's work in the world. Thomas Hooker ex-

[12] Sermon No. 81 opens the text of Matthew 7:20—"By their fruits, ye shall know them"—a text popular with Puritans because it declares visible signs to be indexes of regeneration.

plained: "Mutual subjection is as it were the sinews of society, by which it is sustained and supported. . . . It is the highest law in all Policy Civil or Spiritual to preserve the good of the whole." Regenerate men, Hooker elsewhere declared, naturally seek out like-minded men for mutual strength and brotherhood: "Oh then get you to the Saints of God, and get them to your houses, and lay hold upon gracious Christians, and say, I will live and converse with you, for the Spirit of Christ is with you." The English Puritan William Ames had also kept strictly to the injunctions of St. Paul regarding the vigilance—indeed fastidiousness—necessary in choosing acquaintances. "No man capable of blessedness," Ames wrote, "ought to be removed from the embrace of our love"; but he cautioned that "Some men are more to be loved than others, namely, those nearer to God and in God to ourselves. Gal. 6:10, *Let us do good to all, but especially to those who are of the household of faith.*"[13] Later Jonathan Edwards further defined the emotional grounds of "true virtue" as a "disposition to benevolence towards being in general"; but he continued to insist that the *truly* virtuous are drawn instinctively to men of a like disposition and that one cannot truly appreciate a benevolence one does not possess.

Standards for church membership had lost their rigor by Emerson's day. But he retains the impulse to search out and cleave to good men as a way of cultivating love of God and detecting through social involvement intimations of God Himself. In true friendship, he says in Sermon No. 26, we love not the friend's body but his "spiritual properties." Our very expectation of perfection in friends is a holy sentiment: "Consider that every good man, every good thing, every good action, word, & thought that you love, is only a *fragment of the divine nature.* Thus does our Father make himself known to his children. This is the hourly revelation by which our minds are instructed in his goodness." He goes further, in Sermon No. 121, to declare that men save or damn themselves by the company they keep. Bad men "seek . . . companions who love the same things. They shun the society of good men precisely as the lustful, the glutton, the miser, the robber[,] the murderer here shuns the society of wise & pious men." Correspondingly, the good seek out the good: "It is a law

[13] Hooker, *A Survey of the Summe of Church-Discipline* (London, 1648), part I, p. 188; *The Soul's Exaltation* (London, 1638), p. 53. Ames, *The Marrow of Theology*, trans. from the Latin by John D. Eusden (Boston, 1968), p. 302.

of spirits, wholly independent of time & place, that *like shall be joined with like,* & it holds of the good, as of the evil." The responsible Christian attempts to discern goodness as a way of growing in assurance. Emerson could be speaking of the Antinomian when he complains, "We sit still & hope that our salvation will be wrought out for us, instead of working out our own." With patience, faith, obedience to the Law, and a willingness to use this world for good, a man prepares for that perfect understanding which now belongs only to God but which one day will be accessible to the true Christian.

Intertwined with Emerson's concerns for friendship and society is his concept of the destiny of America. In his jeremiads he speaks of church and nation interchangeably, seemingly unaware that America's geographical, economic, and political expansion is evolving outside the sphere of influence of Boston Unitarianism. On the contrary, he often takes comfort in the conviction that his church is the saving remnant upholding the standards of the Puritan Fathers. The opening of Sermon No. 80, "Patriotism" (July 4, 1830), resembles Bulkeley's reminder at the conclusion of *The Gospel-Covenant* that New England as "a City set upon an hill" is a beacon for the world. Because of this privilege, New England owes God special obligations, obligations met only by inspired communal effort. Of Independence Day, Emerson declares: "The return of this anniversary cannot fail to awaken in our minds the recollection of Gods peculiar favors to our country & to quicken our religious feeling . . . [to rejoice together] is in our eye more godlike, & what mysterious grandeur in the consciousness of sympathizing with vast numbers of men, in acting on the feeling that is shared by a nation in the same hour." In Emerson's fusion of spiritual and political mission, the American Revolution is held up as an inspiration not only in this land, but also "on both sides of the Andes, in France, in Greece & throughout Europe." To the fact of actual corruption in his New Jerusalem, he has a ready solution: redefinition. He simply makes a distinction between the *true* patriotism that "binds him to the best citizen" and "draws him to the purest action," and "The America of the selfish & ambitious man," which by implication is not "real." Rather than bemoan or rail against evil, Emerson simply denies that evil is *inherent* in the *true* America.

We have only recently been made aware that the American jeremiad from the beginning was not merely a lamentation. Sacvan Bercovitch has demonstrated that the promise of America as a redemptive land rendered the thought of actual failure unthinkable. The New England Puritan imagination improves on reality, keeping the promises alive in the heart of the regenerate Christian.[14] For Emerson too the inbred conviction that the New Jerusalem is always still to be achieved feeds the myth that our corporate mission is ongoing, always vital. "[T]he present generation," he says in Sermon No. 80, must "determine for themselves the character of their country"; indeed, the *real* America is an "idea" in each man's mind, implicitly protected from adverse events.

That America's destiny is unfinished makes her, confident of past and future, able continually to respond to fresh challenges. Thus Emerson can make a cult of the Puritan Fathers while at the same time updating the myth to encompass the ideals of the American Revolution. He warns of the danger of America being loved for "convenience" and "calculation": "O my friends [let] not this low corrupt unhonoured America be the image in our hearts[.] It was not such an one that fiftyfour years ago was declared free. It was not such an one that the Puritans sought to build the cities of their Zion in its untrampled snows." Although one side of the nineteenth-century mind stereotyped the Puritans as sour-faced, hypocritical witchhunters, Emerson appeals to that other side of the nineteenth-century imagination that sentimentalized America as "that hallowed asylum of religious liberty which heroic men persecuted in their own country sought & found." That legacy still informs Emerson's "America": "Let it be the country consecrated by the unaffected piety of our fathers by their anxious desire of the spiritual good of their posterity[.]"

In order to make his Puritan heroes palatable to liberal Unitarians, Emerson often scrubbed them of their sterner Calvinistic colors, in effect making them suitable progenitors of Thomas Jefferson (a process Perry Miller blamed on Vernon L. Parrington and James Truslow Adams). But in Sermon No. 113, "Fasting, Humiliation, and Prayer," which Emerson notes was written for "FAST DAY, 1831," he makes no excuses for Puritan severity but lambastes his contemporaries for falling short of Puritan standards. He admits that many

[14] *The Puritan Origins of the American Self* (New Haven, 1975), pp. 115, 125.

criticize the continuation of the Fast Day custom "as a relic of an ancient race, which has outlived its day." But he cajoles his parishioners: "There are, it may be hoped, a great number yet remaining who hold in honour the memory of that old people, that self-denying race, who redeemed England, & planted America" ("self-denying" is inserted over a scratched-out "generous"; Emerson seems to have felt that to humanize the Puritans too lavishly was either sentimental or condescending). "It has become fashionable to praise them," he goes on. "Our self-love leads us to extol our ancestors. But far better would it be that we should praise them with understanding,—that we should value what they valued."

He explains away the Puritan's reputation for fearsome sternness: "He that thinks so profoundly, he that acts so habitually in reference to the principles of the first class as to give all his life & manners the expression of simple gravity, may be excused if he have little playfulness in his conversation, & little elegance in his circumstances[.]" The Puritans had "faults as a party," he admits; "But they had *enthusiasm*." Emerson is not advocating the *heresy* of "enthusiasm"; he is recommending a cure for nineteenth-century ennui and the craving for purposive action in the religious community during a brawling, materialistic, democratic era. The Puritans "tho't life had something worth contending for. They lived & died for sentiments & not for bread only. To these apostolical men, the cross was a dear emblem, who knew how to suffer themselves, their idea of Jesus was an indwelling thot, which manifested itself in every action—in the house; & in Church & in State."

For Emerson the Fast Day is no hollow relic; it grows from the human propensity to sin. "Penitence," he suggests, is "needed for our public & our personal safety." The strenuous life is both appropriate to the human condition and a guarantee of social order. In terms Emerson seldom rivalled for severity, he declares, "The house of mourning is better than the house of feasting. The hair cloth, solitude, & bread & water, are safer courses for tempted man, than much company, & rich clothes, & easy living." He expresses the fear that America's greed may lead to civil war in terms that resemble both the first American Puritans' quest for self-contained uniformity and Jefferson's principles of military and political self-sufficiency: "It needs no strange or impossible foreign influence or marvellous series of external events. It needs only certain change in the speculative principles which we ourselves entertain." The American dream can be destroyed only by negligent Americans. He goes on to list the symptoms of the national malady: the government's mistreatment of the Indians, "a barefaced trespass of power upon weakness" which is sanctioned by law and is met with a distressing "general indifference" by the American people; "the ferocity of party spirit," which contaminates even the courts; a love of quick money and vain "display"; the "hunger for excitement" and willingness to "sacrifice the holiest principles to any popular cry." All this Emerson sees as both a declension from Puritan ideals and a betrayal of public purpose. Citing Jeremiah, he suggests that "These are bad tokens for the permanence of our institutions."

Quentin Anderson has shown that Emerson spoke for a generation that in the wake of Jacksonian levelling was profoundly insecure with respect to its institutions. Anxiety about the disintegration of the social order served to throw men back upon the isolate self as the only reliable source of value, the last refuge from anarchy. While Anderson admits that Emerson was aware "of our incapacity for a final absorption into being," he is critical of the stance of Emerson's audience: "It was a creation of the age, antinomian man, gathered into the antinomian congregation." Anderson explains the danger of Emerson's posture: "Secular incarnation involves a denial of history, membership in a generation, charity, reform, institutional means of every sort, and at the same time an extreme antinomianism, a claim for the supreme authority of the moment of vision."[15] I have tried to show that young Emerson doctrinally was deeply distrustful of any form of Antinomianism.

And Professor Bercovitch has broken new ground for our understanding of the self in the American Renaissance by stressing that Emerson's "concept of representative heroism denies the tenets of antinomianism, in any meaningful sense of the term. . . . If Emerson differs from the chauvinist by his Romantic self-reliance, he differs equally from the Romantic Antinomian by his reliance on a national mission" (*Puritan Origins,* p. 175). Bercovitch shows how Cotton Mather protected the Puritan dream from temporal failure by

[15] *The Imperial Self* (New York, 1971), pp. 24, 46, 54.

equating the inspired believer/perceiver with the "true" America, and we have seen how young Emerson used the same strategy.

Emerson's solution for declension is implicit in his complaint. He reminds his audience that America's plight cannot be blamed on external causes such as the Constitution or our "public officers." The cause of our problems, he goes on in Sermon No. 113, is that "every man is no better than he is." The private life of the soul and the health of the community are ineluctably wed. America's institutions are viable. But to sustain them, to keep them worthy of America's promises, our visible forms must be enlivened by the spirit of regenerate men; for the condition of a man's soul "in the end, determines the intercourse of men, the elections, the laws." In drawing upon the cult of the Puritan Fathers, Emerson revitalizes the Puritan prophecy of America redeemed in time and place: He declares that "the *fear of God* in the community . . . is the salt that keeps the community clean" and is the very "foundation" of society.

IV

Throughout his ministry and more or less throughout his life, Emerson retained both his complex view of the relationship between grace and effort and his inspired vision of the corporate ramifications of the spiritual life. The challenge and the burden of his career after 1832 was, as has long been known, to find viable substitutes for unworthy institutions, to find a new personal "vocation," and continually to define the regenerate individual as representative of the ideal America. What changed during his years at Second Church, what made inevitable his resignation, was his concept of Christ and the function of sacraments in preparing men for Christ. But Emerson's most famous sermon, "The Lord's Supper," is often misunderstood. George Santayana, one of the most astute readers of Emerson, was misleading when he wrote that Emerson "separated himself from the ancient creed of the community with a sense rather of relief than of regret."[16] On the contrary, Emerson's break with Second Church resulted from a conscientious examination of doctrine in terms that, ironically, made use of Puritan modes of thought.

[16] *Selected Critical Writings of George Santayana*, ed. Norman Henfrey (Cambridge, England, 1968), I, 126.

According to Puritan typology, New Englanders were participants in a cosmic drama that existed in the mind of God. Secular events, properly viewed, were prefigured in the Bible. But Puritan typology went beyond the mechanical associations of symbol and allegory, granting to historical events the status of being "real" and unique, however absorbed, ultimately, into God's atemporal scheme. Thus New England, prefigured in the Old Testament, was part of the unfolding of the divine plan. New England in turn prefigured future victories over Satan; and individual New Englanders took part in an inherently valuable temporal, historical experiment.

The Bible held for Emerson eternal truths, essences to be rescued from the dead letter of symbolism in order to regain efficacy for modern man. Sermon No. 43 opens the text of Acts XVII.28: "For in him we live, & move, & have our being," Emerson declaring that contemporary religious liberals "have grown wiser than to fear the *materialism* of the Calvinists [and we] no longer interpret literally the figurative language of the Scriptures which surrounded God with clouds & darkness—& thunders." We have seen that Emerson feared that to indulge in the "mercy" of God can lead to "laxity." But he accuses the "literal" method of the "Calvinists" of delivering a dead letter to modern times: it denies nineteenth-century Christians the opportunity to perceive God face to face; it fails to move the faculties, the affections, the will; and in so doing it denies Emerson's generation its uniqueness in history. He does not advocate reading the Bible as poetry but urges us to seek the compelling spiritual truth that renders biblical figures vital and efficacious.

Emerson's evolving concept of Jesus illustrates the point. He depicts Jesus conventionally in Sermon No. 5 as possessing "a greatness of soul" and "a magnanimity" that are virtually unattainable by man. The true Christian is a child of "sorrow"; the best that can be said about mankind is that many people did keep vigil at the Crucifixion despite the "deep depravity" of human nature. Sermon No. 5, first delivered on June 24, 1827, was given frequently; but not after July 27, 1828. In the middle of Emerson's ministry, his view of Jesus changed gradually. Paradoxically, as he exalted the importance of Christlike qualities, he found the idea of superhuman mediation no longer viable. By Sermon No. 89, for example, he is proclaiming the Hebrew notion of an angry God to be "unreasonable." Innate is man's ability to achieve Christ's greatness of spirit: "the *sources of happiness are always at hand*."

Emerson is now moving toward his Transcendental belief that each man has direct access to the Over-Soul without need of mediation or church guidance. But Sermon No. 95 shows clearly how Emerson's "new views" derive from traditional Puritan concepts. In this sermon he still worries about the by-products of sin. Man, in his view, continues to need regeneration, for which Christ must still somehow be the agent. But how best to appropriate the truth of Jesus? Emerson, always Pauline in matters of the Spirit, finds two distinct scriptural interpretations of the nature of Christ: The evangelists referred to his "*bodily person*," while the "writers of the epistles" spoke of him in a spiritual sense. Emerson finds that the words of Jesus himself confirm the more truly religious dimension of the latter view: "He uses his own name for his religion as he uses the name of Moses for the law of Moses[:] 'Not I, but Moses accuseth you.'" From this Emerson concludes: "It is obvious that Christianity, or the religious truths brot by Christ to men are meant. I understand then that the expression of the text is one of the same import, that *the truth which came by Jesus Christ shall judge the world*." He does not in this manner secularize Jesus; he tries to insure that the typological significance of Jesus will not be lost to his time. Emerson is careful to anchor himself to experience, resisting the lure of quietism or Antinomianism; he goes on in the sermon to suggest that it is *because* human nature falls so far short of Christ's perfection that each man's soul "must be judged according to its deeds." Still, to reduce Christ's divinity to a spiritual essence would seem to take great liberty with traditional typology, would seem radically contrary both to Puritanism and Unitarianism, which retained at least token respect for the "orthodox" concept of Christ as mediator. Further, to do so would seem in Puritan terms to oversimplify the spiritual life; for Thomas Hooker "a *smoking* desire after Christ, and a longing desire after grace" had been only first steps in an arduous spiritual process.[17]

Emerson's definition of Jesus holds, however, striking parallels with the view orthodox Puritans had espoused in the 1630's. The Antinomian "Errorists" had denied the efficacy of man's role in achieving assurance of salvation, arguing that "A man may have all

[17] *The Soul's Vocation or Effectual Calling to Christ* (London, 1638), p. 201.

graces and poverty of spirit, and yet want Christ" (Hall, p. 226). Such ministers as Hooker, Shepard, and Bulkeley, while they had no intention of diminishing the gap between Christ and man, disagreed. They shared the belief that one must participate in the spiritual life and that, to avoid anxiety, one must be able to measure the extent to which one possessed Christ. Peter Bulkeley went so far as to argue that justification through Christ is *not* the same thing as assurance of salvation. Believing that the Antinomian willingness to leave all to Christ ignored the needs of the heart, Bulkeley added this postscript to a letter to John Cotton: "There must be some difference betwixt Christ's righteousness, and that which doth manifest it unto me as mine; but these two you seem to confound."[18] Bulkeley knew that to put sanctification before justification would indeed constitute the Arminian heresy; but he saw no reason why evidence of salvation should not follow in terms man can discern. John Winthrop recorded the Synod's similar judgment, that Christ is indistinguishable from Christlike qualities; indeed, "he that hath righteousness and true holiness, hath learned the truth, as it is in Jesus, and therefore hath Christ" (Hall, p. 226). As Jesus (and Emerson) equated Moses with the *law* of Moses, so the Puritans identified the saving power of Christ with possession of his *attributes*.

The Puritan conviction that a man must be able to gauge his progress in growing to Christ, that Christ's saving grace is not a single moment of overpowering seizure, was grounded deeply in typological habits of mind. It was a commonplace of Puritan doctrine that, as Peter Bulkeley declared, the Jewish and Christian "are but one Church." He preached that we are all "children" of Abraham if we walk "in the steps of *Abraham's* faith." In spiritual substance Passover and the Lord's Supper, baptism and circumcision, are identical. Thomas Hooker too argued that one is not excluded from a holy covenant because one does not carry its outward trappings. He quotes St. Paul: "*He is not a Jew that is one outwardly*." Though circumcision is a seal that represents certain outward "prerogatives and privileges" of the Jewish nation, one need not follow Jewish law to follow in Abraham's steps: "Abraham *is the father of the circumcision, not to them who are of the circumcision only*; but he is the father of the

[18] Bulkeley to Cotton, Department of Rare Books and Manuscripts, Boston Public Library. Quotation is by courtesy of the Trustees of the Boston Public Library.

circumcision if they have faith." In the end, "*all outward privileges, as the hearing of the Word, the partaking of the Sacraments, and the like, are not able to make a man a sound Saint of God.*" The sacraments are seals; but they are impotent until a man "not only enjoyeth the privileges of the Church, but yieldeth the obedience of faith according to the Word of God revealed, and walketh in obedience." As non-Jews can fulfill Abraham's example, so Abraham anticipated New Testament revelation as "so fruitful a Christian." In the unfolding of redemptive history, particular rites were unique and valid for particular times and societies; but forms lack efficacy until enlivened by the Spirit, which follows saving faith.[19]

When in "The Lord's Supper" on September 9, 1832, Emerson explained his resignation from the Second Church pulpit, he did so in terms that simply carried out certain implications of Puritan typology.[20] The text of Romans 14:17 suggests to him that the Spirit, not forms, is the only requisite for salvation: "The Kingdom of God is not meat and drink; but righteousness, and peace, and joy in the Holy Ghost." He finds the necessity of the Lord's Supper unsupported by scriptural evidence on two counts. First, because Jesus "always taught by parables and symbols," we must not infer that he intended at the Last Supper "to establish an institution for perpetual observance"; Jesus was simply celebrating the traditional Passover feast. Second, because he was convinced that the value of a particular rite is relative to its spiritual efficacy, Emerson thinks it "not expedient" for Unitarians to observe a ceremony that began in a foreign culture as a symbolic "local custom"; such formalism undermines the Pauline concern with the Spirit in the nineteenth century.[21]

Later in the sermon Emerson undercuts his own scriptural explanation for his disaffection from the church in terms that are often mistaken for cavalier indifference: his critique of the Lord's Supper, he says, was done merely "for the satisfaction of others"; internal proof, he goes on, is the only compelling reason for a decision such as he

[19] Bulkeley, *The Gospel-Covenant*, pp. 131–134; Hooker, "The Activity of Faith: or, Abraham's Imitators," *Theology in America*, ed. Sydney E. Ahlstrom (New York, 1967), pp. 116–118, 122–123.

[20] Ursula Brumm has pointed out that Emerson's rejection of Unitarianism was based upon "his reading the Bible in the radically literal manner of the Puritans." *American Thought and Religious Typology*, trans. John Hoaglund (New Brunswick, N.J., 1970), p. 6.

[21] *The Complete Works of Ralph Waldo Emerson*, ed. Edward Waldo Emerson. Centenary Edition (Boston, 1903–1904), XI, 9, 4–5, 12, 19–20. Cited hereafter in the text as *W*.

has made. This attitude is itself Puritan. Indeed, Emerson is quick to add that Paul, Jesus, and other martyrs were motivated also by hostility to "formal religion." He has admitted that "Forms are as essential as bodies; but to exalt particular forms," he declares, "to adhere to one form a moment after it is outgrown, is unreasonable, and it is alien to the spirit of Christ" (*W*, XI, 22, 20).[22]

Emerson's leaving Second Church was no simple Antinomian rejection of form. Orthodox Puritans too had valued the Spirit above the letter and had sought merely to insure through forms that the Spirit might have footsteps in the world to guide personal and national destiny. Seventeenth-century Puritans would not, to be sure, have tolerated Emerson's conclusions about the validity of the Lord's Supper. But even John Winthrop allowed, when Antinomianism threatened, that the usefulness of certain rites *is* a relative matter. When the radical literalist John Wheelwright denied the efficacy of public fasting and predicted a "combustion" in church and state, Winthrop declared that his "Fast-Day Sermon" was untimely, for "every truth is not seasonable at all times." The Bible provides much evidence, Winthrop argued, that Jesus and God are aware of man's inability to perceive absolute truth; but doctrines and rituals, useful in aiding man's understanding of spiritual facts, are often expedients adapted to particular occasions: "the same *Paul* would not circumcise *Titus,* though he did *Timothy,* so the difference of persons and places, made a difference in the season of the doctrine." Hence, he concludes, Wheelwright's disruptive sermon was out of "season." To Winthrop, the sermon seemed a diatribe calculated for a particular, dangerous end (Hall, pp. 295–296).

Winthrop's reasoning reveals an ambivalence latent in Puritan typology, an inconsistent attitude toward forms which by the nineteenth century would completely alter the meaning of the New England experiment. When Peter Bulkeley declared the Jewish and Christian "are but one Church," he was thinking not of leveling denominational distinctions with a simple platonic correspondence

[22] Lawrence Buell notes that "one of Unitarianism's chief weapons against Orthodoxy was a strategy of redefinition by appealing to essence." *Literary Transcendentalism: Style and Vision in the American Renaissance* (Ithaca, N.Y., 1973), p. 114.

Karl Keller has traced Emerson's evolving metaphysics through what he sees as a "melting" of Christian typology into Transcendental ideas by the use of "conceit" and "metaphor." "From Christianity to Transcendentalism: A Note on Emerson's Use of the Conceit," *American Literature,* XXXIX (March, 1967), 94–98.

of ideas but of the historical anticipation/fulfillment within God's eternal scheme which characterized traditional typology. But all Puritans were latent Antinomians to the extent that they considered forms subordinate to the Spirit they were meant to minister to the world. Winthrop, we have seen, was willing to judge Wheelwright's political gesture by comparison with what he deemed Paul's relativism in the use of circumcision—a sacrament Puritans esteemed as typologically equivalent to baptism itself. What in Emerson often sounds like freewheeling platonism derives from the Puritans' craving for the *spiritual substance* of sacraments that enables one truly to walk in Abraham's footsteps. He could write on March 13, 1831, for example, that Paul and Peter were inspired by the same truth: "There is one Spirit through myriad mouths"; all truth "is from God" and is indivisible (*J*, III, 236). Emerson continued to believe, we have seen, that the Fast Day observance was not an empty memorial but an occasion for public reflection on individual and social spiritual health; to this extent he was heir to the Puritan vision of religion as a communal venture. But he also implicitly followed to its logical conclusion Winthrop's fatal ambivalence toward sacraments when he rejected the Lord's Supper itself as a mere ritual, an observance inappropriate to America in 1832.

In the seventeenth century, typology was not the tool only of Antinomian firebrands attacking formalism. Rather, orthodox Puritans could argue that Antinomian absolutism, by radically assaulting all forms and letting Christ perform all in salvation, altered the meaning of typology. Sudden seizure by Christ short-circuited a man's participation in truths embodied by types that, though they transcended time, united all moments in time and provided for patterns of spiritual growth and conduct under scriptural and ecclesiastical guidance. Emerson inherited and rigorously applied authentic typological methods to revitalize for his time the spirit of Jesus. He believed, as did Hooker, Shepard, Bulkeley, and Winthrop, that one must personally *experience* the truth of which Jesus was only one, albeit a perfect, example. But for Emerson, in a day when orthodox strictures concerning original sin and the privileges of church membership were being abandoned, genuine Puritan typology led inexorably away from the last relics of orthodoxy. Christ was best appropriated for the nineteenth century not through dead sacraments but as an immediate spiritual essence.

Although Emerson resigned as minister of Second Church, he continued for years to occupy various pulpits as a visiting minister; he did not resign from the ministry as such. He spent the rest of his life searching for new ways to inspire and uplift a broader "congregation," to show all men that revelation is a living fact. When Emerson left Second Church, he did not soar off into a Transcendental empyrean in a lighter-than-air balloon. His ministry was a pervasive legacy in the form of a check to the more extravagant tendencies of Transcendentalism.

Emerson's thought is marked, of course, by a steady commitment to intuition and inspiration. Nineteenth-century romanticism fed this impulse once the restraints of Puritan doctrine had fallen away. Romantic doctrine continued to speak of rebirth, but in terms that replaced God with Nature, soul with Self, grace with imagination.[23] But while Emerson celebrated the mediatory role of Nature in the divine scheme, he never gave himself over totally to a sentimental enthusiasm for Nature: "We may easily hear too much of rural influences," he cautioned; "let us be men instead of woodchucks" (*W*, III, 183).[24] Even *Nature* (1836) is not the purely Antinomian effusion that the "transparent eyeball" passage seems to suggest. Emerson is careful here to define Nature as the "NOT-ME," keeping the soul theoretically separate from the corruption of world and flesh. But he also meticulously describes the Transcendental conversion as a process of growth in which proper use of the world leads to divine

[23] M. H. Abrams treats primarily the British and continental aspects of romanticism's appropriation and transformation of Christian metaphysics in *Natural Supernaturalism: Tradition and Revolution in Romantic Literature* (New York, 1971).

[24] Randall Stewart accuses Emerson of a romantic "Nature-worship" that confuses itself with "God-worship": "The basic theological error here is the confusion of the Creator with the Thing Created." *American Literature & Christian Doctrine* (Baton Rouge, 1958), pp. 44–45.

However, Joe Lee Davis, in distinguishing between "Enthusiastic" and "Mystical" sensibilities, implicitly shed different light on Emerson's attitude toward nature. Enthusiasts, Davis observed, inclined toward "a kind of emotional Deism, a pantheism so crudely stamped with the pathetic fallacy that it would have made a Ruskin weep," while Mystics (with whom he associates "the orthodox Puritans") looked at nature more rationally. Although scholars do not now generally term the Puritan mind "mystical," Davis's distinction is useful: Emerson, despite his famous enthusiastic pronouncements, was clearly aware of the danger of nature-worship and, in this sense, "orthodox" in his uses of nature. Davis, "Mystical Versus Enthusiastic Sensibility," *Journal of the History of Ideas,* IV (June, 1943), 301–319.

power; man apprehends through his faculties the law of God in Nature.

Emerson does not reveal a thoroughgoing Antinomian frame of mind until some of the middle and late essays in which, J. A. Ward has said, he resorts to an optimism in which the conversion process "loses much of its psychological complexity," as when in "Experience" he tries "to affirm a faith independent of experience."[25] Emerson believed that the "intellect" (as mind or spirit), being "antinomian or hypernomian," is a source of both isolation and, potentially, impregnable comfort (*W*, III, 79). He looked in transcendence of materialism for unequivocal "grounds of assurance" for "The Transcendentalist" (*W*, I, 330). But the modern idealist, he knew, had not yet mastered his own vision or realized his talent. He said ambiguously that the Transcendentalist "easily incurs the charge of antinomianism" by placing himself above "every written commandment" (*W*, I, 336). Indeed, Emerson's measured, third-person stance in the essay is not simply a prudent rhetorical strategy to mollify an audience reluctant to endorse the new "collectors of the heavenly spark." It indicates his own hesitance to commit himself wholly to the camp of those who would in the world live on "angels' food" (*W*, I, 358, 338).

The urgency to reach a disembodied audience often betrays Emerson into enthusiastic pronouncements that do not deliver his whole vision. For example, he proclaims that the Over-Soul cannot be tapped by an act of will, for "visions" derive from "some alien energy"; the soul "is not a faculty, but a light" (*W*, II, 268, 270). And he sees in the history of religious awakening "A certain tendency to insanity" because of the finite mind's contemplation of the absolute, revealed above human words (*W*, II, 281–282). Despite such Antinomian utterances, however, he acknowledges the solid otherness of the world. Like the sailor described by Melville's Ishmael, in danger of toppling from the mast-head when his pantheistic daydream makes him doubt the reality of the world, Emerson occasionally has to "pinch" himself to "preserve the due decorum" neces-

[25] Ward, "Emerson and 'The Educated Will': Notes on the Process of Conversion," *ELH*, XXXIV (1967), 506, 511. Lawrence Buell also has noted that in the later essays, as Emerson's tone becomes more personal and cozy, his concept of the poet changes from one of active imagination to "a mere medium (though a glorious one)." *Literary Transcendentalism*, p. 290.

sary for social life; but he knows that "this is flat rebellion," that "Nature will not be Buddhist" (*W*, III, 235–236). The healthy man must "occupy" the middle ground between the life of the spirit and the flesh. To live only a sensuous life is "low and utilitarian"; to live a purely spiritual life is "too vague and indefinite for the uses of life" (*W*, I, 182).

It is true that Emerson's concept of the conversion process began to lose its tension. But he compensated for this loss—even as his essays dealt more often with single extremes of experience such as Prudence or Intellect—with a growing interest in "polarity." This perception that extremes are *complementary,* part of a cosmic system of checks and balances, was but another manifestation of the lessons of his ministry. He continued to believe that vision is gradually prepared, man's faculties being fostered by a source beyond his comprehension; but, though truth comes "unannounced," it comes "because we had previously laid siege to the shrine." This Puritan dialectic includes the "law of undulation," which requires that you both "labor with your brains" and "forbear your activity and see what the great Soul showeth" (*W*, II, 332). Antinomian seizure was never for Emerson a viable means of revelation. As late as 1870–1872, in "Inspiration," he could still both lament that trusting wholly to vision leads to a destructive lack of "consecutiveness" and reaffirm the radical importance of insight: "I hold that ecstasy will be found normal" (*W*, VIII, 272–273, 275). He had discovered as a minister that faith must be grounded in experience. It was the burden and the ballast of his later career that he could not completely forget this truth.

Though Emerson held instinctively to a balanced, if not complex, view of conversion, he labored to define the public implications of his new "vocation." He valued the speech of man to men above all forms of communication; but, like the Antinomians who found the influx of the Spirit independent of hearing the Word of God, he often found silence more efficacious than human utterance. He was capable, for example, of a keen analysis of political euphemism (*W*, XI, 259–260). Yet he came to regret his impassioned letter to President Van Buren protesting a deceitful government treaty with the Cherokee Indians, deprecating his political gesture as "this stirring in the philanthropic mud" (*W*, XI, 571).

However unsatisfactorily Emerson defined his own public role, he never in theory isolated the self from other men. In the Divinity

School Address he declares the loss of "public worship" the greatest "calamity" that can befall a nation, for "Then all things go to decay" (*W*, I, 142–143). The inspired individual assumes the burden of rediscovering the spiritual base of society that the demise of Puritanism had left to erode. Emerson is as scrupulous in "Self-Reliance" as in his sermons to remind us that our "isolation must not be mechanical, but spiritual, that is, must be elevation" (*W*, II, 72). Indeed, for the Transcendentalists it is "the wish to find society for their hope and religion,—which prompts them to shun what is called society" (*W*, I, 347).

It is conventional to contrast Emerson's lofty, even frosty, ideals of society with Hawthorne's defense of the human heart, with all its imperfection. We forget that Emerson sees in "Compensation" as clearly as Hawthorne did in "Young Goodman Brown" that one who lives solely for revelations of the soul forfeits companionship, family, love. Transcendentalists seem often to make friendship and community into monstrously disembodied abstractions. But the urgent intensity with which Emerson sought to define his spiritual brotherhood derives from the orthodox Puritan habit of fastidiousness in selecting true Christians for companions. Living in a democratic age, Emerson is forced inward to people his imagined congregation with worthy nineteenth-century saints. Much was at stake. An inspired man is inwardly compelled to share his vision. And a man's true nature is automatically revealed by his words and his company, for "friends are self-elected," not consciously chosen (*W*, II, 209).

Emerson always craved a more vigorous translation of ideals into action than he felt capable of performing. He privately confessed that his own power and vision of the nation were unstable: "Most of my values are very variable. My estimate of America, which sometimes runs very low, sometimes to ideal prophetic proportions. My estimate of my own mental means and resources is all or nothing: in happy hours, life looking infinitely rich; and sterile at others" (*W*, VIII, 423 n). As Bercovitch has shown, Emerson's doctrine of the representative self would not allow him to admit uncertainty publicly. But he occasionally resorted in his anxiety and ennui to a vision of his forefathers, who, though "tormented with the fear of Sin and the terror of the Day of Judgment," had a "bounding pulse" and knew what they were about in the world (*W*, I, 282, 285).

The archetypal Puritan (rarely are individuals named) joins David,

Paul, Jesus, and a variety of secular representative men in Emerson's Transcendental typology. History is mere secular destiny only to the unregenerate. In the final analysis, a man best carried on the Puritan mission when he could appropriate the spirit of Jesus to his own life and time. The challenge is to "be ourselves the children of the light" (*W*, I, 221). Indeed, Emerson's appropriation of the Puritan past is not mere sentimentality but the latest form of Puritan typology; for he insists that our sense of tradition be not hero-worship but a challenge: "Let us shame the fathers, by superior virtue in the sons" (*W*, XII, 210).

Emerson's desire to see his ideals embodied led to his desperate effort to define John Brown as the modern Puritan champion come to purge and purify the land. He even fed the myth of the hero of Harpers Ferry by describing him, incorrectly, as a direct descendent of Peter Brown of the *Mayflower*. Generally, however, Emerson was a shrewder judge of the Puritan legacy in New England. In journal entries for 1824 he noted that the "Wild Anabaptists" had put themselves above the order of the community. But the "Puritans of 1620 had not a rash or visionary thought about them." We can learn as much, he thought, from "the wise & fortunate legislators" who established New England as from modern radicals (*J*, II, 210, 211, 215). He condemned the "holy fury" of the "Antinomian fanatics of Cromwell's day" (*J*, VI, 147). And it was not Puritan individualism that he celebrated in his Historical Discourse but the force of the church covenant, under which all "were united by personal affection." Benevolent men like Bulkeley and Winthrop provided strong leadership and loving guidance under "the ideal social compact." This national impulse continued down to the Revolution, in which "A deep religious sentiment sanctified the thirst for liberty." The heroic incidents of the Battle of Concord were not "an extravagant ebullition of feeling," but a communal acting "from the simplest instincts" (*W*, XI, 45, 72, 75). In the rhetoric of the jeremiad, he found those principles wanting in the 1830's when Concordians doted over the pastness of the town's traditions.

As a prophet of America's unfolding mission, Emerson relished the thought that "a good principle of rebellion," "some thorn of dissent and innovation and heresy to prick the sides of conservatism," had been a Boston trademark since the days of Wheelwright and

Hutchinson (*W*, XII, 203, 207). He always held that *enthusiasm* for purposeful action was needed to cure America's mediocrity. Paradoxically, he never trusted *enthusiasts*. In his journal he acknowledged that a predominance of good is as "unnatural" a human condition as a predominance of evil (*J*, I, 124–125). Too often, he felt, New England reformers failed of their aims because they miscalculated man's potential for perfection; and he saw that "the fertile forms of antinomianism among the elder puritans seemed to have their match in the plenty of the new harvest of reform" (*W*, III, 253). Although he considered many reformers oddballs, he maintained that ferment was crucial for America's health. Thus he granted the validity of the Abolitionists' singlemindedness ("They are the new Puritans, & as easily satisfied," *J*, IX, 447). Yet he could not bring himself to cast his lot fully with these literalist sons of the Puritans. The Puritan legacy for Emerson was an ambiguous mix of radical prototypes and orthodox restraint. A highly traditional radical, he cheered on nineteenth-century reformers from a careful distance, while directing his own energy toward uplifting the whole human condition.

Thomas Carlyle clearly put the question of cultural continuity to Emerson when he wrote on July 19, 1842: "The disease of Puritanism was *Antinomianism*;—very strange, does that still affect the *ghost* of Puritanism?" Carlyle had just met Bronson Alcott, whom he considered the modern embodiment of Antinomianism, "a kind of venerable Don Quixote" who was "all bent on saving the world by a return to acorns and the golden age."[26] Although Emerson appears not to have answered Carlyle directly, he had the same reservations about his beloved neighbor Alcott. Emerson knew, with the first-generation divines and Jonathan Edwards, that spiritual enthusiasm poses an American dilemma: to be *possessed* by visionary excitement makes one, like Alcott, "a pail of which the bottom is taken out"; but to be unduly *suspicious* of enthusiasm is to become a Whig, who is "a pail from which you cannot get off the cover" (*J*, IX, 208). Emerson challenged America to transcend both the democratic "herd" and the mercantile/political establishment. But he found the Antinomian legacy to the nineteenth century inadequate, whether it took the form

[26] *The Correspondence of Emerson and Carlyle,* ed. Joseph Slater (New York, 1964), pp. 326–327.

of the reformer's self-righteous intensity or Alcott's fluffy idealism.

That Emerson always retained a sense of balance in spiritual matters can be attributed to the fact that he always saw himself as, in essence, a Christian, one who came to grips with the meaning of the Spirit through Puritan habits of mind. We have seen that orthodox Puritans argued that, insofar as a man possessed Christlike qualities, he may be said to have Christ. Emerson too, even while he tried in the Divinity School Address to reduce the significance of the historical church and to remove "the laws of the soul" from time and space, continued to believe that a man had to be able to measure his spiritual estate: "If a man is at heart just, then in so far is he God." This principle leads not to unbridled individualism, but to social cohesion: "Character is always known. . . . See again the perfection of the Law as it applies itself to the affections, and becomes the law of society. As we are, so we associate. The good, by affinity, seek the good; the vile, by affinity, the vile. Thus of their own volition, souls proceed into heaven, into hell" (*W*, I, 122–123). As late as 1869 he expressed the Augustinian belief that Christianity is not historical, but essence. Yet Emerson, like the Puritans, also maintained an experiential gauge for conversion that had moral and prophetic ramifications, and that he still found compatible with belief in "the *doctrine* of Christianity" (Emerson's italics). Christian revelation could be perceived through Transcendental Nature. And Christian conversion could be reconciled to democratic romanticism: "the history of Jesus is the history of every man, written large" (*W*, XI, 486, 488, 491). Thus Emerson expressed his own inspired confidence in America's mission in terms that transcended the Jacksonian common denominator by maintaining democratic touchstones of moral and spiritual regeneration.

In all matters except literal church polity, Transcendentalism reconstructed the Puritan world view as it was concerned with the nature of the Spirit, human faculties and affections, moral conduct, and national mission. It was no mere rhetorical flourish that led Emerson often to measure his time against the New England past. He was not simply mollifying the old Calvinist when he wrote Aunt Mary on September 21, 1841, that "the new is only the seed of the old," that modern reform movements are "but the continuation of Puritanism though it operate inevitably the destruction of the Church in which it grew" (*Letters,* II, 451). He continued to believe in the essential moral truth of Puritanism, that of "an unregenerate person . . . all his good works are sin. It is a new illustration of what I perceive to be a fact[,] that all the errors of Calvinism are exaggerations only & may generally be traced directly to some spiritual truth from which they spring" (*J*, III, 225).

Emerson shared with orthodox Puritans a lifelong dedication to the spiritual life while refusing to confuse a glimpse of heaven with self-perfection. In spite of occasional indulgence in Transcendental hyperbole, he remembered the basic truths about human nature he had learned as a minister: man, being finite, needs rebirth; but he must never rest assured of salvation to the point where he stops using created means to self-improvement; through his faculties a man grows in spiritual awareness; and the inspired American is the keeper of the national dream. Emerson changed his mind about the role the Church plays in guiding men to truth; but he never opted for the easy Antinomian solution to man's spiritual longing. In reviving the Puritan tradition for the nineteenth century, Emerson did more than devise the "latest form of infidelity." He rediscovered the dynamic synthesis of spirit and world, grace and effort, private revelation and communal destiny, which had always been the mark of Puritan integrity.

Emerson's Essay, "Immortality": The Problem of Authorship

Glen M. Johnson

An unanswered question in Emerson scholarship involves the provenance of his last book, *Letters and Social Aims.* Although the volume was conceived in 1870 and part of it had reached proof by 1872, it was not published until December 1875. By then Emerson's mental powers had declined; *Letters and Social Aims* required Ellen Emerson's help and, finally, editing by James Elliot Cabot to reach print. Cabot's preface to an edition published after Emerson's death gives the book ambiguous status in the Emerson canon: "There is nothing here that he did not write, and he gave his full approval to whatever was done in the way of selection and arrangement; but I cannot say that he applied his mind very closely to the matter. He was pleased, in a general way, that the work should go on, but it may be a question exactly how far he sanctioned it." [1] Edward Waldo Emerson, commenting after Cabot's death, added that "Mr. Emerson always disclaimed the credit for *Letters and Social Aims*, and in speaking to Mr. Cabot always called it 'your book' " (*W*, VIII, viii).

In his preface, Cabot singles out "Immortality," which concludes *Letters and Social Aims*, as an example of how "selection and arrangement" apparently worked in the composition of the volume:

[1] Preface (1883) to *Letters and Social Aims*, rpt. in *The Complete Works of Ralph Waldo Emerson*, Centenary Ed., ed. Edward Waldo Emerson (Boston: Houghton Mifflin, 1903–04), VIII, xiii. All quotations from the printed "Immortality" are from the Centenary Edition, cited as *W.* Quotations from the working manuscript of "Immortality" are by permission of the Ralph Waldo Emerson Memorial Association and the Henry W. and Albert A. Berg Collection, New York Public Library. Quotations from loose sheets relating to the lecture "Immortality" and from unpublished letters and manuscripts of Ellen and Edward Emerson are by permission of the Ralph Waldo Emerson Memorial Association and the Houghton Library, Harvard University. Quotations from James Elliot Cabot's letters are by permission of the Houghton Library, with thanks to Hugh and Natalie Cabot.

American Literature, Volume 56, Number 3, October 1984. Copyright © 1984 by the Duke University Press. CCC 0002-9831/84/$1.50

"Nor indeed did I attempt, in preparing the copy for the press, to adhere always to a single manuscript. . . . What [Emerson] desired was simply to bring together under the particular heading whatever could be found that seemed in place there. . . . In this way it happened sometimes that writing of very different dates was brought together: *e.g.*, the essay on Immortality, which has been cited as showing what were his latest opinions on that subject, contains passages written fifty years apart from each other" (*W*, VIII, xii–xiii). If this statement is taken at face value, then "Immortality," if not most of *Letters and Social Aims*, deserves a status closer to journals—raw material—than to Emerson's other works.

Edward Emerson wrote in 1903 that his father gave away the manuscript of "Immortality" and that "no loose sheets" remained (*W*, VIII, 434). Neither of these statements is accurate. A manuscript of "Immortality"—working copy for *Letters and Social Aims*—is now in the Berg Collection of the New York Public Library; a letter still with the manuscript indicates that Cabot kept it until 1890, when Edith Emerson Forbes presented it to Charles Eliot Norton. In addition, the Houghton Library at Harvard holds a folder of loose sheets, about sixty pages of writing relevant to the essay. Most of these sheets at Harvard are lecture material rejected during the preparation of the book. So Cabot's generalizations can be tested against the pages with which he and Ellen Emerson worked. The provenance of "Immortality" turns out to be more complicated, and its status less clear-cut, than the early editors' statements indicate.

Analyzing the Berg Collection's manuscript and the Houghton's folder recovers four distinct stages in the development of "Immortality" as we now have it: (1) a version close to the original lecture read before the Parker Fraternity in Boston, 29 December 1861; (2) an expansion of the original version, probably approximating the lecture as read for the last time in 1872; (3) a radical reorganization of version (2), made with Ellen Emerson's and Cabot's help during 1875; and (4) the printed essay, a revision of version (3) made in proofs that evidently have not survived. The concern of the present analysis is primarily versions (2) and (3), the clearest evidence of whether "Immortality" is Emerson's work or an editorial agglomeration.

"Immortality" was not included in the list of potentially publishable works that Emerson made shortly after *Society and Solitude* appeared in 1870, and as late as March 1875 he was listing the title as only "perhaps" suitable for *Letters and Social Aims.*[2] So "Immortality" likely did not figure in Emerson's efforts during 1872, when he at least thought he had a full volume in view.[3] "Immortality" as we now have it is a product of 1875, when Ellen Emerson and then J. Elliot Cabot were full partners in Emerson's literary production. Their involvement is crucial, and their personal attitudes toward the topic are relevant not only to the finished essay but to the very fact that "Immortality" is in the volume at all.

Emerson himself evidently thought of "Immortality" in a special category. Of the nineteen scheduled readings of the lecture between 1861 and 1872, thirteen were on Sundays; the most frequent audiences were churches or groups like the Parker Fraternity with a religious interest. There were exceptions—for example, "Immortality" concluded the 1866 series "Philosophy for the People"—but mostly Emerson treated the piece as a secular sermon.[4] So it would be understandable for him to hesitate, even when pressed for copy as he was in 1875, about presenting "Immortality" outside of the contexts for which it was intended. The decision to include "Immortality" as the valedictory piece in Emerson's valedictory volume was almost certainly made finally by the editors.

Ellen Emerson's involvement is especially crucial for "Immortality," since in religious matters her opinions differed from her father's, and she seems to have welcomed signs of mellowing in him. She was "pleased" when in his last years he started attending church regularly; in 1880 she opposed, as hasty, Edward Emerson's

[2] *The Journals and Miscellaneous Notebooks of Ralph Waldo Emerson*, ed. William H. Gilman and others (Cambridge: Harvard Univ. Press, 1960–82), XVI, 156–57, 318; this edition is cited below as *JMN*. In a letter to Samuel Longfellow, 28 Jan. 1868, Emerson spoke of "Immortality" as unfinished, though long written, and said he intended someday to revise it. I thank Eleanor M. Tilton for information about this letter.

[3] *The Letters of Ellen Tucker Emerson*, ed. Edith E. W. Gregg (Kent, Ohio: Kent State Univ. Press, 1982), I, 694; this edition is cited below as ETE *Letters*.

[4] See the pocket diaries in *JMN*, vols. XV and XVI, and William Charvat, *Emerson's American Lecture Engagements: A Chronological List* (New York: New York Public Library, 1961).

public letter denying rumors that their father had returned to orthodoxy; and following Emerson's death she maintained, against biographers, that he had not really intended to resign from the ministry in 1832 and had been surprised and saddened when his church let him go.[5] Ellen would not have misrepresented her father's opinions; but she would have regarded "Immortality" as a particularly important, even portentous, statement, and to the extent that she was involved in composing its final form, the influence of her more conventional attitudes should be looked for.

Recently published and unpublished evidence—including the manuscript, where most editorial annotations are in her hand—indicates that Ellen's involvement in *Letters and Social Aims* was more extensive and more fundamental than has been credited. She wanted to keep secret the fact that Emerson had help with the book, but she seems to have acquiesced later in ascribing whatever credit was due to Cabot alone. But she had worked closely with Emerson during July and August 1875, and Cabot's arrival in Concord during the last week in August was evidently at her insistence—as, indeed, his role was originally her idea three years earlier (ETE *Letters*, II, 187, 181–83; I, 692). Cabot made several visits to Concord between August and November, each stay lasting several days. Ellen credited him with providing a "broad view" and with distinguishing between " 'needed' " and " 'not needed' " passages (ETE *Letters*, II, 185): he finished the process of "selection and arrangement" that had always been the essence of Emersonian "Composition." But Cabot's letters of those months make clear that Ellen Emerson remained a full collaborator, working with her father or on her own during Cabot's absences. As late as 1 November 1875, Cabot was responding to her recommendation that the anecdote from Bede which opens "Immortality" be cut or moved so as not to detract from what followed; he reassured her, and the story remained.[6]

No evidence suggests that Cabot and Ellen Emerson differed between themselves about the philosophy of "Immortality." Nancy

[5] Ellen Tucker Emerson, *The Life of Lidian Jackson Emerson*, ed. Delores Bird Carpenter (Boston: Twayne, 1980), p. 186; Ralph L. Rusk, *The Life of Ralph Waldo Emerson* (New York: Columbia Univ. Press, 1949), pp. 503–04; and Ellen Emerson's unpublished manuscript, "What I can remember about Father," Houghton Library. For Ellen's religious opinions, see Carpenter's introduction to the *Life of Lidian*, pp. xxxiv–xxxvii.

[6] Letter dated 1 Nov. 1875, Houghton Library.

Craig Simmons's scholarship has recently made Cabot less enigmatic to us, but his reticence and his self-deprecating persona still complicate determining precisely what his beliefs were.[7] In his writing about Emerson and in his communications with Ellen Emerson he seems to have agreed with, or adopted, her notions. For example, Cabot's statement that "Immortality" contains passages written nearly fifty years apart is almost certainly inaccurate: parallel journal entries range between 1842 and 1861. Yet the fifty year figure neatly spans the entire period from Emerson's entering the ministry to *Letters and Social Aims*, and so at least implicitly parallels Ellen's belief that Emerson's break with orthodoxy was less radical or less ideological than usually thought. A more overt statement about Emerson's beliefs comes in Cabot's *Memoir*, holding that in later years, "when his mind was quiescent, and nothing happened to stir up reflection," Emerson "went back with complacency to the sentiments and the observances of his youth." The older Emerson, Cabot thought, showed "unconscious drift" toward conventional faith.[8] Then there is Cabot's account of the farewell between Emerson and Lidian: "To his wife he spoke tenderly of their life together and her loving care of him; they must now part, to meet again and part no more" (Cabot, *Memoir*, II, 683). The source of this report is not apparent; it does not agree with Edward Emerson's account, written in 1886 for Cabot's use, of his father's last days.[9] The deathbed scene is trite and unconvincing, a curiosity in Cabot's studiously straightforward *Memoir*.

It would be foolish to claim that Ellen Emerson somehow coopted Cabot on matters involving her father's religion. Nevertheless, one sentence in a letter from Cabot to her, written just after they started collaborating, is suggestive. Speaking of certain items that ought or ought not to be published, Cabot wrote about one: "The dithyramb to Bacchus perhaps, but then I should wish

[7] See "The 'Autobiographical Sketch' of James Elliot Cabot," *Harvard Library Bulletin*, 30 (1982), 117–52; and "Arranging the Sibylline Leaves: James Elliot Cabot's Work as Emerson's Literary Executor," in *Studies in the American Renaissance 1983*, ed. Joel Myerson (Charlottesville: Univ. Press of Virginia, 1983), pp. 335–89. The latter article should be consulted particularly for its accounts of Cabot's relationships with Ellen and Edward Emerson and his work on posthumously published volumes of Emerson's works.

[8] *A Memoir of Ralph Waldo Emerson* (Boston: Houghton Mifflin, 1887), II, 629–30, cited below as *Memoir*.

[9] Letter dated 17 Oct. 1886, Houghton Library. There is no parallel scene in Ellen's *Life of Lidian* or in any of her letters that I have examined.

it followed by an explicit acknowledgement of the beneficent providence that refuses to grant the prayer."[10] The language here is as trite as the reported deathbed farewell. Considering that Ellen was both a believer in beneficent providence and a committed advocate of temperance, Cabot's letter is either a declaration of similar belief or an act of deference.

This secondary evidence ought not to suggest a conspiracy by Ellen Emerson and J. Elliot Cabot to soften Emerson's views or to orchestrate in *Letters and Social Aims* an accommodation with orthodox belief about immortality. It does provide important background information for understanding what they did with the manuscript—specifically, why they chose to regard a virtually complete lecture as disjointed, opening the way for a reorganization that shifted Emerson's statements, sometimes radically, out of contexts he placed them in. Each editor brought to work on the essay beliefs more conventional than Emerson's had been. More important, Ellen Emerson and Cabot shared an interpretation that Emerson, "unconsciously" or not, was in older years moving toward mellower religious views. They were responsible editors, but the essay they produced was, in fundamental ways, not Emerson's composition.

II

The manuscript pages now in the Berg Collection and at Harvard provide evidence about the composition of "Immortality" in four areas. First, handwriting supports, in the most literal sense, Cabot's claim that "there is nothing" in the essay which Emerson "did not write." Within the manuscripts are several passages not in Emerson's hand—the writing is Ellen's in each case—but these passages are copies of writing by Emerson found elsewhere in the lecture. In the working manuscript, Ellen's copies obviously were made to assist in rearranging materials by breaking up the lecture's contexts. The Houghton's folder contains several pages of Ellen's copies of material not used in the published essay. These unused copies may indicate the difficulty Ellen had in trying to reorganize "Immortality" before Cabot took hold with judgments of "needed" and "not needed." The important point here is that the substance of the essay, as far as that is found in the working manuscript, is

[10] Letter dated 2 Sept. 1875, Houghton Library.

entirely Emerson's; the editors' contribution, it appears, was indeed limited to "selection and arrangement." [11]

Other manuscript evidence includes: two sets of page numbers in Emerson's hand, making possible substantial reconstruction of his lecture versions of "Immortality"; marginal annotations by the editors, indicating the kinds of things they did and, to a lesser extent, giving some idea of how much Emerson was involved in the work of 1875; and the order of pages in the Berg Collection's working manuscript, showing how Cabot and Ellen Emerson developed new contexts for specific statements in Emerson's original.

Many manuscript pages are numbered, usually in pencil, in top corners—Emerson's usual practice. Another set of numbers, in red pencil, appears top center on many pages. Red numbers appear in other lecture manuscripts of Emerson's, where, as here, they indicate a later version than the corner numbers. In "Immortality," however, the two number sequences are parallel: working on the lecture over the eleven years he kept it active, Emerson cut some and added quite a lot, but except for minor transpositions he did not reorder. The red-number lecture is an expansion of the original, but it is not—using Emerson's definition of the term as "putting together"—a new composition. The published essay *is* a new composition: in the Berg manuscript the red numbers, after the first few sheets, become a random pattern.

The red-number sequence runs from 1 through 227, almost all odd numbers because only obverses are numbered. There are no duplications, and of the one hundred fourteen odd numbers between 1 and 227, only four are missing when the Berg and Houghton pages are collated.[12] The lack of duplicate numbers makes unlikely the origin of these pages in separate lecture manuscripts; so Cabot and Ellen Emerson apparently had at their disposal a lecture version of "Immortality" that was, according to numerical sequence, ninety-six percent complete. Cabot's published recollection of how "Immortality" took shape is therefore misleading: the

[11] Collating the working manuscript with the published essay shows considerable revision in proof, but the revisions do not include substantive additions that challenge the validity of this statement. Ellen's copies among the loose sheets may have been made after Cabot became involved, with the idea of using the passages elsewhere—but I find no evidence of such uses.

[12] Two apparent exceptions prove this observation: one duplicated number shows identical material on both pages; in another duplication, one of the sheets is blank except for a heading.

lecture pages may have been in disarray, though Emerson had done very little public speaking since the last delivery of "Immortality" in 1872, but Emerson's "Immortality" was not irrecoverable. Beyond that, all of the published version comes from pages in the red-number sequence, so Cabot's claim that the essay comprises "writing of very different dates" must be construed as referring only to the genesis of specific passages. Cabot did not insert in "Immortality" any material that Emerson had not himself used in the lecture of that title.

The lecture "Immortality," recoverable in the red-number sequence, makes interesting reading today. Proportions seem off among some topics, but the lecture as a whole is coherent. That the published essay is so different in composition reflects, almost certainly, a decision by Ellen Emerson and Cabot in 1875 to regard the manuscript as lacking "fixed limits" (*W*, VIII, xii). Most likely, as the discussion above has suggested, they found the lecture inadequate less as a coherent statement in its own terms than as an expression of Emerson's views on immortality as they understood them.

The most obvious sign of the editors' work in the manuscript is the presence of marginal notations. There are relatively few of these—about twenty-five in 163 written pages of the Berg manuscript, for example; they range from a single "X" to suggest a deletion to succinct recommendations for specific revisions. The handwriting cannot always be conclusively identified and some notations are mostly erased, but to the extent that identification is possible the marginal writing is mainly Ellen Emerson's. That again suggests her primary involvement, at least in time, in the editorial manipulations of "Immortality." Almost all of the notations are straightforward editorial advice, corrections and deletions. One notation, in Ellen's hand, provides the only case of what might somewhat grandly be called attempted censorship. Emerson, speaking about the difficulty of using intellect to "ground" faith in immortality, wrote as follows: ". . . the reasons are all vanishing & inadequate. You cannot make a written theory or demonstration of this, as you can an orrery of the Copernican astronomy. Tis the *gai science* & must be sacredly treated." [13] Ellen's marginal comment is: "I'm astonished"—a reaction seemingly beyond noting

[13] Quoted from manuscript; cf. *JMN*, XV, 157, and *W*, VIII, 346.

Emerson's anachronistic use of a synonym for Provençal poetry or his repetition of the term from "Poetry and Imagination" (*W*, VIII, 37). More likely involved is Ellen's objection to using a term with erotic connotations in a discussion of religious faith. In any case, the phrase that astonished her is cancelled in the manuscript and does not appear in the essay. Emerson's statement was not altogether clear, but provocative. The cut-down passage that survives is almost a truism; editorial interference has made a more conventional, blander essay.

It is impossible to know if Emerson himself cancelled in the manuscript the reference to *gai science* or agreed to the deletion. Cabot remembered that Emerson gave "full approval" to all of his editors' activities. The available letters between Cabot and Ellen Emerson speak between themselves as if Emerson were nowhere near; on the other hand, as late as August 1877 Emerson apparently was reading proofs for publication of "Perpetual Forces" in the *North American Review*.[14] The manuscript of "Immortality" suggests that the editors went to some lengths to encourage Emerson's involvement in what they were doing. One marginal notation suggests correcting an indefinite article (in "an use"); another insists on having "of" inserted in the phrase "30,000 years." Notations on such minor stylistic issues make little sense except as calculated attempts by the editors to keep Emerson involved—or as a reflection of their literal determination that everything in the text, including articles and prepositions, be Emerson's work. The evidence of their success is mixed: "an use" remains in the manuscript, though the essay reads "a use." The passage containing "30,000 years" is cancelled in the manuscript, with the diagonal slashes characteristic of Emerson. The editorial (Ellen's) insistence on "of years" made little sense to begin with, because the passage is not incorrect or awkward as Emerson wrote it. Emerson may have been expressing puzzlement when he deleted the whole passage—or perhaps he was avoiding showing puzzlement. In either case, there is no evidence to contradict Cabot's statement that Emerson approved, "in a general way," what his helpers did. But there is also reason to underline Cabot's clarification: "it may be a question exactly how far he sanctioned" the changes.

[14] See Ellen's letter to Emerson, 13 Aug. 1877, Houghton Library.

Cabot's question has greater force in relation to the reorganization of the manuscript—the shuffling, for which Cabot claimed responsibility, of the pages of the lecture into new orders. That shuffling was radical, as is made clear simply by noting that, in the Berg manuscript, the red numbers that identify the lecture's order are mostly random. In only one case is there any overt evidence of Emerson's involvement in the reshuffling, and it comes at the first point where lecture and essay diverge. The two versions run parallel through what is now the fifth paragraph of the essay. The bulk of this material comes from Emerson's address of 1855 at the opening of Sleepy Hollow Cemetery, the germ of "Immortality." The Sleepy Hollow material traces a roughly chronological series of illustrations that "there never was a time when the doctrine of a future life was not held" (*W*, VIII, 324). In the lecture, Emerson added more illustrations, including Swedenborg and the world of "sixty years ago. . . . under the shadow of Calvinism and of the Roman Catholic purgatory." The published version follows that far, but then offers a generalization that appears much later in the lecture (the red numbers jump from 41 to 95): "A man of thought is willing to die, . . . because he has seen the thread on which the beads are strung." The new composition is smoothed by an added phrase: he who lacks the vision is terrified, "and is the victim of those who have moulded the religious doctrines into some neat and plausible system, as Calvinism, Romanism or Swedenborgism, for household use" (*W*, VIII, 329). Those twenty-six words begin at the bottom of a manuscript page and were first written in pencil, then traced in ink. Both pencil and ink are in Emerson's hand, but that he may have had prompting is suggested by the next eight words on the page, "It is the fear of the young bird", in pencil only and in Ellen Emerson's hand. These eight are, in effect, catchwords, directing what will come next. The red numbers now jump from 95 back to 45; and on manuscript page 45 is found the same phrase, in Emerson's hand, heading the discussion that, indeed, follows in the essay. It appears, then, that the impetus for reorganization came at least partly from an editor. But, at least in the early stages, Emerson was sufficiently involved to write (and presumably compose) an effective link between two statements originating in diverse contexts.

This early transition is the only evidence in an extended manuscript that Emerson had any part in the reorganization of material.

Because his habit was to put on each separate sheet of paper a syntactically complete discussion, shuffling was relatively easy. In the discussion below, the assumption is that reorganization of these units—the only part of making the essay that Cabot claimed credit for—was done with minimal involvement by Emerson, though probably with his assent at some stage. Certainly, internal evidence suggests that the thematic assumptions behind the reorganization were more Cabot's and Ellen's than Emerson's—at least than Emerson's at the time he first formulated "Immortality."

III

At some point in the history of the lecture "Immortality," Emerson divided the manuscript into topical groupings, using folded cover sheets into which he inserted loose pages of text. The groupings were labeled, in order: "Morale," "Love of Stability," "Evidence from Intellect," "Vouchers," "Evidence of Moral Sentiment," "Realism," and "Hindoo Yama." The first and last of these headings identify two illustrative anecdotes, the story of Senators Lewis Cass and Albert Tracy and the fable from the Katha Upanishad that ends "Immortality." "Vouchers" enclosed a series of quotations from various sages. The remaining topics—"Love of Stability," "Evidence from Intellect," "Evidence of Moral Sentiment," and "Realism"—are an outline of the lecture's argument, a sequence through increasingly more complex or fundamental epistemological categories to an ethical stance resulting from the ascending inquiry.

In the Berg manuscript (the order of the published essay), these four cover sheets appear in the same sequence as in the lecture.[15] Each substantive topic is addressed in the same order; Cabot and Ellen Emerson respected Emerson's ascending pattern: perception of stability, evidence gained through intellect, evidence gained through moral intuition, and ethics of "Realism." Nevertheless, the editors freely shuffled, added, and subtracted within and among categories, so that many units of discussion appear under different topical headings than originally and most units appear in different contexts. How Cabot and Ellen Emerson patterned the essay can

[15] The cover sheets have red numbers but no corner numbers. Only "Vouchers" has a different order in the Berg manuscript, shifted from before "Moral Sentiment" to after.

be seen in the following analyses of "Evidence from Intellect" and "Realism."

"Evidence from Intellect" discusses immortality as perceived by the understanding, an intermediate step between instinctive "delight" in stable things and intuitive moral sentiment. In Emerson's red-numbered lecture version, the cover sheet enclosed seventeen units of discussion. ("Unit," here and below, means a separate piece of paper comprising a syntactically complete passage.) Disregarding two gaps in the red-number sequence, "Evidence from Intellect" forms in the lecture a continuous discussion of about 1600 words. In the rearrangement, only four of the original seventeen units remain within the cover sheet, with two more immediately preceding it. These six units, plus an inserted quotation from Montaigne, give the essay a continuous discussion of about 500 words. Cabot and Ellen Emerson cut the topic by about two-thirds.

"Evidence from Intellect" is disproportionately long in the lecture, so cutting made sense. Still, what the editors did to the section deemphasizes intellect as an agent of belief in immortality. Cut are the more emphatic statements about the role of understanding, including Emerson's suggestion that "power to believe in immortality" might be lacking for those "who had not already a revelation of it in the phenomena of intellect." The editors also excised a quotation from Plotinus: "Intellect is not at all in want of another life, or of other things." In both cases, less direct suggestions of these notions remain, but the cutting of the most overt statements—an argument out of line with the Biblical definition of faith—appears to be a pattern.

Another cut markedly alters the context of what originally followed. The anecdote about Empress Anne, who brought together the genius of Russia to build a snow palace, appears in both lecture and essay. In the lecture it is preceded by a discussion of natural science and by: "Whenever we are in a high state of intellectual excitement, we believe. Every good book suggests the immortality. We see that we are wiser than we were,—we are older. Can Nature afford to lose such improvements? Is nature suicide?" In the essay, the anecdote of the snow palace is introduced by this: "For the Creator keeps his word with us. These long-lived or long-enduring objects are to us, as we see them, only symbols of somewhat in us far longer-lived. Our passions, our endeavors, have something ridiculous and mocking, if we come to so hasty an end. If not to *be*, how like the bells of a fool is the trump of fame!" (*W*, VIII, 336). An observation about intellectual excitement at scientific discovery has been made an evidence of Divinity.

The anecdote about Empress Anne was moved entirely out of the topical grouping "Evidence from Intellect." The same is true of another unit, which in the lecture follows a discussion of the "scholar or thinker": "You shall not say, 'O my bishop, o my pastor, is there any resurrection?' . . . What questions are these! Go read Milton, Shakspeare, or any truly ideal poetry. . . . Let any master who can codify the moral laws. Simply recite to the ear of thoughtful men the substantial laws of the intellect, &, in the presence of the laws themselves, you will never ask such primary-school questions" (quoted from manuscript; cf. *W*, VIII, 346–47). By juxtaposing "laws of the intellect" and "moral laws," this passage anticipates in the lecture the next upward step in the argument. In the essay, two sentences are telescoped: the "truly ideal" is made equivalent with laws of intellect, and the middle term "moral laws" is dropped. The editing in effect redefines "intellect" and again deemphasizes the role of understanding in belief. So it is not surprising to find this passage removed from its original context and placed near the end of the essay, where it is introduced not by a discussion of scholarly endeavor but by something well beyond: "We cannot prove our faith by syllogisms. The argument refuses to form in the mind. . . . It must be sacredly treated. . . ." In context, the reason why one does not ask questions of the pastor becomes quite different: what originally evidenced a breakdown of intellectual discipline has become a lack of faith in the "truly ideal."

It is well to emphasize that the statements about faith and the ideal are Emerson's and were part of the lecture. The point is not that conventional language or a religious perspective was added to Emerson's material, but that in the lecture such a perspective was clearly located and defined in argument as part of an epistemological process. In revision, primarily through rearrangements, such conventional statements were aggrandized and placed so as sometimes to seem the end beyond argument, the thread on which everything was strung. Examining the topic "Realism" will further clarify how the change worked.

"Realism" comprised the final fourth of Emerson's lecture "Immortality," with the Hindu anecdote serving as an illustration of the topical discussion. The culmination of Emerson's lecture is, then, a "knowledge" that, he wrote in his journal about the time the lecture was first given, leaves people "astonished & angry when it is spoken in church"—as "Immortality" often was (*JMN*, XV, 156). In his journal for 1865, Emerson defined "Realism" and indicated its importance to his later thinking: "Especially works on me at all times any statement of Realism, &, old as my habit is of thrumming on this string, I must continue to try it, till, in a manlier or a divine hour, I can see the truth, & say it. The sum of it is, the time is never lost that is devoted to work. If you are well at work on your design, you can well afford not to have customers for the present" (*JMN*, XV, 66; cf *W*, VII, 294). That Emerson made this doctrine of Realism the end of his investigation of immortality, following both intellectual and moral considerations, suggests that the ethical imperative is what the work is most fundamentally about. Realism is the string on which the lecture is strung, structurally as well as thematically. Indeed, the initial historical survey of religions concludes with a call to "the duties of today" and a rejection of any impulse to "waste life" in fruitless speculations about an afterlife (cf. *W*, VIII, 328). The Hindu myth that ends the essay makes a similar point with some wit. Granted by Yama three wishes, Nachiketas asks to know what lies beyond death. He gets, first, advice to choose another wish, and then, when he persists, an answer that is rhetorically impressive but obscure. On one level, supported by the structure of "Immortality," the anecdote is satirical; its moral is: don't ask.

Cabot and Ellen Emerson decided to end the essay "Immortality" with the anecdote about Yama and its Sphinx-like conclusion; the lecture's four-page peroration was deleted. The anecdote indeed makes a striking finish, but its enigmatic qualities lend themselves to somewhat wider implications than the original, more specifically illustrative, use had. What the editors' version emphasizes is not the illustration of Realism or the satirical dimension of Yama's comment, but the more conventional perspective in which Nachiketas is "a house whose door is open to Brahma" and in which he learns that "the soul is not born; it does not die." The emphasis is there largely because of alterations in how the immediately preceding discussion of Realism develops. A new perspective is created by juxtaposing passages that originally were distinct.

Of the three paragraphs preceding the anecdote about Yama in the published essay, the third (essentially an introduction to the story) is identical in lecture and essay. The other two paragraphs, fourth and third from the end of the essay (*W*, VIII, 347-49) were rearranged. Analyzing these paragraphs into original units yields this outline:

> [A] "Is immortality only an intellectual quality, or, shall I say, only an energy? . . . He has it, and he alone, who gives life to all . . . where he comes. . . ."
> [B] "Future state is an illusion for the ever-present state. . . ."
> [C] "But see how the sentiment is wise. Jesus explained nothing, but the influence of him took people out of time, and they felt eternal. . . ."
> [D] "It is strange that Jesus is esteemed by mankind the bringer of the doctrine of immortality. He is never once weak or sentimental. . . ."
> [E] "How ill agrees this majestical immortality of our religion with the frivolous population! Will you build magnificently for mice? . . ."
> [F] "But this is the way we rise. Within every man's thought is a higher thought. . . . He is rising to greater heights, but also rising to realities; . . . he entering deeper into God, God into him. . . ."

This sequence is a factitious construction, as is made clear simply by collating the red numbers (lecture order) of the six units: 173, 193, 167, 165, 183, 197. The original contexts were quite different. Units [C] and [D], for example, denying that Jesus preached "immortality" as a future consummation, originally came immediately before the cover sheet of "Realism." In that lecture use, Emerson's denial of "sentimental" notions about the afterlife, in favor of a "great integrity" that "makes a day memorable," forms the transition between intuitions through moral sentiment and the injunction to work in the real world—in other words, to *make* the day memorable. Unit [E], with its Mark Twain-like observation that people would find insufferable the heaven they anticipate, follows within the lecture a segment that Cabot and Ellen Emerson cut. Having noted that "we live by desire to live" (cf. *W*, VIII, 345), Emerson added in the deleted unit: "And the question arises, whether all are in like manner immortal? He who would live hereafter must live now. This sublime hope of man refuses to deal with men in masses, in races; it severs the individual soul from the whole world, to deal with him alone." And so in context unit [E], following immediately in the lecture, is more or less a direct slap at churches, which swallow up individuality and promise afterlife through "masses" (an obvious pun) or institutions.

Most striking in the published sequence is the juxtaposition of units [E] and [F], implying that "our religion" (the manuscript originally read "our popular religion") is part of a rising process that leads to God. In fact, in the lecture "the way we rise" has nothing to do with beliefs that Emerson has, after all, just called "weak" and "sentimental"; the way we rise is ethical, and the passage affirms Realism. The editors cut entirely three units that originally intervened between [E] and [F]. Excerpts from the excised passages show how Emerson built his argument: "The other world & all worlds will resemble this, in eternal preparation & toil for everything worthy." "Heaven is the exercise of the faculties, the added sense of power; to the architect, it is architecture; to the traveller new journeys. . . ." "We are concealed in our bodies. 'The body is an integument which is dissolved in order that man may truly live. . . .' "[16] In Emerson's composition, heaven is emphatically an everpresent state of mind; the relationship between the corporeal and the eternal is clearly and precisely stated. In Cabot's and Ellen Emerson's rearrangement, the relationship is fuzzy; even sentimental and "frivolous" conceptions are allowed their place—despite the fact that these popular conceptions contradict Emerson's notion of a Unitary eternity and make anomalous his ethical lesson that one should work, not toward the future but within the eternal present.

The editors' rearrangement makes Emerson's definition of "immortality" vaguer and thus allows for a different, more conventional interpretation of Yama's statement that "the soul is not born; it does not die." The essay accommodates a perspective that the lecture rejected. Compare to the confident sequence that Cabot and Ellen Emerson arranged the unit that Emerson, in the lecture, placed just before the introduction to the Yama anecdote (and

[16] The first two units are from the Houghton folder, the third from the Berg manuscript. The quotation is from Swedenborg.

which the editors moved elsewhere): "There is one drawback to the value of all statements of the doctrine, and I think that one abstains from writing or printing on the immortality of the soul, because, when he comes to the end of his statement, the hungry eyes that run through it will close disappointed: the listeners say, 'That is not here which we desire' " (cf. *W*, VIII, 345). Emerson here is obviously setting up a parallel between his own lecture and the enigmatic statement of Yama that follows. I cannot satisfactorily answer your question, Emerson says with Yama, at least partly because you are asking it in the wrong terms. It is precisely the distinction of terms that Cabot's and Ellen Emerson's rearrangement confuses.

IV

Emerson was fortunate in his early editors. Ellen Emerson and J. Elliot Cabot, and later Edward Emerson and Waldo Forbes, did their work responsibly and respected the integrity of Emerson's thinking as they understood it. Cabot's recollection of how *Letters and Social Aims* took shape finds general support in the two manuscript gatherings relevant to "Immortality." Emerson wrote everything in the essay; and, although evidence here is less conclusive, there are signs of consultation and no reason to doubt that Emerson approved, at least "in a general way," what they did. Their work was, as Cabot said, primarily that of "selection and arrangement," but the *re*arrangement of Emerson's lecture "Immortality" was so comprehensive as to make the essay a new composition. Thus Cabot's honest qualification: although Emerson approved his editors' working, they could not say that he fully sanctioned the product.

That qualification should be emphasized because two of Cabot's recollections are, when tested against the manuscript of "Immortality," incorrect or at least misleading. Emerson's lecture was not "without any completely recoverable order or fixed limits," since a virtually whole, consecutively paged lecture is available even today. And Cabot's claim that "the essay on Immortality . . . contains passages written fifty years apart from each other," suggesting an editorial fabrication from diverse sources, is belied by the fact that all materials in the essay are found in the sequential lecture manuscript that Emerson himself assembled between 1861 and 1872.

External and internal evidence suggests that Ellen Emerson and J. Elliot Cabot chose to rework "Immortality" less because it was incoherent than because they thought it inadequate as a statement of Emerson's beliefs at the time *Letters and Social Aims* was appearing. Both editors detected in Emerson a growing accommodation to conventional belief, an "unconscious drift" toward orthodoxy. Whether that actually occurred in Emerson's life is debatable, but the drift clearly *is* present in "Immortality" as the editors reconstituted it during 1875. Primarily through changes in context and through juxtaposition of statements originally carrying different implications, the editors aggrandized a perspective that the lecture at best deemphasized and at worst dismissed as "sentimental" and "weak." Emerson's careful organization through ascending epistemological stages is blurred, and his conclusion in "Realism" is submerged in a homogenized perspective that seems less concerned with ethics than with justifying popular beliefs as "the way we rise."

What, then, should scholars' attitudes be toward the published essay? Recent trends might suggest upholding the recoverable lecture manuscript as an "unexpurgated" "Immortality." That would be extreme: Emerson certainly authorized *Letters and Social Aims* and approved "Immortality," even though his approval was probably mainly passive. The essay should remain in the canon with its collaborative nature acknowledged. Yet publication and analysis of the lecture is essential for evaluating Emerson's late thinking and habits of composition. The lecture is a different work from the essay. What Ellen Emerson and James Elliot Cabot presented to the world may well accurately reflect the Emerson they knew, but the whole Emerson is still not fully available to us.

Emerson, Kneeland, and the Divinity School Address

Robert E. Burkholder

"It is plain from all the noise that there is Atheism somewhere. The only question is now, which is the Atheist?" Emerson wrote in his journal on 20 October 1838.[1] In Boston in the first half of the nineteenth century, atheism seemed to lurk behind every pillar, and the charges of non-belief, infidelity, and even blasphemy, like that of witchcraft in the seventeenth century, were levelled often in the press, and from the pulpit and podium. But to an American of that time such a charge would imply much more than it does to us today. In *The Age of Jackson*, Arthur Schlesinger, Jr., explains that the Federalists valued the clergy and the judiciary "as a great stabilizing influence in society, hoping thus to identify the malcontent as a foe of both God and the law." In the first quarter of the nineteenth century the Federalists and their political successors, notably the Whigs, conceived of America as "essentially and legally a religious nation" in which church and state would work together to maintain the existing social order.[2] Ronald P. Formisano quotes Henry Cabot Lodge, who suggested that the Federalists could be called "the Puritan party," and he contends that the same might be said of the Whigs: "The Federal and Whig parties both expressed the ancient Puritan concern for society as a corporate whole; both attempted to use the government to provide for society's moral and material development."[3] In his 1835 *Political Reminiscences*, John Barton Derby, a disaffected Boston Democrat, characterized the age as one in which:

[1] *The Journals and Miscellaneous Notebooks of Ralph Waldo Emerson*, ed. William H. Gilman et al. (Cambridge: Harvard Univ. Press, 1960–1982), VII: 112. Hereafter cited in the text as JMN.

[2] *The Age of Jackson* (Boston: Little, Brown, 1953), p. 350.

[3] *The Transformation of Political Culture: Massachusetts Political Parties, 1790's–1840's* (New York: Oxford Univ. Press, 1983), p. 289.

American Literature, Volume 58, Number 1, March 1986. CCC 0002-9831/86/$1.50

> Old principles of eternal truth, established by the wisdom of ages, are now proclaimed, by unfledged politicians hardly out of faction's nest, as the relics of barbarous times,—the monstrous errors of an age of darkness. The right of property is crumbling to pieces; liberty is not believed to be founded on law and order; an independent judiciary is considered a national evil; the patriots who framed the Constitution, are estimated by beardless statesmen who are not yet old enough to have got rid of the smell of bread and butter, as infinitely inferior in learning and talent to themselves; and even the Christian religion, which fortunately survived the assaults of Hume and Voltaire, it is now expected by many will knock under to Abner Kneeland.[4]

Therefore, charges of atheism or infidelity implied not only an anti-establishment religious stance but also similar anti-establishment social and political views, and those who challenged accepted religious views and practices were thought to be attacking social and political stability as well. Opposition to these attacks was particularly pronounced among Boston Unitarians, whom Daniel Walker Howe has argued carried "the political attitudes of eighteenth-century Whiggery through most of the antebellum period"; that is, they believed in "approved patterns of social deference and the near monopoly of political office by an educated and prosperous elite."[5] Religious and political order was intended to support such a belief.

The idea of the social and political implications of Emerson's Divinity School Address and the resulting controversy has never been of immediate concern to literary scholars, but it is important to note that one of the first critics of the Address, Andrews Norton, the so-called "Unitarian Pope," identified the "New School" with social upheaval: "They announce themselves as prophets and priests of a new future, in which all is to be changed, all old opinions done away, and all present forms of society abolished. But by what process this joyful revolution is to be effected we are not

[4] *Political Reminiscences, Including a Sketch of the Origin and History of the "Statesman Party"* (Boston: Homer & Palmer, 1835), p. 157.

[5] *The Unitarian Conscience: Harvard Moral Philosophy, 1805–1862* (Cambridge: Harvard Univ. Press, 1970), 206. In his discussion of the formation of political parties in Massachusetts during this period, Ronald P. Formisano states that the "Unitarians were . . . almost always respectable and usually Whig. But more important, they were associated with wealth, power, and secularism. In the 1830s and 1840s many Orthodox and other citizens continued to distrust the Unitarians as a powerful, exclusive, and domineering elite" (*The Transformation of Political Culture*, p. 291).

told."[6] Norton's criticism of Emerson may seem narrowminded and unreasonable to us, but it is consistent with, if not a bit more reasonable than, responses to other assaults on the religious order of things in the 1830s.

Invariably such responses indicate a strong identification of religious nonconformity with social and political nonconformity and suggest that the concerns of church and state were really the same—maintaining the status quo. In Connecticut in 1828, for instance, a Federalist judge threw out the lower court testimony of a Universalist because, the judge reasoned, disbelievers felt no accountability to God or an afterlife. In Massachusetts in 1838 a Whig report to the Senate on the competency of nonbelievers to serve as witnesses in court cases stated that atheism was not only hostile to religion, "but to all decency and regularity, to the peace of all communities, and the safety of all governments."[7] The concerns of the conservatives are admirably summed up by Samuel Gridley Howe when in recounting the changes in America in the previous ten years, he equated the rise of Andrew Jackson and his levelling democracy with a concomitant rise in atheism and argued that proponents of such thought should be socially ostracized and economically sanctioned.[8]

Howe's article deals in particular with the case of Abner Kneeland, who on 18 June 1838 began serving a sixty-day sentence in the Suffolk County Jail in Boston for blasphemy. Kneeland was the last person convicted of that offense in Massachusetts' history, and his story serves as the best example of how the state acted as the secular arm of established religion in Boston in the 1830s. But even more than that, the knowledge that Kneeland was sitting in a cell in Boston, convicted of a crime against religion, at the very moment Emerson stood at the podium in Divinity Hall on 15 July 1838, adds a depth to our understanding of that moment and the subsequent months in Emerson's life and suggests some insights into Emerson's tenuous relationship with the idea of democracy.[9]

[6] "The New School in Literature and Religion," *Boston Daily Advertiser*, 27 Aug. 1838, p. 2.

[7] Both examples are from Schlesinger, *The Age of Jackson*, p. 351.

[8] "Atheism in New-England," *New-England Magazine*, 7 (Dec. 1834), 500–01. Howe's article is concluded in the next number of the *New-England Magazine*, 8 (Jan. 1835), 53–62.

[9] Two useful discussions of Emerson and democracy are Perry Miller, "Emersonian Genius and the American Democracy," *New England Quarterly*, 26 (1953), 27–44; and part

If one were to accept Henry Steele Commager's 1935 interpretation of Kneeland's life and trials, he would view the man as a benign old eccentric who managed, almost despite himself, to get caught up in the gears of the machinery of Boston conservatism.[10] Kneeland's writings in the weekly newspaper he also edited and published, the *Boston Investigator*, would suggest something altogether different, since for nearly a decade he had stabbed at the vitals of Boston conservatism by publishing his essentially pantheistic views on religion, advancing the social theories of Robert Dale Owen and Fanny Wright, supporting the work of Dr. Charles Knowlton in educating the public about birth control, disseminating the Rationalism of Voltaire and Paine, and championing the causes of Jacksonian democracy and the working class. Any one of these crusades might have resulted in trouble for its advocate in Boston in the 1830s, but together they were dynamite, and Kneeland added insult to injury by conducting Sunday "services" for the "First Society of Free Enquirers" at Julien Hall and later at the Federal Street Theater, often to audiences of two thousand.[11] He also became a popular lecturer throughout New England, attracting large audiences wherever he went. As Roderick French has contended, "Kneeland was at the center of a very vital movement of change in American society."[12]

If we were to use the term generically, we might call Kneeland a "Transcendentalist," even though he might have been hooted out

---

of the chapter on "Jacksonian Democracy and Literature," in Schlesinger, *The Age of Jackson*, pp. 384–86.

[10] "The Blasphemy of Abner Kneeland," *New England Quarterly*, 8 (March 1935), 29–41. An excellent source is Leonard W. Levy, "Satan's Last Apostle in Massachusetts," *American Quarterly*, 5 (1953), 16–30; reprinted as the "Introduction" to *Blasphemy in Massachusetts, Freedom of Conscience and the Abner Kneeland Case: A Documentary Record*, ed. Levy (New York: Da Capo, 1973). The best single source for studying Kneeland's life and trials is Roderick Stuart French, "The Trials of Abner Kneeland: A Study in the Rejection of Democratic Secular Humanism" (Diss. George Washington Univ. 1971), which serves as the basis for French's "Liberation from Man and God in Boston: Abner Kneeland's Free-Thought Campaign 1830–1839," *American Quarterly*, 32 (1980), 202–21.

[11] Derby, *Political Reminiscences*, p. 144, states that "The Federal-street Theatre, where he [Kneeland] holds his Sunday meetings to scoff at the Bible,—to ridicule everything we hold sacred, and to sneer at the Deity, is usually crowded from top to bottom. It is said that 2000 have been present at once"; Howe, "Atheism in New-England," pp. 504–07, describes a typical service, which included the singing of hymns, readings from the Bible of Reason, and a sermon, which Howe observes was usually aimed at preaching "the doctrines of the French infidels" (p. 506).

[12] French, "The Trials of Abner Kneeland," p. 10.

of the proper drawing rooms of Concord and Boston where Emerson and his circle met. Like Orestes Augustus Brownson, Kneeland served several religions before becoming a zealous proselyte for the one he finally adopted—Free Enquiry. For a brief period he was a Baptist preacher, but through a friendship with Hosea Ballou, he converted to Universalism and for twenty-five years served as a minister in that church, holding important pastorates in Philadelphia and New York, until his outspoken religious doubts caused the Universalists to consider him *persona non grata* in 1829.[13] Like Emerson, he fought against the cold formalism of established religion. And like Amos Bronson Alcott and George Ripley, he attempted to establish a utopian community—Salubria, in the Des Moines valley of Iowa.[14] If Emerson had been looking for someone to exemplify the concept of Self-Reliance, Kneeland might have served him well: He was self-taught in Greek, Hebrew, and Latin; he devised and published his own phonetically rational spelling system; he knew enough law to argue his own case before the Massachusetts Supreme Court and enough medicine to deliver some of the twelve children his four marriages produced; at various times during his life he had been a farmer, a carpenter, a legislator, a teacher, a preacher, and an editor, and even the briefest of biographical sketches suggests that he more than satisfied the Emersonian ideal of the "One Man."[15]

What separated Kneeland from the Transcendentalists were his politics and the zeal with which he promoted his favorite causes. To Kneeland politics and religion were essentially the same. In 1827 when his radical religious views alienated the conservative members of his congregation at the Prince Street Universalist Church in New York City, he organized the Second Universalist Society of New York and for a time held his weekly meetings at Tammany Hall.[16] A disgusted John Barton Derby contended that

[13] "The Trials of Abner Kneeland," pp. 62–63.

[14] "The Trials of Abner Kneeland," pp. 196–200, 251–56.

[15] See Commager, "The Blasphemy of Abner Kneeland," p. 30; and Mary R. Whitcomb, "Abner Kneeland: His Relations to Early Iowa History," *Annals of Iowa*, series 3, 6 (1904), 340. For the concept of the "One Man," see "The American Scholar," in *The Collected Works of Ralph Waldo Emerson*, ed. Alfred R. Ferguson (Cambridge: Harvard Univ. Press, 1971–), I, 53.

[16] French, "The Trials of Abner Kneeland," p. 57.

in Boston "nineteen-twentieths of the followers of Abner Kneeland were or are now Jacksonmen," that Kneeland himself had publicly declared his support for Jackson in the newspapers, and "that the Van Buren party throughout the Union, embraces in its ranks the Infidels and sceptics of all the states."[17] One can only imagine how Kneeland might have responded to Emerson's admiration for that arch-Whig, Daniel Webster.[18]

It was Kneeland's zeal that resulted in the charges of blasphemy, four subsequent trials and an appeal hearing, and a legal controversy that would last four years and end in what Leonard Levy has called "one of the worst opinions ever written by Chief Justice [Lemuel] Shaw" of the Massachusetts Supreme Court and with Kneeland's imprisonment.[19] The charges were based on a 1782 law that defined blasphemy as "denying, cursing, or contumeliously reproaching God," denying Jesus Christ, or denying God's creation, government, final judgment, or holy word.[20] Ironically, Kneeland's statement was not aimed at Unitarianism or an even more conservative sect but at Universalism and particularly at another disciple of Ballou, Thomas Whittemore, who as publisher of *The Trumpet*, the leading Universalist weekly, "was to grow into a doughty defender of Universalism."[21] Although the original indictment cited three articles in the 20 December 1833 issue of the *Investigator* as the basis for the charge against him, the question of Kneeland's guilt rested on his response to Whittemore's request that he clarify his position in relation to Universalism. Kneeland responded with a statement that included the following:

1. Universalists believe in a god which I do not; but believe that their god . . . is nothing more than a chimera of their own imagination. 2. Universalists believe in Christ, which I do not; but believe that the whole story concerning him is as much a fable and fiction as that of the god

[17] Derby, *Political Reminiscences*, p. 143.

[18] See Leonard Neufeldt, "Daniel Webster as Representative Man," in his *The House of Emerson* (Lincoln: Univ. of Nebraska Press, 1982), pp. 101–02.

[19] *The Law of the Commonwealth and Chief Justice Shaw: The Evolution of American Law, 1830–1860* (New York: Harper and Row, 1967), p. 43.

[20] Commager, "The Blasphemy of Abner Kneeland," p. 32; see also Levy, 'Satan's Last Apostle." p. 17.

[21] Ernest Cassara, *Universalism in America: A Documentary History* (Boston: Beacon Press, 1971), p. 133. For more on *The Trumpet* see Frank Luther Mott, *A History of American*

Prometheus. . . . 3. Universalists believe in miracles, which I do not; but believe that every pretension to them is to be attributed to mere trick and imposture. 4. Universalists believe in the resurrection of the dead, immortality, and eternal life, which I do not; but believe that all life is material, that death is an eternal extinction of life.[22]

If Kneeland's declaration sounds at all familiar, it is probably because in his attack on Universalism he rather admirably, but with less rhetorical flourish, sums up Emerson's complaints about Unitarianism as enumerated in the Divinity School Address nearly five years later. But Kneeland was jailed and Emerson was not.

One reason for prosecuting Kneeland and not Emerson was that Kneeland was eminently more dangerous: he was preaching "Free Enquiry" to huge crowds every week and disseminating religious, social, and political radicalism to more than two thousand subscribers to the *Investigator*. By comparison Emerson was not much of a problem: his influence was limited to a small group of mostly Harvard-trained intellectuals, almost all of whom had some ties to the conservative establishment themselves, and to those who attended his lectures and who had bought and read *Nature*. Emerson's following was hardly the sort to storm the Bastille. Furthermore, Emerson was a member of the establishment himself,[23] whereas Kneeland seemed to represent every known threat to the social order of Boston. That is not to say that Emerson was entirely safe from prosecution. The chief protector of the social order of Massachusetts in Kneeland's case and the prosecutor in his third and fourth trials and in his final appeal hearing before the Massachusetts Supreme Court was James Trecothick Austin, state Attorney General and a staunch defender of the faith. Austin's view of Christianity, like that of many of his Unitarian contempo-

---

Magazines 1850–1865 (Cambridge: Harvard Univ. Press, 1938), p. 72; and Jean Hoornstra and Judy Heath, *American Periodicals 1741–1900: An Index to the Microfilm Collections* (Ann Arbor: University Microfilms, 1979), p. 215.

[22] See French, "The Trials of Abner Kneeland," pp. 266–318, for the most clear and accurate account of the complexities of Kneeland's case; Kneeland's response to Whittemore is quoted from Levy, "Satan's Last Apostle," p. 18.

[23] See Catherine L. Albanese, *Corresponding Motion: Transcendental Religion and the New America* (Philadelphia: Temple Univ. Press, 1977), pp. 33–38, for discussions of the conservative social and political climate in Boston and Emerson's conservative credentials.

raries, was that its principal function was to enhance the social order. "The duty of Christianity," Austin wrote in 1835, "is not to excite strong abhorrence in one portion of the community, which may lead them to break the bonds of moderation and prudence, nor to excite in another angry and hateful feelings."[24] It is little wonder then that Austin, when invited to speak at a memorial meeting for the abolitionist minister and publisher, Elijah Lovejoy, who was murdered by a mob in Alton, Illinois, placed the blame squarely on Lovejoy. Before the crowd at that meeting, which was unquestionably sympathetic to Lovejoy's cause, Austin asked, "Why then should we be called on to make this occurrence at Alton an occasion for public expression of condolence, in Faneuil Hall? To sympathise with those who had been mobbed, when their rashness, and folly and imprudence have stirred up the vindictive passions of the multitude, and made the mob which they affect to deplore, is not the way to prevent mobs for the future, or preserve the peace of society and the majesty of the laws."[25]

Clearly Austin perceived the reformer as the cause of pro-slavery mobs and class dissatisfaction and as such the reformer was dangerously close to violating the laws that Austin believed were in place to protect the tranquility of the existing order. Therefore, it was not difficult for Austin to attack peaceful men of conscience who advocated reform, as he did when William Ellery Channing published his argument against slavery in 1835.[26] In his response to Channing, Austin suggested that his work planted the seed of rebellion in the minds of slaves, and he publicly charged Channing with publishing "*the doctrine of Insurrection*."[27] The rationale for such a charge was a curiously Unitarian one, that the rules of good conduct and good taste must supersede perceived morality if social order was to be maintained. "Under the administration of a free government," wrote Austin, "there is the stronger obligation for personal restraint, because it is to the personal, and not the public power, that the good order of society is mainly entrusted."[28] Such

[24] A Citizen of Massachusetts (pseud. for James T. Austin), *Remarks on Dr. Channing's Slavery* (Boston: Russell, Shattuck, 1835), p. 7.

[25] *Speech Delivered in Faneuil Hall, December 8, 1837, at a Meeting of Citizens Called on the Petition of Willam E. Channing and Others* (Boston: John H. Eastburn, 1837), p. 11.

[26] *Slavery* (Boston: James Munroe, 1835).

[27] Austin, *Remarks on Dr. Channing's Slavery*, p. 14.

[28] *Remarks on Dr. Channing's Slavery*, p. 22.

was the climate when Emerson delivered his Address at Divinity Hall.

Given these circumstances it is difficult to accept interpretations of the Divinity School Address as "barefaced effrontery" and easier to see why Emerson was motivated to take great care in tailoring his ideas and his rhetoric to his audience in Divinity Hall.[29] He did not compromise his truth, only state it in a way that would make it less offensive, and this acquiescence to audience must have made the resulting furor that much more surprising and disheartening to Emerson.

Immediately following the Divinity School Address and for several months thereafter, Emerson found himself in an untenable situation. Even though he had resigned his pastorate in 1832, he still identified with Unitarianism—the religion of his father, and, more important, his class—and there is no reason to suspect that he went to the Divinity School on that July evening with any less formidable a task in mind than the reform of Unitarianism away from narrow formalism toward a broader sort of religion based upon his recognition of the divinity in nature and in man. In mid-October 1838 Emerson chided himself in his journal for not realizing beforehand that those burdened by "the insanity that comes of inaction and tradition" would find fault with his ideas and reject them—and him—completely, with a "Babel of outcries" (JMN, VII: 105). This rejection was all the more baffling because he had intended those ideas to be the salvation of *his* religion, offered out of concern and friendship. As he said in the same journal entry, he saw that "the divine features of man" were

[29] Joel Porte, *Representative Man: Ralph Waldo Emerson in His Time* (New York: Oxford Univ. Press, 1979), argues that the vocabulary of the Address is a "barefaced effrontery" intended to shock the audience (p. 144); Mary Worden Edrich, "The Rhetoric of Apostasy," *Texas Studies in Literature and Language*, 9 (1967), cites Emerson's use of irresponsible and exaggerated language in the Address (pp. 550–56), which also has a testiness of tone indicative of Emerson's unwillingness to compromise; and David Robinson, *Apostle of Culture: Emerson as Preacher and Lecturer* (Philadelphia: Univ. of Pennsylvania Press, 1982), states that in the Address Emerson "was certainly making no effort to soften his attack on historical Christianity based on miracles" (pp. 125–26). Among those who suggest that Emerson's intent was anything but effrontery are Stephen E. Whicher, *Freedom and Fate: An Inner Life of Ralph Waldo Emerson* (Philadelphia: University of Pennsylvania Press, 1953), pp. 73–76; Carol Johnston, "The Underlying Structure of the Divinity School Address: Emerson as Jeremiah," *Studies in the American Renaissance 1980*, ed. Joel Myerson (Boston: Twayne, 1980), pp. 41–49; and B. L. Packer, *Emerson's Fall: A New Interpretation of the Major Essays* (New York: Continuum, 1982), pp. 121–29.

hidden by a disguise, "& he felt that he would dare to be so much their friend as to do them this violence to drag them to the day & to the healthy air & water of God, that the unclean spirits that possessed them might be exorcised & depart." But the exorcism failed, and the exorcist was denied. Suddenly many of those who shared his religion, his politics, and his view of society no longer wanted him. He had violated the sacred proprieties, committed an act in bad taste, and was no longer respectable. As Convers Francis reported in his journal in September 1838, in the homes of the inner circle, "the straitest sect of Boston conservatism," people had been taught "to abhor and abominate R. W. Emerson as a sort of mad dog."[30] Even his venerated uncle, Samuel Ripley, begged Emerson not to publish "the wicked thing" because he did not "want to see you classed with Kneeland, Paine &c, bespattered and belied."[31]

That Ripley would fear Emerson's being placed in a class with Kneeland and Paine is itself a revelation of Emerson's predicament following the Address. Conservative Boston's rejection of his theology, their calling it "atheism" or "infidelity," had the effect of making Emerson seem the ally of the infidel Democrats, and while his views may have been altogether different from Kneeland's, the transgressions of the two men were linked as though they sprang from some common source of destructive infidelity. It is little wonder, then, that Emerson protested on 29 September that "I hate to be defended in a newspaper" (JMN, VII: 95), since such defenses underscored his differences with the conservatives, tended to solidify his image as a radical, and kept the entire matter in the minds of the public that bought tickets to his lectures. It added to his embarrassment to be defended in the pages of papers identified with Jacksonian democracy, notably the *Investigator* and the *Boston Morning Post.*[32]

This identification with zealous religious as well as political and social radicalism was not one that Emerson fancied. Perhaps

[30] Joel Myerson, "Convers Francis and Emerson," *American Literature*, 50 (1978), 28.

[31] Samuel Ripley to Emerson, August 1838, in *The Letters of Ralph Waldo Emerson*, ed. Ralph L. Rusk (New York: Columbia Univ. Press, 1939), II: 148 *n* 169. Hereafter cited in the text as L.

[32] See Z. (Horace Seaver), "Rev. Mr. Emerson," *Boston Investigator*, 29 Sept. 1838, p. 3; and the review of the Divinity School Address by G. T. Davis in the *Boston Morning Post*, 31 Aug. 1838, p. 1.

because of his social station, Emerson reacted to Kneeland in much the same way that any member of Boston's inner circle would have. In his journal he referred to "the miserable babble of Kneeland & his crew" (JMN, V: 71) and to "the orgies of the Julien Hall" (JMN, IV: 326). In April 1834 Emerson wrote: "Good is promoted by the worst. Don't despise the Kneelands & Andrew Jacksons. In the great cycle they find their place & like the insect that fertilizes the soil with worm casts or the scavenger bustard that removes carrion they perform a beneficence they know not of, & cannot hinder if they would" (JMN, IV: 281). By June 1838, however, Emerson apparently saw enough injustice in Kneeland's imprisonment to be one of the 167 signers of a petition written by Ellis Gray Loring and sponsored by Dr. Channing that argued that religion and government should be separated and Kneeland released.[33] To some, especially after the Divinity School Address, Emerson's signature on that petition would further solidify his identification with Kneeland, the Free Enquirers, and the Democrats.

Emerson's journal entries in the months following the Address reveal a man hard at work attempting to re-establish his own political and social conservatism, at least in his own mind. One such entry appeared under the heading "Vanburenism" on 9 October 1838. In it Emerson denounced Democrats, whom he referred to as "jacobins," for reducing all the accomplishments of men to "Numbers of majorities," and he suggested how his view of things differed from that of the "modern jacobin": "It seems the relations of society[,] the position of classes irk & sting him. He will one day know that this is not fluent or removeable but a distinction in the nature of things, that neither the caucus, nor the newspaper, nor the Congress, nor the tax, nor the mob, nor the guillotine, nor the halter, nor fire, nor all together can avail to outlaw, cut out, burn, or destroy the offence of superiority in persons" (JMN, VII: 99).

But if Emerson found fault with Kneeland and the political and social philosophies of the Democrats, they, at least as represented by Kneeland and the *Boston Investigator*, were initially not all that willing to accept him either. Until the fall of 1838, Kneeland

[33] William Henry Channing, *The Life of William Ellery Channing*, pp. 504–05; and French, "The Trials of Abner Kneeland," pp. 308–09.

tolerated and even featured the views of Brownson, the most politically radical of the Transcendentalists,[34] but Emerson's blue blood, close ties to the establishment, and mysticism would make him suspect. In 1837 Kneeland complained that "When people resort to mystery, or 'transcendentalism' alias mysticism for proof it evidently shows that they have nothing more to say on the ground of common sense."[35] The same theme was revived by Kneeland in March 1838 for a discussion of Emerson's Phi Beta Kappa Oration: "it is altogether too bombastical, metaphysical, caballistical, allegorical, rhetorical, figurative—yea, too full of every thing but plain common sense, to be useful to the common reader. If such a style is to constitute our future 'American Authors,' we hope they will be 'like angels' visits'—few and far between."[36] Only six months later, as Emerson denounced the Democrats in his journal, the *Investigator*, with its babbling crew of atheists, came to his defense, and Emerson became one of Kneeland's causes, joining Free Enquiry, utopian socialism, birth control, and Jacksonian democracy as an issue to be defended in the pages of the *Investigator*.[37]

On 30 August 1838 Emerson attended the Phi Beta Kappa exercises at Harvard, and the fear of conservative Boston was made all too apparent to him in the "odium, and aversion" with which he was greeted and which he recorded in his journal the next day (JMN, VII: 60). To make matters worse, Kneeland's disciple, Horace Seaver, writing in the 29 September *Investigator*, cited the

[34] See, for example, "Proposed Discussion," *Boston Investigator*, 31 March 1837, p. 2, in which the background for a discussion between Brownson and Kneeland "on the cause or causes of infidelity" is delineated. Brownson proposed three topics: "1. Does man know, or can he know, any thing which is not observable by one or more of his *five* senses? Or, 2. Can all phenomena of consciousness be traced back to sensation? Or, 3. Is all knowledge derived from sensation?" The second question was agreed upon and a series of articles titled "A Discussion on the Question, *Can all phenomena of Consciousness be traced back to Sensation?*" appeared in the 7, 14, 21, 28 April, and 5, 12, and 19 May numbers of the *Investigator*. In the 26 May number Kneeland informed his readers that "Mr. Brownson having backed out from a discussion, which was of his own seeking, (and which he has closed none too soon), our readers will be relieved from his further lucubrations, which, however intelligible they may be to himself, reflect no light whatsoever to a rational mind." For more on the relationship of Brownson and Kneeland see French, "The Trials of Abner Kneeland," pp. 179–96.

[35] *Boston Investigator*, 3 Feb. 1837, p. 3.

[36] "Philosophy and Common Sense," *Boston Investigator*, 9 March 1838, pp. 2–3.

[37] According to French, "The Trials of Abner Kneeland," p. 244, Kneeland even "devoted two Sunday evening lectures to a review of Emerson's Divinity School Address" in the early fall of 1838.

"enlarged and liberal mind" of the man who only six months before had been a bombastical and caballistical rhetorician, and claimed Emerson as a "free enquirer."[38] Surely it was better to be called an atheist by Andrews Norton than to be welcomed into the fold of atheism by the atheists themselves! But the *Investigator* pressed the matter, perhaps as a way of vindicating Kneeland. In the 12 October number of the *Investigator* Emerson was praised for preaching "a different and a better doctrine" that was "no longer sectarian," and the sectarian accusers were themselves indicted with the words of the same law Kneeland had been tried and convicted for violating: "The more sectarian a religious man becomes, the greater his infidelity—the greater his disbelief in the boundless capacities and energies of the mind, which is the worst infidelity and the worst blasphemy conceivable, since it is treason and slander and 'wilful and contumelious reproach' of the only true, omnipotent, omniscient, omnipresent GOD!"[39] Finally in the 2 November issue, Kneeland himself congratulated Alcott, Brownson, and Emerson, whom he still identified with the conservative establishment, for managing to stir up trouble, noting that "although there may be as much fancy as real fact in their crude notions, yet, by the aid of these very chimerical notions, they become bold in asserting what they believe to be true."[40]

Throughout the fall of 1838 Emerson feared that he was being too closely associated in the press and in the public's mind with Kneeland and his followers, and in his journal and in letters he expressed concern over what that association might mean to his career. Reasonably secure in the armor his social standing provided him he did fret about the potential loss of his lecture audience and his livelihood, as well he should since social ostracism and economic sanctions were the principal weapons of his detractors. On 15 September he rationalized the possible effect of a loss of income as a result of urging "the doctrines of human Culture on young men," and concluded that he would "continue to spend the best of my time in the same way as now, rich or poor" (JMN, VII: 71). His

[38] Z. (Horace Seaver), "Rev. Mr. Emerson," p. 3.
[39] Z. (Horace Seaver), "Mr. Emerson and the Unitarians," *Boston Investigator*, 12 Oct, 1838, p. 3.
[40] "Our Religious Opponents," *Boston Investigator*, 2 Nov. 1838, p. 2.

fears are also suggested in a 29 September letter to his brother William in which he stated his intention to lecture in Boston during the coming winter, "& perhaps the people scared by the newspapers will not come & pay for my paper and pens" (L, II: 162). However, Emerson misjudged the effect of the criticism;[41] Kneeland was, after all, lecturing to thousands every Sunday, and in all likelihood Emerson benefited from the curiosity the controversy had aroused about him and his views. By late December, he was able to proclaim to William, "the lecturing thrives. The good city is more placable than it was represented & 'forgives,' like Burke, 'much to the spirit of liberty' " (L, II: 176–77).

Emerson's use of the quotation from Burke is indeed ironic in light of the prosecution and imprisonment of Kneeland, and Kneeland himself was quick to point out a similar irony in letters to the *Investigator* from his prison cell, which he emphasized was within sight of the Bunker Hill Monument. In Emerson's terms the entire episode indicates that Boston did indeed forgive those whom it deemed forgivable, while the Kneelands and Theodore Parkers took perhaps too much liberty to expect forgiveness. In 1840 Kneeland left Boston and went to Iowa, where his utopian community never materialized and where he dabbled in politics, held a political office, and even found the peace of a sort of benign acceptance. For Emerson, forgiveness faded into success and eventually even an adoring acceptance by the same Boston that for a few months in 1838 he feared had written him off as one of the Democratic rabble.

[41] See Lawrence Buell, *Literary Transcendentalism: Style and Vision in the American Renaissance* (Ithaca: Cornell Univ. Press, 1973), p. 32, who suggests that the Divinity School Address received general acceptance among middle-of-the-road Unitarians.

Index

Notes on Contributors

Raymond Benoit (1936—). St. Louis University, 1965—. *Single Nature's Double Name,* 1973.

William Braswell (1907-1985). Purdue University, 1935-1973. *Melville's Religious Thought,* 1943; ed., *Thomas Wolfe's Purdue Speech: Writing and Living,* 1964.

William E. Bridges (1933—). Pine Manor College, 1958-1966; Mills College, 1966-1974. *Spokesmen for the Self: Emerson, Thoreau, Whitman,* 1971; *The Seasons of Our Lives,* 1977; *Transitions: Making Sense of Life's Changes,* 1980; *A Year in the Life,* 1982.

Robert E. Burkholder (1950—). The Pennsylvania State University, 1980. Ed., *Critical Essays on Ralph Waldo Emerson* (with Joel Myerson), 1984; *Emerson: An Annotated Bibliography* (with Joel Myerson).

Frederic Ives Carpenter (1903—). Harvard, 1929-34. Editor, *The New England Quarterly,* 1928-1938. University of California, 1934-1976. *Emerson and Asia,* 1930; *Ralph Waldo Emerson,* 1934; *American Literature and the Dream,* 1962; ed. *The Emerson Handbook,* 1953; *Robinson Jeffers,* 1962; *Eugene O'Neill,* 1964, 1979.

Vivian C. Hopkins, (1901—), SUNY, Albany, 1941-1971. *Spires of Form: A Study of Emerson's Aesthetic Theory,* 1951; *Prodigal Puritan, A Life of Delia Bacon,* 1957.

Paul R. Jackson (1932—). Columbia, 1961-1962. Northwestern, 1963-1966. Temple 1966—

Glen M. Johnson (1947—). Grinnell, 1976-1977. Louisville, 1977-1981. Catholic, 1981—. Editor (with R. A. Bosco), *The Journals and Miscellaneous Notebooks of Ralph Waldo Emerson,* Vol. 16, 1982.

Wesley T. Mott (1946—). Thomas College, 1974-1978. University of Wisconsin-Madison, 1978-1987. Worcester Polytechnic, 1987—. Books in press: *"The Strains of Eloquence": Emerson in His Sermons* (1988); editor, *The Complete Sermons of Ralph Waldo Emerson,* Vol. 4 (1991).

Joel Myerson (1945—). South Carolina, 1971—. Editor: *Studies in the American Renaissance, an Annual,* 1978—. *The American Renaissance in New England,* 1978; Editor, *Emerson Centenary Essays,* 1982; *Ralph Waldo Emerson: A Descriptive Bibliography,* 1982; (with R. E. Burkholder) *Critical Essays on Ralph Waldo Emerson,* 1984, and *Emerson: An Annotated Bibliography,* 1985.

David B. Robinson (1950—). Georgia College, 1982—

William T. Stafford (1924—). Kentucky, 1950-1954. Purdue, 1965—. Editor:

Modern Fiction Studies, 1955—. *Melville's "Billy Budd" and the Critics,* 1961, 1968; *Twentieth Century American Writing,* 1965; *Perspectives in James's "The Portrait of a Lady,"* 1967; *Studies in "The American,"* 1971; *A Name, Title, and Place Index to the Critical Writings of Henry James,* 1975.

Frederick B. Tolles (1915-1975). Swarthmore, 1941-1975. *Meeting-House and Counting-House: The Quaker Merchants of Colonial Philadelphia,* 1948; *Slavery and the Woman Question: Lucretia Mott's Diary,* 1952; *George Logan and the Culture of Provincial America,* 1957; *Quakers and the Atlantic Culture,* 1960.

Thomas R. Whitaker (1925—). Oberlin, 1952-1954. Goddard College, 1964-1966. Iowa, 1966-1975. Yale, 1975—. *Swan and Shadow: Yeats's Dialogue with History,* 1964; *William Carlos Williams,* 1968; *Fields of Play in Modern Drama,* 1977, *Tom Stoppard,* 1983.

David M. Wyatt (1948—). Virginia, 1975-1982. Maryland, 1987—. *Prodigal Sons: A Study in Authorship and Authority,* 1980; *The Fall Into Eden: Landscape and Imagination in California,* 1986.

Library of Congress Cataloging-in-Publication Data
On Emerson.
(The Best from American literature)
Includes index.
1. Emerson, Ralph Waldo, 1803–1882—Criticism and interpretation. I. Cady, Edwin Harrison. II. Budd, Louis J. III. Series.
PS1638.05 1988 814′.3 88-3750
ISBN 0-8223-0861-4